Farming the Cutover

Farming the Cutover

A Social History of Northern Wisconsin, 1900–1940

Robert Gough

University Press of Kansas

Published by the University Press of Kansas (Lawrence, Kansː
which was organized by the Kansas Board of Regents and is operated
and funded by Emporia State University, Fort Hays State University,
Kansas State University, Pittsburg State University, the University of
Kansas, and Wichita State University

Library of Congress Cataloging-in-Publication Data
Gough, Robert
    Farming the cutover : a social history of Northern Wisconsin,
1900–1940 / Robert Gough.
      p. cm.
    Includes bibliographical references and index.
    ISBN 0-7006-0850-8 (alk. paper)
    1. Wisconsin—History—1848– 2. Wisconsin—Social conditions.
3. Cutover lands—Wisconsin—History—20th century. 4. Agriculture—
Wisconsin—History—20th century. 5. Farm life—Wisconsin—
History—20th century. I. Title.
F586.G68 1997
977.5'041—dc21   97-14712

Excerpt from *Land of the Free*. Copyright 1938, © renewed 1966 by
Archibald MacLeish. Reprinted by permission of Houghton Mifflin Co.
All rights reserved.

British Library Cataloguing in Publication Data is available.

Printed in the United States of America

10 9 8 7 6 5 4 3 2 1

The paper used in this publication meets the minimum requirements of
the American National Standard for Permanence of Paper for Printed
Library Materials Z39.48-1984.

Contents

Acknowledgments

I do not have a scholarly background in rural history and have never lived or worked on a farm or even milked a cow. Therefore, while this book may benefit from an outsider's perspective, it may contain some mistakes. I am thankful to the numerous people who have tried to help me avoid these errors, but take complete responsibility for those that remain.

Two of my graduate school teachers, Lee Benson and John Shover, did important work in rural history. While their scholarly interests were elsewhere when I studied with them, their example impressed upon me the significance of the history of rural America.

In the twelve years I have been working on this project, numerous colleagues and staff members at the University of Wisconsin–Eau Claire have assisted me. Ronald N. Satz, now Dean of the College of Professional Studies, provided encouragement and financial assistance in his capacity as head of university research. At the William D. McIntyre Library, the interlibrary loan assistance of Kay Henning was indispensable. The library's Area Research Center is a rich trove of resources and has access to the even greater treasures of the State Historical Society of Wisconsin. My use of these materials was facilitated by the center's current staff, Lawrence Lynch and Rita Sorkness, and by its previous head, Richard Pifer, now at the State Historical Society. Over the years a dozen or more student assistants have checked footnotes, done bibliographical searches, tabulated data, and performed other chores. From among them I wish to thank especially Cathy Inderberg, now a graduate student at the University of Chicago, who researched part of chapter 5 and later critiqued a draft of that chapter.

Portions of chapters 3 and 5 appeared previously in the *Wisconsin Magazine of History* and a portion of chapter 6 in *Essays in Economic and Business History*. They benefited from suggestions by the journals' respective editors, Paul Hass and Edwin J. Perkins, and are reprinted here by permission. Deborah Kmetz of the State Historical Society encouraged me at an early stage and facilitated my research. The maps were skillfully prepared by Alice Thiede of Carto-Graphics. Robert Peters graciously allowed me to quote from his poetry. The photographs which illustrate the text appear by permission of the Drummond Historical Museum and the State Historical Society of Wisconsin. Two colleagues at the University of Wisconsin–Eau Claire, James Oberly and Jane Pederson, read portions of earlier drafts, and David Danbom of North Dakota State University thoughtfully critiqued the entire manuscript. The staff at the University Press of Kansas transformed the manuscript into a book with great professionalism.

I am deeply indebted to the men and women who lived in the cutover before 1940 and who, in the late 1980s, took me into their homes and churches and guided me around their communities while sharing accounts of their experiences. They must remain anonymous, but have my gratitude.

My wife, Deborah Mathias Gough, read earlier drafts and helped prepare the final version of manuscript for publication. With difficulty, I might have found professional assistance of similar quality elsewhere, but no one else could have provided me the emotional encouragement and support I needed to finish this project. I hope that my gratitude can match my love for her.

Introduction

In the spring of 1993 Virginia and Jerry Darrow operated the only remaining farm in their township. "We both liked farming anyhow and weren't that happy with our jobs in town or anything," was Jerry's explanation of what brought the couple to the town of Wilkinson, in the Blue Hills of Rusk County in northern Wisconsin. "We just didn't like factory work, and we were raised on farms and liked that kind of life." For several years after beginning farming in 1981 the couple also kept their factory jobs seventeen miles away in Rice Lake, a city of eight thousand, but by 1993 made their living exclusively from their two hundred acres, seventy-five of them cleared, and herd of fifty-five dairy cows.[1] For the Darrows, northern Wisconsin offered the opportunity to work for themselves, close to a natural environment they liked, in a way that allowed them to express their individuality.

Early in the twentieth century, thousands of eager settlers came to this "cutover" region, many for the same reasons that attracted the Darrows to their farm. Some of their descendants, as well as newcomers like the Darrows, carry on their spirit in the 1990s. But for the most part, their attempts at farming were not successful. There were thirteen farms in Wilkinson in 1925 and twenty-one by 1940, but only the Darrows' in the 1990s. In 1940, 148 people lived in Wilkinson, all of them on farms; in 1990, the town's population was just 51, making it the second smallest of Wisconsin's 580 municipalities. Most people in Wilkinson, said Walt Gordon, who was born in the town in 1911, are "just surviving. You won't find a much prettier place to live, but as far as making a living here, forget it."[2] Throughout Rusk County in 1940, 2,430 farmers worked over 265,000 acres; by 1990 there were only about 750 farms on less than 200,000 acres. Across the cutover, there was only about one fourth the number of farms and only about one half the acreage in farms in 1990 than there had been a half century previously. As early as 1949, recalling his boyhood in an area perhaps ten miles south of the Darrow farm, B. M. Apker pointed out that because of reforestation it was not possible to ride a horse within a mile of where he had gone to school in 1884.[3]

While some of their legacy may now be invisible or in decay, the settlers who came with optimism to the cutover between 1900 and 1940 created a history. Their story is the subject of this book. Previous scholarship has examined the cutover primarily as a region whose history shows the importance of some process or pattern—for instance, the closing of the frontier, the wisdom of government planning in attacking rural poverty, the social costs of environmental mistakes, the resistance to assimilation shown by immigrants to the United States, the usefulness of core/periphery models in explaining internal development within the United States. A different perspective emerges by focusing on people and the meaning they gave to the space that was northern Wisconsin. By their thinking and their actions, humans created the cutover as a series of places.[4] The agricultural settlers of northern Wisconsin were just one of a number of human groups which experienced northern Wisconsin differently as a consequence of their historical circumstances. The experiences of American Indians, timber barons, eager farmers, and urban critics of rural America each in turn affected what kind of place the cutover would be for other groups. For each group, therefore, the cutover was a different place.

The way in which agricultural settlers worked on the cutover's land defined their relationship to its space and made it their own place. They worked to bring to northern Wisconsin the style of yeoman farming that had flourished in nineteenth-century America. They expected to secure economic independence by owning their own farm; they were willing to work hard, depending on the labor of their own families and trading work with neighbors; they were satisfied with owning only the small amount of acreage which could be worked under such conditions; they respected individuality while wanting to become members of a community that would provide most of their economic and social needs; and they accepted the need to balance economic success with the other benefits of a rural lifestyle. At the beginning of the twentieth century, as an era of extensive commercial timbering ended in northern Wisconsin, physical and social space still existed for new settlers with this vision. "Many people came up here from the older settlements down south because of the fishing, the hunting, the wild berries, the cheap land," according to Harold Buchman, who was born in the town of Springbrook, Washburn County, in 1899. These settlers were largely from immigrant backgrounds, and relied on the strengths of their ethnic traditions to create the kinds of farming communities they wanted. Buoyed by the optimism characteristic of American agriculture in the first two decades of the twentieth century, they were confident they could build a new agricultural region which would replicate the social and economic patterns of existing family farm regions in the United States. After assessing its possibilities, "my father thought that this was the best country in the world," Buchman remembered.[5]

Agricultural experts experienced the cutover in other ways, developed an alternative vision for it, and eventually transformed it into a different place. Urban-focused and native-born, they reflected the Progressive social and political attitudes widespread in turn-of-the-century Wisconsin. They believed that with their expertise in farming practices, household work, public education, rural credit, local government management, religious life, environmental protection, and many other areas, they could engineer the cutover so that its inhabitants could live better lives. At the beginning of the century they felt their engineering would build yeoman farming communities, but they became disillusioned as economic problems developed nationwide in rural America after 1920 and the limitations of the physical geography of parts of the cutover became apparent. By the 1930s their vision folded the cutover into a complex of rural "problem areas," including Appalachia and the Dust Bowl, for which the federal government initiated ameliorative policies. Ultimately the social engineers decided that the cutover should be depopulated and that forests should be replanted to attract tourists to a different sort of place. Yeoman farming rapidly (but not completely) faded from northern Wisconsin, anticipating its demise across the United States in the decades after World War II.

But before it faded, agriculture was significant in northern Wisconsin for several decades. The accomplishments of the men and women who tried to farm in the cutover need to be recognized. As one of them pointed out, from the perspective of "those of us who helped clear a stump-farm from the cut-over, there is nostalgia for the events of those times; for the feeling of pride when another acre of clover was added, for the excitement of a burning pile of stumps, or for the drama when a wild-fire swept across the nearest hill."[6] Just as the settlers of the cutover wanted to build a society like that preceding them in rural America, their history also deserves a place in growing scholarship of the "new rural history."

In significant respects, however, the experience of the cutover's settlers differed from the image we have in our minds of most farmers in new regions of the United States. Perhaps reflecting Frederick Jackson Turner's idea of the frontier as a place for Euro-Americans to overcome challenges, the story of rural settlement in the eighteenth and nineteenth centuries has been one of successful communities and prosperous regions. The history of the cutover was different. Its significance was that its settlers were unable to replicate the style of farming which had previously characterized American history. This failure presaged the accelerated spread after World War II of a more commercialized, highly capitalistic agriculture, based on wage labor, specialized crop production, heavy mechanization, reliance on chemicals and genetic engineering, greater involvement in world markets, higher capitalization, and dependence on government subsidies. This style of agriculture involved far fewer independent operators: where there had been over six million farms in the United States in 1940, there were barely two million in 1990.[7]

As counterpoint to the general pattern of success in settling new areas in the United States, stories of failure such as those in the cutover can provide much useful information. Sociologists have recently focused on the significance of rural regions in the United States with persistent poverty. For them, such places as Appalachia and the Ozarks in the 1990s seem to refute the predictions of neoclassical economic theory that rural poverty should disappear as people out-migrate for better jobs and industry in-migrates in search of low wages. Rather, theories of dependence and internal colonization appear better able to explain the continued existence of such areas.[8]

Studying the history of the cutover illuminates the significance of these poor regions. Northern Wisconsin's history parallels in some ways that of other depressed, "problem" regions, but is also different. Like Appalachia, northern Wisconsin has sections with soil and terrain that discourage agriculture and encourage social isolation. But settled as it was in the early twentieth century, the cutover was never a place of subsistence agriculture, as Appalachia was for over a century. Furthermore, in the cutover the impact of outside-owned, corporative-organized, resource-extractive industry came *before* agricultural settlement, instead of subsequently impacting it. Like the Great Plains, where water resources limited crop production, the short growing season was a barrier to agriculture in the cutover. But settlement in northern Wisconsin never displayed the boom-or-bust pattern of the Plains. Farming in the cutover was smaller scale, less mechanized, and more harmonious with the environment than on the Plains. It had none of the speculative aspect of suitcase farming. Furthermore, government programs beginning in the 1930s did not enable farming in northern Wisconsin to rebound after the travails of the Depression, as they did for Plains farmers, but encouraged its demise. Like the tenant farmers and sharecroppers in the Cotton Belt, cutover farmers were poor but, for better or worse, they owned their farms. This aspect of yeoman farming in turn encouraged in them a less dependent attitude toward public officials, bankers, and agricultural experts. The number of people working on the land did decline dramatically in northern Wisconsin after World War II, as it did in the Cotton Belt, but farm mechanization played a less direct role in the cutover, given the style of agriculture cutover farmers practiced. In sum, the limits of the environment, the impact of technological change, and the expansion of capitalistic values affected all these "problem" regions, indeed agriculture everywhere in the United States. They played themselves out in a unique way in the cutover, however, as the values and actions of settlers desiring to become yeoman farmers interacted over half a century with those of agriculture experts who wanted to engineer the cutover in a different direction.

The first chapter of this book describes northern Wisconsin and its people in 1900, the place that American Indians and lumber magnates had shaped. It identifies the legacies these people left for agricultural settlers: native peoples pushed aside, land cutover by commercial timber harvesting, an infrastructure developed for resource extraction, not agriculture, a booster mentality about the region in the minds of opinion-makers throughout the state, landowners eager to unload land. Hopeful settlers, eager to duplicate in the north the pattern of yeoman farming successfully established in the rest of Wisconsin, understood these conditions only imperfectly, as did the experts who encouraged them to move to the cutover. Chapter 2 describes the partially successful efforts of these settlers to build yeoman farming communities in the first two decades of the twentieth century. A system of work dependent on family labor and work exchange with neighbors was central to their economic survival, social cohesion, and development of community institutions. Chapter 3 turns to the views about the cutover and its settlers expressed by outside "experts" in the first quarter of the twentieth century. In line with the nationwide Country Life movement, people interested in northern Wisconsin from both the public and private sectors increasingly worked together to control farm settlement in the region.

By the 1920s many of them were skeptical, if not fearful, of farming in the cutover. Their fears were magnified as they saw what happened to the cutover as first the agricultural depression of the 1920s and then the Great Depression of the 1930s took its toll on the region, as chapter 4 recounts.

Cutover settlers were not just passive victims of economic events in these decades; they protested, adapted, made do, and sometimes even prospered. But public officials and agricultural experts were concerned with the high rates of public assistance and municipal fiscal insolvency which characterized the region by the end of the 1930s. The dangerous and exotic qualities of the cutover, epitomized by its use as a refuge by gangsters, made the region appear threatening to outsiders, as chapter 5 shows. Social engineers therefore developed and implemented a vision for the cutover different from that of settlers who wanted to farm and the boosters who encouraged them at the beginning of the century. They decided that reforestation and tourism would help the cutover's struggling farmers, improve the physical environment of the region, and protect economically all of the residents of Wisconsin. Public officials implemented this vision in the 1930s by policies creating public forests, zoning rural areas to exclude agriculture, and encouraging relocation of failing farmers. These programs became part of the thinking of New Deal agricultural policy makers, discussed in chapter 6. New Deal farm programs discouraged small-scale farming like that in the cutover in order to boost commodity-producing commercial farming. The impact of these programs outweighed efforts in the cutover by some federal government agencies to help small producers, such as the Farm Security Administration's attempt to build a subsistence homesteads project which combined farming and forest work for its residents. By the end of the 1930s, parts of the cutover had developed into successful yeoman farming communities, but their future was tenuous because they were seen by outsiders to be part of a region in which agriculture should be discouraged.

The epilogue briefly sketches the effects after World War II of the new public programs of the interwar years. It concludes with the view that the decline of farming in the cutover was not entirely the consequence of unfavorable environmental conditions and certainly not the fault of the settlers. Rather, if farming had begun a half- or even a quarter-century earlier in the cutover, when public attitudes and policies towards yeoman farming had been different, success would have been more likely. The epilogue also points out that the vision for the region of the social engineers of the interwar years was not achieved. The cutover remained a place where some people continued to try to live like the settlers who wanted to bring yeoman farming to northern Wisconsin in the first decades of the twentieth century.

The impact of the attitudes and values of these settlers continues to be found in the cutover in the 1990s. Residents of northern Wisconsin, farmers and nonfarmers alike, value personal independence within a community framework, maintain an attachment and appreciation for the land around them, have limited economic goals, and preserve many traditional social customs. They are skeptical about the benefits of agricultural change. Many "old time pioneer homesteaders," such as Ed Pudas, who was raised on a farm in the town of Oulu in Douglas County in the first decade of the century, wonder "who really profits from the modern style of farming. The farmer, the implement dealer, or the finance people?"[9]

Rural people in the cutover recognize that many of the practices and values of the "sustainable agriculture" movement of the 1990s recall the experience of cutover farmers before 1940. Knute Anderson, the third generation to work his family's farm in the town of Luck in northern Polk County, observed in 1989 that "what they did before" in the cutover in the 1920s resembled the contemporary calls he heard for less reliance on machines, chemicals, and high capitalization and more emphasis on diversification of crops and low-intensity uses of the land. If Wendell Berry is correct, these farming practices should encourage community among rural people, resembling the "one big family" which Knute's father recalled existed in Luck when he operated the Anderson farm.[10] Our renewed appreciation of this style of farming should encourage a closer look at the history of the settlers who tried to farm the Wisconsin cutover in the first decades of the twentieth century.

1 | The Cutover in 1900

Come to Sunny Southern Sawyer
There's a future here for you
Mother Nature's always smiling
And the skies are rarest blue.
Where the crops are always "bumper"
And the taxes always paid
And you've got a dollar waiting
When you've got a dollar made

Anonymous[1]

The *Milwaukee Journal*'s issue of March 12, 1900, was a special "Northern Wisconsin Edition." The banner headline on the front page was "Milwaukee's Future Lies to the North." Articles on the inside pages described the history and existing conditions of the northern part of the state, projected a rosy future for the region, and outlined what roles the city of Milwaukee should play in the region's development. In just ten to twenty years, reported a correspondent based in Rice Lake in Barron County, the "agricultural resources" of northern Wisconsin "will equal any part of the state." A *Journal* editorial concluded that, with "agricultural and stock possibilities yet unmeasured," northern Wisconsin was "bound in time to be the richest part of the state."[2]

The boosterism tone of these newspaper articles about northern Wisconsin was widely shared in the state at the beginning of the new century. On a visit to Chicago in 1902, U.S. Secretary of Agriculture James Wilson exclaimed that northern Wisconsin was "going to be a great agricultural country." When Wisconsin's first agricultural extension agent came to Oneida County he reported back to Madison breathlessly, "This is a wonderful country. I never saw anything like it." A scientific study of the soil in some of the very northernmost counties of the state concluded that "the greater part of the land is fair to excellent in quality and susceptible of the highest agricultural development" and would also promote the physical and mental health of the settlers. Therefore, "we in the north need no pity," asserted a Clark County judge, for "the coming 25 years will be marked by surprising agricultural development." The proof of these claims appeared to be seen in dollars and cents. "Farm lands in this county have more than doubled in the last eight years and we predict that they will double once more in the same time," reported a small-scale land dealer in Lincoln County. "Any man who buys a farm . . . in this country stands absolutely no chance of losing." Lumberman John G. Owen summarized well the consensus about the potential of northern Wisconsin land: "There is some good hard work in prospect before a man gets it cleared up, but it pays him big profit in the end."[3]

This land of rapture—most significantly the millions of acres commercially logged over during the last third of the nineteenth century (whence the name "cutover")—was put to many uses during previous centuries, the legacies of which were not fully and accurately understood in 1900, but promoters at that time confidently proceeded to retail cutover land to farm settlers. Their methods were tailored to the conditions of the cutover, received government encouragement, and showed the influence of contemporary science and marketing practices while also reflecting the strongly ingrained optimism of Americans about their nation's continued capacity for growth and re-creation. From what they learned about the cutover from these sources, settlers believed that they could create for themselves in northern Wisconsin small-scale family farms in largely self-sufficient and socially integrated rural neighborhoods.

The eighteen northernmost counties of Wisconsin contain 11,767,080 acres, one third of the state's land area (Figure 1.1). They correspond closely with the northern highland physiographic division of the state, an extension from Canada of the Laurentian Shield; 90 percent of the cutover is part of this division, and 90 percent of the northern highlands are part of the cutover. The northern highlands are dome-shaped, with elevation declining in all directions from about seventeen hundred feet above sea level near Land O' Lakes in Vilas County. They are underlaid by Precambrian crystalline rocks, chiefly granites and basalts which were uplifted and exposed by erosion of sedimentary rocks about one million years ago—the Blue Hills in Rusk County are one of a half-dozen hilly outcrops of Precambrian rocks in the cutover. In more recent geological times, most of the northern highlands was covered by glacial deposits, responsible for the region's gently rolling terrain, numerous lakes, and scattered swamps. The greatest concentration of such lakes is in the northernmost counties of Vilas and Oneida. Here some two thousand lakes cover about one sixth of the surface area. At the north-

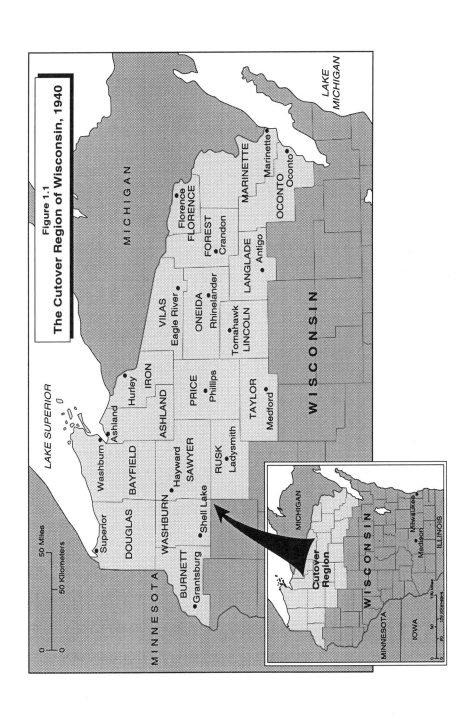

Figure 1.1
The Cutover Region of Wisconsin, 1940

west corner of the northern highlands an escarpment drops 300 to 400 feet. At the bottom is a plain 10 to 20 miles wide, the Lake Superior lowland, a separate physiographic division situated mostly on Precambrian sandstone which covers the northern edges of Douglas, Ashland, Bayfield, and Iron counties bordering on Lake Superior.[4]

From the underlying rock formations, the processes of climate and glaciation produced the soils that covered northern Wisconsin in 1900. Broadly speaking, these are chiefly cool-climate forest soils which, consistent with the underlying geology, are related to the soils of southern Canada (as well as other places such as Scandinavia and Scotland), in contrast to the grassland soils characteristic of southwestern Wisconsin and the woodland soils of the southeastern part of the state. At the beginning of the century, scattered rocks of various sizes covered the surface of most of these soils. Agricultural agent Ernest Luther sarcastically reported, regarding Oneida County, that "God got a little careless with his work of sowing and in some spots did not get the stone on." The presence or absence of rocks, as well as the nature of the terrain, complicated the evaluation of the capacity of northern Wisconsin soils. Furthermore, snow obscured them for almost half of the year and, most important, their quality varied greatly within a relatively small area. When asked, Fred Etcheson, who came to the town of Limrick in Sawyer County as an infant in 1891 and farmed there beginning in the 1920s, described the quality of the land: "Some places it's awful good; some places it's no good. . . . I got 60 acres that's practically level. . . . There is no rock, and again you can probably go half a mile from there or a mile and you take a piece of land that's almost the same size, you couldn't get the rock off from it all summer."[5] In the 1990s soil analysis classifies about 45 percent of the cutover as of medium or better soil productivity, when managed intensively, compared to over 90 percent of the rest of the state in such classifications.[6] In 1900 informed opinion rated northern Wisconsin soils as more comparable in quality to those of southern Wisconsin.

In the centuries following the end of glaciation about nine thousand years ago, northern Wisconsin became almost completely forested. Whereas prairie grasses mixed with oak, elm, sugar maple, and basswood trees covered southern Wisconsin, by the nineteenth century a mixture of pine and hardwoods predominated in the northern part of the state, providing a transition to the conifer-dominated forests north of Lake Superior. In northern Wisconsin hardwoods grew on the better clay and loamy soils—sugar maples on drier, hillier sites and hemlocks and yellow birch on heavier soils and wetter sites. Especially in drier areas, magnificent white pines, with diameters sometimes in excess of fifty inches, towered above the hardwoods, and predominated, in conjunction with red (or Norway) pines, in places such as in the headwaters of the Flambeau River in Oneida and Vilas counties. Smaller jack pine growth characterized the dry, sandy soils of the "sand barrens," two diagonal strips cutting through Burnett, Douglass, and Bayfield counties in northwestern Wisconsin, and Oconto and Marinette counties in northeastern Wisconsin. Spruce, tamarack, and cedar trees also grew in northern Wisconsin in wetter, swampier locations. In scattered places, especially in Marinette and Oconto counties, white spruce and balsam fir grew, typical of the boreal forest dominated by conifers which ranges only a few hundred miles farther north.[7]

At the beginning of the twentieth century, commentators emphasized the "healthy," bracing quality of the region's climate. They pointed out that, with its location in the center of the North American land mass, northern Wisconsin fully experienced all four seasons. Indeed, the monthly range of temperatures at Rhinelander, in Oneida County, in the center of the region, goes from 11 degrees Fahrenheit in January to 68 degrees in July. Precipitation averages around thirty inches a year, about half as rain in the summer. But summers are short—100 to 120 frost-free days in most locations away from the shores of Lake Superior and Green Bay. Much of the precipitation, therefore, comes as snow— the cutover corresponds closely with the part of Wisconsin that receives more than fifty inches annually. Snow usually covers the ground from November through March. It was these long, snowy winters that made an impression on many early settlers different than that emphasized by northern Wisconsin boosters. Writing in the third person, Robert Schlomann recalled as a five-year-old having to use the outhouse for the first time on the December day he arrived in town of Grow, near Rhinelander. "He almost forgot what he came for as the spine-tingling chills ran up his back when the skin met the boards. Zip—two quick pages from the Sears-Roebuck catalog. He didn't bother to button his pants. One hand held them as he ran to the shack."[8]

The settlers attracted to northern Wisconsin by the optimistic reports circulating in 1900 were not, of course, the first humans to live in the region. Over several thousand years, Native American peoples had lived there by successfully adapting to the region's ecological conditions. In historic times, bands from Algonquian-speaking tribes, chiefly Chippewa

(Ojibway) but also some Menominee, lived in northern Wisconsin. In the century following European contact with the Americas, largely in response to opportunities in the fur trade, the Chippewa had expanded from a region around northern Lake Huron and eastern Lake Superior into much of what is now Ontario, Michigan, Minnesota, and Wisconsin. Since the Chippewa generally planted corn only where there was a minimum of 120 frost-free days, this crop was of little significance to them in northern Wisconsin. Subsistence came instead from hunting deer, moose, caribou, and elk; from fishing in the Great Lakes; and from collecting wild rice on the numerous lakes of northern Wisconsin. Indeed, wild rice was the staple in the Chippewa diet, perhaps providing more than half of their caloric intake. The large wild game the Chippewa hunted were never abundant in Wisconsin; deer tended to inhabit an area to the west for which both Chippewa and Sioux contested. This reliance on wild rice distinguished Wisconsin bands of the Chippewa from bands north and east of Lake Michigan, who relied most heavily on fishing, and the more agricultural Sioux to the west. The Menominee also extensively harvested wild rice. By 1900 they were concentrated on the edge of the cutover in Oconto and Shawano counties, on the far northern edge of their original homeland.[9]

By the beginning of the twentieth century, the intrusion of Euro-Americans had altered the cutover's vegetation and corresponding habitat for animals in such ways that native peoples could no longer live independently by relying on the resources of their environment. By a series of treaties negotiated during the second quarter of the nineteenth century, Wisconsin Indians had ceded their land to the federal government. Washington's intention was to relocate these Native Americans to west of the Mississippi, as it did with most eastern tribes during this period. Tribal people from southern Wisconsin, such as the Fox and the Kickapoo, did make the move, but when the time came for the Chippewa to relocate, Washington reconsidered the wisdom and effectiveness of the removal policy—too many Indians were filtering back from their new homes, and those who did not come back threatened to become the focus for a pan-Indian movement west of the Mississippi. In the 1854 treaties, therefore, four bands of Chippewa—Red Cliff, Lac Court Oreilles, Bad River, and Lac du Flambeau—as well as the Menominee were assigned to reservations in northern Wisconsin (Figure 1.2). The Chippewa were left in an economically inviable situation. Confined to about 275,000 acres, they lost the mobility necessary to practice their

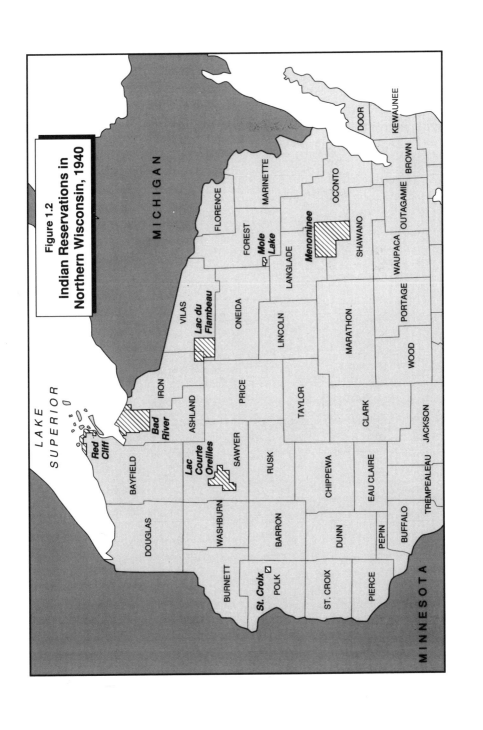

Figure 1.2
Indian Reservations in
Northern Wisconsin, 1940

traditional hunting, trapping, fishing, and rice gathering. Not until the 1980s would the federal courts acknowledge that under the 1854 and earlier treaties the Chippewa had reserved off-reservation hunting and fishing rights in the ceded territories. The complaint by a Minnesota Chippewa chief about the treaties was typical of the situation in Wisconsin: "It requires many of us to give up good homes for poor ones. [It] . . . gives us little but swamps or marshes. . . . True, we may find a little rice and a few fish, but not sufficient for my people, not enough to save them from starvation."[10] Federal government policy, beginning in 1887, of breaking reservations up into individually owned allotments undermined the integrity of the Indian communities and led to plots on the reservations falling into the hands of white vacationers seeking lakeside summer homes and lumber companies eager to remove the land's timber. With these developments came the introduction of exotic fish species into lakes, the loss of habitat for game by removal of the forest, and the degradation of wild rice beds by the artificial manipulation of water levels. An Ontario official in the 1890s reported an experience similar to many in Wisconsin: "Lumber men have been damming up the creeks, and then letting the water out and raising the water in the lakes and killing the growing rice stems."[11] (Wild rice grows best in three or four feet of stable, slowing moving water.) Faced with these unwelcome changes, Native Americans clung to traditional economic practices as best they could, but when they gathered wild rice, for example, it was increasingly for commercial rather than subsistence purposes. Indian men had to rely on casual labor as fishing guides for the tourists or woods workers for the lumbermen. These interactions with whites and their cultural practices led to further social disorganization among Native Americans in northern Wisconsin. Mabel Greenhazen recalled that as a young girl she helped her father, who operated a tavern in the town of Stone Lake in Washburn County in the 1880s, illegally sell liquor to Indians.[12]

Negatively affected by these conditions, the number of Native Americans in northern Wisconsin declined. Precisely accurate counts are lacking, but the state census of 1905, at the time which appears to have been the demographic nadir of American Indians in general, identified just 4,619 Indians in the cutover counties, only about 2 percent of the region's population. Similarly, censuses taken in 1900 by Bureau of Indian Affairs officials at Bad River, Lac du Flambeau, La Court Oreilles, and Menominee reported 4,054 Native Americans.[13] American Indians, therefore, would not be an "obstacle" to the settlement of the cutover by white farmers; their numbers were relatively thin and increasingly confined to reservations.

Under these circumstances, it was easy for whites to ignore Indians in northern Wisconsin. An 1881 antiquarian history, referring to Bayfield County, reported that only "solitary companies of these aborigines wander over the country to the present day, like ghosts of departed rulers."[14] Whatever attention whites did bestow on them was usually in the form of caricature. For example, an antiquarian historian of Langlade County, writing in the early twentieth century, triumphantly claimed that "we see the ideal farmhouse . . . where once the Indian tepee comforted the restless and impulsive red man. Where the Indian made his temporary abode, we find prosperous farms and contented communities."[15] In nineteenth-century America, Indians had generally been eliminated from territories by white settlement. By contrast, in the cutover, native peoples remained in close proximity to the whites who tried to replace them on the land. The new settlers, however, did not seek to learn anything from the people who had lived there for centuries. As the language of the local historians just quoted suggests, white attitudes were of superiority and disdain. Furthermore, the interrelated changes which had come over both the traditional Indian way of life and the natural environment of northern Wisconsin obscured the ability of white settlers to appreciate how well the Native Americans had been able to live in the region. None of the promotional or advisory literature for prospective cutover farmers suggested that they should harvest the wild rice themselves or deliberatively sow beds. Perhaps successful ricing depended on knowledge of local waterways and seasonal changes which newcomers did not possess. (When paddy rice cultivation did finally emerge in the 1960s, little of it was in Wisconsin.)[16]

Commercial lumbering had brought the raw forces of capitalism to northern Wisconsin in the nineteenth century and produced enormous change in its natural environment, especially the vegetation on which Native Americans had based their way of life. The settlers who subsequently came to the cutover to farm, therefore, were not like nineteenth-century American farmers faced with problems such as the commercialization of the countryside by impersonal market forces requiring agricultural specialization, by rapacious landlords, or by protoindustrialization. Rather, they came in the wake of large-scale, immensely profitable commercial lumbering,[17] which had been far more disruptive than the mining and fur-trading activities preceding agricultural settlement in nineteenth-century America. Settlers had to deal with the legacy of this lumbering, but perhaps because nineteenth-century models were in their minds, they did not fully appreciate its significance. Thus, they greatly limited themselves by disdaining American Indians and ignoring what had happened to them. Seemingly oblivious to the fact that the same interrelated forces of intensified commercialization and ecological change which had decimated and disorganized native peoples in northern Wisconsin could also affect them, they confidently believed that what they wanted to do with northern Wisconsin was inevitably preordained to succeed. Lumbering had been devastating, admitted a booster of northern Chippewa County on the edge of the cutover, but it was "also the beginning of the industry which is to eventually place the section of Northern Wisconsin first in wealth and beauty—the farming industry." For farming to follow lumbering was part of "a stupendous and well-ordered campaign in the eternal, onward march of civilization."[18]

As part of the march of civilization, in the quarter-century following 1873 an estimated sixty billion board feet were cut by Wisconsin sawmills.[19] This product was almost entirely shipped out of Wisconsin, contributing to both the physical growth and more elaborate business structure of distant communities such as Chicago but providing little basis for long-term economic development in the cutover.[20] This business also increasingly came into the hands of large-scale enterprises. Edward P. Hines, a Chicago-based lumberman, operated as many as seventeen sawmills in northern Wisconsin, including one at Park Falls in Price County which could produce two hundred thousand board feet of lumber a day, equal to seventy-eight miles of 1"× 6" boards. These activities produced enormous profits. Lumbermen such as Hines, Owen, Orrin Ingram, and Frederick Weyerhaeuser emerged from the woods as wealthy men. The precise dimensions of their fortunes are obscured by the surviving records of their complex, interrelated enterprises, but the immense Victorian homes they built in Eau Claire, Chippewa Falls, Wausau, Stevens Point, and other cities on the edge of the cutover, many still standing, testified publicly to their success. One example of a medium-sized enterprise is suggestive. In 1882 John A. Humbird organized the White Pine Lumber Company with timberland in the town of Mason in Bayfield County (Weyerhaeuser held a one-eighth interest in the enterprise). On an initial investment of $460,000 the company paid dividends to its shareholders of over $2,000,000 during the next twenty-three years, and then was sold to Hines for $2,620,000.[21]

What did all this activity do to the land in northern Wisconsin? "Coming to Ashland in 1889 through 200 miles of continuous forest interspersed with lakes, it seemed that the supply of timber was inexhaustible and yet in a few years the timber was exhausted," recalled J. M. Dodd. When lumbering reached its peak, the four billion board feet cut in 1892 alone required the clearing of over five hundred square miles, 3 percent of the surface area of the cutover. In 1898 federal forester Filbert Roth estimated that in the twenty-seven northern counties he had surveyed only about 13 percent of the original pine remained standing.[22]

A booster at the beginning of the twentieth century was proud that "a few more years will see the last of our forests."[23] But after being logged over, the land of northern Wisconsin was devastated. Brush, limbs, tops, and unwanted logs littered the ground, which still contained millions of stumps (Figure 1.3). With less vegetation, runoff increased, lowering stream levels, drying up marshes, and creating flood problems. In streams with lower levels and increased silting, increased penetration of sunlight changed the habitat for fish. There was also less cover for

Figure 1.3. Brush, stumps, and small trees remaining on recently cutover land in northern Wisconsin in the early twentieth century. (State Historical Society of Wisconsin, photo WHi (X3) 50583)

game. Consequently, caribou and moose, for example, were extinct in northern Wisconsin by 1900.[24]

The language used to describe the subsequent appearance of the cutover suggests the destruction that had come to the region. Writers attempting to convey the experience of World War I, with its scarred and treeless battlefields in France and Belgium, had used arcadian images to highlight ironically what war had done to the land.[25] In a twist on this use of language, after the war visitors and settlers in northern Wisconsin used images of warfare to convey the appearance of the region's natural environment. A visitor to Price County in 1921 explained, "One who has not seen cut over country can hardly imagine the task of clearing its stumps. It's almost like asking a man to transform the war scarred fields around Verdun into fruitful farms." In their later years, when people who saw the cutover at this time sought words to describe it, they turned to the wars more recent in their memories. In 1988 a seventy-two-year-old resident of the town of Drummond in Bayfield County, who had worked on his family farm while growing up, stated that with a comparative wartime perspective, "now I can tell you" that the cutover landscape "looked like those islands out in the Pacific in World War II." A half-century after he settled in Gleason in Lincoln County in 1902, a physician looking for language with maximum impact hyperbolically explained that the cutover had "presented a picture of destruction wrought by a score of Hiroshimas."[26]

The commercial lumbering of the late nineteenth century irrevocably altered the forest of northern Wisconsin known to the Indians and early white fur traders. White pine trees did not grow up to replace the great stands harvested by the lumbermen, which in some places had grown for twenty-five generations over a period of 6,000 to 8,000 years. Felling all white pine in a section eliminated the seed supply from adjacent trees, which had naturally regenerated white pine areas where trees had been downed by fire or windfall. Brush fires followed commercial lumbering much more frequently than would have occurred naturally and further eliminated seed sources. Where cheap nursery stock was imported to compensate for these problems, it introduced from Asia white pine blister rust, often fatal for American white pine. In its place after the lumber harvest flourished species with characteristics more adapted to the new ecological conditions of the cutover (Figure 1.4). Jack pine and aspen spread widely and remained because lumbermen did not value them and their seed supplies were well adapted to survive

Figure 1.4. Second-growth birch and other trees on land where pine forest had been cut over near Lake de Flambeau Falls, 1929. (State Historical Society of Wisconsin, photo WHi (W63) 11799)

post-logging fires. Referring to the aftermath of a fire in Door County, on the edge of the cutover, an old-time settler recalled that "in the spring of 1872 the whole burned area was covered with poplar, aspen, and white birch trees seeded thick as grain in a field, and grew fast."[27]

This blooming regrowth of vegetation in the cutover, especially in the aftermath of fire in the brush that lumbermen left behind, actually encouraged new settlers often to have positive views about the region's fertility.[28] Blueberry and raspberry bushes, for example, quickly sprang up everywhere. Some animals, such as deer, rapidly multiplied in this habitat. Albert Stouffer, who moved in 1886 as a ten-year-old to the town of Bashaw in Washburn County, remembered that "fish and game were plentiful. . . . Deer fed on our rutabaga patches and it was only necessary to go up the river a few bends to get all the mallards we wanted." Charlie Carlson recalled "blueberries, blueberries, fish, and venison. That's what we lived on." Wild hay was also abundant; grasses such as timothy initially produced large yields from only semicleared cutover fields. Even exotic plants and weeds introduced on the sides of lumber roads grew impressively. Gus Gensler, coming to Three Rivers in Oneida County in the early 1890s, found that the "land was fertile and bounteous."[29] Most settlers, however, did not recognize the consequences of this brief post-logging blooming. In the long run, the intensified browsing by larger deer herds which it encouraged inhibited the growth of trees such as hemlocks and opened the way for the proliferation of such species as jack pine. Furthermore, the initial encouragement from fire for regrowth was only temporary and many severely burned areas suffered permanent damage.

At the beginning of the twentieth century, the landscape of one significant section of northern Wisconsin remained largely unchanged from what it had been for hundreds of years. The 230,000-acre Menominee Indian Reservation, home to about seventeen hundred American Indians in Oconto and Shawano counties, had not been cut over (Figure 1.2). For anyone traveling through the reservation or, later, flying over it, its landscape presented a striking visual reminder of how the forest of northern Wisconsin looked before the logging era. The Menominee was one of the few tribes to reject the federal government's allotment program initiated in 1887. "We accepted our present reservation when it was considered of no value by our friends," Menominee Chief Neopit explained in 1882. "All we ask is that we are permitted to keep it as a home." Over the next several decades the tribe actively resisted attempts by loggers and government agencies to exploit this land commercially. By the end of the nineteenth century the Menominee people certainly had lost many aspects of their traditional life—separated from their historical source of wild rice on Shawano Lake and without even a basis in their treaties to claim off-reservation gathering rights, they no longer included rice in their diets or gathering rituals in their social life. A faction within the tribe became assimilated to Euro-American ways. But the Menominee still used the resources of the forests on their reservation. Maple-sugar production in the 1860s and 1870s was reported at sixty tons per year. Federal legislation in 1890 allowed the Menominee to cut two million board feet of timber a year, the proceeds benefiting the tribe collectively. The subsequent selective cutting of the forests provided work for tribal members and early in the twentieth century began to support a sawmill at Neopit which became a source of further employment.[30] The Menominee could not avoid some of the poverty and social disorganization characteristic of most Native American communities. But they had maintained the integrity of a part of their traditional lands, from which they could use natural resources in the self-sustaining ways their people always had. Furthermore, to the extent they engaged the market economy that was growing around them, they did so as a group, not as individuals.

White Americans, however, ignored this alternative land use for northern Wisconsin. The lesson they seemed to learn from the logging experience, instead, was that the natural environment of northern Wisconsin had been violently—and from the lumberman's point of view, successfully—altered. Settlers coming to farm the cutover intended to alter it again, successfully, they expected. Indeed, some agricultural settlers and promoters saw it as their task to "redeem" the region from the damage that logging had done to it. In doing so, they followed the long American tradition of "improving" an environment through human action, in part by using its natural resources.[31] But the specific environmental conditions of the cutover at the beginning of the twentieth century made their efforts problematic. In eighteenth- and nineteenth-century America, pioneer settlers had been seen as overcoming a pure, orderly, and beautiful wilderness, usually forested.[32] In the twentieth-century cutover, nature did not have these qualities to encourage settlers and legitimize their efforts in the eyes of other Americans.

Over time different peoples had shaped and reshaped the natural environment of northern Wisconsin, both on the ground and in their imaginations. It was this legacy of how the land had been used, more than its inherent qualities, that challenged the agricultural settlers of the cutover.

The logging era also left social and political legacies which influenced the future settlement of the cutover. Old lumber company towns were scattered across northern Wisconsin, and on the edge of the cutover medium-sized cities such as Eau Claire, Wausau, and Stevens Point owed their existence to lumbering. Their merchants, bankers, and newspaper editors were eager to find new economic bases to support these communities as logging wound down in the 1890s. Encouraging farmers to settle in the surrounding countryside was one way to do this.[33]

Lumbering, and mining on the upper peninsula of Michigan, had encouraged railroad construction across the cutover, which was responsible for the development of several small cities in the region (Figure 1.5). By the beginning of the twentieth century, the Chicago and Northwestern system, through its Omaha subsidiary, had connections through

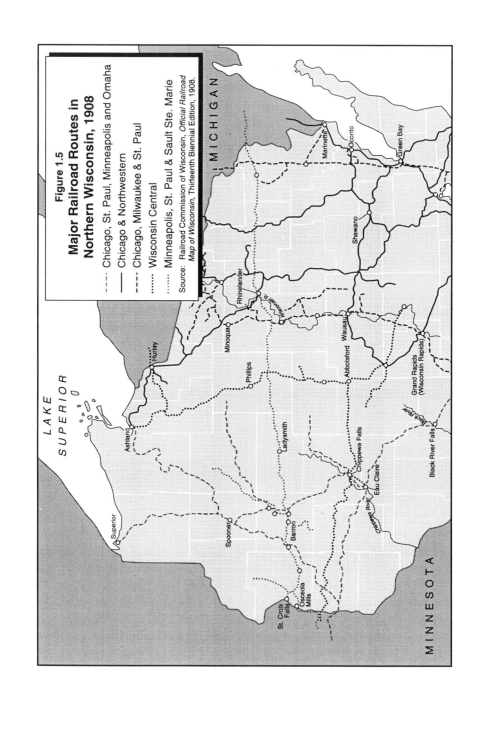

Figure 1.5
Major Railroad Routes in Northern Wisconsin, 1908

-·-·- Chicago, St. Paul, Minneapolis and Omaha
──── Chicago & Northwestern
------ Chicago, Milwaukee & St. Paul
········ Wisconsin Central
········ Minneapolis, St. Paul & Sault Ste. Marie

Source: Railroad Commission of Wisconsin, *Official Railroad Map of Wisconsin*, Thirteenth Biennial Edition, 1908.

LAKE SUPERIOR

MICHIGAN

MINNESOTA

Superior

Ashland

Hurley

Minocqua

Rhinelander

Phillips

Ladysmith

Spooner

Barron

Chippewa Falls

Eau Claire

Abbotsford

Wausau

Shawano

Marinette

Oconto

Green Bay

Grand Rapids (Wisconsin Rapids)

Black River Falls

St. Croix Falls

Osceola Mills

Chippewa River

Black River

Wisconsin River

Eau Claire to Ashland and Superior. The Chicago and Northwestern had also built through Rhinelander to Ashland and to the upper peninsula of Michigan. Its rival, the Chicago, Milwaukee, and St. Paul system, had built lines northward through the center of the cutover from Wausau to Minoqua and through northeastern Wisconsin from Green Bay into the upper peninsula. The Wisconsin Central had track extending northward into the cutover, from Abbortsford in Clark County through Phillips in Price County to Ashland and Hurley. The Wisconsin Central also operated an east-west route on the edge of the cutover, from Abbortsford through Chippewa Falls to St. Paul. The Minneapolis, St. Paul, and Sault Ste. Marie—known locally as the Soo line—had also built in an east-west pattern through northern Wisconsin as part of a route from St. Paul through Canada to the Atlantic ports designed to carry prairie grains in winter when the Great Lakes were frozen. A motivation for the initial construction of several of these railroads, perhaps most notably the Omaha and the Wisconsin Central, had been to earn federal land grants designed to encourage railroad construction. At the end of the nineteenth century, agricultural settlers could buy this land from the railroads and use it to grow crops whose shipment would begin to replace sawed logs as railroad traffic.[34]

Another legacy left by loggers for agricultural settlers was a system of minor civil divisions. The relatively few settlers in northern Wisconsin in 1900 had already organized an elaborate governmental system. In some instances timber companies had encouraged this pattern: in 1895 lumberman William Knox manipulated the creation of the new town of Knox in Price County, dividing the existing town of Brannon, in anticipation of his timber lands receiving a lower assessment in the new town. But in many cases, it was settlers who schemed for the creation of new units of local government because most of the taxes they would levy would be the responsibility of lumber companies, whose managers and stockholders lived elsewhere. In 1900 the cutover contained only about 10 percent of Wisconsin's population but had seventeen (soon to be eighteen) of its seventy counties and more than its share of towns, villages, and cities. Nine of the cutover counties had less than ten thousand people, but only two counties in the rest of the state were so thinly populated. Many of these units of government had freely taken on indebtedness to subsidize railroad construction through the community and for other purposes. In the 1880s, when it still had only eight hundred residents, Ashland County had an indebtedness of over $200,000.

With the demise of lumbering, these debt burdens from a preceding era became an ongoing responsibility of agricultural settlers.[35]

Agriculture had not been totally absent from northern Wisconsin during the lumbering era. Lumber companies discouraged settlers, who would want to tax timber company land for roads and schools. But sawmill and lumber camp workers had to eat. Timber companies needed an estimated two million bushels of wheat and fifteen thousand tons of hay annually in the 1880s and 1890s. The companies themselves, therefore, often maintained corporate farms to provide potatoes, vegetables, and beef for their employees. In 1889, the Phillips Lumber Company had fifteen hundred acres in potatoes and one thousand in root crops.[36] Later settlers sometimes got started with this farmland as their basis— for instance, in 1903 Homer Levake and his brother bought several hundred acres in the town of Stone Lake in Washburn County that the Dobie Logging Company had used for its stock. There were also some opportunities for independent operators to develop farms and sell their products to lumber camps. For example, Hans Skinvik was an 1891 Norwegian immigrant who worked in lumber camps around Minong in Washburn County but also slowly developed a farm during summers on which he grew potatoes and beans which he sold to lumber camps. Bernhard Bay combined woods and railroad work with dairy farming near Glidden in Ashland County, and by 1890 had a fourteen-cow herd furnishing milk for lumber camps. Dismas Frank began farming in the town of Worcester in Price County in 1885. In 1886 he initiated the first milk delivery route for the nearby city of Phillips and continued to farm until about age sixty in 1920. Overall the number of cows on farms in Price County grew from 224 in 1889 to 934 by 1898. In neighboring Lincoln County, part-time farmers in the 1880s gathered large wild ginseng roots and sold them for between fourteen and twenty-two dollars a pound.[37] Many of these lumber workers were eager to start farming because they had been attracted to northern Wisconsin by immigration appeals designed to meet the labor needs of the lumber industry but emphasizing the agricultural opportunities of the region.[38] To optimists, the farms they initiated were just the beginning of the anticipated general spread of agriculture in northern Wisconsin in the twentieth century.

Lumbering did not end completely in 1900. Massive cutting of white pine, and the bonanza profits associated with it, was finished. But smaller tracts of land, particularly those forested with hardwoods, remained to be cut. Timber that had been passed over when there were more profitable alternatives now began to be brought to market. Edward Hines, for example, promoted fibrous hemlock as equal to smooth-grained white pine and bland-textured yellow birch as "the mahogany of the north." Cutting several hundred thousand acres in northeast Rusk County, western Price County, eastern Sawyer County, and southern Ashland and Bayfield counties, Hines sent birch to his mill at Rice Lake, which operated until the early 1930s, and hemlock to Park Falls, which sawed timber for another decade.[39] While they operated, these activities provided part-time employment in the forest or in the sawmill for many of the settlers coming to the region to farm. But they also encouraged many settlers to choose locations more for their propinquity to off-farm employment opportunities than for their agricultural potential.

The logging era experience was also significant for the agricultural future of the cutover because it determined the way in which settlers acquired their land. Land was not "free" for settlers on nineteenth-century frontiers or in the twentieth-century cutover. However, in both cases settlers were usually able to own their land instead of having to lease, rent, or sharecrop it.[40] But the process by which newcomers to the cutover acquired ownership was different than that on previous frontiers. In the nineteenth century many settlers claimed or purchased their land directly from the state or federal governments. At the time the cutover opened up for agricultural settlement, such homesteading possibilities were the main methods of settlement in the western Dakotas and Montana and across the international border in Saskatchewan and Alberta.[41] In these situations, at the minimum, the government provided an alternative to the private market as a source of land. In northern Wisconsin, by contrast, despite the universal practice still in use of referring to farms as "homesteads," settlers acquired almost no land by any form of government entry. The opportunity for this sort of purchase did not exist: what public land there had been was almost entirely in private hands by 1900. Only about three hundred thousand acres remained of the more than ten million acres of United States land that had been in the public domain in 1867.[42] The state of Wisconsin, for its part, under pressure to finance its fledgling university and hesitant to appear as a land speculator, quickly sold over five hundred thousand acres assigned to it by the Morrill Act of 1862 for only about fifty cents per acre.

Consequently, timber, mining, and railroad companies benefited from nineteenth-century public policies designed to put the public domain into private hands as rapidly as possible. It was from these enterprises rather than the government that almost all cutover settlers acquired land. The quick transfer of land into private hands in the nineteenth century had been absolute, and not as part of a comprehensive plan or incumbered with restrictions such as land classification—the federal 1892 Stone and Timber Act had little impact in Wisconsin since the timber-cutting era was almost over. (In Canada, by contrast, title to the Great Lakes forest was retained by the crown, and the land only leased to timber companies.) Once in private hands land in northern Wisconsin was exploited quickly to extract its natural wealth. Therefore, in contrast to their nineteenth-century predecessors, immigrants to the cutover bought land that had been extensively used and altered.

There had been little public concern with the accumulation by a few individuals or companies of large tracts of land or what would happen to this land once it had been logged over. To begin with, land was a major source of capital, especially significant in a society where liquid capital was limited. The entrepreneur who could accumulate land therefore was an individual to be encouraged by government largesse and emulated. Lumbering consequently followed a quick-return mentality which further inhibited the market from developing the ability to assess the long-term value of northern Wisconsin and identify the economic activities best suited for it. Techniques of economic theory, accounting methodology, and soil science did not have the opportunity to develop sufficiently to provide a longer-term perspective and challenge the generally believed but casually formulated assumption that profitable agriculture would naturally follow the timber harvest. The quick-return mentality also meant that timber companies did not have a long-term commitment to northern Wisconsin. From the companies' perspective, short-sighted state and local taxation policies impelled them to log off the land as quickly as possible and then rapidly dispose of it for other uses. They could not afford, they argued, to hold land until the forest regenerated itself and could be harvested again.[43] The significant point is that farmers coming to the cutover at the beginning of the twentieth century inherited this legacy of an unregulated, ill-informed, short-sighted, and loosely managed system of land distribution.

This casual manner of land distribution was one factor in making the cutover the diverse region it would become in the first third of the twentieth century. Its features of physical geography would also play a role. The agricultural potential of the sand barrens of Burnett County was much different than that of the loamy soils of Langlade County.

There would be diversity among the settlers of the region as well. For some, life in the cutover would be a postscript to lumbering. For others, it would be the opportunity to initiate farming in a new region. Some of these settlers would locate in regions easily accessible to markets for farm products, at Superior or St. Paul or Green Bay, or along railroads linking them to still more distant markets. But others would find themselves in remote locations, influenced more by where lumbering had flourished than by where agriculture could prosper. As we shall see in chapter 2, these differences encouraged levels of farming intensity that were not the same in all parts of the cutover. In chapters 4 and 6 we will also learn that there were different degrees of economic success among cutover farmers.

But in important ways the cutover was also a single region. Its vegetation at the time of European contact differentiated it from the rest of Wisconsin and provided the basis for an extractive industry focused in the region in the late nineteenth century which profoundly altered its ecological makeup, indigenous population, and political organization. Even more significantly, largely as a result of its nineteenth-century history, Americans perceived the cutover in 1900 as a single region. Indeed, the promoters of the region wanted it thought of in this way. They tended to be indiscriminate in projecting the undeniably positive resources it contained and the accomplishments of some of its settlers onto the entire region and its population. The picture they created served their immediate need of encouraging settlement, but it also provided the basis for a counterweight with an equally negative and indiscriminate stereotype of the entire region which would become dominant by the 1930s, as we shall see in chapters 3 and 5.

Critical to the future of northern Wisconsin in 1900 was the way it was portrayed to outsiders. Land salesmen would be expected to exaggerate its potential. But what about the opinions of scientists, other trained observers, and government officials entrusted with advancing the public good?

There were a few doubts at the end of the logging era about the agricultural future of the cutover, but they were still an ignored minority. As early as 1821, Henry Rowe Schoolcraft reported in his *Travels* through the Great Lakes region that some parts of it could "never be rendered subservient to . . . agriculture, or traversed by roads." At the beginning of the logging era, an 1867 report to the Wisconsin legislature by Increase Lapham recommended the adoption of what today would be called sustained yield practices for the northern Wisconsin forest, warning that otherwise its residents would "revert to conditions of barbarism." Going beyond such utilitarian concerns, in the 1890s Beloit College professor J. J. Blaisdell developed what today would be called an ecological approach to conservation. He argued that preserving forests in northern Wisconsin as part of a balanced land use system would benefit the "physical and mental life" of Wisconsinites. In 1898 forester Filbert Roth concluded that there was "no prospect that our denuded lands will be put to agricultural uses." Efforts to do so would only attract "crackers," foreign immigrants with "very low standards of living," characterized as "ignorant and unambitious." State forester Edward Merriam Griffith in 1906 recommended "guided" settlements in forest areas and the formation of public forests closed to farming.[44] As a possible model, New York state amended its constitution in 1894 to create a "forever wild" state park in the Adirondacks. However, an effort by the Wisconsin legislature to form a state forest in the cutover was struck down as unconstitutional by the state supreme court in 1915. Both the public and the judiciary remained attached to the nineteenth-century rejection of state-mandated economic planning and wanted to maintain a romantic vision of the forest as the locus for individual challenge and success. More specifically, the economic interests of community leaders in the cutover depended on having new settlers with whom they could do business come to the region rather than waiting forty years for the forest to become ready to recut; newspaper editorial opinion in northern Wisconsin opposed reforestation in the early decades of the twentieth century.[45]

Despite the skepticism expressed by men like Lapham and Roth, a larger body of informed scientific opinion at the beginning of the twentieth century stressed the positive aspects of the cutover for agricultural settlement. This view was expressed during controversies over conservation policy, which had their Wisconsin counterparts to those on the national level during the Taft presidency. For example, in 1908 Hiram Chittenden of the U.S. Army Corps of Engineers questioned the benefits of reforestation in northern Wisconsin for flood control.[46] This attitude was also shown in a series of reports on soil and agricultural conditions throughout the state published over the first two decades of the century by the Wisconsin Geological and Natural History Survey. The volumes that focused on the cutover ranged from cautiously optimistic to strongly bullish about the region's resources and possibilities, provided that settlers followed recommended "methods of improvement." For example, in a 1914 report on the Bayfield area, A. R. Whitson and his colleagues recommended reforestation of less than 4 percent of the region while describing the success of fruit cultivation near Bayfield on admittedly sandy soils and dairying near Ashland on Superior Clay soil on which "magnificent crops of clover, timothy, alfalfa, and pasture grasses can be grown."[47] Two years later Whitson was even more effusive in a report that covered Vilas, Oneida, Iron, Price, and parts of Ashland and Rusk counties. Except for the corner of Rusk it included, the report rated the soils of the region at six, five, or four on a scale descending in quality from six to one.[48] In a 1921 summary volume to the series, Whitson confidently reported that "one hundred thousand farms of 80 acres each are waiting the farmer in upper Wisconsin." Over 80 percent of the region was characterized as "good farm land," with the remainder fit "only for pasture and forestry."[49] These reports do not differ significantly from those of Roth and later more critical investigators in respect to the chemical properties or other scientific features of particular units of soil, but differ rather in how subjectively to characterize it—Whitson described as "excellent" the same soil that would later be rated as "mediocre."[50]

The University of Wisconsin's College of Agriculture was a leader in these efforts to appraise the agricultural potential of the cutover and encourage its settlement. At the direction of the legislature, in 1895 William A. Henry, dean of the college from 1891 to 1907, personally authored *Northern Wisconsin: A Hand-book for the Homeseeker*, a best-selling booklet in which he marshaled evidence—including staged photographs—to assure his readers that "Northern Wisconsin will not revert to a wilderness with the passing of the lumber, but will be occupied by a thrifty class of farmers" (Figure 1.6). The state distributed fifty thousand copies of this publication, and in 1903 Henry proudly boasted that as a result of his handbook, "the new-comer will have but few privations to suffer."[51] Henry also supervised the establishment in 1905 of three temporary substations of the college's Experimental Station which became centers in the cutover for agricultural research and extension work. Two years later, E. J. Delwiche, a recent graduate of the college, began a series of winter meetings with farmers in Bayfield and Ashland counties, out of which developed a formal annual statewide series of Farmers Institutes. Between 1910 and 1913, for example, about 20 percent of these institutes were held in communities in the cutover.[52]

Harry L. Russell, who succeeded Henry in the dean's office in Madison in 1907 and was both a distinguished scholar and a personal investor in cutover lands, encouraged these developments. Two permanent experimental substations were soon established in the cutover, at Ashland Junction in Bayfield County and at Spooner in Washburn County. By 1913 Russell was able to report regarding the Ashland substation that "the experimental fields showing the adaptability of this soil to wheat, pea and clover culture are in full view of every passing train. . . . [This] has proven of much more value in encouraging the settlement of the surrounding region than has the expressed opinion of even the oldest inhabitant."[53] Russell also used a 1909 state law authorizing the appointment of "itinerant" instructors and "traveling schools" to bring agricultural expertise to the cutover. By 1915, eight of thirteen such positions were in cutover counties, and three others in adjacent counties. This program was expanded and formalized with the appointment of county agricultural agents. Russell assigned the first such agent in Wis-

Figure 1.6. Shoulder-high oats growing on the farm of Edward Dascam near Antigo, July 30, 1895. This photo was taken on Dean Henry's tour of northern Wisconsin and used in his *Hand-book for the Homeseeker*. (State Historical Society of Wisconsin, photo WHi (H44) 34)

consin, Ernest Luther, to Oneida County in 1912.[54] "I think that it is up to me now," wrote Luther confidently, "to show the world how to farm jack pine land. The world has waited a long time for this fellow. HERE HE IS."[55] Russell concentrated the first agricultural agents in northern Wisconsin counties, while encouraging his faculty in Madison to work on the development of forage crops adapted to the short growing season in the cutover.[56] Studies at the Conrath experimental substation, for example, led Delwiche to conclude that even wheat had a future as a crop in northern Wisconsin: red clays in the Lake Superior lowland, he reported, "excel, in their ability to produce wheat, any section of the state."[57] Science increasingly impacted agriculture throughout the United States in the late nineteenth century, but nowhere more clearly than in the Wisconsin cutover, seemingly a blank slate for the application of the newest ideas and technologies. Science also conferred legitimacy on the idea of the cutover as a promising region for agricultural settlement.

The activities of the College of Agriculture were part of a pattern of governmental verification that the cutover was potentially a good place to farm. As early as the 1860s, the legislature—concerned with providing a labor force for the timber industry—chartered private companies to encourage immigration to northern Wisconsin. In 1895 it established a state Board of Immigration, which encouraged settlement of the cutover by sending representatives to fairs and meetings, distributing promotional literature, referring potential purchases to land dealers, and working with organizations like the Northern Wisconsin Development Association and the Northern Wisconsin Farmer's Association (which in 1906 sponsored an exhibit in a train car that traveled through Illinois, Iowa, Indiana, and Ohio). The state board also coordinated the efforts of county immigration agencies. By 1897 thirteen county boards were appropriating money to attract settlers.[58] In Vilas County, for example, the Board of Immigration published its own *Hand Book for the Homeseeker*, explicitly modeled on Henry's work, which emphasized that "all information contained herein is vouched for by the Board as being accurate and reliable in all respects." For his county's Board of Immigration, newspaperman Edward L. Peet prepared *Burnett County, Wisconsin*, which described "unlimited agricultural resources" as promising as those in southern Wisconsin. In Price County, the County Board's Committee on Advertising placed newspaper advertisements, focusing on the Chicago papers; responded to inquiries by sending back a promotional booklet and list of farms in the county for sale; and encouraged the county school superintendent to send prospects a follow-up letter boasting about the county's educational program. As the Vilas County board emphasized, it was important that a potential settler did not "think because you are coming to Northern Wisconsin that you are going into the wilderness, away from all the comforts and privileges of civilization."[59]

Government also sponsored fairs to promote the agricultural potential of northern Wisconsin and encourage the efforts of its farmers. The state assisted northern Wisconsin counties by subsidizing fairs. The Northern Wisconsin State Fair, at Chippewa Falls, one of several designated "district fairs," was founded in 1897 largely as a showplace for northern Wisconsin agricultural products; the state raised its initial subvention of $2,500 to $3,250 in 1901, and through the 1920s the Northern Wisconsin State Fair received the most state aid of any fair in Wisconsin. There were corresponding activities at the county level. In Forest County, for instance, the county board sponsored booths at the Wisconsin State Fair. It also subsidized the Forest County Agriculture Association's annual fair and local community fairs. Its appropriation for these activities in the 1920s reached $5,000 annually.[60]

In sum, government would not direct the agricultural settlement of northern Wisconsin. It would not even significantly regulate it. Even in a politically progressive state like Wisconsin, there was a strong belief that a major problem like what to do with cutover stumpland would best be solved by private enterprise. The role of the government in the cutover would be to encourage agricultural settlement, using twentieth-century methods, from propagandistic use of promotional pamphlets to the publication of scientific bulletins.

Timber companies and other purveyors of northern Wisconsin land took advantage of government-supported efforts to boost northern Wisconsin as a place to farm. By 1900 they knew they had to find a use for their land other than lumbering. From a peak production level of 3.4 billion board feet in 1899, the output of lumber in Wisconsin fell in half by 1912. White pine, in particular, was exhausted: 70 percent of the 1899 production had been white pine, but only 20 percent in 1912. What timber remained to be harvested was largely lesser-value hardwoods, much of which had been passed over in previous decades by lumbermen questing for the higher returns from white pine. Lumber and timber prod-

ucts had been the largest industry in Wisconsin by value of product produced in 1900; by 1925, with the dollar value of its products unchanged
in a quarter-century, the lumber and timber industry had become only
the state's eighth largest industry.[61] Having used up their land for the
purpose they had bought it, and unwilling to pay taxes on it for forty
years until it was ready to log again, timber companies were therefore
eager to unload their land as quickly as possible.

There were several methods to dispose of cutover land: companies
retailed the land directly, pooled it for sale by a consortium, or sold it
to middle men for resale, many of whom hoped for speculative profits.
For example, John S. Owen began selling his lands in northern Clark
County in 1893, and had dispersed over one hundred thousand acres
by 1926, with thirty thousand still for sale. He had less success with his
properties in Bayfield County. Selling only a few thousand acres a year,
while still acquiring new land, resulted in a net reduction between 1918
and 1929 from sixty-five thousand to just fifty-six thousand acres. This
slow pace of sales occurred despite the fact Owen's land in Bayfield
County was particularly well consolidated, or "blocked up." Other lumber companies, and railroads in particular, had more scattered holdings.
The Daniel Shaw Lumber Company, for example, had little success
beginning in the late 1890s in selling its relatively scattered holdings
throughout the Chippewa River valley in northwestern Wisconsin. After
a series of unsatisfactory relationships with land agents, the Shaw Lumber Company began to work in conjunction with the Gates Land Company, which assembled by purchase and exchange large blocks of land
for sale to potential farmers. Cornell University also transferred to Gates
fifty thousand acres of its unsold northern Wisconsin domain. Overall,
"Stumpland" Gates sold 456,000 acres between 1898 and 1902.[62]

A typical multi-enterprise land development scheme at this time was
the assignment of twenty thousand acres in Price County of land owned
by the Wisconsin Central Railroad, the American Immigration Company,
and the Good Land Company to the Johnson Stock and Farming Company. Johnson agreed to spend $3,000 per year on promotion, and within
2.5 years settle at least twenty-five families on plots of not less than forty
acres. These settlers would pay at least $7.50 an acre—more if some of
their land was already clear—with ten years to pay at an annual interest
rate of 6 percent on their balance if they actually moved onto their farms.
The railroad agreed to remove stumps on part of some plots, for which
the price would be higher, and in conjunction with the other vendors

agreed to build a Catholic church, rectory, and schoolhouse. The vendors would get the first $7.50 on every acre sold and the developer the next $5, with any income above $12.50 an acre split 50-50.[63]

The most significant cooperative selling effort was undertaken by the American Immigration Company (AIC). A consortium of nine lumber companies organized in 1906, AIC sold 438,000 cutover acres, generally to actual settlers rather than the land dealers who bought from Johnson Stock and Farming, before liquidation in 1939. However, despite its title, AIC did little aggressive recruiting anywhere, much less outside the United States. An affiliated enterprise with that goal, the American Colonization Company, failed and was liquidated in 1907. In general, both Gates and AIC focused on selling land and showed limited interest in more comprehensive programs to assist settlers and develop or maintain community feeling among them.[64]

There were other companies at the beginning of the twentieth century, however, which tried to develop "colonies" of planned, supervised settlements in the cutover, going beyond the "extras" offered by enterprises like Johnson Stock and Farming. Fred R. Rietbrock, a Milwaukee lawyer and lumberman, developed a model farm near Athens in northwestern Marathon County. This Athens Advancement Association sought to attract dairy farmers to Marathon County, assist them with information on modern farming techniques, and develop brickworks and sawmills as supplementary sources of income for them. From 1905 to 1908 Rietbrock employed D. O. Thompson to give his settlers advice, test their cows for disease, and provide them with bulls for free stud service. In another example, in 1908 Hans P. Petersen began operating a business in Merrill, in Lincoln County, which became the Cloverland Colonization Company. Petersen focused on attracting German-Americans by advertising in German-language newspapers in Milwaukee, Chicago, and elsewhere in the Middle West. Cloverland sold farms to settlers on land contracts; then, when they had accumulated sufficient equity, it gave them title, financing the settlers' purchases by taking back mortgages on the properties. Petersen also published a monthly *Practical Advisor* for his settlers, and attempted to develop a demonstration farm and supply settlers—for a fee—with ready-made houses. A third example of a company assisting development was the experience of the Good Land Company in selling its six thousand acres in the town of Pilsen in Bayfield County, largely through Bohemian-, Slovak-, and Hungarian-speaking agents. With the impetus of depressed urban conditions in the aftermath of the Panic of 1907, the company attracted about forty-five settlers between 1908 and 1915, chiefly immigrants who had been farmers in Europe. Showing a paternalistic spirit, the company loaned settlers money for buildings and livestock, started the Moquah Fair to improve their agricultural practices, and arranged courses of instruction to get them qualified as citizens.[65]

Whatever their goals, organization, or methods, these purveyors of cutover land portrayed their offerings in lavish terms. They were encouraged to exaggerate by competition from the promoters of "free" land in the Dakotas, Montana, and the plains provinces of Canada.[66] The sales manager for the Edward Hines Land Company, based in Winter in Sawyer County and which began operating about 1905, recalled the literature he mailed in response to inquiries: "It was written so that anyone could understand it. . . . The soil analysis was there, pictures of settlers' homes, their names, in fact I believe that the folder contained about 50 pages."[67] While based on the scientific studies of the College of Agriculture staff and other researchers, this promotional literature included few of the qualifications that hedged the academic reports. Even Dean Henry admitted that there was some bad land in northern Wisconsin, encouraged settlers not to try growing wheat there, and warned them to purchase land only after a close personal inspection.[68] He and his colleagues would certainly have blanched, therefore, to learn that the prior existence of heavy forestation was proof of good soil. "It is well known," asserted a Burnett County promoter, "that where trees grow, the soil, properly cultivated, will produce in abundance any grain, grass or vegetable suited to the climate." Referring to the soil in Forest County, propagandists for the Keith and Hines Lumber Company claimed that "the original crop of dense forests of big hardwood trees . . . is in itself conclusive evidence of its productiveness." The promotional pitch dismissed inconvenient features: in Burnett County, the "climate is changing," prospective settlers were assured, because "as the land is cleared, the climate and other unfavorable conditions will change." In Vilas County, "clearing the forest has mitigated the rigors of the climate." Where Delwiche had promoted wheat as a crop for the Superior lowlands, developers in Forest County—where the growing season is weeks shorter—claimed that "all experience has shown that conditions are very favorable to its growth." There was even less restraint, if that was possible, about the possibilities for dairying: a publication of the AIC predicted that the cutover would produce "rivers of milk, lakes of cream, and mountains of butter and cheese." Newspaper editorialists, local bankers, and organizations such as the Wisconsin Advancement Association joined the chorus promoting the cutover for agricultural settlement. Cheap land on reasonable terms, abundant moisture, fertile soil adaptable for almost any crop, a healthy climate, opportunities for supplemental off-farm work, convenient transportation to markets, communities already with schools and churches—what more could a prospective settler want? "Nothing is surer than that the experience of other sections of the country is to be repeated here" was the confident conclusion of the Keith and Hines Lumber Company. "In a few years the best of these find lands . . . will be gone like the rest"—now was the time to buy.[69]

These appeals did not just tell settlers that northern Wisconsin was going to become a booming region economically. They emphasized equally that the cutover offered settlers independence, security, and community life with compatible people. In Vilas County, a farmer "can be a free man" according to the Board of Immigration. "No matter how hard the times may be, [he] is sure of enough for himself and family to eat and a roof to cover them that he can count his own." Promoters described the cutover as the perfect place for both city workers dissatisfied with the discipline of factory labor, and farm renters and hired men with no opportunity to work for themselves. In northern Wisconsin they would find "a liberty loving community" eager to build schools, churches, and other accoutrements of "civilization." The promotional pamphlets were filled with the success stories of settlers who had already made the move to northern Wisconsin, not just to highlight their economic success, but to "convince the home seeker that Burnett County has within its borders many people who will make good neighbors." New settlers would find "a law-abiding community, where your family can live in peace and enjoy the comforts of civilized life, and where your children will find good schools and grow up in a clean, moral atmosphere."[70] For new settlers, therefore, life in the Wisconsin cutover would replicate the ideals of rural America in the nineteenth century: independent living as part of a community of persons with similar backgrounds and values, material success tempered by obligations to that community and its members, and accumulation of property in order to become integrated with these community expectations rather than to escape them.[71]

Land vendors intensified their sales efforts when face-to-face with possible customers. Some settlers, despite repeated warnings by the

Division of Immigration (chapter 3), bought land sight unseen. However, a visit to the cutover to select a farm, perhaps taking advantage of low-fare "homeseekers excursions" offered by the railroads, usually preceded relocation. Some settlers, like Robert Schlomann, who moved with his family to the town of Grow in Rusk County in 1919, came to believe that all this meant was that a "desolate, raped area . . . was being unloaded upon unwary people." Martin Herman was one such disillusioned purchaser. About 1910, after reading a promotional article in an Omaha newspaper, Herman took a train to Rhinelander to look at land for sale. Land agents typically clustered at the depot to greet such new arrivals. Herman was met and taken on a tour of the town of Cassian by A. P. Crosby, who had Crosby Lumber Company land to sell. Herman was impressed by a forty-acre piece of level land with a stream, a "particularly attractive feature for a westerner," which was also very inexpensive by Nebraska standards. Despite the fact that deep snow covered the land, Herman purchased it only to learn the following June that it was largely swamp. A few years later Crosby admitted to an interviewer that most land buyers "really do not know what they want and do not have a sufficient knowledge of the characteristics of good land to enable them to make wise selection of land."[72] Even when land quality was clearly good, sellers often required buyers to include some hilly or swampy land in their purchases or directed settlers to remote locations, anticipating that consequent public road construction would increase the value of adjacent unsold land.

Vendors, understandably, publicly characterized their land sales practices differently. Michael F. Beaudoin, who directed the disposal of Hines Lumber Company land from a headquarters at Winter in Sawyer County, sold land only after the snow had melted. Beaudoin explained: "When the settler came to Winter, he was given attention by a man who understood the country. He would give them his time to look at the land, no high pressure methods were used, and we did turn away several whom we thought were not suitable or would not make a success." Beaudoin was proud that beginning in 1915 Hines brought in five hundred settlers, the "majority" of whom remained on the land and were "doing nicely" in 1950.[73] It is difficult to evaluate the sincerity of the land vendors, which doubtless varied. Until about 1920 they had some reason to feel their consciences were clear, but even during this period at least some developers had their doubts about what they were doing. In 1913 the president of a mortgage loan company specializing in cutover business told his board of directors, in contrast to the boosterish public position of the company, that he was not in "an easy frame of mind" because in Wisconsin "the farms that have not made the owners well off are not desirable farms to loan on." Their operators only "make interest payments." Indeed, his company would make a $36,000 profit in 1915 on revenues of $85,000, but would be bankrupt less than twenty years later.[74]

Settlers generally bought cutover land in forty- or eighty-acre units. Some paid cash or traded for an existing farm. In most cases, however, purchase was by land contract, as with the previous example of the Johnson Stock and Farming Company. In this arrangement, the buyer made a downpayment, generally 10 to 25 percent of the purchase price, and usually had five to ten years to pay the balance and receive a deed. Generally there were no other fees required of purchasers. Payments of principal might be in annual or semiannual installments. In reality the sellers expected little cash payment beyond the downpayment: payment of principal was often deferred by the contract for the first few years and in practice many settlers never paid any scheduled installments. Many contracts, furthermore, specified payment of principal only as part of a final, balloon payment. Generally, sellers charged 6 percent annual interest on unpaid principal. The normal practice was that at or before the date of the expiration of the land contract the purchaser would buy the land from the original seller, obtaining the needed cash by then mortgaging the land to an individual investor or mortgage loan company. This pattern of transactions depended on land values rising between the time of the original purchase by land contract and the refinancing by mortgage, because mortgage lenders generally at most loaned 50 percent of appraised value of cutover farms. This needed increase in land value came both from the settler's clearing and improving of his property, and from the general rise in land value as the district became more densely settled. In general, lenders did not press for payments of principal, understanding that both settlers and lenders benefited from the settler's investing what cash he could into improvements on his farm. The president of Eau Claire's Union Mortgage Loan Company repeatedly assured his mortgagees that they "need not be afraid of a mortgage" and that if necessary "you can renew it when it becomes due for any such portion as you wish."[75] As a consequence of these practices, owning your farm was feasible for many settlers, and renters or sharecroppers were few in the cutover; however, these cutover farmers were less likely than others in Wisconsin to own their property outright. In 1920 only 5.3 percent of cutover farmers were tenants compared to 14.4 percent statewide, but only 32 percent of these owners worked property clear of encumbrance compared to 38 percent statewide. Cutover farmers also had to pay higher interest rates to secure their mortgages. In 1930, when statewide the ratio of charges to mortgage debt on farms was 5.49 percent, the range in cutover counties was from 5.82 percent to 6.69 percent, the highest burden in the state (except for the tiny number of farms in Milwaukee County).[76] The cutover did provide settlers with land to call their own, as the promotional literature promised, but their hold on that land was not secure.

Ownership was feasible because cutover land was relatively inexpensive. In 1918, when congratulating a land dealer for selling "a bum farm" for $10,000, a farm mortgage executive observed that "some people will never learn the real value of land, especially here in northern Wisconsin, where a man could have bought half of the state for a few pennies only a few short years ago."[77] Statewide in Wisconsin in 1900 farm land, exclusive of buildings, was valued at $26.71 an acre; it was higher in well-developed sections—$41.20 an acre, for example, in Dane County.[78] By contrast, Kim Rosholt, who sold land optioned him by timber companies, averaged $6.65 an acre on seventeen sales in Clark County between 1890 and 1894 (Table 1.1). The Holt Lumber Company, centered in Oconto County, priced its cutover lands most suitable for agriculture at $8 to $10 an acre. On the basis of land quality, terrain, soil quality and type, and the presence of surface water, the company classified most of its holdings into three lesser categories, which were priced even lower. Similarly, when AIC was organized in 1906, it classified its lands into five categories, valued from $2 to $7 an acre.

As farmland values rose, both in the cutover and statewide, the cost of "wild land" for sale increased also. By 1911 Holt had priced its best land at $15 to $20 an acre, and in 1914 combined its two least expensive categories, in which land had previously been priced at $1 and $3 an acre, into one category selling for $6 to $8 an acre. Its 114 sales between 1911 and 1915 averaged $8.64 an acre. Similarly, the mean value, by year, of land sold by AIC was $8.40 an acre for 1906–1915 and rose to $11.65 an acre for 1916–1924. In response to a questionnaire from the economics department of the University of Wisconsin, land companies with sales in five cutover counties in 1917 reported a range of prices centered just below $20 an acre. A social scientist who examined four communities

Table 1.1. Sales of Undeveloped Cutover Land, 1890–1924

	n =	Vendor/Company	County	Price per Acre
1890–1894	17	Kim Rosholt	Clark	$6.65
1906–1915	(n.a.)	American Immigration	(general)	8.40
1911–1915	114	Holt Lumber	Oconto	8.64
1914	60	Northwestern Lumber	Clark/Chippewa/ Taylor	17.74
c. 1910–1920	150	(various)	Marathon/Oneida	18.00
1910–1920	(n.a.)	Northwestern Lumber	Clark/Chippewa/ Taylor	22.71
1916–1924	(n.a.)	American Immigration	(general)	11.65
1917	15	Hill and Sergent	Rusk	12.50–25.00
1917	16	Homemaker Land	Price/Clark/Wood	15.00–20.00
1917	170	Baker Land	Polk/Burnett	15.00–25.00
1918	52	Northwestern Lumber	Clark/Chippewa/ Taylor	24.22
1918–1919	37	John S. Owen Lumber	Clark	24.02

Source: See nn. 79 and 80, p. 240.

where most of the settlers had arrived between 1915 and 1920 (two in the cutover and two in adjoining Marathon County) found that $18 an acre had been the average sale price.[79]

The pattern was similar with land owned by the John S. Owen Lumber Company, based in Owen in Clark County, adjacent to the cutover. The company sold thirty-seven properties to individuals during 1918–1919, averaging $24.04 an acre. Altogether this company sold over one hundred thousand acres between 1893 and 1926 for an average of $16.55 an acre. Referring to their operations farther north, near Drummond in Bayfield County, an Owen official reported in 1919 that "we have already sold at Drummond, in retail lots, over 4,000 acres, no sale exceeding 160 acres; largely Forties and Eighties at prices ranging from $18 to $24 an acre." Similarly, the Northwestern Lumber Company, based in Stanley, twenty miles west of Owen, averaged $17.74 an acre on sales in 1914 and $24.22 an acre by 1918. Altogether, during the 1910s, Northwestern sold 51,300 acres at $22.71 an acre.[80]

However, while prices rose as time passed, they did not particularly burden new settlers because, as per farm values quadrupled in all but one cutover country between 1900 and 1920, they were easily able to obtain mortgages and pay off their land contracts. Of the sixty contracts in the 1914 Northwestern Lumber Company sample, only four were canceled. Settlers successfully completed payment on the remainder, in forty of fifty-two cases before the scheduled end of the contract (the remaining four sales were for cash). Similarly, all but two of Holt Lumber Company's 114 sales between 1911 and 1915 were paid off. Referring to his company's operations, John G. Owen boasted in 1909 that "in fourteen years we have never been forced to foreclose on a settler's property."[81]

This success was in part due to the fact that during these first two decades of the century, settlers found that they generally could easily refinance their farm purchases and gain title to their land by obtaining a mortgage loan and paying off their land contracts with part of the proceeds. Union Mortgage Loan, organized in Eau Claire in 1905 and one of five such institutions in the city in 1920, averaged over one hundred farm loans annually in Wisconsin between 1913 and 1922, with a total value greater than $2,000,000. From loaning about $70,000 in 1908, the company expanded its business to over $300,000 in both 1919 and 1920. Data in a sample of sixty loans given during 1911–1913 show that Union Mortgage Loan's typical mortgagee had lived on his eighty-acre plot (valued at about $2,500) for five years. He received a $750 loan and told the company that the proceeds went to pay off an existing land contract or mortgage. For example, Frank Trott bought forty wild acres in Rusk County for $600 in 1911 from the Gates Land Company. By 1915, with ten acres claimed as "under cultivation," he valued his farm at $1,800. Although Union Mortgage Loan's appraiser concluded that Trott "overvalued" his property, the company still loaned him $600 of the $650 he wanted to pay off the $400 still owed to Gates. Union Mortgage Loan's lending record was good: before 1912 it had to foreclose on only three of eight hundred loans, and never more than three in a single year before 1918. Other lenders had similar records. William J. Starr was a small land dealer in Polk County; surviving records of one hundred mortgages he gave on land he sold, mostly in the early 1910s, show no foreclosures before 1920.[82] The general success of mortgage-based lending for land sales encouraged the extension of the practice to the financing of livestock purchases. About 1915 farmers began to buy cows with loans from the bank in Iron River secured by mortgages on their herds. This "Iron River Plan" quickly spread to other communities.[83] All in all, the comment made some years later by a Rust-Owen

Lumber Company executive that "for some years the new settlers were able to get along nicely" could apply to most of the cutover before 1920.[84]

Did the lumber companies and other land sellers profit excessively from the dispersal of their cutover lands? Is that why eventually some settlers encountered financial problems? Many distressed settlers thought so. "There are so many that want to *rob* the fellow that is pinched," wrote one distressed farmer to the Union Mortgage Loan Company. Basil Stefonik, a grandson of an immigrant farmer who settled in the town of Sugar Camp in Oneida County, related in a 1993 interview an example of what he thought was such "robbery." "The Brown Brothers Lumber Company bought 27 forties for total of $500," Stefonik explained. "They sold each logged off forty for $500. Five hundred dollars for a forty of stumps. . . . The foreigners were really taken advantage of."[85] The perspective of the lumber companies was understandably different. "The sales were not very profitable—mostly at liquidation prices," insisted an executive of the Holt Lumber Company (perhaps conflating post-1920 and pre-1920 sales).[86]

The experience of the American Immigration Company directly addresses the question of the profitability of selling land because that was its entire business. After a close examination of its extensive records, the company's historian has concluded that it "showed a moderate profit" (Table 1.2). However, since the company was initially capitalized at about $1,800,000–$1,640,000 in land and $160,000 in working capital, it is unclear how, when liquidation was complete, dividends and distributions to the participating companies of $1,538,639 constituted a profit.[87]

Critical to establishing the profitability of this and other land sales operations is determining the initial cost of the land from the point of view of the seller. Should it be the market value of the land when first made available for sale, as seems to have been approximately the case with AIC? Or should it be the assessed value of the land, which was often higher than the market value because most towns assessed all but the worst waste land in the cutover at at least $10 an acre in the early years of the century? Or should the calculation be based on the actual cost of the land to the seller, which often had been only $1–2 an acre in the nineteenth century? In that case, the value should be depreciated, since the principal factor in establishing the initial cost of the land—its timber—had been removed.

The land sales records of the Holt Lumber Company provide an unusual opportunity to examine this question, since they allow the match-

Table 1.2. American Immigration Company
Operations, 1906–1939

Number of acres sold	437,945
Income from land sales	$3,322,601
Expenditures	
Taxes	$1,147,961
Advertising	62,817
Commissions	214,559
Other	591,619
Total	$2,016,955
Net income	$1,305,646
Dividends and division of capital in liquidation	$1,538,639

Source: Lucile Kane, "Selling Cut-Over Lands in Wisconsin,"
Business History Review 28 (1954): 247, table I.

ing of the sales price of each piece of land with its initial cost to the company. Between 1911 and 1918 the company sold for $111,535 land which had cost it $75,687. Of course, selling the land and getting paid for it were separate points, but Holt, like most vendors, successfully collected its money during this period from all but a handful of buyers. Holt actually grossed $81,556 in cash from its land operations during these years. Of course, the company had expenses for sales, marketing, and taxes. Furthermore, post-1918 sales, while still above initial cost, were certainly less profitable because it appears that in these years at least a third of individual buyers canceled their contracts before completing purchase. By the end of 1922 the company had sold 24,326 acres but still had 90,076 in its inventory.[88] As individual purchasers all but vanished after 1920, most of this remaining land went at lower prices to businesses such as Northeast Power, which bought 6,360 acres in 1925 at Holt's 1908 cost, and eventually in the 1930s to the federal government, which paid about $1.25 an acre for cutover land. But all these calculations are based on an undepreciated value of the land, and certainly the company's pre-1920 land business would have to be categorized as highly profitable if that factor were taken into consideration.[89]

Tax considerations further complicate the analysis. Especially as they began to move into liquidation, timber companies tried to characterize payments to their shareholders as distributions of capital rather than dividends from profits on current operations. After the adoption of the federal income tax in 1913, this practice was particularly advantageous to shareholders, especially if it could be made to appear that the companies were taking capital losses so that the distributions would not be subject to any income tax. Of course, the higher the initial value assigned to the land as capital, the more likely it would appear to have been sold at a loss. Today, generally accepted accounting rules, not to mention the Internal Revenue Service, would require the companies to systematically depreciate land after it was cut for timber, but that was not always the practice with Wisconsin lumber companies before 1940. Consequently, as the vice-president of the Northwestern Lumber Company explained to stockholders regarding land sales, "we should continue just so long as we can get anything more than the back taxes."[90]

It is difficult to evaluate fairly the question of whether lumber companies charged "exorbitant" prices to settlers for purchase of cutover land. Incomplete records, obscure accounting systems, complex corporate organizations deliberately designed to make subsidiaries look profitable or unprofitable, and corporate manipulation of the tax laws handicap analysis. Certainly the profitability of selling cutover land varied from vendor to vendor and decreased as time passed. A cautious conclusion would be that overall the companies profited from cutover land sales, but not to bonanza dimensions.

Settlers on new lands in nineteenth-century America were never entering a virginal environment on their own, frontier mythology notwithstanding. But the settlers who came to the cutover in the early twentieth century were particularly at the mercy of the unplanned consequences of what in 1900 was still seen as a great achievement of American capitalism, one that certainly had integrated northern Wisconsin into the national economy. The settlers' expectations, however, encouraged by the promises made to attract them to the cutover, were still those of independent nineteenth-century yeoman farmers. Furthermore, there were sharp constraints on what these settlers would be able to do in northern Wisconsin. Newcomers were entering a region in which the physical environment recently had been radically altered, and consequently was still poorly understood both by scientists and laypeople. Their success or failure would be affected by the preexisting financial situation of lumber companies and municipal governments focused on the near-term and relying on guesses, hopes, and imperfect historical analogies to predict a successful agricultural future for the cutover. As the last stages of commercial lumbering continued around them into the twentieth century, settlers would both benefit economically and be distracted from farming. In this situation there was no shortage of people to give them advice and assistance. The government, however, would not sell settlers cheap land or loan them money for purchases and development. It would not even indirectly classify land for future economic use by putting land unsuitable for agriculture into parks or forests, although private enterprises had sophisticated classification systems for the land they were marketing. The encouragement and advice that the state and its agents, such as the university, were eager to give could easily turn into paternalism and even social control. As settlers began to struggle with the unique conditions of the cutover, experts from outside the region would increasingly introduce policies to overcome the deficiencies the settlers had nothing to do with. But for a quarter-century settlers and promoters alike had good reason in their own minds to believe that farming could flourish in the cutover.

2 | Building a New Life in the Cutover, 1900–1920

Don't see all stone—See the land
between the stone that grows more
grass to the acre than any land in
Wisconsin without the stone.

    C. E. ("The Land Man") Tobey[1]

With high expectations and the encouragement of public and private agencies, tens of thousands of farmers and their families moved to northern Wisconsin in the first two decades of the twentieth century. They developed ways to survive, physically and economically, in the scourings left by the lumbering era. Especially for settlers in more favorable locations, a modest prosperity even emerged by 1920, based on family labor on the farm, exchanging work with neighbors, and off-farm supplemental work. Cutover settlers also began the process of replicating the social patterns of the rural communities which previous generations of yeoman farmers had built across the United States during the nineteenth century. By cooperation, sharing, and exchange they increased their ability to survive independently on their own farms and build up community institutions such as schools and churches.

In 1900 Wisconsin's eighteen northernmost counties occupied the bottom eighteen positions among the state's seventy-one counties when ranked by percentage of land in farms. With only about 210,000 residents, the cutover was also thinly populated: it contained one third of the state's land area but only about 10 percent of its population. Except near a few cities such as Superior and Marinette, located on the Great Lakes bordering the region, and in a few other locations, population density was less than five persons per square mile. Indeed, three entire counties—Forest, Rusk, and Sawyer—fell below this level.[2] Over the next two decades, as American agriculture went through an Indian summer phase buoyed by generally high prices for its products, the number of farms grew nationwide by 12 percent.[3] The cutover was one of the fastest-growing regions in the nation during these years. By 1920 its population had expanded to over 320,000, and the number of its farms had more than doubled to over twenty-five thousand. Where only 10 percent of the cutover had been in farms at the beginning of the century, 23 percent was by 1920. In a 1922 editorial, "Northern Wisconsin—Revelations of the Fourteenth Census," the *Wisconsin Magazine of History* proudly pointed out, "Little did our fathers dream that such a result would follow the destruction of the 'pineries.'"[4]

This development was not the work of professionally managed, absentee-owner farms. Attempts to expand the corporate farms previously operated by some lumber companies generally did not succeed. In 1918 Walter B. Clubine, a son-in-law of lumber baron Edward Hines, built a concrete barn for 120 cows in the town of Iron River in Bayfield County. Culbine envisioned a large-scale commercial enterprise manufacturing its own butter and cheese, but it never became operational. Similarly, the Anson Eldred Co. Farm, a 350-acre enterprise worked by hired labor near Stiles in Oconto County, showed a profit in only two years between 1900 and 1915. These efforts could not provide a model for other such businesses.[5]

Agriculture in the cutover would be instead the domain of family farmers, comprising a disproportionately large number of immigrants: 24 percent of the region's population was foreign born in 1920 compared to 18 percent statewide, and another 43 percent had at least one foreign-born parent (Figure 2.1).[6] These immigrants were largely European peasants who found limited economic opportunity offered by mining and industrial work and experienced an uncongenial lifestyle in urban America. In 1915, for example, of twenty-seven farmers from Conrath, Rusk County, who applied to refinance their land purchases, twenty-three were foreign born, eighteen from Poland. Before purchasing farms, they worked, on average, for ten years in the United States, mostly in mining, factory, or railroad work. Only three had previously worked on farms in the United States, although most had in Europe. Typical was Josef Sokolowski, a 1901 immigrant from Austrian Poland where he had worked on his father's farm. Sokolowski bought forty acres near Conrath in 1911 after working in the Pennsylvania coal fields and saving $360 of the $600 purchase price of his farm. Land developers targeted immigrants like Sokolowski, especially through immigrant community newspapers. B. M. Apker, a major land promoter around 1912,

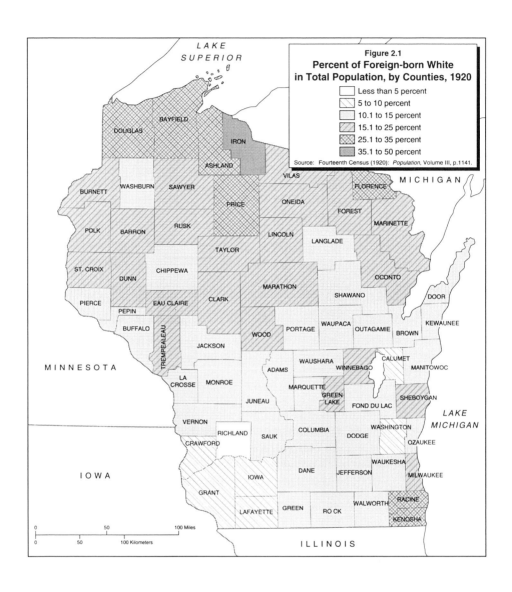

Figure 2.1
Percent of Foreign-born White
in Total Population, by Counties, 1920

Less than 5 percent
5 to 10 percent
10.1 to 15 percent
15.1 to 25 percent
25.1 to 35 percent
35.1 to 50 percent

Source: Fourteenth Census (1920): *Population*, Volume III, p.1141.

recalled that "we built in southern Rusk County two very large Polish colonies in which we sold to nobody except Polish people."[7]

Such sales practices reinforced the tendency seen everywhere in nineteenth-century America for immigrant groups to cluster among themselves.[8] Lars Kailberg recounted that when his father came in 1891 to the Rice Lake area from Sweden, he settled where he could "club together" and share work with people who spoke the same language. Observers believed Swedish immigrants to be attracted especially to the "Nordic countryside" of neighboring Burnett County, where in 1905 38 percent of the residents of the town of Trade Lake were Swedish born. As late as 1920, 12 percent of the county's inhabitants had emigrated from Sweden. A similar nostalgia for the landscape of their homeland reportedly brought over fifty Lithuanian families from Chicago to the towns of Newbold, Woodboro, and Crescent, in Oneida County.[9]

Like Kailberg, immigrants of many nationalities settled together to ease the transition to a new country and to lighten their load by work-sharing. Hans Pederson's father came to the Drummond area, in Bayfield County, as part of a group of twelve or thirteen farmers from the same neighborhood in Norway. Desiring to escape military service, they came to "where they knew people." After working in the Rust-Owen Lumber Company's lumber mill, Pederson's father began farming in 1932. William C. Ritzer, for his part, was twenty when he immigrated from Germany to the United States in 1886, and came to the Three Lakes area in Oneida County in about 1900 to work in a lumber camp. After marrying in 1907, he began to develop an eighty-seven-acre farm while still working during the winter in the woods. "Near neighbors were an important part of making it in the country," he recalled. Referring to the German settlement in the Spirit River valley in Price County, Carl Rhody emphasized that "the new settlers depended on one another. Little differences and petty quarrels had to be forgotten. . . ." Such cooperation contributed to the development of positive attitudes among immigrants which led to the phenomenon of "chain migration." Jack C. Plano identified "word of mouth" as the principal reason why Germans came to the Merrill area in Lincoln County. "Those who came," he recounted, "wrote to their relatives and family about the available land and opportunities." Consequently, the state census of 1905 reported that over 14 percent of the population of Lincoln County was German born. Local concentrations of Germans were even greater—in neighboring Taylor County over one third of the residents of the town of Rib Lake had been born in Germany.[10]

Rural settings helped new immigrants maintain their traditional customs and group identities. Regarding language, for example, a prospective settler in the Merrill area was cautioned, "I presume you have not forgotten how to speak German, as that is a factor here. We have a heavily German community, especially out in the country." In the early years of the century, the *Phillips Times* in Price Country regularly published a "German Department" containing articles written in the native language. Robert Schlomann, who was born in 1915 to immigrant parents, recalled speaking only German at home and not learning English until he started school. Critics believed that such "backwoods" Germans did not even use English in the public schools. World War I inhibited the public use of German—Roy Meier recalled that Zion Lutheran Church in the town of Spirit in Price County dropped German-language services at that time—but other groups maintained their native tongues for decades. At East Denmark Lutheran Church in Luck, services were conducted in Danish until the 1940s.[11]

Finns were one of the most distinctive immigrant groups in northern Wisconsin. A social scientist who surveyed Price County in the summer of 1921 described them as "largely out of touch with American ways of life." An unsympathetic neighbor of Finns in Knox, Price County, where they comprised 38 percent of the town's population in 1905, even more bluntly characterized them as "atheists," "fighters," and "drinkers."[12] Finnish settlers in this region included men such as Otto Hakola, who in 1915 moved to a wild, eighty-acre farm in the town of Reseburg in Clark County, having worked as a plasterer in Minnesota mining communities for a decade after immigrating to the United States. By 1925 he had become a full-time farmer.[13] Many Finns also settled in the northwest corner of the state: in 1905 one third of the population of the town of Oulu in Bayfield County was Finnish born, as was over a quarter of the population of the town of Brule in Douglas County. Referring to both immigrants and their children, an Iron County newspaper reported in the 1920s that "a majority of the farmers in the county are Finnish."[14] The vernacular architecture of these Finns left its mark on the landscape (Figure 2.2). Finns also converged in the lake region of Vilas and Oneida counties, according to one contemporary observer because "it resembled their homeland" so much. In 1920, more than 5 percent of the residents of Vilas County were Finnish born.[15]

Figure 2.2. Davidson Feed Mill near the Amnicon River, southeast of Superior, 1935. This wind-powered mill was constructed in 1900 by Finnish immigrant Jacob Davidson and reflects the continuing impact on the landscape of immigrant practices. (State Historical Society of Wisconsin, photo WHi (X3) 34263)

In the early twentieth century, Poles in particular sought out the cutover. Men like Josef Sokolowski settled in Rusk County; as early as 1905, one third of the town of Strickland was Polish born. Blazus Kolowski, for example, had been working as a skilled laborer in a Ford plant in Detroit in 1917 when, not satisfied by Ford's good wages and wanting to live on a farm as he had in Europe, he moved to the town of Radisson. In 1919 the local newspaper reported him as "healthy and happy" and by 1930 he had twenty-five acres planted in crops.[16] To native-born Americans, these Poles lacked self-discipline, like Finns; were Catholics, like many Germans; and seemed stupid, like Swedes. But in addition, unlike the other immigrant groups, they were characterized as dirty and lazy. A social scientist reported after a firsthand survey of the cutover that Poles were "quarrelsome" with a "low standard of living." The young woman who taught the 1923–1924 school year at the Oakland school in Strickland remembered being shocked at "discovering the children were lousy." She emphasized her predicament with these foreigners by recounting that "one Polish lady reminded me that children weren't healthy unless they had lice." Like Finns, Poles were seen as cliquish. Referring to the Polish-born neighbors of his family's farm in Vilas County, Robert Peters recalled that "the Kulas made little effort to fit American ways; they might just as well have been tilling fields near Krakow."[17]

Not all cutover settlers were foreign born. As potential farm land in older rural areas of the Midwest became fully settled in the late nineteenth century, land values rose, precluding easy purchase by sons of farmers unfortunate enough not to inherit from their fathers.[18] The cutover therefore beckoned to some young men and women who had grown up with the experience of living in a yeoman farming community. Glenn Wymore, who moved with his parents from Iowa to Rusk County in 1926, explained that "cheap land looks good to a high-priced renter." Henry Kater moved to the Bruce area from Iowa in 1915 with his son because he "desired a larger farm." Reportedly, he subsequently influenced eleven other Hawkeyes to move to the neighborhood. In the early 1920s, a visitor to Price County found similar people when he reported "two new settlements . . . made up of native-born Americans recently arrived from Indiana and Illinois" located near the village of Lugerville.[19] Still other settlers moved to the cutover from the rural Midwest for different reasons. Julie Paylin's father, for instance, found that farming in Illinois had become too intense and specialized.[20] Other settlers came to northern Wisconsin from the Great Plains, in the aftermath of farming fluctuations there in the 1890s related to unstable wheat prices and unpredictable weather.[21]

The organization during these years of the Forest County Potawatomi community paralleled in interesting ways the migration of Euro-Americans into northern Wisconsin. Nineteenth-century treaties expected the Potawatomi, unlike the Ojibway and the Menominee, to leave Wisconsin, and most resettled in Kansas and Oklahoma. Scattered groups of Potawatomi, however, remained behind, shifting their settlements and squatting on land in central Wisconsin, along Lake Michigan and Green Bay, and in upper Michigan. In 1894 a group settled in the cutover in Forest County, homesteading under the Indian Homestead Act of 1884. They were joined by other Potawatomi from Wisconsin, Michigan, and even Kansas. A 1910 federal report identified 457 Potawatomi living in the Wabeno area, in southwestern Forest County. Largely through the lobbying efforts of Lutheran minister E. O. Morstad, in 1913 United States Senator Robert M. LaFollette, Sr., arranged for a federal appropriation to buy land and build houses for these people. This did not create a reservation—federal Indian policy was in a reservation termination phase, and Morstad wanted to Christianize the Potawatomi. Rather, the Potawatomi were given scattered holdings, with the expectation that they would therefore assimilate Euro-American culture. This did not happen, however. Despite some geographic intermixing, Indian and white people had little social interaction. Interestingly—and ironically, in view of Morstad's goals—the Potawatomi emerged as the most culturally conservative of Wisconsin's Indians, maintaining at mid-century a dream dance and a peyote cult.[22] Just as European immigrants and their children found that they could maintain some of their folk practices better in northern Wisconsin than in urban America, the Potawatomi took advantage of the relative isolation of the cutover to preserve their traditional ways.

In addition to the presence of American Indians, at the beginning of the twentieth century northern Wisconsin resembled a frontier in other ways. The demographic patterns of its Euro-American settlers were like those of settlers on nineteenth-century American frontiers.[23] Males predominated—more so, in descending order, than in older rural areas in Wisconsin such as Trempealeau County, the state as a whole, and all of the United States (Table 2.1). The physical demands of clearing land and developing farms also meant that the cutover attracted younger adults. In 1920 only 19.9 percent of the residents of northern Wisconsin were at least forty-five years of age, compared to 22.5 percent of the rest of Wisconsin's population. The relative shortage of women in younger age groups, furthermore, meant that disproportionate num-

Table 2.1. Sex Ratios, 1900 and 1920

	1900	1920
Cutover	131.0	117.0
Trempealeau County	109.1	110.4
Wisconsin	106.7	106.4
United States	104.4	104.0

Source: U.S. Bureau of the Census, *Historical Statistics of the United States, 1607–1976*, 1:15; Jane Marie Pederson, *Between Memory and Reality: Family and Community in Rural Wisconsin, 1870–1970* (Madison, 1992), 181; *Wisconsin Blue Book* (Madison, 1903), 170; U.S. Bureau of the Census, *Fourteenth Census (1920)*, vol. 1: *Population*, 666–67.

bers of young men had to remain bachelors. For example, among a group of Latvian immigrants who settled in Lincoln County between 1901 and 1908, 25 percent of the men never married.[24]

These Latvian men had a limited pool of potential marriage partners because at first they tended to restrict their choice of spouses to women from their own ethnic group. Most immigrants followed this pattern: a 1907 description of the Danish settlement near Luck in northern Polk County reported that forty years after initial settlement "the Danes are all nearly unmixed."[25] At the beginning of the twentieth century "new" immigrants in particular—Latvians, Poles, Bohemians, Finns—still practiced endogamous marriage. These nationalities tended to settle in northern Wisconsin where the thin ratio of population to land enabled them to find the space to cluster together. Consequently, between January 1, 1905 and September 30, 1906, when marrying, 66 percent of foreign-born individuals in the cutover wed another foreigner, while only 52 percent of foreigners in the rest of the state so married.[26]

The unbalanced sex ratios meant that some men had to remain unmarried, but to operate a farm in the cutover you all but had to be part of a family. Lars Kailberg recalled an uncle who wanted to farm but was thwarted in part by being single, and instead went to work in a Pittsburgh steel mill. In fact, in 1900 in the town of Dewey, in what would soon become Rusk County, a married couple was present on 86 percent of the 44 farms, and on 89 percent of the 162 farms in 1910. Similarly, in the towns of Radisson and Ojibwa in neighboring Sawyer County in 1910, 93 percent of ninety-seven farms had a married couple present.

Men recognized that they were at a disadvantage trying to farm in the cutover without a wife. "It is not very advisable for me to keep the Place," explained a farmer near Ladysmith, in Rusk County, about why he wanted to sell, "as I am single."[27]

Settlers in northern Wisconsin also showed the demographic characteristics of a frontier region in their marriage and fertility decisions. Predictably where the sex ratio is unbalanced, women married at relatively young ages: in 1913, 26 percent of brides in the cutover were age nineteen or younger, compared to only 22 percent in the rest of the state. Early marriage encouraged larger families in the rural cutover. Recalling the area around the village of Thorp in northwestern Clark County, lifelong resident Robert Rasmussen related that before 1930 "the nearby farms often had large families." In 1920, in fact, there were 999 children aged six and under living in the cutover for every 1,000 women between ages eighteen and forty-four; statewide the ratio was only 763. For the earlier years of the century data are not available to calculate such fertility rates, but cruder information suggests that cutover families were relatively large in this period as well. For instance, from 1908 through 1912, on average there were 49.1 reported births for every thousand women in the cutover, compared to 46.9 reported births for every thousand women statewide. At least part of this relatively high fertility is explained by the disproportionate presence in the cutover of immigrants, who in general bore more children than native-born Americans. For example, in the town of Roosevelt in Taylor County in 1910 Polish-born women between the ages of forty-five and fifty-four had averaged 8.6 births.[28]

These parents and their children usually lived in nuclear families. Despite the fact that chain migration often involved kin—Hans Skinvik emigrated directly from Norway to the Minong area in 1891 after receiving encouraging letters from his brother Olaf—the process of relocating to the United States inevitably meant both separation from relatives in the old country and the impossibility of cohabiting with those already in the new.[29] In 1900 in the town of Dewey, 82 percent of the farm families were nuclear (just parents or parents and their children); only one was three-generational. Ten years later, 78 percent were nuclear and only three were three-generational. In the towns sampled in neighboring Sawyer County in 1910, 83 percent of farm families were nuclear and three generations were present only twice. Nor was it likely that nonkin would live with cutover farmers: in the towns just identified, only 7 percent had hired help and 7 percent had boarders. Structurally, nuclear families have always been the rule in the United States, but seem to have been particularly characteristic of the early-twentieth-century cutover. For example, nationwide in 1900 about one in sixteen households contained three generations; the corresponding figure on farms in the cutover was about one in thirty-three.[30]

If the cutover was like the Nebraska frontier at the beginning of the twentieth century, the prevalence of nuclear families may have *contributed* to the region's high fertility. Nebraska frontier farm women in nuclear households, desiring the companionship of children and lacking sources of birth control information, bore significantly more children than women living in expanded households (defined to include those with both nonnuclear kin and nonkin).[31] Nellie Peters recalled, "When Mom was barely twenty, without any other women to talk to, she was saddled with two tots" on a small farm in Vilas county. Her first three children provided enough companionship for Mrs. Peters but, ignorant of effective contraception, she bore three more kids. Alluding to the most common method of birth control used by cutover couples, Nellie Peters admitted, "I should have run down Mom's leg when Dad spurted the seed." Her sister-in-law "gave Mom old French-Canadian folk remedies for miscarriages," including "a mix of kerosene laced with pig grease and pepper." Mrs. Peters "tried every way she could to jar the foetus loose." But "nothing worked."[32]

In sum, patterns of family structure, sex ratios, nuptiality, and fertility in the cutover in the early decades of the twentieth century resembled those of previous American agricultural frontiers. But as we shall see, the settlers were confident that in these and other respects they could transform their frontier into a land of yeoman farmers.

Cutover settlers were poor. In Hans Pederson's words, they just "didn't have anything when they came." Social scientists who investigated new settlers in the cutover between 1915 and 1920 reported that at time of arrival they generally had a net worth of less than $1,000. The region's farms, consequently, were smaller and less valuable than those in the southern part of the state. In 1900, cutover farms had only 83 percent of the acreage of the average Wisconsin farm and 39 percent of the value of the average farm's land, improvements, and buildings. In fact, 28 percent of cutover farms were smaller than fifty acres, and only 29 percent of the acreage of cutover farms was improved.[33] During the next two decades, however, through their labor and that of their family members, these farmers cleared land, grew crops on which to subsist, and began to find commercial crops, while supplementing their income with off-farm work.

The 1920 United States Census reported the results of two decades of work: the value of land, improvements, and buildings on cutover farms had increased to 47 percent of the state average, and 33 percent of the acreage of cutover farms was now improved. There was even more impressive agricultural development in the counties adjacent to the cutover—Barron, Chippewa, Clark, Polk, Shawano, and Marathon counties together added as many improved acres between 1900 and 1920 as the whole cutover, over one hundred thousand acres alone in Marathon.[34] The counties that had already been most developed in 1900—Oconto and Marinette along Lake Michigan and Burnett along the Mississippi—added the most improved acres in the twenty years, over one third of the entire increase in the cutover. But development was also impressive in Lincoln and Langlade counties, on Antigo soils, which were the best in the cutover; in Taylor County around Medford and to the north along the Wisconsin Central line; in Rusk County along the Soo and Wisconsin Central lines which dissected the county into fourths; and in Bayfield County, especially along the shores of Lake Superior (Figures 1.1 and 1.5).

But the cutover was still a relatively poor region in 1920; the value of the average farm's land and buildings was only $6,585. These farms produced crops worth $1,563, only two thirds of the state average.[35] Some farmers were success stories. Swedish immigrant Victor Johnson started farming in Bayfield County in 1897; by 1915 he had forty-two of his eighty-five acres free from stumps and cultivated and had a herd of nine dairy cows, justifying a self-evaluation of his farm at $9,150. Perhaps more representative was the experience of twenty-seven farmers in the Conrath area of Sawyer County who were surveyed in 1915 by their mortgage lender. After five years on their land, these farmers had four acres under plow and another 4.5 brushed, a herd of eight dairy cows, and land and buildings valued at $2,580, an increase from $840 at the time of purchase.[36] But for every farm operator whose years of hard work was increasing the value of his farm, two or three new settlers were beginning to farm forty-acre plots worth less than $1,000, retarding the overall increase in farm values. And there were still large sections of the cutover which were little more than wilderness: in the three northernmost counties with no shoreline on lakes Superior or Michigan—Forest, Florence, and Vilas—less than 10 percent of the land area was farmland at all, and less than thirty thousand acres had been cleared between 1900 and 1920.[37]

This land-clearing occupied the intense labor of cutover farmers and their families for their first several years in northern Wisconsin. Referring to his father, who began to farm in the town of Bashaw in Washburn County in 1886, Albert Stouffer remembered that "it seemed that he and Mother worked night and day, clearing land." Advertisements for northern Wisconsin land might emphasize that it was "easy to clear," but the truth was usually otherwise. Even before a settler could attempt the arduous job of breaking the soil for planting, he had to gather into piles the rocks which lay scattered over so many cutover fields or build them into stone fences. "Oh, what a back-breaking job we had picking rocks off of the farm," was the bitter memory of the child of one settler. Also, the brush and other debris left behind by loggers had to be taken off and, most significantly, tree stumps removed. This was a particular obstacle for cutover settlers because pine stumps, unlike those of hardwood trees, do not rapidly disintegrate naturally. Mechanical stump pullers were available: a walking team of horses would turn a large screw or a wheel on a tripod that would mesh with a block or a shift which, when raised or turned respectively, would pull up a stump to which it had been chained (Figure 2.3). After World War I, Dean Harry Russell of the College of Agriculture secured surplus military dynamite and provided it, with demonstrations, for stump removal in the cutover. Farmers in Price County bought 138,000 pounds of low-cost dynamite in 1920 alone. The local newspaper, in an understatement, reported "Lots of Noise in Price County." Still, no settler could hope to stump more than a few acres a year, even if he could afford dynamite. Ed Pudas claimed that "my father used more money for dynamite to blast out the stumps than the fabulous stumpage price of $1,500 he got for the pine forest on his 160 acres." Typical of this situation was the response of the Swan family (like the Stouffers early settlers of the town of Bashaw). "In the beginning in cultivating our land [we] left the stumps in and cultivated around them" (Figure 2.4).[38]

To clear brush and to accelerate the weathering process of stumps, many cutover settlers resorted to fire, after which their land seemed to blossom with rich new growth. "When the territory began to be opened up and settlers located on the cut-over lands," explained a lumber executive, "the clearing process necessitated burning." This technique

Figure 2.3. Mechanical stump-puller in use on a northern Wisconsin farm in the early twentieth century. Uprooted stumps are evident, especially in the right foreground. (State Historical Society of Wisconsin, photo WHi (X3) 50582)

could easily get out of control: in 1925 alone 1,400,000 acres burned in the cutover districts of the Great Lakes states. Forest fires are natural, of course, especially in a brush-filled environment like that in the aftermath of lumbering. Sparks from the numerous railroads which extended across northern Wisconsin also contributed to the problem. But commentators at the time, and scholars today, put the blame for most fires on individual settlers. When "people would clear their land by setting it on fire," admitted Lars Kailberg, it was "bad business." Death was one consequence of this burning: over eight hundred people died in the infamous 1871 fire at Peshtigo in Marinette County, and no reminiscence or novel based on life in the cutover is without a scene based on a family member narrowly escaping from a fire. In the late summer of 1898, for instance, a contemporary newspaper reported, "Nels Nelson, a farmer who lived 8 miles west of [Rice Lake], went down into his well to save his life, but the well house caught fire and Nelson's burned body was taken from the well." "I remember several times after I rode a bicycle seven miles to attend high school in Shell Lake," Albert Stouffer recalled,

Figure 2.4. McCormick mower ready for use between stumps remaining in hayfield. (State Historical Society of Wisconsin, photo WHi (X3) 26540)

"the principal would dismiss school for the day on account of the nearness of forest fires, and I would have to ride back home through smoke so thick I could hardly see the road." If they did not lose family members, cutover settlers often lost their farms to fires that got out of control. Referring to the 1893 forest fire in Lincoln County near Pine River, a settler's daughter recalled years later that "the hills and valleys were as black as a piece of coal and a number of families were burned out." As this comment suggests, fire in the cutover also affected the landscape. More intense fires actually damaged rather than nurtured the land and—perhaps more significantly—left it with a negative appearance, especially to outside observers. "In the 1890s and 1900s," commented the lumber executive previously quoted, "a ride on the Omaha railway from Chippewa Falls north through Spooner afforded a depressing sight . . . sickening . . . like a charnel house." No wonder promoters of the cutover seldom mentioned to potential settlers anything about the role fire would play in their lives if they moved to northern Wisconsin.[39]

Albert Stouffer's comment about his mother working alongside his father highlights an important point: land clearing—indeed, all farm work in the cutover—was a family activity.[40] One woman remembered that in the early years of her marriage on a Price County farm around 1915, "the two of us picked 21 to 22 loads of rocks a day." John Samadrak, who settled in southern Sawyer County in 1918, admitted that his wife was "nearly as good" as he was at land clearing. He credited his family with being responsible for the twenty acres which had been cleared on his farm in hardly a year. "Clearing land is a work [sic] that women and children enjoy," he told a local newspaper reporter. However, it was not always remembered that way by the children: sixty years afterwards Larry Garneau groaned as he recalled the work he and his brothers did picking up rocks on his family's farm in Washburn County in the 1920s— "that land was just solid rocks." That task was not limited to boys—Edna Hatlestad Hong, in a positive memoir of growing up in Taylor County in the 1920s, remembered children of both sexes in the fields every spring picking up rocks. In an explanation that applied to all farm work done by women and preadolescent children, Samadrak claimed, "This is one of the big advantag[es] of land clearing. It provides employment for the other members of the family, and at wages far beyond what they can obtain on the open market."[41] The whole family needed two or three summers of work to build a rough house, put up a small barn, dig a well, stump and clear a half acre or an acre for a garden to meet as much of the family's food needs as possible, and clear and brush a few acres for stump pasture for a team of horses, or perhaps oxen, and a milk cow for home consumption. Cutover settlers were similar to other midwestern farmers in the decades before World War II in this reliance on family labor, but their motives were somewhat different. They worked together not so much to save money to buy more land to pass on better farms to the younger generation, but to get started as farmers and survive their first years in frontier settlements.

As much as possible, settlers made use of the resources they saw around them. The berries flourishing on burned-over land were both an important food source and a commercial opportunity. When he was growing up, Larry Garneau's family canned up to one hundred quarts of strawberries a year. Berrying also offered small-scale commercial opportunities. An early settler in the Minong area of Washburn County remembered that "it was profitable for all participants, as whole families could pick, and blueberries were plentiful and always in demand in the large city markets." Dora Brewer, who operated a store and post office in the Nancy Lake area west of Minong in 1914, bought, packed, and shipped over two thousand cases of blueberries, which went by rail from Minong to Superior or the Twin Cities.

Many cutover farmers earned a few dollars to help get them through their first few seasons by selling potatoes or rutabagas. Hans Pederson recalled that around Drummond in the 1920s, "potatoes and rutabeggies [sic] seemed to be the big thing." Eldon Marple's father found that by the third year on their farm "a cash crop was necessary to augment the casual income derived from the eggs and the butter," and in Sawyer County "potatoes became the bonanza." In the three Sawyer County towns of Lenroth, Ojibwa, and Radisson, where most settlers had arrived within the previous decade, 81.5 percent of the 205 farms grew some potatoes in 1925 (Figure 2.5). Overall in 1920, 20 percent of Wisconsin's

Figure 2.5. Sawyer County booth at the State Potato Show in Madison, 1917. (State Historical Society of Wisconsin, photo WHi (X3) 50584)

potatoes were grown in the cutover. Carl Rhody estimated that, on the Price County farms around where he was raised, families themselves could consume as much as a ton of potatoes a year.[42]

Some cutover settlers never developed their farms much beyond this stage. "Many of our neighbors lived . . . for many years," explained Eldon Marple, "almost self-sufficient with a few animals and the crops to feed them and a garden to help feed [themselves]." On Albert Haas' family farm in the 1920s in the town of Wilson in Rusk County, "we raised all our own food except sugar, flour, coffee and tobacco." "Taxes could be worked out on the town roads," Marple explained, and "surplus eggs and butter [traded] with the stores in town to buy cloth, tools and the few commodities which they could not produce on the farm." Even clothing needs could be met by home production. According to Ed Pudas, in the town of Oulu in Bayfield County in the 1900s, "all the settlers raised sheep for the wool for clothing." As late as 1930, the United States census classified 7 percent of cutover farms as "self-sufficient" (whose residents consumed most of what the farm produced), compared to 2 percent in the rest of the state. Forest and Vilas counties had over 20 percent of their farms categorized as "self-sufficient."[43]

Some settlers did not develop their properties because they were primarily part-time farmers. By preference, or necessity because of their limited resources, they worked in the woods—like Mary Bedore's father—or in sawmills, devoting themselves only seasonally to farm work. On several of the Apostle Islands in Lake Superior near Bayfield, Norwegian immigrants combined fishing with raising orchards and dairy farming. Other settlers, such as the Finns in Douglas and Iron counties or the Croatians in Vilas County, were miners or worked on the railroads. Finns "surely did not settle here with the purpose of making a living out of agriculture," an Iron County newspaper explained. Instead, as a result of labor agitation in the mines, "a number of these settlers were compelled to come here by the black-list to cut logs, and thus support their families." Economic downturns or structural changes in their primary employment could take away the resources these part-time farmers needed to develop their farms. "I went there to be a lumberjack," admitted Herb Jolly, a farmer in Vilas County in the 1920s. "But the big timber companies had cut every thing clear. . . . I just settled on forty acres in the sticks, and grubbed along raising pigs, chickens, cows, kids, and taters." Even when off-farm work was intended to finance improvements on the farm, events sometimes intervened to produce a different outcome. Lillian Mishler King, who was born in 1892 in the town of Springbrook in Washburn County, explained: "Dad made good money in the woods every winter but, like most of the lumberjacks, he would stop off in the saloons at Hayward or Springbrook when he came out and spend most of his money. As a result all of us [fourteen] kids lived from hand to mouth."

In the cutover, therefore, nonagricultural employment was often not part of a transition to a more commercialized economy as it was for participants in the putting-out economy of the early nineteenth century in which some stages of manufacturing were done in rural households. Rather, it retarded greater market involvement. This difference was in part due to the gendered nature of the work involved. Women had often been involved in putting-out work (or went to work in the early textile factories), leaving their husbands to work to bring their family farm into the more commercialized economy which was spreading across the countryside. In the cutover, by contrast, nonfarm work was largely done by males, often at the cost of commercial development of their farms.

Some cutover settlers never cleared much land because limited agricultural activities satisfied the desire for security, independence, and a close relationship with the natural environment that had attracted them to the cutover in the first place. A Rusk County schoolteacher later recalled that, early in the twentieth century, "Hunting and fishing were the general hobbies; sometimes I used to think they were the vocation and farming was the hobby. No farm responsibility could hold one of those folks if the urge to go fishing seized him." A farmer near Hayward, in Sawyer County, who took over the farm started by his father in 1891, admitted that a major reason for farmers' failures was that they "had too much fishing to do." In welcoming a new settler in 1919, the Radisson newspaper pointedly noted that the man he bought his farm from had "answered the call of the wild" and had only "hunted and fished for seven years."[44]

However, many cutover farmers and their families seriously applied themselves to farming and gradually became more integrated with the market economy. The factors of geographical isolation and poor transportation which kept Appalachia a subsistence agricultural region into the twentieth century were absent in the cutover.[45] Cutover settlers moved toward a style of rural life which had come to predominate in Trempealeau County, seventy-five miles south of cutover, a half-century before northern Wisconsin began to be developed for farming. An anonymous letter in the Phillips newspaper at the beginning of the twentieth century admitted that the settlers of the town of Worcester were only "poor farmers," but emphasized that they were determined to work themselves up to the level of their counterparts in southern Wisconsin. "They achieved their aim," the writer pointed out, "and I guess by a little perseverance and elbow grease we can do the same."[46]

Farmers needed capital to move towards more commercial farming. For instance, W. J. Davies, who moved from Ohio to near Shell Lake in Washburn County in 1905, had to spend most of his first two seasons in the cutover "working out" for other farmers, getting only a half-acre clear for a garden on his own property—"it was pretty tough sledding." But in 1907 he received a small inheritance and was able to buy a plow and a team of horses, which enabled him to clear land full-time. "As soon as I got a little land cleared and broke," he recounted, "I planted corn and potatoes with hand planters, and got some land in hay to feed the stock. Now I was in business!"[47] Some farmers, like Eldon Marple's father, used cash brought with them to the cutover to pay for the land clearing and equipment necessary to develop more market-focused agriculture, while others relied on savings from off-farm work, especially in lumbering, once they had settled in northern Wisconsin. If a farm itself still had some standing timber, that could be logged and sold for pulp. Furthermore, as land prices steadily increased until 1920, many cutover settlers were able to refinance their land contracts with mortgage-backed loans (chapter 1) and use some of the proceeds to develop the commercial orientation of their farms.

More market-oriented farms became more specialized. County agents and other experts told cutover farmers to get half their income from one product and the rest from three others. Consequently, some farm operators expanded the small potato plots they had planted for quick income in the first few years on their land and specialized in raising potatoes. Forty or fifty potato farms developed in the town of Argonne, north of Crandon in Forest County. A few miles to the east, near Three Rivers in Oconto County, retired major league baseball player Fred Luderus started the eighty-acre Luderus Potato Farm in 1920.[48] By the 1920s Barron County and the section of Langlade County around Antigo produced most of the potatoes grown in or on the edge of the cutover. These locations joined a large section of Portage and Waupaca counties farther south as the chief potato-growing regions in the state. For instance, by the early 1920s, Paul Thompson, who had come to Langlade County as a seventeen-year old in 1897 to work in the woods, operated City View Farm near Antigo, raising potatoes and horses on reportedly one of the finest farms in the county.[49] During the early decades of the century when railroads dissected northern Clark and Chippewa counties and southern Rusk County, farmers around the villages of Stanley and Sheldon intensively cultivated potatoes, cabbages, cucumbers, and peas as cash crops.[50]

Cranberries were another important cutover crop. Cranberry bogs were created near Nancy Lake, in Washburn County, and in Price County; these counties ranked fifth and sixth in cranberry production in Wisconsin by 1920.[51] Growing cranberries required intensive labor: marshes had to be scrapped clear to the peat soil and ditched and the soil loosened, beds needed to be planted by hand with stems cut from existing beds and then required constant attention, harvesting the marshes involved flooding and then skimming the beds with hand rakes—ten men were needed to harvest one acre in two days. It took up to six years for beds to develop fully their potential yield. Harvested cranberries went to processing plants like that in Eagle River, where young women working seasonal jobs sorted out by hand as much debris as possible before the berries were canned.[52] Market-oriented farmers, such as cranberry growers, also began to organize themselves in associations which reflected their specialized interests. For example, between 1912 and 1918, Langlade County farmers developed a beekeepers' association, a potato growers' association, a poultry association, and a purebred cattle association.[53]

The quest to find a viable cash crop led some cutover farmers in exotic directions. Marathon County farmers, adjacent to the cutover, cultivated ginseng, a root crop with a market in eastern Asia as an aphrodisiac. Carl Rhody recalled that in the Saga Valley area in Price County in the 1920s ginseng was "a lucrative business . . . one harvested acre would bring a small fortune." Another group of settlers, 1890s German immigrants from Ukraine to the area around White Potato Lake in Oconto and Marinette counties, grew and processed cucumbers. Early in the twentieth century, numerous Price County farmers also contracted to plant an acre or so in cucumbers to supply the Henry Weichert Company of Chicago with pickles. Ukrainian-Germans also tried their hand at raising sugar beets, as did cutover farmers from elsewhere, such as those around Moquah in Bayfield County, but the growing season in northern Wisconsin was generally too short for this crop. The *Phillips Times* boosted sugar beet cultivation early in the twentieth century, but had to admit after the 1904 crop that the "experiment . . . has not been satisfactory." By the 1920s, sugar beet production in Wisconsin was concentrated in the southeast part of the state.[54] Attempts to introduce commercial livestock-raising to northern Wisconsin were also generally unsuccessful. Schemes to raise sheep on cutover lands around Fifield in Price County in the first decade of the twentieth century came up against disease, predators, and the weather. One ranch lost over five thousand sheep and lambs to a late spring snow.[55] Sheep were still widely distributed on farms in all parts of Wisconsin in 1920, but in declining numbers.[56] Their numbers remained low because of the development of specialized sheep-ranching in parts of the western United States; unlike the situation with potatoes, no particular section of Wisconsin was suitable for large-scale commercial sheep-ranching.

As cutover farms developed commercially, dairying got the most focus, not only because of the suitability of the climate but because, relative to growing field crops, dairying was labor- rather than capital-intensive, an attraction to settlers with limited means. "Dairying was the object of all the settlers when they took up land at Moquah," reported the town's historian, an old-time settler. An Oulu resident wrote in 1911 in a Finnish-language newspaper, "Experience has taught us that dairying is the best and most profitable occupation. But it requires work and energy. First we must clear more land for hay; and secondly, we must procure the best milking herd." In general, successful dairy farms in the cutover had herds of ten or more cows; at least an acre of hay for each cow; and an accessible market for their milk. C. A. Paul showed the attitude needed for successful dairy farming when he wrote to the Union Mortgage Loan Company in 1915. Paul had been operating a forty-acre farm in Rusk County mortgaged to Union Mortgage Loan since 1907. Believing that potatoes were unreliable as a cash crop, he wanted to concentrate on dairy and cattle production. This necessitated acquiring more pasture and enlarging his herd to at least fifteen cows. "I am not satisfied on a forty," he emphasized in asking for an increase in the size of his mortgage loan. Similarly motivated were Nellie Balsewicz and her husband, who in 1917 traded their tavern in Chicago for a farm in the Lithuanian settlement in the town of Crescent in Oneida County, and eventually milked thirty-two cows on 240 acres.[57]

In parts of the cutover in the first two decades of the twentieth century, dairy farming began to provide good financial returns to settlers. Prices paid for Wisconsin butter and cheese almost doubled in the two decades before World War I, creating a demand which could be met only by the less developed northern part of the state.[58] In the area in northern Polk County settled by Danes in the late nineteenth century, the local historian reported in 1907 that during the previous decade, farmers "little by little have gotten their farm management brought to such a point that they now have good incomes. Many now have twelve to sixteen good milk cows. . . . In 1906 milk and cream was delivered from 100 farms from 800 cows." Ed Pudas proudly recalled that by about 1910 in Oulu, people did "not refer to the homesteaders any more as settlers, but small farmers as they made most of their living from dairy cows rather than forest work. Forest work began to be more a side line for additional income." By 1920 there were 139,073 dairy cows on cutover farms, and although the herd size on these farms was smaller than the state average, it had increased from 4.3 to 5.3 during the previous decade.[59] During these decades Marathon and Clark counties, adjacent to the cutover on the state's central plain, successfully made the transition from dependence on lumbering to profitable dairying—in fact, in the 1990s these were the two leading counties in Wisconsin in value of dairy products produced.[60] Suggesting that this development would continue northward, the number of cows grew most rapidly in adjoining districts of southern Taylor, Lincoln, and Langlade counties.

The expansion of dairying accompanied a transformation from home production to creameries and cheese factories. Harold Buchma recalled that on his family's farm in Washburn County as late as 1910, "there was no market for milk or cream or eggs. Mother was a good butter maker; so we traded it in for groceries." Especially among Scandinavians, buttermaking was a skill often used by women in home production. Ed Pudas explained that "milk and cream was separated by gravity process, cream was churned by hand, to make butter, mother worked the butter and mixed in the proper amount of salt and packed the butter in pound crocks" to trade in town.[61] The remaining skim milk could be fed to calves, sheep, hogs, or other livestock found in small numbers on almost every cutover farm. By 1909 farm butter production in northern Wisconsin had increased by about one third in a decade and made up 13 percent of the state total (Table 2.2). But home production of butter peaked statewide in the 1890s and shortly after 1910 in the cutover. On the Buchma farm the introduction of a cream separator encouraged change: "we separated our cream from the milk and shipped the cream in cans to Bridgman and Russel in Duluth and to Minneapolis" for $4.50

Table 2.2. Measures of Cutover Butter Production, 1889–1930

	PRODUCTION (LBS.)		PERCENT OF STATE PRODUCTION		
	Home	Factory	Home	Factory	Total
1889	1,002,892		2.2		
1895		1,809,297		2.4	
1899	2,310,750		5.2		
1905		1,544,054		1.7	
1909	3,550,287	3,171,007	13.1	3.0	4.8
1915		6,875,536		5.5	
1919	2,401,236	8,021,303	27.7	8.2	9.8
1925		14,824,797		8.8	
1929	1,118,831		37.1		
1930		16,824,415		9.9	

Source: Walter Ebling et al., "A Century of Wisconsin Agriculture 1848–1948," *Wisconsin Crop Reporting Service Bulletin,* no. 290 (Madison, 1948), 109–10.

a can. Even more significantly, creameries opened in northwestern Wisconsin and cheese factories in northeastern Wisconsin, where they became outlets for farmers' milk. Only 16 of Wisconsin's 951 creameries were located in the cutover in 1896; subsequently, the number of creameries declined in southeastern Wisconsin but increased in the cutover, reaching 67 by 1924. The Buchma family eventually began to ship their milk, for example, through the Co-Operative Creamery at Springbrook. Factory butter production in the cutover quadrupled between 1895 and 1920 while increasing by less than a third statewide. By 1919 the cutover produced 8.9 percent of the state's factory butter and 6.4 percent of its factory cheese; the region had produced only 2.4 percent of the state's butter—and essentially none of its cheese—in 1895 (Table 2.2).[62]

This increase in output and shift from home to off-farm production of milk products highlights that cutover settlers were not peasants, as some scholars have tried to characterize eighteenth- and even nineteenth-century American farmers. Commercialization would have been resisted in a peasant economy since it is zero sum: one farmer's additional cow on the common meadow means one less cow for another farmer or less milk produced by all the other farmers' cows. In the cutover, by contrast, settlers encouraged and helped one another to develop their farms. Roy Meier, for example, recalled the older farmers in his neighborhood as a major source of information for the improvements we have seen he made on his family's farm. In the cutover, increased production by one farm operator did not hurt his neighbor. Indeed, it helped to increase the value of the neighbor's land, which in turn increased all land values in the neighborhood.

Growing reliance on butter and cheese factories also altered the lives of northern Wisconsin settlers. Home production steadily declined both absolutely and relative to factory production. As herds increased in size, farm activities became more and more focused on them. Roy Meier recalled that when a creamery opened in the town of Spirit in Price County in 1910, his father bought a separator and began to expand dairying operations. At this time, Meier's father abandoned selling the cabbages and other commodities on which he had previously relied for a small cash income. This growing dependence on a milk check challenged the independence of cutover farmers. The crops they planted also reflected this change: more and more acreage was devoted to hay to feed the cows and less to corn and other crops. This pattern was statewide but particularly pronounced in the cutover. By 1927 about half the cropped land in the cutover was in hay, compared to only about one third statewide.[63]

Women's roles also changed in response to more intensive dairying. They were increasingly relieved from the heavy labor involved in clearing rocks from fields and making cheese at home. Subsequently their less direct involvement in agricultural production may have reduced the mutuality which tended to exist initially between settler spouses, undermined the perception of the importance of women on cutover farms, and increased patriarchy.[64] Previously in dairy regions of New York state, the transition from home to factory cheese-making in the 1870s, the spread of creameries in the 1880s, and the advance of the cash economy led to the decline of neighborhood labor exchange systems and the family economy, in which women's work was essential.[65] In the long term, especially after World War II, this may have happened also on cutover farms. As immigrants assimilated the Victorian ideology of separate spheres in gender roles, many settlers came to see the barn and the field as not the proper place for women. While "overburdening of women is an old custom with the Finns," a Finnish-language publication admitted, it should not continue in the United States.[66] But for the most part in the early decades of the twentieth century, increasingly commercialized dairying and other types of agriculture were compatible with yeoman farming and its central role for women's labor.[67]

Women on cutover farms continued to be indirectly essential to agricultural production. Their cooking, washing, canning, and other activities in the farmhouse and farmyard contributed to family self-sufficiency and freed up male resources for more commercial endeavors. In addition, as the diary of Marathon County's Anna Pratt Erickson shows, many women reduced the need for off-farm purchases and kept cash available for investment in agricultural production by trading potatoes, vegetables, garden products, and other items within their rural neighborhoods.[68]

Some women also continued to be involved more directly in agricultural production. As creameries opened, a few women found jobs as butter-makers. Johanne Ravholt was the first butter-maker when a creamery opened in the Danish community in Luck in 1886. For many women, furthermore, the release from home butter production meant more time was available to milk the farm's larger herds, a role that was common for them on cutover farms. For women of Scandinavian descent, this was a continuation of traditional European practices. Lars Kailberg's mother "loved cows. She grew up with cows in Sweden and cows liked her too. And she wasn't happy without some cows." He explained that "in Sweden men never milked. So my father was interested in cash crops anyways, didn't care for animal husbandry." Even on German-American Roy Meier's farm, where his mother "had no knowledge of running a farm," she "wouldn't do chores except to milk (and take care of the chickens)."[69]

Raising poultry was another way cutover women like Meier's mother played a productive role in the cash economy of their farms. "Every farm was equipped with a chicken coop," claimed Elise Kramolis Lajcak about Bayfield County farms at the beginning of the twentieth century. Cutover women—like their farm sisters everywhere—took responsibility for poultry. Mary Bedore, who grew up in southern Oconto County in the 1890s, remembered that "Mother raised large plots of onions and garden stuff, chicken and turkeys, and they used to drive to Oconto with loads of butter, vegetables, apples, green onions."[70] Especially where incomes were low, as in the cutover, the cash or credits earned from chickens and eggs could be critical to the survival of a farm family.

Some cutover women, furthermore, earned a small cash income from midwifery. Both a 1919 United States Department of Labor survey of Marathon County, adjacent to the cutover, and a recent scholarly examination of Price County found numerous midwives, themselves usually immigrants, serving the needs of women of their own nationality in their communities, earning as much as $5.00 per delivery. In the town of McKinley in Taylor County, between 1915 and 1927, twenty-one deliveries were assisted by a midwife and only eighteen by a physician (only spouses or others assisted in seven cases, and one woman delivered unassisted).[71] While for the most part immigrant agricultural traditions quickly faded everywhere in the United States in the face of a new landscape and increasing market demands, ethnic traditions (which remained particularly strong in the cutover) continued to have impact in the much more private realm of childbirth. Opportunities therefore remained for women to play more public—and remunerative—roles in such activities.

Did the experience of settling in northern Wisconsin in the early twentieth century in any way "liberate" women? From the point of view of women themselves who came to the cutover, the answer must be mixed. As had been the case with most migration to nineteenth-century frontiers, the initial decision to move to northern Wisconsin was usually made by men; wives often followed reluctantly, hesitating to abandon those aspects of the female sphere—networks of kin and friends, churches—that they knew would be difficult to replicate at least initially in the cutover. Referring to one family which moved to the community in 1916, the historian of Stone Lake explained that "Mrs. Ross wasn't too happy about leaving her friends in Onalaska" in La Crosse County in southwestern Wisconsin. But some women were enthusiastic about the move and were even the persons behind it. The Bednarczyk family moved to Lublin in Taylor County in 1912 when Anna Bednarczyk, who liked farming, told her husband to quit working in the Pennsylvania coal mines or she would return to Poland. The parents of Ed Jones moved in 1905 to a farm three miles outside of Shell Lake in Washburn County because his mother disliked the altitude in Colorado where they had been living.

The pattern was similar for women once they had settled in northern Wisconsin. Certainly some females were unhappy with the life they found in the cutover. The first priority had to be farm operations, and improvements for women's work and life in the house were neglected. Roy Meier remembered his mother lamenting, "I'll never get the sewing machine; I'll never get the cook stove," when his father decided in the 1890s to invest time and money into developing a business wholesaling butter to Tomahawk stores. Settlers who gave up their cutover farms and moved elsewhere after a few years often blamed their wives' dissatisfaction for their move. But many cutover women, invoking the Victorian norm of female submission to fate, quietly accepted their situation and worked hard to help their families succeed. When asked whether women were as satisfied as men among northern Wisconsin settlers, Hans Anderson admitted, "I know my mother wasn't satisfied. . . . She said the food tasted so much better" in Sweden. "But of course she had nothing to say about it," he pointed out. Margaret Pike explained that "Mother didn't really like some things about farm living; but she worked hard." Alvina Schmitt remembered that "when we moved out to the farm" near Bloomer in Chippewa County "after we married" in the 1920s, "we didn't have much furniture. We didn't have anything in the living room, so I just shut the door." But "I knew I would get eventually. . . . We needed machinery and feed first." Families negotiated the allocation of resources. Roy Meier's father, for example, agreed to let his wife keep her "surplus earnings" from selling produce so as to be able to buy the things she wanted. Attitudes changed—Mrs. Ross "got to love it here so much that the family had a hard time getting her to go anywhere for any length of time." Carl Rhody's mother was one of many women who felt great satisfaction in seeing her family establish a new home in the cutover.[72] In sum, at least as many cutover women came to feel a proud sense of ownership in their work like that of the women in Union County, Illinois, studied by anthropologist Jane Adams, as they did a "chronic dissatisfaction" like that of the oppressed Nebraska farm women examined by historian Deborah Fink.[73]

Just as the slowly growing commercialization of cutover farming did not significantly marginalize women, at least before 1940, it did not completely eliminate earlier subsistence practices. Bartering with storekeepers in town remained common into the 1940s. Charles Patterson, a Rice Lake grocer, recalled "a big farmer west of town" and his wife, who as a "sideline" to their large dairy farm, brought three thirty-dozen cases of eggs a week to his store. They received groceries for about two thirds of the value of the eggs, cash for the remainder. When farmers had nothing to trade, storekeepers often extended them credit for gas, medicine, and groceries. "You paid your bills when you had the money," recalled Stanley J. Pero about life in the town of Hughes in Bayfield County as late as the 1930s. Of course, each side in such relationships sometimes thought the other was trying to take advantage of them. Patterson remembered the time he embarrassed a farmer by insisting on candling a pail of eggs brought in to trade and finding all of them rotten. But such face-to-face bartering also worked to bond merchants and farmers socially and to strengthen community feeling by limiting urban-rural tensions. As Adams found for Union County in southern Illinois, successful yeoman farming depended on and encouraged the integration of country and village people. Recalling patterns of forty years earlier, when interviewed in the 1980s Patterson was still proud that a regular rural clientele patronized his store.[74]

In sum, in the first two decades of the twentieth century, increased land clearing, rising land values, and more effort at producing products for the market helped make cutover farmers more like the yeoman farmers they desired to become. Some cutover farms remained more subsistence-oriented while others focused more on the market. As the practice of bartering with storekeepers illustrates, however, one pattern did not replace the other; the two overlapped. Furthermore, depending on market conditions, the family cycle of the farm family, the degree of development in the neighborhood, and other factors, a cutover farm might go through stages of greater-or-less involvement with the market. Yeoman farmers were neither hard-nosed profit-maximizers nor backward peasants.[75]

Regardless of the extent of its engagement with the market, a cutover farm was basically a family enterprise. To ensure its vitality, each family enterprise in turn had to mesh with others in the community. Consequently, the productive aspects of cutover farms were shaped by the strictures of a family- and neighborhood-based labor system that was closely integrated with the social life developed by the settlers.

The labor force on a northern Wisconsin farm consisted overwhelmingly of members of the farm operator's family. Robert Schlomann recalled his father insisting that "we don't have money to hire anybody" to work on the family's farm in the town of Grow in Rusk County. It was unusual for a cutover farm family to have a hired man living with them, or even to be assisted by a paid laborer who lived on another farm and might be trying to accumulate cash to get started developing his own farm. The continued presence in the cutover of a few corporate farms owned by lumber companies and staffed by hired laborers distort the figures in the 1905 state census, but these numbers still suggest the relatively limited significance of nonfamily farm labor: in the cutover there were 483 agricultural laborers for every 1,000 farms compared to 554 statewide. For example, in Catawba in Price County, a newly opened area where farming was the predominant activity, only seven agricultural laborers worked for 75 farms; in the town of Florence in Florence County, where the continued association of many farmers with mine work limited the commitment to agriculture, only twelve agricultural laborers worked on 123 farms.[76] Although American Indians occasionally harvested cranberries for a few days for cutover farmers, no agricultural proletariat existed in northern Wisconsin as it did elsewhere. Early in the twentieth century corporate sugar-beet farms in eastern Wisconsin and the Saginaw Valley in Michigan exploited first Belgian and eastern European immigrants and then, after World War I, Mexican-Americans. Elsewhere in the Midwest, even family farms which grew products such as fruit often depended on migrant labor.[77] Cutover farmers neither desired to operate or work for wages on such farms; those enterprises represented the antithesis of their yeoman farmer ideal.

On northern Wisconsin farms the family cycle often affected farm operations. On his farm in the town of Spirit, Price County, Carl Rhody's father decided to cut back on working in the woods and concentrate on farming in the mid-1920s, enlarging his herd and planting more potatoes and rutabagas; he reasoned that his two adolescent sons could help him with land clearing and field work but were not yet old enough for woods work or other off-farm cash employment. Indeed, when evaluating farms for creditworthiness, appraisers for Union Mortgage Loan Company noted favorably the presence of adolescent boys.[78]

But girls also did important work. Mary Bedore began doing chores when she was six, and remembered that "most every girl I knew did the milking and I did because my Mother disliked the job." If older brothers had been present, which they were not by the time she was thirteen, Mary might have escaped such "barn chores," but almost all girls assisted with poultry, gardens, potato debugging, and orchards. "I mostly collected eggs from the chicken house," recalled Anne Martin, whose family farmed near Minong in Washburn County, "and, oh yes, the garden always needed tending to." Nell Peters and her sisters and brothers sold wildflowers to tourists, debugged potatoes, hoed and picked corn, and entered animals and vegetables in competition at the Vilas County Fair.[79]

All family members worked to the maximum at harvest time. Albert Haas recalled that at the Wilson Center School in Rusk County, seventh- and eighth-graders would be absent from mid-September to late-October "to help with the farm work and help our family make a good living." In the late nineteenth century men still harvested hay by cutting it by hand with a scythe while women and children followed behind them, raking the hay with wooden rakes and building hay cocks.[80] In the early twentieth century, as farming developed in the cutover, horse-drawn hay mowers and rakes became more common (Figure 2.4).[81] "Mothers were often pressed into service at haying time," recalled Paul Nagel, who grew up near Jump River, in northern Taylor County, in the 1920s. It was "sometimes to drive the team on the wagon in the field, sometimes to receive and stack the wagon and often to drive the team at the barn" when the hay was unloaded.[82] Children also often helped by driving the team or helping their father spread the hay in the barn. Grain harvesting was similar. Albert Stouffer's father was the first farmer in the town of Bashaw in Washburn County to buy a grain binder, which replaced cutting by hand with a cradle and mechanically tied grain into bundles with binding twine. Stouffer went with his father to use the machine on neighboring farms. "I was about 12 years old," he recalled. "It was my job to ride the left hand horse of the lead team, and many the hot day I rode that horse until I was so sore, I could hardly sit down."[83]

In sum, different family members usually concentrated on kinds of work thought to be suitable to their age and gender—men in the fields, women in the barn, children in the garden. But their work roles were mutually supportive and could be flexible, depending on individual interests and abilities, the products being produced, and the immediate needs of the family. In the Midwest before World War II, flexibility in work roles was greatest on smaller farms, as in the cutover. The physical demands of dairy farming, which was becoming the norm in the cutover, in contrast to the demands of cattle-ranching or large-scale wheat-farming, also allowed roles to overlap. Furthermore, immigrants, which farmers in the cutover tended to be, were often more flexible in work roles than were native-born farmers.[84]

Because family and work were so deeply intertwined, the interruption of the family cycle had important implications for labor on cutover farms. When Jens Ingretson, who farmed for several decades in the town of Crystal in Washburn County, wrote that "Pearl and I and the children got about fifty acres cleared and under cultivation on our farm before Pearl died in 1936," he underscored the centrality of family labor to farm operations. Jens implied that Pearl's death ended the developmental stage of the farm's history. More often death claimed the adult male in the farm family, and even more often in the cutover he would be absent for extended periods, working in the woods or elsewhere. In these circumstances cutover farm women had to rely on themselves and their children to keep their farms operating. "We had to do all the chores while dad was in the logging camp . . . before we headed off to school," Larry Garneau remembered. When his father died in a woods accident, Larry remained on the farm, as his family seemed too large to move into town. "We all worked like tigers," he said, and recalled how his mother would come in from the fields and collapse for an hour while the rest of the family ate the dinner prepared by his eldest sister. But "we done better than they that sat there and waited," he emphasized.[85]

Garneau also "worked out" for cash income to help his family. This practice of a family economy was common in both urban and rural areas of nineteenth-century America and continued into the twentieth century in poorer regions like the cutover where family cohesiveness, reinforced by conservative immigrant values, remained strong. It was the rule in intact as well as female-headed families like Garneau's.[86] Boys found work doing chores on farms in the neighborhood where the operator had no adolescent sons, or went with their fathers into the woods in the winter. In their later teenage years, they could work seasonally on wheat-harvest crews in the Dakotas. Although fewer in number, there were also such opportunities for girls, more often in nonfarm work and farther from home, as was characteristic of the Midwest before World War II. Within the Polish community around Lublin in Taylor County, for example, teen-aged farm daughters often went to Chicago to work as domestic laborers. Assisted by a relative in Chicago, Helen Ciesliek left Lublin at fifteen to work in the laundry of the Hotel La Salle in Chicago. At her mother's insistence, she sent home $2.00 a week of her earnings.[87] Such income from children was critical when there was no adult male in the household. For example, Veronika Helstein was the only adult on her farm in the town of Grow in Rusk County in 1910; her six children lived with her, the eldest of whom—fourteen-year-old Dufel—worked in a sawmill. Dufel's labor for his family was not without reward—Veronika eventually enlarged the farm and was still operating it in 1940.[88]

The practice of the family economy required children to temper their ambitions. After finishing eighth grade, Carl Rhody pleaded with his father for permission to go on to Phillips High School but was told in no uncertain terms, "You stay home and help me." For Ann Johnson, who grew up in the town of Grant in Rusk County, studying at the county teacher's school in Ladysmith about 1920 meant not only walking four miles and back to town but "getting up at four in the morning, helping my father milk the cows, feed and water them. Then at night when I came home [I] helped clean the barn and do any other necessary chores." Ada Blake Nelson had nearly graduated from nursing school in St. Paul when her brother enlisted to serve in World War I and her "father sent for me to come home and help him with the farm work" in the town of Evergreen in Washburn County. "I remembered how bitterly disappointed I was," Ada recalled, "but I was a dutiful daughter, and gave up my career." For Robert Schlomann a few years later, the norms of the family economy meant delaying going to high school for one year, and later delaying going to college for several years, so as to do unpaid work on the family farm and off-farm construction work for pay. But when his younger brother was fifteen and able to be his father's "second man," Robert went off to River Falls State Teachers College. A loan from his younger sister, who had gone to work as a nanny, first in Ladysmith and later in Pittsburgh, helped Robert pay his expenses. When he got a job teaching agriculture, Robert then repaid his sister, who went on to study to become a medical technician.[89]

Family obligations did not necessarily end with marriage. The daughter of an Iron County farmer saw her father have a nervous breakdown when she and her sister married within weeks of one another—he "thought he had lost the whole world." So she and her new husband abandoned their plan to move to the state of Washington, stayed in Wisconsin, and went into "partnership" with her father to work his farm.[90]

Off-farm work and cycles within the family economy were central to the development and operation of the Meier family farm in Price County. Karl Meier, a German immigrant, settled on 160 acres in 1883 and married in 1886; thirteen children followed (an extreme example of high fertility on the frontier). Karl worked in the woods while slowly developing his farm; in the first decade of the twentieth century, his wife and children churned milk from about ten cows into butter for sale in Tomahawk. Then between 1907 and 1917 "tremendous" change occurred on the farm, in the words of Roy Meier, born in 1902. The Meiers constructed a new barn, enlarged the farmhouse, increased the herd to fifteen Guernseys; put twenty-five acres under cultivation in oats, corn, and hay, and began to sell milk to a creamery. Off-farm work, mostly by Karl (including income from part-time municipal employment) supplied critical funds to the farm's operation in 1911, for example, when significant expenses were made for additional livestock (Table 2.3). These

Table 2.3. Balance Sheet, Meier Family Farm, Selected Years 1911–1921

	1911	1916	1921
Receipts			
Farm			
Butter/cream	$165.36	$305.83	$356.85
Meat/animals	96.82	231.76	143.53
Timber/bark	211.71	1138.39	328.53
Other	15.67	76.93	27.96
Subtotal	$489.56	$1802.91	$856.37
Other			
Off-farm work	$571.48	$2.00	$217.00
Boarders	0	0	32.00
Interest received	36.50	0	9.60
Miscellaneous	48.81	46.70	3.50
Subtotal	$646.79	$48.70	$262.10
Total receipts	$1146.35	$1851.61	$1118.47
Expenses			
Farm			
Feed	$63.93	$45.90	$0
Equipment	75.81	22.42	3.90
Services/supplies	26.29	128.12	61.81
Insurance	64.50	16.81	37.22
Hired Help	50.60	16.50	0
Livestock purchase	141.00	6.00	0
Subtotal	$422.13	$235.85	$102.93
Family			
Groceries	$161.23	$252.12	$39.71
Dry goods/merchandise	131.91	186.98	550.40
Medical	0	5.00	69.40
Telephone	0	12.00	15.00
Furniture	0	51.64	0
Piano/radio	0	310.00	31.98
Children	63.76	0	100.00
Other	89.98	60.10	32.29
Subtotal	$446.88	$877.84	$838.88
Other			
Auto purchase	$0	$636.50	$0
Auto operation	0	39.43	100.16
Taxes	30.95*	0†	221.99
Interest paid	50.00	0	103.00
Miscellaneous	76.20	112.17	27.71
Subtotal	$157.15	$788.10	$452.86
Total expenditures	$1025.76	$1909.84	$1373.71
Net income (deficit)	$120.59	($58.23)	($254.84)

*Taxes for 1911 paid December 31, 1910.
†No record of taxes for 1916.
Source: Calculated from data in the Roy R. Meier Papers, ARC, UWEC.

capital improvements provided the foundation for more than doubling the farm's income from agriculture by 1916. By that year, the family could afford to cut back off-farm work, which gave them the time to take advantage of high war-induced prices and log off and sell timber still standing on the farm. The Meiers also paid cash that year for a piano and automobile, and in general increased expenditures for family consumption. But Karl became ill and cows had to be sold to pay living expenses, and after his death his widow and his son Roy were left to operate the farm. According to Roy, his mother could not now control his older brother and sister, who took the car and spent money on "carefree times." In these circumstances, made worse by the impact of the agricultural depression beginning in 1920, farm income in 1921 dropped to half what it had been in 1916 (despite substantial inflation in the intervening years). The family therefore curtailed expenses, and three children contributed cash to the family budget from off-farm work. But a determined Roy Meier continued his father's dairying enterprise, which is evident in the 1921 income figures. Roy rebuilt the herd, bought a new mower, and built a silo in 1924 so as to get "a milk check in winter." When interviewed in the late 1970s, he still operated the farm.[91]

The assistance of neighbors—"trading work"—was an essential supplement to family labor in yeoman farming. Such assistance characterized American farming in general before 1940, but was particularly significant in the cutover because the relative poverty of the region meant that a settler had few alternatives but to turn to his neighbors for help. Trading work helped to bind together rural neighborhoods and could overcome divisions within them. "Everyone helped someone else," recalled Stanley J. Pero, who moved to a farm in the town of Hughes in Bayfield County in the 1930s. Neighbors often temporarily housed new settlers while a rough farmhouse was being built for them. The Schlomann family experienced this sort of assistance when they moved from North Dakota to the town of Grow in Rusk County in 1919; the Polish Pavlik family let the German Schlomanns stay in a shack on their farm during the newcomers' first winter. In the next stage of developing a cutover farm, neighbors assisted with the construction of barns and permanent houses. Susan Slaton recalled that after her family moved to the town of Bass Lake in Washburn County in 1897, "the next spring and summer the neighbors from all around came to help us build a cabin on our place." These sorts of activities had a social as much as an economic function. Lars Kailberg inadvertently acknowledged this when he described a "barn-raising spree; barn-raising bee I should say"; what was no doubt on his mind was the "keg of beer" which he admitted followed such "bees." "Trading work" was a responsibility of living in the community, and was not calculated on a cost/benefit basis. Milford Keepers, who farmed near Jump River in northern Taylor County, admired "neighbor Bell" not only because he "never turned me down when I needed help" but because he "never left me feeling that I owed him anything."[92]

Work-sharing was also central to the lives of cutover women. Stripping geese feathers for quilts, canning beans, sewing, weeding the garden, learning new canning techniques—whenever possible, small groups of women did these tasks together. This cooperation reduced the total amount of labor which had to be done but, perhaps even more important, brought the women together socially. "We had such fellowship, or sisterhood, or whatever you call it," recalled an Ashland County woman about her cooperative canning group in the 1920s. "Many winter evenings were spent with the neighbor women and girls congregating at one home to strip feathers," Elise Kramolis Lajcak remembered. "The women would speak in Czechoslovakian, laughing and telling jokes."[93] For women as well as men in the cutover, labor was not isolated from but rather was directly dependent upon involvement with neighbors.

In the early decades of the twentieth century, the introduction of new farm machinery increased interdependence among men and women in cutover neighborhoods. The cost of this machinery often had to be shared by several families. In the 1920s in a settlement apparently in Florence County dubbed the "Sorenson Community" by a social scientist, farmers shared a grain binder, grain drill, corn binder, corn planter, and potato digger. The operation of some of this machinery then required a team of workers. In potato harvesting, neighbors "got together quite a bit" remembered Lars Kailberg, "especially after the potato digger was invented, because it took four horses to pull those and most of us had only two."[94]

The introduction of the steam-powered thresher for harvesting grain was perhaps the most dramatic technological change which increased labor cooperation.[95] Ed Pudas recalled Oscar Abrahamson buying the first thresher in the town of Oulu just after the beginning of the twentieth century. Most threshing in northern Wisconsin was done by Abrahamson and other farmers doing "custom work" for their neighbors, not by professional itinerant threshers. But in either case, with steam-powered equipment threshing was done in a day or two of intense labor rather than spread throughout the winter (Figure 2.6). Herman Swan, a Washburn County farmer, explained, "The old-fashioned threshing machine required a large crew. Two men changed off feeding the machine. There were several teamsters. One man cut the bands on the bundles. One man pitched the bundles from the stack. One man took the grain from the machine in sacks. One man stacked the straw. Two men carried the grain from the machine to the granary." To meet this need for more workers at one time, "rings" of six to twelve families worked together, moving from farm to farm in the neighborhood over a two-to-three-week span in the late summer. The communal midday dinners, prepared by the host farmer's wife, were a memorable feature of working on the ring. Olaf Severson recalled working on a ring around Luck in the 1930s as "really enjoyable"; he learned who were the good farmers and who were the good cooks. For Roy Meier, "this [was] perhaps the happiest time of life for farming, when you could work together." Adult men operating the threshing machines, adolescent boys stacking bundles on wagons in the fields to be brought to the machine, wives cooking in the farm-

Figure 2.6. Steam-powered threshing operation on a farm near Rice Lake, Oct. 17, 1895. (State Historical Society of Wisconsin, photo WHi (H44) 29)

house, and girls bringing water to the men in the fields and barnyard strikingly highlighted the age- and gender-specific but also integrated nature of work on cutover farms, and the essential contribution made by every family member and the family's neighbors.

At threshing time and throughout the year, therefore, not only labor requirements but the need to be part of a rural community encouraged cutover farmers to temper their desire for autonomy and independence with a significant degree of cooperation among themselves. When asked as an old man, "What is a successful farmer?" Meier replied by emphasizing community, church, and 4-H involvement. "I wouldn't class him by the size of his milk check," Meier emphasized (although he worked hard at obtaining that, as we have seen), "because perhaps their milk check was used for interest . . . [more] than it was for family living."[96]

Their work practices also led northern Wisconsin farmers to form organizations which encouraged community bonding and mediated between individual families and latently powerful market forces. In Forest County, for instance, among the groups formed by settlers were the Guernsey Club of Mole Lake, the Forest County Beekeepers Association, the Cow Testing Association, and the Forest Country Co-Operative Dairy Company. The last group was perhaps the most significant. Cooperatives drew on immigrant traditions, especially among Scandinavians, and were encouraged by the Progressive spirit in public life in turn-of-the-century Wisconsin. Indeed, the Finns and Danes of Bayfield County were leaders in the development of the cooperative movement in the state. In the cutover, as throughout Wisconsin, cooperatives rapidly increased in number between 1910 and 1930.[97]

In the words of Oulu farmer Ed Pudas, cooperatives gave farmers "a little at least to say about their every day economic situation." For example, the Medford Co-operative Creamery, organized in 1915, shipped about 1.5 million pounds of butter and had revenues of $943,000 in 1925, over ten times greater than in 1917. The Flambeau Valley Farms Cooperative in Ladysmith, in Rusk County, began as a milk-producers cooperative in 1924, built a new plant in 1927, and purchased another plant in nearby Stanley in 1939. It initially concentrated on butter production, but as time passed added cheese, fluid milk, and dried milk to its product lines. By 1940 it had about fifteen hundred "patrons."[98]

From handling agricultural products, cooperatives in northern Wisconsin expanded into livestock, retail products, automobile fuels and home heating oil, and publishing. They benefited their members as consumers as well as producers.[99] Cutover farmers also organized themselves into mutual fire insurance companies. There were ten such organizations in the cutover by 1914, the largest of which was the Trade Lake Town Mutual Fire Insurance Company, writing policies in Burnett and Polk Counties. From a group of twenty-five formal organizers in 1890, this company expanded in the number and size of its policies. By 1920, about eighteen hundred policies, with average coverage of $2,100, were in force.[100]

Through their involvement in cooperatives, therefore, cutover farmers connected themselves to the expanding market economy. They wanted the benefits, such as the Meiers' piano, that this economy could bring to them and their families. But cooperatives allowed northern Wisconsin farmers to engage this market somewhat on their own terms and as part of the communities they were trying to build. Involvement in cooperative activities directly increased community involvement—363 of the 596 members of the Medford Creamery attended the 1926 annual meeting. Eldon Marple recalled a "spirit of brotherhood" in the Northern Lakes Consumer Cooperative in Sawyer County during the 1920s. Cooperatives also promoted community identity. Lars Kailberg proudly claimed that the Barron County Cooperative Creamery, to which he shipped milk, was the largest in the United States.[101] By buffering individuals from the direct impact of market forces, cooperatives allowed cutover settlers to organize themselves as groups in the ways they wanted.

Many cooperatives were rooted in the common ethnicity of their members. As late as 1920, the Trade Lake Town Mutual Fire Insurance Company still required that "the proceedings, except the application and policy, shall be made in the Swedish language." But over time larger cooperatives in particular tended to integrate members of different ethnic groups. Manager Erich Lenz at the Merrill Cooperative emphasized that his board of directors was balanced with Norwegians, Swedes, and Poles, as well as Germans from the majority community in the region, and that twenty-seven of the twenty-eight farmers in an Italian community north of Merrill joined the cooperative.[102] It was in the cooperatives, therefore, that cutover settlers worked out one of the tensions inherent in their settlement practices: strong ethnic ties brought them to particular localities in northern Wisconsin and buffeted them from the cultural threats of the new environment, but success at farming the cutover depended on developing functional social and economic integration in the rural neighborhoods that the settlers developed, regardless of the nationality of the neighbors.

Reinforcing the economic interdependence they showed by labor-sharing and forming cooperatives, cutover farm families developed among themselves a rich social life, both formal and informal. "I knew every neighbor," Harvey Dueholm proudly emphasized. It is true that the relatively thin population of the cutover meant that, even by 1920, many families lived miles from the nearest neighbors. But neighborliness was highly valued, and newcomers expected that the cutover would come to resemble yeoman farming areas elsewhere in rural America where overlapping patterns of social visiting, labor exchange, and trading of farm-produced products created integrated neighborhoods.[103] The growth of more market-focused farming at least initially encouraged this development—men mixed with their neighbors while making deliveries to the new creamery, while women freed from home production of butter had more time to participate in neighborhood activities.[104]

The introduction of the automobile, by effectively reducing distance among farms, actually increased rural sociability. By 1930 73 percent of cutover farms had cars, almost equal to the statewide rate of 84 percent. Newspaper advertisements for cars even told cutover settlers that "Every Farm Needs Two," one open and one closed! Automobiles increased the number of contacts by rural people in the cutover with people from beyond their immediate community, to be sure, but at least initially these contacts may have also strengthened social ties within rural neighborhoods. For example, when Anna Pratt Erickson and her husband, who farmed near Athens in Marathon County adjacent to the cutover, got their first car in the early 1920s, they increased the frequency of their trips to town but usually in the company of friends from their rural neighborhood. In sum, the increased use of automobiles in the cutover, like the introduction of telephones which also characterized these years, illustrates historian Elizabeth Perkins's point that the growth of consumerism and the accompanying greater presence of material objects can enhance rather than negate community feeling among rural people.[105]

Also a result of these transportation improvements, farmers knew that in case of illness or other emergency assistance would come from the neighbors. Early in the century a physician in the town of Lake Nebagamon in Douglas County observed that, "Necessity made it a custom to help each other in sickness, and often times it would seem that the entire neighborhood was there to help." "If anyone needed something," Ellis Smith remembered about his neighborhood near Jump River in northern Taylor County, "the neighbors saw to it that they got it." A Ladies Aid, organized in 1921, took on much of this responsibility. Indeed, through organizations such as this as well as informal patterns of visiting, women played vital roles in building farm neighborhoods in the cutover.[106]

Community gatherings such as Fourth of July picnics or school celebrations were festive times, organized by the settlers themselves. In the words of a young woman who moved to the town of Atlanta in Rusk County to teach for three years in the first decade of the twentieth century, "everyone went and no one had to be invited or urged." In the Sentinel Ash district of this town around 1930, one resident recalled, "The school was the central interest of the neighborhood . . . pie socials and other entertainments were held—drawing big crowds. . . ." Similarly, in the town of Washington "the community centered around the school," one settler recalled. "The last day of school in May, a community picnic was held with the entire neighborhood attending." Halloween and, especially, Christmas programs were the major school events of the year. Participation was not limited to families with children in the school—Anna Pratt Erickson and her son attended school picnics each year long after her children had grown. Managing the affairs of these one-room country schools also involved the community in democratic decision-making. Voters at the annual school district meeting set the school term, authorized construction and repair of school buildings, contracted (usually among themselves) for supplies and services, and hired a teacher and perhaps a janitor (or assigned the janitorial responsibilities to the teacher!).[107] In Price County, there were seventy-one school districts operating seventy-seven rural schools in the 1919–1920 academic year. Public education therefore reached cutover children: despite the newness of settlement, 74.4 percent of children aged fourteen and fifteen were in school in the cutover in 1920, comparing favorably with the statewide percentage of 77.8 (Figure 2.7).[108]

Churches were close to schools in importance as a focus of social life. The new Presbyterian pastor found that his church was "the center of life" in Cornell, in northern Chippewa County, around 1920—his parishioners "had to hang together." Church picnics, women's guild activities, and Lutheran Young People's meetings were important to many

Figure 2.7. Representative example from the 1890s of a one-room school in the
Brandon district, west of Antigo, and its student body. (State Historical Society
of Wisconsin, photo WHi (W6) 21473)

settlers (Harvey Dueholm fondly recalled that the last provided good
opportunities to play "grab the girl in the dark"). Women frequently
involved themselves in church activities as this was a public role permitted them by even the most conservative adherents of Victorian gender
roles. Indeed, many of the small churches of northern Wisconsin survived only because of the commitment of their women members. "At
all times the women have been active," at the Union Congregational
Church at Three Rivers in Oneida County, emphasized Alice Rydzewski
in 1918. "Harvest Dinner, Mother-Daughter Dinner, bake sales, ice cream
socials, to name a few." Church membership rates were a little lower in
the cutover than statewide (the force of law did not bring people to
church anywhere in Wisconsin, of course, as it did bring children to
school), but were still impressive for a frontier region. In the mid-1930s
about 45 percent of people in northern Wisconsin were affiliated with a
church (compared to 53 percent statewide), up from about 38 percent
in 1916 (when half the state's population had a church affiliation).[109]

One farmer's organization which had a particular impact in northern Wisconsin was the Grange. When the Grange changed its focus from politics to social activity in the first decade of the century, its greatest growth in Wisconsin came in the cutover. Roy Meier remembered that the Grange "encouraged cooperation of farmers." Granges involved women as well as men, and tended to be initiated from within communities themselves rather than by county agents or other outsiders, as with organizations like the Farm Bureau. Regular Grange meetings with speakers, assistance projects for members in need, dances, and Fourth of July picnics attracted increasing membership. Between 1912 and 1922 a cutover location was the site for all but one of the annual meetings of the Wisconsin Grange.[110]

Informal socialization was also important to northern Wisconsin settlers. "Entertainment was simple" in the 1920s, recalled Walter Hubin about life in the town of Beaver Brook in Washburn County. "Every Saturday night there was a party at some neighbor's house. They'd roll up the rugs, pile the babies on beds, and dance." Larger dances, sometimes with professional bands, were held in barns or schools. "There will be a dance and a general good time at no. 2 school house in the town of Georgetown on Nov. 3d, 1900," read a typical Price County newspaper announcement. "Everybody is respectfully invited to attend." Over four hundred public dances were licensed in Price County in 1928. At Larson's Hall in the town of Spirit silent movies complemented the dancing in the 1920s, while men gathered and drank moonshine liquor at a "blind pig" behind the hall. Similarly, Spirit's Fourth of July celebration in 1904 brought together hundreds of "people from miles around" for a parade, horse and foot races, fireworks, "literary exercises," and dancing until dawn.[111]

The observance of ethnic traditions also brought together many rural people in the cutover. Mary Christianson and Ida Peterson remembered Mayfires—a Scandinavian tradition to drive away evil spirits—as an annual event celebrated just before Memorial Day around Trade Lake in Burnett County as late as the 1920s. "The young people gathered around a huge brush pile," reported Ida, which "was set afire, and by its light, the young adults played ring games. This was followed by roasted wieners and partaking of a lunch." Between 1912 and 1923 in the village of Cameron in Barron County hundreds of settlers from surrounding communities gathered annually to celebrate a "forsmaling," a festival brought to America from the district around Lake Bandak in southern Norway.

In the Croatian community of Velebit in the 1920s, festivities featuring Kolo dancing to the accompaniment of traditional instruments and feasting on roast lamb took place at the Jug Hall community center. In Price County, the Bohemian Farmers Association regularly held dances and picnics at Viola Villa Hall. Young people in the cutover also followed the traditional European custom of the charivari as a way to acknowledge the union of a newly married couple. "Newly weds would expect to have a Chavaree [sic]," in Rusk County. "The neighbors would all gather at the home of the newly weds and shoot guns." When Anna Pratt Erickson remarried in 1922, her new husband was expected by custom to give $12 to buy treats to such a group when they came to the newlywed's house on their wedding night for a charivari.[112]

Not everyone got along with all their neighbors, of course. Northern Wisconsin had its share of Saturday-night bar fights among men, which received disproportionate attention in the news coverage of the cutover by papers from outside the region (chapter 5). Gossip taken the wrong way by women canning or sewing together led to quarrels. But as Harvey Dueholm observed about Scandinavian women in Polk County, they quickly made up after fighting because "they just about had to— [they] were responsible for each other." Dueholm related a dramatic incident at a 1925 Lutheran Young People's meeting in which his cousin Elsie was murdered by her married lover. He had impregnated her but had become frustrated by Elsie's attempts to end the relationship. But there "didn't get to be bitterness between the two families—[it was] one of those things that happen," Harvey explained. There was too much interdependence among families to allow permanent estrangement. In a situation recalling the pattern of colonial New England women acquitted of witchcraft continuing to live for decades in the same village, Elsie's sister was living next door to the murderer's brother a half-century after the incident.[113]

An expanding national agricultural economy, concerted governmental efforts, aggressive land marketing, and the strong desire of many foreign immigrants to return to a rural lifestyle brought substantial migration to northern Wisconsin in the first two decades of the twentieth century. These settlers still saw around them in 1920 influences from the past—Indian peoples resistant to assimilation, miners, loggers, and others who were not-too-serious farmers; continuing commercial logging activities, destructive brush fires, and a physical landscape which in most places was still dominated by post-lumbering debris and stumps. But the settlers were able to begin clearing land and building farms while maintaining their values of personal independence and community responsibility. There were no bonanza farms or suitcase farmers in the cutover. Family security was the primary goal even of more commercially oriented farmers. These settlers tried to develop farms of the type and scale that expert opinion told them was suitable for the physical environment of the region. Through the passion many of them had for hunting and fishing and the bywork they often did in the woods, they remained close—not hostile to—this physical environment.

Clearly the cutover was still in a frontier stage in 1920 and its settlers were poorer than other residents of Wisconsin. But the new migrants to northern Wisconsin were confident that they could replicate the style of yeoman farming and the rural communities associated with it which had characterized nineteenth-century America, and which they saw in the early twentieth century in the fully developed areas of southern Wisconsin. "Gradually we cleared and improved our farms, going mostly into dairying," reported Herman Swan, Jr., who took over his family's farm in the town of Dewes in Washburn County in 1910. "We built our schools and churches, and with the passing of years became a church going, law abiding, reasonably prosperous farming community, a good place in which to live and raise our families."[114]

3 | The Shaping of the Cutover by Agricultural Experts, 1895–1925

Late-twentieth-century Americans still largely see the settlement of new regions of the United States in the nineteenth century as an example of successful self-reliance and individual initiative. The reality was different. Federal and state governments and other organizations played major roles in assisting frontier development. Governments gave land to farmers or leased it at below cost to ranchers, railroads built with government subsidies brought in settlers and connected them to national markets, federal troops helped the settlers drive off Native Americans, and reclamation and dam construction projects financed by Washington made the new lands viable for the settlement.

There were similar influences on the settlement of northern Wisconsin. But the involvement of government officials and other outsiders affected the cutover differently in the early twentieth century than it did the trans-Mississippi United States in the nineteenth century. Progressive-era confidence in governmental and social science expertise encouraged the development of programs that not just facilitated or encouraged development but benevolently directed the activities of individual settlers. A belief that rural America in general was in crisis—backward, inefficient, and dangerously susceptible to radical political ideas—encouraged this pattern. Hence in the first decades of the twentieth century, across the United States the Country Life movement encouraged an activist government to reorganize and systematize economic and social life in settled rural areas. The need for such programs seemed even greater for rural areas still in the frontier state, as the failure of farming in newly opened regions such as the west country of South Dakota, the staked plains of New Mexico, and the deserts of California and Oregon seemed to show.[1]

This chapter examines the impact of outsiders on the cutover from the 1890s to the mid-1920s. The views of these outsiders gained weight from the increasing respect given to professional expertise during these decades. In addition, given the enhanced role of the public sector in

Wisconsin during the Progressive era, their views were often at least semiofficial in character. State officials recruited settlers for the cutover, agricultural extension agents gave them advice, university professors worked with developers to plan their communities. These outsiders genuinely believed that opportunities still existed for small farmers in frontier regions like northern Wisconsin, but that in the twentieth century settlers in such places could not succeed on their own the way that Americans imagined them to have done during the nineteenth century. As professional experts on rural America associated with the Country Life movement studied the cutover more closely they also observed patterns that alarmed them. Therefore, during the first decades of the twentieth century, expert thinking increasingly emphasized the need for limits and controls on cutover settlers. It also began to patronize, if not disdain, the settlers. In doing so, it laid the foundation for the public policies which would later discourage agricultural settlement in northern Wisconsin.

For many cutover settlers, the first contact they had with northern Wisconsin was through the state Board of Immigration. Beginning in 1895, the board recruited settlers for the cutover (chapter 1). A new board was organized in 1907, and during the next twenty years this agency played an active role in assisting new settlers in northern Wisconsin. In 1911 B. G. Packer became secretary of the board, later taking the title of Commissioner of Immigration. Packer's training was as a lawyer and his immediate background was as secretary of the Farmers' Institute and Festival Association. In this job he persuaded farmers to improve their dairy herds and plant new varieties of corn recently developed by the College of Agriculture.[2] Predictably, therefore, the thrust of the board's programs in the next fifteen years was on the professional and business direction of settlers in the cutover rather than their indiscriminate recruitment, which had previously been characteristic of the board's work. This thrust was increasingly indicative of the way in which outside individuals and agencies related themselves to farmers in northern Wisconsin.

The publications of the Board of Immigration remained positive about farming possibilities in the cutover but became more instructional than boosterish. In "An Empire in Waiting," a speech given in the early 1920s, Packer gushed, "What a privilege to live in a state that has not accomplished its full bloom of development." Packer emphasized that northern Wisconsin was "in the midst of good markets," with a "desirable" climate and "highly productive soils." But he also cautioned that "Not every man who raises crops is a farmer, though he lives on the land all his life." True farmers needed the advice of the Board of Immigration and other state agencies to which the board referred prospective settlers. Packer told such prospects that they should buy no more than eighty acres; bring $1,200 in cash in addition to their down payment, build inexpensive houses, regardless of their wives' desires, focus on dairying, construct a silo, start a garden immediately upon arriving, and so forth.[3] Packer also arranged for specialized pamphlets—for instance, *Beef Production in Wisconsin* (1914)—to be sent to prospective settlers based on their experience and interests. "The work develops more and more into a clearing house of information," Packer wrote in his 1915 biennial report.[4] The board now emphasized that it did not put prospects in touch with land dealers; implicitly, *it* wanted to guide them to the place and into the activities for which it felt they were best suited.

Packer emphasized that "No state gives so much personal service to the intending settler as does Wisconsin."[5] This attention included personal interviews of prospective settlers by Packer and his assistants. For example, on October 6, 1923 Packer sent letters to 270 Chicago-area residents who had recently sent inquiries to what had become the Division of Immigration. He invited them to meet with him in Chicago the following week. In early December a similar letter from assistant director G. M. Householder went to 143 Twin Cities prospects.[6] In these meetings Packer both provided information to the prospects tailored to their background and interests and evaluated their potential as successful settlers. In his mind, making good in the cutover required sufficient capital, physical strength, commitment to remain on the land, and willingness to accept advice. His agency reported that "almost daily" it was "compelled" to warn off settlers from "land proposals where the man, family, pocket book, and the chances failed to fit." For example, when a potential settler from Chicago received a pitch from the Burnett County Abstract Company to buy land on "good soil" at below assessed value and was urged to buy now since "these bargains are not going to be on the market for any length of time," he asked the advice of the Division of Immigration. The blunt response told the prospect that "you cannot afford to settle on that land and try to farm if they gave it to you for nothing."[7]

The Division of Immigration implied that some types of people were more suitable than others as settlers. While essentially eliminating advertising in foreign-language publications, Packer sent exhibits and representatives to state and county fairs in neighboring midwestern states. The division bragged that in 1924 it "discouraged a negro settlement project in Jackson County on unimproved sandy land." Packer emphasized that inquiries to his agency came from "hundreds of experienced corn-belt farmers, good folks, possessed of some means, a large measure of hope, and a heap of determination." City-dwellers could succeed, too, if they were northern European immigrants (or their children) who had had farming experience in Europe and were "not the type who have failed at everything else." Householder made clear what was meant by "the type" the Division of Immigration did not want to attract when he discouraged a prospect from buying poor land in Burnett County: "In Portage County there are a great many Polish people that exist on this kind of land," he wrote. "You cannot live as cheaply as those people who have a very low scale of living."[8]

The Division of Immigration stayed in contact with farmers once they had settled in the cutover. It mailed instruction bulletins and pamphlets to a follow-up list of settlers which had over twenty-three hundred names by 1924. These settlers also periodically received questionnaires, and the division used the survey results to make their informational and guidance programs more effective. In 1923 the division reported that it had received over two thousand "reports of progress." Overall, the paternalistic spirit of the Division of Immigration was well reflected by the title of a favorable article on its activities in a national journal: "Protecting Immigrant Settlers."[9]

Once they had settled in northern Wisconsin, farmers most often received advice from county agricultural agents. From its beginnings, discussed in chapter 1, the system of agricultural agents spread statewide by the 1920s. The agents shifted the focus of their activities from classroom instruction to one-on-one conferences and field demonstrations.[10] The agents assigned to cutover counties encouraged farmers to clear more land, buy larger dairy herds of purebred stock, test their cows for tuberculosis, build silos, adopt better seeds, use lime, plant alfalfa, join a cooperative, and so forth. They urged cutover farmers to specialize in one cash-generating commodity, usually dairy products, but also to grow one or two other cash crops, such as potatoes or a vegetable. Agents also insisted that cutover farmers produce not only for the market: they wanted the farmer to grow as much as possible of what his family consumed, speaking derisively of farmers who "ate out of cans." They repeatedly brought this message directly to northern Wisconsin farmers. For example, in a county with about two thousand farms, the Price County agent officially reported 2,396 farm visits, office calls, and phone calls with farmers in 1928, and 3,280 such contacts in 1931.[11]

The agents held faculty rank in the state university's College of Agriculture, and their message reflected the production-oriented agricultural philosophy of its dean, Harry L. Russell. A nationally known scientist and agricultural educator, Russell took a particular interest in northern Wisconsin as part of his larger vision for agricultural research. Especially after the passage of the Adams Act in 1906, bountiful federal funds were available for research at agriculture colleges, but the benefits needed to be apparent immediately. Russell was confident that his programs for northern Wisconsin, including first-rate scientific research at branches of the Experiment Station in the cutover, would increase agricultural production and lead to the lower food prices demanded by consumers in urbanizing America.[12]

Statewide, there was a mixed evaluation of Russell and his programs.[13] As Ernest Luther, who was assigned to Oneida County in the cutover as the first county agent in the state, wrote, Russell "was a man of the world when matters of commercial business were up . . . always at home among men having large and small business connections." On the other hand, Russell was the target of criticism from individual small farmers, politicians of liberal sympathies, and farm organizations which in the 1920s came to believe that production had to be limited to boost agricultural prices. The dean had a "lack of sympathy with that sort of democracy" associated with people "who might not be able to write a readable letter," Luther pointed out.[14]

Northern Wisconsin farmers had a similar mixed response to Russell's efforts at agricultural extension. The agents, or at least the more sensitive ones, tried to be diplomatic and portray their roles as consultants to farmers rather than omniscient overseers. Some cutover farmers responded positively to their involvement and advice. Lars Kailberg, who took over the farm his father bought in the late-nineteenth century near Rice Lake, developed a close relationship with E. J. Delwiche at the Spooner Experimental Station. Following his advice, Kailberg began to use only certified seeds for his potatoes and soybeans, purchased more land, and, as soon as his son was old enough to help, concentrated on dairy production.[15] Other cutover settlers were less enamored of the College of Agriculture's representatives in the north. The work of the agents was financed on a cost-sharing basis between the county and the university, and at times of fiscal stringency taxpayers often tried to eliminate the agent, sometimes with success.[16] These settlers were bothered by the attitude of at least some agents. Luther, for example, aroused criticism for greed by submitting several winning entries in his county fair's crop competition. He insensitively dismissed his critics as "crazy" and explained away his conflict of interest by claiming that the competing "exhibits were terrible" and needed his example to improve. "Farmers up here do not know how to work," he had previously claimed; "most of them would prefer to come to town to take a few too many glasses for the good of farming."[17] It was no doubt in reaction to such attitudes that in 1925 Felix Framer started a new publication, *Upper Wisconsin Farmer,* which he announced was to correct the "misrepresentations" of men who had studied at "agricultural schools."[18]

The most significant academic influence on the cutover came from the work of Richard T. Ely, head of the economics department in the state university's College of Letters and Sciences, and the best-known economist in the United States in the first quarter of twentieth century. Ely came to Madison from Johns Hopkins University in 1892. Labelled a Christian socialist, he enjoyed a reputation of activity in reform and Social Gospel causes focused on advocating a positive role for government in reform through business regulation; he also possessed both a record as a successful academic organizer and scholarly accomplishments that had developed in the United States the "new school" in economics, which stressed that economic principles were not inherent in rigid laws as nineteenth-century liberal economists had argued but rather should reflect society's needs at particular historical moments. In many respects Ely continued in these directions over the next three decades, advising successive Progressive administrations in the capitol at Madison. But he was also profoundly affected by the public attacks he received in 1894 for alleged partisanship in a local labor dispute. Although vindicated by the university's Board of Regents after a celebrated "trial," Ely received lukewarm support within the economics profession and subsequently ended his direct involvement in reform activities. He maintained the principles of his economic thought—which in the twentieth century became the "institutional economics" of Thorstein Veblen and John Kenneth Galbraith—but adapted them to the more conservative political environment which particularly developed in the United States during and after World War I. Ely concentrated on the new subdiscipline of land economics as an area of scholarly specialization, at least in part because he saw it as unlikely to involve him in public controversy. Having grown ever more comfortable with capitalism and individual capitalists, outside the classroom he spent his time speculating in land rather than lecturing to church groups.[19]

Influenced by the "Wisconsin Idea"—the program by which university resources were used to assist state administrators and their various constituencies—Ely turned his attention to the economics of land development in northern Wisconsin. Like Packer, he was optimistic about the future of the region. "There are as good opportunities to acquire farms in the United States as there were in the days of free land," Ely claimed referring to the cutover in a 1918 article in the *American Economic Review.* "Good colonization with suitable public control can give hundreds of thousands of settlers better opportunities than those generally enjoyed by the pioneer farmers even in the Mississippi Valley." But, like Packer, Ely believed that unassisted settlement by individual farmers would not help the region accomplish its potential. Simply transferring land ownership from unwilling land companies to unsophisticated new farmers would not work. Deeply rooted in Ely's thought was an abhorrence of the dangers of excessive individualism, which could be expressed easily in the cutover. Cutover settlers, Ely believed, needed to settle close together and share collective facilities. But Ely's growing antipathy to government's hand in the economy and sympathy for the benefits of private enterprise discouraged him from advocating a direct public role in accomplishing this. The government should license real estate dealers, Ely allowed, but settlement should be directed by private land companies. With 20,000 to 25,000-acre projects, these organizations could supply advice and demonstration farms, intelligently match individual settlers with specific plots of land, and even sell them ready-made farms. This sort of assistance was needed, Ely claimed, because of the "fundamental fact" of "the inability of settlers to choose land wisely." Based on his impressions of three "fairly successful" land development schemes in northern Wisconsin, Ely concluded that, "If guided honestly and if wisely placed and directed, private colonization is generally successful for the settlers" (Figure 3.1).[20]

Benjamin Faast was the best-known individual who tried to develop colonies of settlers in northern Wisconsin in the manner suggested by Ely. Beginning in 1904, Eau Claire–based Faast began to speculate in cutover land, mostly in Rusk County, and retail it to settlers, principally

Figure 3.1. Settler's home near Holcome, 1917. Richard T. Ely's assistants toured this district in the summer of 1918 and noted such tar-paper dwellings. (State Historical Society of Wisconsin, photo WHi (X3) 38213)

through his Benjamin Faast Land Company and Rusk Farms Company. He developed a sympathetic relationship with Dean Russell, who in 1912 chose to locate a College of Agriculture demonstration farm on a Faast Land Company tract near Conrath. Two years later, Faast began a twenty-year term on the university's Board of Regents.[21]

From his experience as a land salesman, Faast developed firm ideas about the proper direction of settlement in the cutover, which he conveyed to university officials, professional real estate associations, and the general public. Faast saw northern Wisconsin as a "new frontier" in which farmers—"modern pioneers"—had to work cooperatively with merchants and manufacturers. There was a major role in the process for colonization companies retailing large blocs of land. In conjunction with state and university specialists, they could perform detailed economic and soil surveys, setting aside land unsuitable for farming, provide easy purchase terms giving settlers as much as forty years to pay for their land, perform rural planning, including providing a prescribed "architectural character" for village buildings in order to make them attractive for settlers, and actually clear small plots and put up temporary buildings so that new settlers could purchase "ready-made" farms.[22]

Faast also had innovative ideas about financing cutover settlers. Unlike the Division of Immigration, he did not stress the need for settlers to bring with them very much working capital. Loans and credits from the colonizing companies themselves could meet this need. In turn, as a way of furnishing capital for the companies, Faast in 1913 helped organize the First Wisconsin Land Mortgage Association. This association operated somewhat similarly to the Union Mortgage Loan Company (chapter 1), but on a smaller scale and with closer direct involvement with both government and land companies, based on Wisconsin's Land Mortgage Association Act of 1913. It made some direct mortgage loans, but most of its business involved purchasing mortgages on the secondary market that land companies had taken back when giving deeds to their settlers. The association's specialty was thirty-year mortgages, which at the time were innovative by their length to maturity and planned amortization. First Wisconsin Land Mortgage then sold bonds backed by the mortgages, which it placed on deposit with the State Treasurer as security. The philosophy behind the association, in the words of Packer's assistant Householder, was that "we must plan to finance and guide our small settlers." But the scheme also assisted Faast's enterprises. Over 80 percent of First Wisconsin Land Mortgage's mortgages were bought from three Faast companies, the Wisconsin Colonization Company, the Chippewa Valley Colonization Company, and the Rusk Farm Company. Its president, T. B. Keith, was vice president of the Wisconsin Colonization Company. The understanding was that local banks in the cutover would step in with small loans and help settlers make payments to First Wisconsin Land Mortgage. At the Conrath State Bank, conveniently, Keith was president and E. G. Kuehl, secretary of the Wisconsin Colonization Company, was a director. At the end of 1919, after six years in operation, First Wisconsin Land Mortgage had bought less than $100,000 in mortgages, but in the postwar optimism of the next three years it financed over $500,000 in mortgages.[23] After 1917, Faast also operated on a larger stage, but for ends similar to those of First Wisconsin Land Mortgage, as a director of the Federal Land Bank of St. Paul. This institution was part of a nationwide scheme initiated by the federal Farm Loan Act of 1916 to expand rural credit through the organization of local farm loan associations.

In sum, with state and federal coordination and regulation, Faast confidently believed that corporate financiers who bought bonds, private land sellers who got cash when their settlers got mortgages, and state banking organizations which provided an institutional framework could develop what he called the "New America of the Middle West." Unburdened by tradition, a "truly American race," in his view, would populate presently undeveloped land in the Middle West. The thrust of Faast's message was consistent with the New Era economic policies that developed in the 1920s, which stressed that economic rationalization could be accomplished by private individuals, organizations, and associations, coordinated but not directed by the government.[24]

Faast's greatest labor was the planned rural community centered on the village of Ojibwa. This was apparently one of three projects from which Ely drew information for his 1918 article (the others were clearly Rusk Farms and the Faast Land Company). In early 1917, Faast's Wisconsin Colonization Company assembled about fifty thousand acres in southern Sawyer County. The centerpiece of this development was the village of Ojibwa, on the banks of the Chippewa River, laid out by University of Wisconsin professor, civil engineer, and town planner Leonard S. Smith, in consultation with the Minneapolis landscape and town planning firm of Morell and Nichols. The plan featured architecturally harmonious buildings in a style vaguely colonial-revival, with a radial street plan and careful adaptation of buildings and streets to local topography. Faast believed that maintaining such aesthetic values was important in making rural life attractive to settlers and keeping them on the land. In the country, the company sold forty- and eighty-acre plots with houses already constructed for $25 to $40 an acre. The settler paid only $250 down, with further payment of principal deferred for three years. At that point, if the company deemed him trustworthy and industrious, it issued him a deed to the land, taking back a thirty-year mortgage on the balance owed the company. The farmer began operation with a cow, some hogs and chickens, and seed furnished by the company. Company representatives operated demonstration farms and gave advice to settlers. They organized contests with cash prizes to encourage farmers to clear land, and Faast lowered the balance owed him by settlers who met land-clearing quotas.[25]

Faast implemented his goals in a number of ways. As a regent, he drew on his connections with the university. Dean Russell became the largest investor in the Wisconsin Colonization Company, owning 17 percent of the company's stock by 1921. Faast put Russell's son-in-law A.C. Fiedler, a recent graduate of the university, in charge of agricultural development for the company. College of Agriculture faculty members prepared bulletins and pamphlets such as *New Land in Southern Sawyer County* (1922). Faast also planted favorable stories about his enterprise with local newspapers.[26] Through constant letters to his settlers he urged "Let us all get together and boost," and tried to keep up morale with a different slogan every year, such as 1918's "Hew the Line and Let the Sunshine In."

The Wisconsin Colonization Company's development around Ojibwa met with initial success. By the beginning of 1920, about 160 farmers had settled on company land and on average operated farms the company valued at $3,364. The subsequent end of the war-induced agricultural boom retarded further development, but the company still reported 350 families on its farms by the middle of 1921, by which time the company had sold about 60 percent of its tract. Tom Kidrowski bought land from the Wisconsin Colonization Company in 1917. Company publicity quickly highlighted him for "What Can a Man Do In a Year on a New Farm" with no capital. Kidrowski had brushed and fenced twenty of his forty acres by the end of 1918 and was growing rutabagas to feed seventy rabbits. He was reported as hoping to get a dairy herd. Indeed, Kidrowski had twelve acres completely free of stumps by 1924, when the First Wisconsin Land Mortgage Association appraised his farm at over $5,000, and milked a herd of six cows by 1925. He purchased an additional forty acres for his farm between 1925 and 1930.[27] Polish-born Stanley Killian had only a "garden" planted in 1922, but had four acres cropped and a herd of four cows by 1925, with eight acres cropped and six cows a decade later. His compatriot Martin Pydo was unusually old at forty-nine when he came to Ojibwa in 1921, but he had eleven acres in crops and four cows on his eighty-acre farm by 1925, which expanded to twenty-one cropped acres and eleven cows by 1935. Faast's employee, B. M. Apker, had these sorts of stories in mind in 1949 when, referring to Faast's operations throughout the Chippewa Valley, he bragged that "now you'll find these beautiful farm houses and good farms and successful farms and I think we have been justified in our pride."[28] The First Wisconsin Land Mortgage Association assisted this development. By 1924 it owned about 180 mortgages on property sold by the Wisconsin Colonization Company. Almost all these mortgages had been issued between 1918 and 1920 on what at the time of purchase had been "wild" land. By

1924 on the average these farms had nine acres "cultivated" (presumably without stumps), which were valued at $100 an acre. Overall, these farms were valued on average at over $4,000, and mortgages were outstanding on them for about half that amount.[29]

Outside observers praised Faast's work. Reporting for *Survey*, Marion Clinch Calkins described Ojibwa as "a town of the future." Calkins was impressed by the plan for the village's well-designed buildings, and pointed out that Faast's long-term mortgage amortization plan meant that it remained in the interest of the land company to stay involved with helping settlers. Estonian immigrant Peter A. Speek visited northern Wisconsin and clearly observed Ojibwa (although he did not mention it by name) in preparing his 1921 book *A Stake in the Land*, which encouraged rapid assimilation of immigrants. Speek praised the work of state agencies as well as operations like Faast's in raising the status of immigrants, in contrast to ethnically based organizations like churches and schools which he felt retarded assimilation.[30]

The son of Austrian immigrants, Faast was not a nativist. But he did show the "wise economic leadership" by the "relatively few superior men in the community" praised by Ely in his 1918 article. This approach was at best paternalistic, at worst overbearing. In designing Ojibwa, for instance, Faast was careful to rely upon sophisticated professional advice, but made no attempt to survey settlers regarding what style or arrangement of buildings *they* desired. Other colonizers were quite explicit about their paternalism. Michael Beaudoin, who worked in land sales for the Edward Hines Lumber Company, related that "we took an interest in the settlers and their families and a large number of the growing children were placed by us in different spots, for instance, in Park Falls in the offices of the city school, some of them we took to Chicago, helped them to get jobs."[31]

Such paternalism could become demeaning to its recipients. For example, Ely learned from assistants doing field work in northern Wisconsin that Wisconsin Colonization Company officials believed that Polish settlers, in particular, would be "quite helpless" without company assistance. The supposed docility of these Poles, however, made them ideal settlers, because they would remain dependent on the company and accept a low standard of living.[32] In discussing the operations of the Tomahawk Land Company, a colonization scheme similar to Ojibwa, Calkins admitted that some settlers resented the company's paternalism. When Ely's assistant visited this project he found the company's representative "dominating" and "disrespectful" and the settlers resentful, rejecting company advice as too restrictive and spurning equipment like stump pullers as too difficult to use.[33]

For his part, Faast interpreted any less-than-complete commitment by one of his settlers to maximizing the agricultural potential of his farm as a character flaw. In a circular letter to settlers after a visit to Ojibwa, Faast primly observed that he was "disappointed" in new settlers who had not cleared any land, and tried to shame them by describing incidents where he "found the man sitting inside smoking while his wife was working." Faast's approach tolerated little criticism. He told his settlers, "The man who fails is usually seen hanging around town kicking about the town board, school board. . . . Very seldom do you find a successful man a knocker."[34]

Stereotyped views of the negative qualities of Poles, in particular, were so strong in the minds of some land men that they went beyond paternalism and made these immigrants into unattractive settlers. Ely's assistant repeatedly heard that Poles drank, quarrelled, and did not follow instructions.[35] Some land vendors who adopted this view of immigrants organized their operations differently than did Faast. The Skidmore Land Company in Marinette County, for example, focused on selling to so-called "high type"—that is, native-born—farmers. This company therefore believed that it could keep itself "in the background," encouraging its settlers to do things for themselves.[36] Similarly, real estate dealer W. D. Jones of Wassau believed that it weakened character for land companies to help settlers too much. When Jones took Ely's assistant Cox to visit one of his settlers, the farmer did not recognize Jones, something that surely never would have happened on a visit by Faast to one of his settlers.[37]

Ely was predisposed to be alarmed by these reports from his assistants about the deficiencies of immigrants, and allowed them to sharpen his view that cutover settlement needed to be actively managed. From a Yankee background, Ely had long advocated immigration restriction, especially of "baser foreign elements" such as the Chinese, who contributed to excessive "diversity" which "renders difficult the growth of . . . the highest civilization." Always confident in the wisdom of academically trained "scientists," he was also sympathetic to the eugenics movement within Progressive reform, exemplified by his close friend and Johns Hopkins student, Edward A. Ross.[38] In 1913 Ely supported the Wisconsin Sterilization Law, and the following year signed a petition to President Woodrow Wilson regarding American Samoa initiated by the prominent eugenicist Charles Davenport. Having been to Samoa, Ely agreed that the natives were a "primitive race," moved by "affections" and not "abstract thought," and lacking the "mental makeup" to adopt American institutions such as private property; they were in need, therefore, of further study and the benign assistance of the federal government.[39] Eugenic concerns reinforced Ely's long-held animosity to individualism; eugenicists, like Ely often fascinated by their own family genealogies, believed that if allowed to intermarry some people could pass on to subsequent generations undesirable social and physical traits. The special object of fear in the classic late-nineteenth and early-twentieth-century eugenic studies was the degenerate hillbilly family in an isolated, often wooded area. Exemplified by the dreaded "pinies" widely written about by Elizabeth Kite in the years around World War I, these people were out of reach of the methods of social control increasingly available to urban professional reformers.[40]

Ely planned to use the information gathered for him by his assistants on their tours of northern Wisconsin in the summer of 1918 in a series of a dozen pamphlets to assist new settlers.[41] In the only pamphlet published, Ely and two colleagues asserted that 60 percent of new settlers in the cutover came with less than $500, in contrast to the $2,000 which was needed. Many purchased unsuitable land from land "sharks." Even if they chose these lands wisely and eventually paid off their initial land contracts by refinancing with mortgages, such farmers lacked the capital to develop their farms. Changes in farm credit arrangements were necessary, the bulletin concluded, to prevent "the chief source of failure" among settlers.[42] At this time, Ely was still optimistic and sympathetic to settlers, but already was writing privately that "what we need is more labor and capital upon land already brought into use rather than the opening up of new land." This message struck a discordant note with Faast, who had never been much concerned with how much working capital his settlers brought with them, and who believed that whatever credit they needed could be furnished by colonization companies and mortgage associations. When Faast saw a draft of the proposed pamphlet, he pronounced it "disgusting" and demanded that Dean Russell suppress it. Russell, to his credit, went against his own immediate personal financial interests and allowed publication with only minor changes; he reasoned that the academic freedom of his faculty members and the needs of potential settlers for accurate financial information took precedence over the influence of a university regent.[43]

This contretemps should not disguise the close alignment which generally characterized Ely's and Faast's views on small as well as major issues. For example, Faast was an advocate of Ely's proposal to educate and license real estate dealers. Ely believed that "the movement to raise the standards of [farm land dealers] to a professional basis" was the kind of "private activity" through which "more could be accomplished for men on submarginal land than could be accomplished through politics."[44] Within a few months of the controversy over the *Credit Needs* bulletin, Ely turned to Faast for support for a proposed undergraduate degree program in land economics.[45] Subsequently, Faast turned to Ely to comment on the draft of a speech he had to present. In replying, the professor assured the regent that he believed colonization "should be a private undertaking rather than a public undertaking" and that "the chief point of all is simply getting together and ironing out differences among the various agencies that furnish credit."[46]

That Ely and Faast shared the New Era belief that government's proper role was to stimulate business by encouraging cooperation among private interests became evident in their common response to proposed plans for post–World War I settlement of returning doughboys on agricultural lands. In Wisconsin, Milwaukee banker Henry A. Moehlenpah, the unsuccessful Democratic candidate for governor in 1918, organized the business community to push for rural settlement programs as a safety value for potential urban discontent.[47] Some cutover land companies expressed support for Interior Secretary Franklin K. Lane's scheme, embodied in the proposed Mondell Bill, which would have appropriated $500,000,000 for the federal government to buy and develop land to be leased for soldiers' colonies. Much of the inspiration for this scheme came from an Interior Department staff member, Elwood Mead, who directed the development of two colonies initiated by the California Land Settlement Act of 1917.[48] Faast reacted negatively to the California-inspired component of the Mondell Bill which provided federal funds for land reclamation—putting more land in competition with the cutover was not a good idea.[49] Ely dismissed Mead as "unduly influenced by working associates with radical proclivities." He helped to steer a committee on postwar land policy appointed by the governor of Wisconsin to oppose state-sponsored soldier resettlement and recommend a toothless Farm Development Board to coordinate colonization activities in Wisconsin. Bruno Lasker outlined Wisconsin's scheme for the readers of *Outlook:* "A federal or state supervisory commission . . . will promote and foster the voluntary movement, and through the cooperation between different owners, . . . new colonization companies."[50] Ely made clear his position in a letter published in the *Wisconsin State Journal* on May 27, 1920, clarifying a recent talk reported by the newspaper. Ely emphasized that he favored settlement in northern Wisconsin because of the "great opportunities there," but that he opposed the use of public funds for land development because that could be done better by private colonization companies.[51] Labeled as socialistic, and opposed by the Department of Agriculture and farm groups more interested in restricting than expanding food production, the Mondell Bill was not adopted.

Ely was not affected by the war-induced cynicism which overcame many Progressive-era reformers. He confidently believed that the science of land economics—in contrast to schemes like Lane's—could successfully guide agricultural policy in the 1920s. He outlined his ideas in an essay published in 1920 in a volume with the revealing title *America and the New Era,* which boasted a foreword by Herbert Hoover. Ely called for a comprehensive national land policy including land classification, encouragement of individual ownership, and opposition to single-tax proposals. "It is important to push forward improvements along lines of development which had already begun before 1914," he wrote, implicitly rejecting programs such as the innovative soldiers' resettlement schemes.[52]

If Ely's (and Faast's) commitment to New Era economic principles was defined by its difference at one end of the spectrum from Elwood Mead, it was also defined at the other end by its difference from lumberman John S. Owen. Owen's activities in dispersing his immense acreage of stump land (chapter 1) included selling land on credit to Faast, who was a high school classmate of his son Ralph. In the early twentieth century Owen continued to express laissez-faire economic principles. He felt that there was no need for a comprehensive plan to settle returning servicemen or any other settlers in northern Wisconsin. Writing to Ely, Owen denied that there was any shortage of food products in the United States, and charged that Hoover and his food administration were cynically using the fear of food shortages to prolong their government employment.[53] Owen was especially critical of the idea of government experts classifying cutover land by suitability for farming (although lumber companies often employed such schemes in their marketing programs). This position put him into conflict in the early 1920s with Ely, for whom land classification was coming to be of premier importance. Owen scoffed at "Soil Survey Boards, Valuation Boards, Agencies of Development, Boards of Settlement, etc." "Don't for a minute think that the settlers can't make a wise choice," he lectured Ely, "or that the Bankers, Land Companies, Etc., can do better, or are more practical. Forget it."[54] Owen, of course, knew that even a generous evaluation of each of his forty-acre holdings would result in much land being classified as unsuitable for agriculture. He preferred to sell large, unclassified blocs of land, which he knew were of mixed value, to speculators, settlers, or the government. These purchasers would just have to take some undesirable blocs in order to get the land they really wanted.

Comfortable as he was with the political economy of Hoover's associational state, Ely adopted increasingly conservative social and political positions in the years during and after World War I. The women's suffrage movement attracted his anger. "Feminism is individualism and that is opposed to eugenics," he wrote in comments on a book manuscript by eugenicist Paul Popenoe. "Strengthen your argument contra!" Ely took the lead among the university faculty in denouncing Robert M. LaFollette's opposition to U.S. involvement in World War I and calling for LaFollette's removal from the Senate. A superpatriot throughout the war years, he organized the Madison chapter of the Wisconsin Loyalty Legion "to stamp out disloyalty and to stimulate a militant love for our country." Having always been a critic of Marxism, he enthusiastically joined in the rhetoric of the Red Scare, denouncing bolshevism as "a more serious menace than Czars and Kaisers were in the last century." Ely played on postwar fears of communism to induce railroad and public utility interest groups to finance the establishment at the University of Wisconsin of an Institute for Research in Land Economics, with himself as its head. The institute was based on the premise that academic study of the ownership and distribution of landed property was necessary to preserve capitalism.[55]

Ely and other observers who viewed politics through the lenses of the Red Scare had reason to be alarmed by what they saw in northern Wisconsin. Cutover voters generally tended to support the Progressive Republican candidates and policies from which Ely had become distant by 1919. For example, in the crucial 1908 referendum to amend the state constitution to allow the legislature to adopt the nation's first progressive income tax, support was 84 percent in the cutover in contrast to 67 percent in the rest of the state. In 1912, 45 percent of cutover voters but only 37 percent of voters in the rest of the state supported a constitutional amendment to give women the vote, an issue which so vexed Ely.

Pockets of political radicalism even existed in the cutover in the early twentieth century. Ely ascribed such "bolshevism" to bad settlement practices which he was working to overcome. In the 1916 presidential election, for example, Socialist Allan L. Benson won pluralities in four towns and captured 5.6 percent of the vote in the cutover, compared to 2.9 percent in the rest of the state outside of Milwaukee and 3.2 percent nationwide. In the Eleventh Congressional District, thirteen of whose fourteen counties were in the cutover, the Socialist candidate won 6.7 percent of the vote, his party's best performance in the state outside of Milwaukee. Four years later, Socialist presidential candidate Eugene Debs's vote in the cutover exceeded his percentage in the rest of Wisconsin excepting Milwaukee. The seven towns in the state with the highest percentage of Debs voters were in the cutover or adjacent counties. Immigrants were often a disproportionate share of the population where there were radical voting preferences. For example, in the town of Knox in Price County, which was 38 percent Finnish-born in 1905, the 1920 Debs vote was 48 percent. Years later, a farmer in a neighboring town related this result to the "communistic ideas" of the Finns, whom he characterized as "atheists," "fighters," and "drinkers." In Ely's views these were settlers who had obtained land "in the wrong way" and therefore had became frustrated and discontented and vulnerable to the appeals of political radicals.[56]

Ely certainly believed that dirt farmers were important, but he was increasingly unsympathetic to the lives of ordinary people. For example, in an analysis of wage levels, Ely characteristically did not invoke market forces. Rather, he argued that cooks, whose "cultural standards are not high," did not deserve wage increases at the expense of "struggling university instructors," who as part of the middle class needed higher income to "command respect" and maintain their "leadership."[57] Not surprisingly, Ely—like Russell—received increased public criticism when Progressives returned to political power in Wisconsin in the early 1920s. The university's regents became alarmed that nonacademic influences might influence teaching and scholarship. In a measure incomprehensible to cash-hungry universities in the late twentieth century, they moved to ban outside financing of activities such as Ely's institute. Now an enemy of public officials rather than their counselor, Ely took his institute and fled to Northwestern University in 1925.[58]

Patronizing reports from outside observers in the early 1920s continued to impress on Ely and others that northern Wisconsin settlers needed their assistance. A representative from the Committee on Social and Religious Surveys, cooperating with the Federal Council of Churches, visited Price County in the summer of 1921. He was staggered by the "cabins . . . in which the stench is as bad as in any city tenement." With a clear nativist perspective, he toured the county and found a "racial caldron" which desperately needed "Americanization." His report published the following year concluded that "Price County needs community organizations with trained leadership which with patience and understanding will introduce American ways and methods to the newcomers to her soil." Organized religion, however, was not providing that directing force because the county was "overchurched." People fractured into too many small congregations because they stubbornly clung to the ethnic religious traditions they brought with them from Europe. This pattern resulted in small congregations that lacked the full-time staff and programs to accomplish the needed Americanization. The large Czech population of Price County, said to have been reluctant converts in Europe to Catholicism, was particularly identified as a group potentially receptive to the Americanizing programs of "the church." Never considering that most Price County immigrant settlers' spiritual needs were being met by the Catholic Church, the report lamented that "less than 10 percent of the people are affiliated with any Protestant church." Full-time, better-educated clergy and cooperation, indeed consolidation, among churches were needed to overcome these problems.[59] Absent in Fry's analysis, as it was in similar surveys of religion in rural America during the interwar years, was a concern with what Price county settlers themselves felt about their churches, and specifically how they saw their congregations as essential parts of their rural communities.[60]

Some views of the cutover during the years around World War I went beyond skepticism about the capabilities of the settlers and suggestions for assisting them. In the view of a few people, whose numbers and influence would grow in the 1920s and 1930s, farmers did not belong in the cutover. This had long been a minority view in Wisconsin, and even

Ely admitted in his 1918 *American Economic Review* article that one third of northern Wisconsin was submarginal for agricultural purposes (that was *why* settlers needed help in carefully selecting their farms). P. S. Lovejoy told Ely in 1920 that he had come to reject the idea that "farms will, ought and must follow forests."[61] Lovejoy used his position as editor of *Country Gentleman* to criticize farming and encourage reforestation in the Great Lakes cutover. As he grew sympathetic to Lovejoy's ideas, Ely increasingly published popular essays on land policy in Lovejoy's journal.

If the account he recorded thirty years later is accurate, Henry C. Taylor had become convinced as a result of an automobile tour of northern Wisconsin in the summer of 1917 that the land settlement movement "as a whole was unsound, that so soon as the war was over and prices began to take their normal level, most of this land that was being sold would be sub-marginal."[62] Taylor's view was important because of his influential position. A student of Ely's, he had established the department of agricultural economics within the College of Agriculture in 1909, and became one of the national leaders in the discipline.[63] His hostility to agriculture in northern Wisconsin could only have increased as a result of his involvement in the 1919 controversy over the *Credit Needs* bulletin. Because of his strong academic interest in rural credit policy, Taylor had been involved in the drafting of the document. He apparently was particularly sensitive to Faast's claims that because he and another coauthor, Benjamin Hibbard, wanted to protect their investments in southern Wisconsin farmland they slurred northern Wisconsin in the bulletin. Taylor left Madison in the summer of 1919, before publication of the bulletin (on which his name does not appear), to head the Division of Farm Management in the Department of Agriculture in Washington. Before doing so, however, he chose to vindicate himself and defend the *Credit Needs* bulletin by launching a counter-smear against Faast. Taylor alleged that Faast used his insider position with the Federal Land Bank of St. Paul to get credit extended to farmers in Faast's land development schemes. University president Edward A. Birge ordered an investigation, which vindicated Faast.[64] The whole episode no doubt convinced Taylor not only of the worthlessness of cutover land dealers but also the worthlessness of the land they were trying to sell. Taylor shared Ely's conservative sympathies, lamenting to him about the "tendency to let the question of personal human rights of the nonproperty classes get too strong a hold on the control of things."[65] When he lost his job in Washington in a policy dispute in 1925, Taylor returned to Ely's land economics institute, now at Northwestern. But his intellectual legacy remained in the reorganized agency he left behind, the influential Bureau of Agricultural Economics, whose studies subsequently stigmatized the cutover and discouraged further agricultural settlement there (chapter 5).

While on the faculty of the College of Agriculture, Taylor encouraged the study of rural sociology. His colleague Charles J. Galpin pioneered the development of the discipline the way that Taylor pioneered the development of agricultural economics. Taylor subsequently brought Galpin to Washington to head a small sociological section within the Bureau of Agricultural Economics.[66] In a 1924 publication, which reflected his experience of living on a cutover farm in Michigan while recovering from an illness, Galpin described a fictive region of sandy soils and jack pines, the "skins," populated by "submarginal people who are pushed by competition off the marginal clearings." The "skins" was a land of "machines with broken handles," shacks, barefoot children, people who "must not worry or overwork," who are the "lame, the halt, the blind." So backward were they that adults spent their time tending cows in common-field meadows. One resident discussed was a "stranded" lumberman named Friday. Another was a blind man, "derelict of derelicts," who was the father of a woman who abused her children.[67] By using literary allusions and transparent bodily metaphors, Galpin apparently was clumsily trying to suggest that his subjects were just as simplistic. In any event, the residents of the "skins" were clearly the eugenicists' worst fears.

In the minds of professors and other experts, cutover settlers were changing from clients to be assisted (Henry's 1895 bulletin, discussed in chapter 1), to victims to be protected (Ely's 1920 bulletin), to waste products to be feared (Galpin's 1924 essay). This progression was possible because, at each stage, the negative view of cutover settlers implied in the previous stage was the basis for an even more inimical view in the next.

Through his own work and increasingly that of his students, Richard T. Ely shaped the transformation of outsiders' views of the Wisconsin cutover between 1895 and 1925. In studying the cutover, Ely based his thoughts on the fundamental principles of his economic theory, which emphasized the importance of pragmatic, institutional, and evolutionary ideas. He sincerely believed that the economic profession could help improve the life of the average American, including pioneer farmers on cutover land. But Ely also consistently showed an eagerness to benefit from accommodation with whatever ideas or individuals could help advance this goal. In the decade straddling 1920, this approach led Ely into increasingly conservative political and social directions. Coming from this perspective, his work influenced the creation of a negative view of farming in northern Wisconsin.

In the first two decades of the twentieth century, observers increasingly described rural Americans everywhere as backward, immoral, and increasingly dangerous. In part because of Ely's influence, this image was particularly applied to the settlers of the cutover. As a nativist, Ely expounded beliefs which discouraged a complete understanding of immigrant settlers. Furthermore, what was condescension in his mind and that of men like the county agents working in northern Wisconsin became hostility in the minds of others. As an exponent of increasingly conservative political views, Ely was also alarmed by expressions of political radicalism in the cutover. This attitude in turn justified "Americanization" programs by public and private agencies. Furthermore, Ely was an elitist whose confidence in the ideas of experts legitimized decision-making for cutover farmers by planners, such as Packer and his staff in the Division of Immigration. This confidence in expertise paralleled Russell's belief that academic science would produce positive social results. In addition, as an antagonist to individualism, Ely fueled the eugenic alarm about the dangers of isolated settlement. Finally, his involvement with developing land economics as an academic discipline precluded Ely from comprehending the noneconomic reasons which partially motivated most cutover settlers. Therefore, especially in the minds of his students such as Henry C. Taylor, settlers in northern Wisconsin became objects rather than people. Consequently, in the 1920s and 1930s, agricultural economists, rural sociologists, and land-use planners—many of them Ely students from the University of Wisconsin or his land economics institute—propagated a grim, hostile interpretation of farming in northern Wisconsin. The popular mind was receptive to this view because the impact of the agricultural depression of the 1920s and the Great Depression of the 1930s created enormous economic and social problems in the region.

4 | Struggles with Adversity, 1920–1940

Behind the blackberry barrens: back of the brush piles:
Back of the dead stumps in the drifting sand:
Millions of acres of stumps to remember the past by—
  Archibald MacLeish[1]

For northern Wisconsin, the first two decades of the twentieth century was a period of growth, and for its settlers a time of optimism and accomplishment. The next two decades would be very different. Nationwide developments—the agricultural depression of the 1920s and the Great Depression of the 1930s—broke apart the nexus of rising land values, increasing in-migration, and growing agricultural output in the cutover. These changing conditions brought into relief the ecological limits of northern Wisconsin and the undercapitalized status of most of its settlers, factors which had been obscured by the prosperity of the previous quarter-century. Some of these settlers lost the expectation that they could replicate the pattern of yeoman farming built by previous generations of farmers in new regions. As individuals and members of communities their lives became distressed and they became more dependent than ever on outside assistance and direction. But for a period in the early 1930s, northern Wisconsin also attracted a small influx of settlers escaping problems in other parts of the country. Public opinion, however, feared that this population movement would only further impoverish the region.

  Despite these setbacks, northern Wisconsin settlers did not abandon the cutover or their vision of its lifestyle that had originally attracted them to the region. For support in this period of distress, they relied on one another and the institutions they had begun to build during the previous two decades. For economic survival they struggled to expand their farm operations while looking for new sources of supplemental income. Many relatively established communities in the cutover weathered the interwar years and emerged intact if not stronger. In these ways, northern Wisconsin settlers were like millions of other American farmers in these decades. But because it was incompletely developed and relatively poor before 1920, northern Wisconsin did not have the political and economic resources which would have enabled its settlers to more fully control their own destinies. Lacking the strengths possessed by farmers in more mature regions, cutover settlers were soon exposed to new public policies. Created in response to rural distress like that found in northern Wisconsin, these policies in the longer run discouraged yeoman farming.

Developers and settlers alike began the 1920s with continued optimism about the future of northern Wisconsin. World War I had boosted prices for farm commodities and other northern Wisconsin products. "The Great War had also brought new prosperity to the area," Carl Rhody remembered. "When the government took over the railroads for the duration of the war and put the tracks in first class condition, it caused the best market for railroad ties anyone had seen" (chapter 2 discussed how the Meier family earned considerable income during the war logging off their own land). Observers expected that postwar demobilization would turn loose ex-soldiers looking for cutover farms. The president of Eau Claire's Union Mortgage Loan Company (UML) confidently expected land values in northern Wisconsin to rise "when the boys come back from the war." In January 1920 a land dealer in Lincoln County reported that "the activity in land has reached the northern country also and prices are showing a strong advance." UML granted 127 mortgages in Wisconsin in 1919, almost twice as many as in 1918. These loans totaled $291,000, more even than in 1915 and 1916 when the company had made more loans than it did in 1919.[2]

But experience did not match these expectations. An economic depression came to rural America in the summer of 1920, ending almost a quarter century of relative prosperity. For example, corn—which had sold for $1.50 a bushel in 1919—brought only $.52 a bushel in 1921. This plunge was part of a nationwide postwar depression, but the price farmers received for their commodities did not rebound in 1921 or 1922 as the national economy turned sharply upward. Worldwide demand for U.S. agricultural exports, especially cotton and wheat, declined as wartime shortages eased and European nations deeply in debt to the United States from the costs of the war became reluctant to import from the United States. The agricultural segment of the nation's economy, therefore, remained depressed throughout the 1920s. On the average farm in the United States, cash receipts from marketing were 28 percent lower in 1930 than they had been in 1920. Meanwhile, the parity ratio (the price of farm products in comparison to the price of manufactured goods farmers had to buy, standardized at 1910–1914 levels) declined from 99 in 1920 to 83 in 1930. Consequently the average farm in the United States lost 26 percent of its value during the decade.[3]

This was not an auspicious time, therefore, to begin farming in a new region like the cutover. A few settlers, such as Henry Kroll, continued to trickle into the cutover. Kroll found himself unpopular in the German community he lived in around Dodgeville in southwestern Wisconsin when he sold war bonds during World War I; in 1921 he felt it prudent to trade for a new farm near Weyerhauser in Rusk County. But nationwide net rural-to-urban migration of 6,250,000 people indicated that most Americans saw brighter futures in cities than in the country. The federal government's restrictive immigration legislation of 1921, 1924, and 1927, furthermore, curtailed the influx of the kind of people who were likely to be attracted to the cutover. B. M. Apker, who worked on several of Ben Faast's development schemes, argued that it was more a lack of people than a lack of prospects for those people that hindered the development of northern Wisconsin. Referring to immigration restriction, he stubbornly believed that "every foot of agricultural land would have been and could have been developed if we had not stopped the people from coming here."[4]

But for whatever reason, people stopped coming to the cutover. UML's president admitted in 1924 that "there is almost a complete absence of demand for farms these days." The total population of the region in 1930 was just 314,000, or some 8,000 less than in 1920. By comparison, during this decade the population of Wisconsin increased by 11.7 percent, and that of the United States by about 16 percent. Similarly, after expanding so spectacularly for three decades, the number of farms in the cutover grew by only 2.6 percent during the 1920s, and acreage in farms by just 4.3 percent. Both figures actually declined after 1925. This farmland, furthermore, was worth less. The per-acre value of farmland (including buildings) declined between 1920 and 1930 in fourteen of the eighteen cutover counties, in seven of them by more than 10 percent.[5]

These figures were grim, and especially shocking in light of what was expected to happen, but they should be kept in perspective. The increase in the number of farms in the cutover was small in the 1920s, but the corresponding number *declined* both nationwide and in Wisconsin. (Sixteen of the twenty counties in Wisconsin that had more farms in 1930 than 1920 were in or adjoining the cutover.) More land was being farmed in the cutover at the end of the decade than at the beginning, less in the rest of the state. The decline in per-acre value of farm land and buildings was much greater outside the cutover—20 percent in Wisconsin, 30 percent in the United States as a whole, and over 30 percent in regions like western North Dakota and eastern Montana. Consequently, the total value of farmland and buildings declined only 6 percent in the cutover, compared to 17 percent statewide. Indeed, eight of the cutover counties increased their total value of farmland and buildings. The increasing importance to the region's farmers of dairying, which escaped the worst impact of the decade's agricultural depression, cushioned economic decline in the cutover somewhat. Cash receipts for American farmers from dairy products were higher each year between 1926 and 1930 than they had been in 1920, and milk cows sold for slightly higher prices in 1930 than they had a decade previously.[6]

In particular, people who had an economic or emotional investment in northern Wisconsin agriculture did not give up easily on their dream of seeing the cutover filled by yeoman farms. Into the mid-1920s, private land sellers as well as officials in the College of Agriculture and the Department of Immigration clung to the belief that land and commodity prices in the cutover would soon return to "normal." Community boosters continued to encourage agricultural development. The *Phillips Times,* in Price County, denounced the "shackles and inertia" and "dry rot" in its community which encouraged some residents to think that "things have been going decidedly wrong." It stressed that "communities grow and prosper only through co-operation of the citizens," specifically including farmers.[7] The paper highlighted the activities of community organizations which, in New Era–fashion, encouraged this cooperation. The Commercial Club, the Advertising Club, and the "Business Men" organized lunches, banquets, speakers, exhibits, and entertainment for Price County farmers. "Farmers Play Big Part in Our Boom," read the *Times* headline, but the paper also emphasized the need for farmers' "reciprocity" by patronizing Phillips merchants.[8] It also stressed that Price County farmers needed to clear more acres. After all, it argued, "pioneers" cleared their land under even more difficult conditions. With this effort, the *Times* assured its readers, "There is NO limit to the amount of milk, butter, cheese, eggs, and potatoes that Price county farmers can sell." To provide models, newspaper feature stories reported the accomplishments of successful farmers.[9]

To farm operators in the cutover, however, a free lunch or movie accompanied by unwelcome advice or the message that they were losing less ground than most American farmers was not helpful. Since cutover farmers started out poorer, even small declines could push them into financial distress. Human suffering often accompanied such financial problems. "Plese dont foreclose[;] give us a chance untill fall," begged one farmer indebted to UML. He received a reprieve, as was usually the case. But his crops failed in the fall of 1921 and he lost his farm. Others held on longer, but equally unsuccessfully. Joseph Phahuta bought a forty-acre farm on an eight-year land contract from the John S. Owen Lumber Company in 1918, paying close to top price—$920, with $225 down. He struggled to make his payments through the 1920s and was foreclosed in 1935 after falling $665 in arrears—approximately the amount he sank (and lost) in the property. Of thirty-seven land sales to individuals made by Owen Lumber during 1918–1919, only sixteen original purchasers eventually secured deeds to their properties.[10]

Problems were especially acute for farmers new to northern Wisconsin like Phahuta. An observer identified "farm places whose owners were fairly started when the change came" as most hard hit. These owners had bought their land at the high price level of the late teens. A few years later when payments on their land contracts began to fall due, they found that—despite their work at clearing and building—their farms had not appreciated enough to warrant becoming security for a mortgage loan. With commodity prices so low, their income was insufficient to cover payments on the contract. In this situation, land vendors had little choice but to liberalize payment terms. In some cases they did not foreclose if the settler continued to pay interest on the principal still due on the contract; in other cases they reduced the amount of principal due. Table 4.1 shows that few purchasers of land from the Northwestern Lumber Company in 1914 failed to complete their purchase agreement and obtain a deed. Significantly, all but three had paid their contracts by 1920. By contrast, purchasers in 1919 paid more for their land, generally had easier terms (eight years to pay, with only interest due for four years), but struggled to meet their payments even as the company reduced the amount they owed. Only three of fifty-eight original purchasers received deeds.

Archie Mallo was one of the 1919 purchasers, buying 140 acres for $3460.80, deferring $2,595 for eight years, with only interest due for four years. Mallo paid the interest and even $60 toward the principal in 1920.

Table 4.1. Land Sales, Northwestern Lumber Co., 1914 and 1919

	1914	1919
Sales	60	58
Price per acre	$17.74	$26.50
Cash sales	4	8
Contract sales		
Paid early (reduced)	40 (0)	12 (1)
Paid on schedule (reduced)	12 (0)	8 (5)
Paid late (reduced)	0	7 (7)
Cancelled	4	19
Unclear	0	4
Purchaser gets deed	50	30
Deed to another individual	6	5
Reverts to NWL	4	19
Unclear	0	4
NWL receives full payment	56	22
NWL receives partial payment	0	13
NWL regains property	4	19
Unclear	0	4

Source: Calculated from Northwestern Lumber Company Records, ARC, UWEC.

But he soon encountered difficulties. Interest payments became late and insufficient, and Northwestern Lumber had to pay the farm's taxes to avoid a tax deed sale which would wipe out both its and Mallo's stake in the property. Mallo saw the company take back thirty acres in 1932. After an unsuccessful attempt to refinance his debt through the Federal Land Bank, Mallo in October 1935 negotiated a new deal with Northwestern Lumber, which accepted $300 in cash and gave him a new land contract on which he had to pay $800. Mallo died in 1936 and by 1938 his widow faced increasingly insistent dunning from the company. In mid-May she pleaded, "If we cant get the money wold you wait till next spring [when] we wold have sale and pay of[*sic*] on place[?]" She explained, "I wold do that now but I know we wold not have enough to pay the morage[*sic*] on the cows and land. . . . I am trying every way to get the money." But two days later she was told that C. D. Moon, vice president of Northwestern Lumber, personally "insisted that this be cleared up before June 1st." On June 3 her farm was sold from under her by Northwestern Lumber for $832 in cash. In nineteen years on the farm, the Mallos had paid Northwestern Lumber more than $2,000 as well as taxes, but now had nothing to show for it.[11]

Businesses suffered as well as individuals. UML had never had to foreclose on more than three loans in a single year before 1918. Then between 1918 and 1922 the company took possession of 105 farms. By August 1923 it had under foreclosure about 20 percent by value of its outstanding mortgages, or about $300,000. Throughout the 1920s at any given time it owned about twenty-five farms and about three thousand acres in Wisconsin; perhaps half of the fifty other mortgages it continued to hold would be delinquent. The company had little success at selling or even renting foreclosed farms. Its president wrote in 1927 that "we are unable to sell at any price." The company had little new business, making fewer loans between 1926 and 1932 than it had in 1919 alone, while red ink mounted. There were only two profitable years between 1924 and 1934. UML finally entered bankruptcy on November 1, 1934.[12]

Ben Faast's dream for a planned rural community in southern Sawyer County met a similar fate. Land sales by the Wisconsin Colonization Company tumbled. It sold only a little more than four thousand acres in 1922 and 1923 together. Settlers were struggling: by 1924 the average settler had cleared only about six acres and was cultivating about ten more acres between stumps. Prospects were so bleak that the company's agricultural specialist took an opportunity to leave and become a county agent. "My neighbors have nearly all left here," reported one discouraged settler. "It is surely a forlorn place to live . . . On every hand are empty houses[,] windows and doors out and gone to ruin." An anonymous informer told the company that even farmers with money from logging and moonshining would not make their payments "but are going to a different place to farm," and remained temporarily in Ojibwa only because "it isn't so easy to put them out." Despite the success at farming we have seen he had achieved, Martin Pydo—a convicted moonshiner—was mentioned as one of this group of deadbeats.

Faast's dream for northern Wisconsin became obscured by the red ink of his business enterprises. The Wisconsin Colonization Company's income was insufficient to meet its financial obligations to John S. Owen and other lumbermen to whom it still owed part of the purchase price of its tract. Faast averted disaster for a few years by getting his creditors to scale down his debt (as he was doing with his settlers) and accept bonds as payment in lieu of cash when principal payments came due. But in 1925 the state Securities Commission tightened its regulations on bonding cutover land, requiring much more reasonable—and therefore lower—evaluations than had been the practice. The First Wisconsin Land Mortgage Association, initiated by Faast to sell bonds backed by mortgages on farms sold by his companies, found itself unable to issue new bonds and without income to meet payments on existing securities. By early 1928 payments were in default on over 80 percent of the mortgages held by the association—over 90 percent of the mortgages acquired from Faast's companies but only 31 percent of other mortgages. On February 1, 1928 the association was taken over by the state Banking Department and was rapidly liquidated. The following year the American Immigration Company, the large consortium of land vendors, demanded that Faast pay overdue notes. American Immigration offered to settle for 25 percent of the outstanding debt, but Faast could not raise the cash, and the Wisconsin Colonization Company entered bankruptcy. Ironically, one of the biggest financial losers in this debacle was cutover-booster Dean Harry L. Russell (who had also been a major stockholder in First Wisconsin Land Mortgage Association), who lost his $35,000 equity investment and had to pay back two bank loans to the Wisconsin Colonization Company that he had personally guaranteed, an obligation he claimed destroyed "a lifetime of savings."[13]

Economic conditions only worsened in the 1930s.[14] At first the national economic downturn which began in the summer of 1929 did not dramatically impact already struggling northern Wisconsin. In the Schlomann family in the town of Grow in Rusk County, "the beginning of the big depression left little impression on the family. It seemed to be more of the same." Clergyman Frank Richardson recalled that he realized the nation was in a depression only when he left Superior in 1932 for a new pastorate in Chicago. "We didn't know what a depression was. . . . We had nothing to compare it with, we were always poor." "It was a little easier for us," recalled Roy Meier about life in the town of Spirit in Price County; "we were the kind of people used to doing without." Consequently the Park Falls newspaper ignored any local problems and confidently reported that national economic conditions were returning to normal. Only in the late summer of 1930 did evidence of local distress appear in print: the city council asked employers to give married men preference for jobs, and the local movie theater reduced its admission price "because of the general business depression." Finally in November, when it printed a record list of fifty-five hundred descriptions of property in Price County vulnerable for unpaid taxes, the paper admitted that "times are not so good and the trend is distinctly not toward occupying the land."[15] Overall, the partial involvement of most cutover farmers with the market economy temporarily shielded them from the economic freefall experienced by many Americans in the first half of the 1930s.

Bad times lasted all through the decade of the 1930s. By 1939 the average cutover farm produced only $815 in farm products, a 40 percent drop from a decade earlier. The decline was statewide, to be sure, but greater in the cutover than elsewhere: in 1929 the products of cutover farms were worth 68 percent of the state average, but in 1939 they were worth only 59 percent. Consequently, in all but three of the eighteen cutover counties the per-acre value of farm land and buildings fell by more than the statewide and nationwide figure, which was around 35 percent; the decline in most counties was around 50 percent. This decline continued in the late 1930s after it had reversed in most parts of the country, including southeastern Wisconsin. The selling price of land plunged because, in the words of the Rust-Owen Lumber Company official in charge of sales, "lands are being offered to settlers on any kind of terms they want." At the John S. Owen Lumber Company, where the sale price of land had been above $24.00 an acre in 1918–1919 (Table 1.1), sales in 1926–1927 averaged $16.39 an acre and averaged only $12.71 an acre by 1932–1933. Even this figure was inflated by the inclusion of "semi-developed" farms (which had been repossessed); by the 1930s the company's completely "wild" land was selling for $6 to $10 an acre. Holt Lumber Company cut the asking price for its wild land, which had been a minimum of $20 an acre for grades #1 and #2 in 1920, to $11 an acre for grade #1 and $3 to $5 an acre for grade #2 by 1930. The company actually sold land for even less. Similarly, Rust-Owen actually sold land in Bayfield County for $2.50 an acre in the early 1930s.[16]

The declining value of their land and the products produced on it left many cutover farmers economically distressed. "It was a terrible time, the depression," recalled Sarah Martin, who farmed with her husband near Minong in Washburn County. "It seemed like John worked all the time and that no money was coming in." Another desperate woman emphasized to her farm mortgagee that she and her husband both had taken off-farm jobs, but they still could not buy needed seed, much less meet mortgage payments. "I don't know what to do," she cried. "It will take time for me to do anything on the interest," reported a farmer from northern Chippewa County to his mortgagee. "The boy ran into the mower which cost a lot of money. . . . I then . . . broke my finger but worked any way until I was layed off." These setbacks in the 1920s and 1930s led some cutover farmers to despair. They were willing to surrender their farms to land companies or mortgage holders—"the place is not worth it," J. J. Roseman wrote with resignation to the First Wisconsin Land Mortgage Association.[17]

This grim mood was reinforced by the seeming intransigence of brush fires in the cutover in the 1920s and 1930s. As clearing for agriculture lessened, large amounts of stump and brush land remained vulnerable to burning. In Price County in 1926 alone, 238 reported fires burned 84,500 acres, over 10 percent of the county's land area. In the 1930s, drought and the arson of men desperately hoping for work in extinguishing fires resulted in a "pall of smoke [which] hung over the city of Merrill for days," in the words of Jack Plano.[18] It seemed that farming was not restoring the physical environment of northern Wisconsin, as boosters had promised early in the twentieth century.

Rural people in northern Wisconsin were not helpless in this situation. Some breathed defiance rather than resignation when threatened with loss of their farms. They challenged the accounting of mortgage and land contract holders. They argued that the payments and taxes they owed were unfair, given the quality of land they had been sold. They taunted mortgage holders by asking them how well they could farm under the circumstances. "If you want to make forclose on that pile of rocks," Martin Pydo raged, "you can any time you want to." They invoked what they thought were their legal rights. "I will deed you the place and throw in my 7 years of labor," Arthur Stapleton told the First Wisconsin Land Mortgage Association, "or you can foreclose as you wish[,] but if you foreclose I am going to retain possession the 21 months the law allows me."[19]

Settlers, however, needed more than a spirit of resistance. For survival in the depression decades, rural people in northern Wisconsin also turned to one another, invoking the family labor and community exchange system, characteristic of yeoman farming in the United States, which they had created in the more developed parts of the cutover. Family members assisted one another. The Martins "learned a great deal about saving food and saving money and especially getting closer as a family." Sympathetic community members also tried to help. Even the crabby *Park Falls Herald* printed an article at the depths of the Depression sympathetic toward the residents of a Hooverville on Lake Superior near Ashland. It described them as clean and self-regulating and concluded that, "These men are meeting an unfortunate situation as best they can." Cooperatives assisted their members as best they could. The

Flambeau Valley Farms Cooperative in Ladysmith, Rusk County, advanced money to members against future milk checks and guaranteed debts they owed to retailers, using the member's stock in the cooperative as security. It chastised a local storekeeper for resorting to a collection agency and assured him that "we can work out some plan." Community organizations also assisted the needy. In Price County, the American Legion took the lead in organizing voluntary assistance, as it did in many parts of rural America. Dances, high school football games, and other fund raisers helped "benefit the poor." In neighboring Taylor County in the town of Jump River, a "Golden Rule Club" helped "abandoned" mothers and children in 1931. The Pine Lake Welfare Club in Oneida County similarly paid for medical and dental care for children in needy families. In the pseudonymous community of Poundville, social science investigators found that residents organized the Polish Farm Club in 1932 for mutual self-help in order to avoid the need for dependency on outside assistance. Like the people in Union County, a poor part of southern Illinois recently studied by anthropologist Jane Adams, residents of northern Wisconsin strengthened their community life in response to the Great Depression.[20]

Cutover farmers also insisted that local government ease its tax burden. In the town of Harmon in Price County in November 1931, farmers organized themselves for "self-preservation and protection of our families" because "the small farmers of Price Co. are on the verge of destitution." In addition to asking the county board to stop foreclosures, they petitioned for tax relief: they wanted the county budget cut 25 percent (targeting for elimination the county fair and county agricultural agent, the representatives in Price County of outside agricultural expertise) and the tax burden somehow shifted to "bankers and large corporations." Reflecting this perspective, throughout 1931 and 1932 editorials and letters to the editor in the *Park Falls Herald* called for reduced county and local spending. Cuts were made: in November 1933, according to the newspaper, by demand "of a large delegation of farmers" the county board cut the salaries of all its employees by 20 percent. Cutover residents received constant verbal encouragements in their struggles—Wisconsin Badger head football coach Glenn Thestlewaite told the Park Falls Commercial Club that the "present economic situation" might be overcome by the kind of teamwork taught by his football program.[21]

However such bromides did not help cutover residents overcome material deprivations. Residents of northern Wisconsin, like Americans throughout the country by 1932, found that private aid and economy in government spending were insufficient to meet the unprecedented hardships of the Great Depression. In early February, 1933, the *Park Falls Herald* had to announce that "no more Red Cross clothing is available." The paper then desperately tried to boost spirits by running articles like the one entitled "Sees Finish of Depression," an interview with a "former Fifield resident and now an astrologer at Minneapolis."[22]

Battered farmers now organized to take direct action to get themselves out of their predicament. In Price County during the first two years of the Depression, local politicians, businessmen, the county agent, and Agricultural Extension representatives had encouraged dairy farmers to organize themselves for cooperative marketing and planned development. About 250 farmers heard such speakers at a meeting in the late winter of 1930.[23] Even the conservative Park Falls newspaper editorially endorsed local involvement in the Wisconsin Cooperative Milk Pool, a statewide group which sought to promote cooperative marketing and raise farm income, and reported that it was supported by Park Falls businessmen.[24] Then in 1932 Price County farmers—like poorer dairy farmers elsewhere in Wisconsin—began to sympathize with the increasingly radical rhetoric of Milk Pool president Walter M. Singler, who railed against large dairies and their supposed ability to manipulate the state Department of Agriculture and Markets. Singler claimed that "farmers by uniting can turn the nation upside down." Milo Reno of the national Farmers Holiday Association, who tried to bring the Milk Pool into his group, spoke at a rally in Ladysmith, the county seat of Rusk County, on August 21, 1932. "No meeting I have held has given me more satisfaction and encouragement," he privately reported afterward.[25] Reno returned to Wisconsin in September and December for rallies at Marshfield, a city bordering the edge of the cutover. The five thousand attendees at the September rally choose Arnold Gilberts of Dunn County, bordering on the cutover, as state president. The message of Singler and Reno—that farmers needed to act themselves to secure direct government assistance—was the antithesis of the message of Richard Ely and his students that farm conditions could be ameliorated indirectly by educators and bureaucrats.[26]

Encouraged by the organizational efforts of the Farmers Holiday and the Milk Pool, cutover farmers took more radical action as the Depression deepened. For their part, Price County farmers participated in large numbers in the three Wisconsin milk strikes of 1933. The first strike, in

February, was reportedly unanimously endorsed by a meeting of three hundred farmers and closed all but one cheese factory in the county.[27] Elsewhere in Wisconsin the milk strikes grew increasingly violent and were met with brutal repression by sheriffs and national guardsmen; but newspaper reports, at least, indicated that in Price County the strikes, while effective, remained peaceful.[28] They made clear, moreover, the unity of small farmers in the county and their commitment to saving their way of life.

Strains of political radicalism continued to be present in northern Wisconsin during the rest of the 1930s. Olaf Severson remembered farmers intimidating a lawyer executing foreclosures near Frederick, in northern Polk County. Many such protests in Polk County were led by George Nelson, the Socialist Party candidate for vice president of the United States in 1936. A particularly dramatic confrontation occurred in the town of Brantwood in Price County in the fall of 1933 when fifty men and women tried to prevent a foreclosure. The Phillips Fire Department and "citizen volunteers" finally "routed" the crowd and the sheriff made six arrests. Brantwood would be a continuous trouble spot during the 1930s: farmers repeatedly sent "demands" to the county board for higher wages for work relief, free seeds for spring planting, and more respect for reliefers from the sheriff and his deputies. Certainly the socialist tradition of the Finnish community in the town encouraged this militant language and behavior, but militancy was not limited to one ethnic community. The group arrested in Brantwood in the fall of 1933 for attempting to block the farm foreclosure included men from the towns of Fifield, Knox, and Worcester, as well as Brantwood, and half did not have Finnish surnames.[29] However, the willingness of the authorities to suppress this and other expressions of radicalism in the cutover did not reflect a unified community as support for the Milk Strike did in Price County. Instead such actions suggested—especially to observers outside the region—that the cutover, rather than being a safety valve for radicalism as intended had become an incubator for destabilizing protests.

In this situation, even the opponents of direct action such as the milk strikes had to acknowledge the necessity of increased public assistance. In an average year in Price County during the 1920s the county supported about one hundred persons with outdoor relief and fifteen to twenty each with soldiers' pensions or aid to the blind, and administered state-funded "mothers' pensions" for a couple of dozen others. The responsibility for general assistance remained with the towns. In these years the rural towns—relative to the cities of Phillips and Park Falls—spread assistance more generally among their residents, but in smaller dollar amounts. This practice perhaps reflected greater shared feelings of community in the countryside. The heavily Finnish, socialist-oriented town of Knox was most generous with its assistance.[30]

In the early 1930s relief rolls exploded, and Wisconsin counties had to assume responsibility for general assistance in November 1932. By the end of the following month, 1,296 people (out of Price County's population of about 18,000) were receiving outdoor relief. Some funds came to the county through the Reconstruction Finance Corporation, but as unemployment swelled in 1933 the relief burden overwhelmed the county's resources. With the milk strikers no doubt on their mind, the county board telegraphed to the state highway commissioner in May, reporting, "Men waiting for relief work. Tension very high. At breaking point. Work needed at once." Through the programs of the Federal Emergency Relief Administration, state and federal funds did come to Price County. In 1934 the county spent $134,000 on unemployment relief (all but $6,000 from Madison or Washington). For many small farmers, now without the part-time work in the woods or elsewhere on which they had depended, the government became the supplemental source of income. They were also eligible for federal loans to purchase feed, and in 1934 the county distributed $55,000 in emergency drought assistance. These programs required recipients to work off their benefits.

Price County residents continued to depend on public assistance into the late 1930s. In April 1936, 885 farmers (out of about 2,500 in the county) still had $56,000 in drought relief loans outstanding. That September 311 unemployment relief cases remained active, probably covering about nine hundred people. This need existed even after county officials, reluctantly faced with the termination earlier in 1936 of general federal unemployment relief, had transferred as many reliefers as possible to other public assistance programs. By September, therefore, 222 county families had a member working for the Works Progress Administration; there were 378 cases active in the new Social Security categorical aid programs for the elderly, dependent children, and the blind. Altogether, taking into account a few soldier and sailor relief cases which remained the county's responsibility as well as temporary and emergency grants, probably over three thousand people, about one-sixth of Price County's population, received public assistance in September 1936. Furthermore, since December 1935 federal aid had been available for rural rehabilitation from the Resettlement Administration (whose activities in northern Wisconsin will be discussed more fully in chapter 6). Although apparently no Price County farmers received such assistance in September 1936, over three hundred had earlier in the year, and as late as 1939 184 farmers received aid between January and April.[31]

Price County's dependence on public assistance programs was typical of the cutover. In 1935, thirteen cutover counties had greater than 18 percent of their population on relief, and the other five at least 12 percent. Of Wisconsin counties with greater than 18 percent on relief, all but one were in the cutover; of the sixteen with 12 to 18 percent on relief, five were in the cutover and two were adjacent.[32] The eight northernmost counties had over 30 percent of their residents on relief. This rate put them, along with parts of Appalachia; drought-ravaged South Dakota; eastern Oklahoma from which Okies were fleeing to California; the Dust Bowl section of New Mexico, Colorado, and Oklahoma; and counties in Minnesota and Michigan also in the Lake Superior cutover, in the unenviable category of the most relief-dependent parts of the United States.[33] Overall, as late as March, 1938, 87,213 northern Wisconsin residents—about a quarter of the total population—received general relief, WPA or Civilian Conservation Corps work, Social Security categorical aid, or Farm Security Administration subsistence grants (by this time the Farm Security Administration had taken over the programs of the Resettlement Administration). Hardest hit was Forest County, on the Michigan border, where most residents were reliefers.[34]

Especially in rural areas and smaller cities, an infrastructure for relief programs did not exist before the Depression. To assist their residents battered by the Depression, northern Wisconsin counties generally did a better organizing job than was done in many such areas.[35] Price County created the position of director of public relief in November 1932. Unfortunately, from the point of view of the board of supervisors, the first director, Martin Knez, turned out to be an alleged communist. Knez reportedly endorsed the Communist Party; favorably compared conditions in the Soviet Union with those in the United States; wanted farmers exempted from taxation and rent payments; and encouraged farmers to kill their cows and go on relief in order to overburden the system and contribute to the collapse of existing institutions. Knez was forced to resign in February 1933, and Price County officials thereafter were more successful in establishing agencies that worked to control rather than ferment social discontent. They opened a centralized "relief and unemployment office" in Phillips in December 1933 to handle county, state, and federal programs. This office evolved later in the decade into a Central Application Bureau which evaluated CCC, WPA, and rural rehabilitation grant applications, distributed surplus commodities, and handled other relief responsibilities. At the direction of the county supervisors' relief committee, the Bureau in December 1937 added the responsibility of overseeing the county's participation in the Social Security program, which previously had been handled by the Pension Department. As much as was feasible, the county committed its resources to public assistance. In 1928 it had spent $21,562.90 of its own money on outdoor relief, mothers' pensions, aid for soldiers and the blind, schools for dependent children, and hospitalization of the indigent. With its residents so battered by the Depression, in 1936 the county spent over 2.5 times that amount on comparable programs. Two years later it found the money to hire a county nurse.

But the local funds that went to public assistance in Price County were dwarfed in magnitude by money from the federal and state governments—80 percent of the cost of the county nurse, for example. In September 1936, for instance, 99 percent of the cost of general relief, 75 percent of the cost of categorical Social Security assistance, and 48 percent of WPA costs were paid by Washington and Madison. As a contemporary study of beleaguered Forest County concluded, "relief costs are high, and the State and Federal Governments are paying practically all of it."[36] Cutover residents had done what they could for themselves, publicly and privately, but by 1940 they were more dependent than ever on outsiders, now for welfare checks as much as agricultural advice or credit to finance land purchases.

Who needed public assistance in the cutover in the 1930s? As the high percentage of population receiving aid suggests, people from all backgrounds found themselves asking for help. In the town of Lenroot in Sawyer County during the depths of the Depression, the relief rolls included Nels Sorenson, a successful farmer who in 1925 after about twenty years of work had 68 of his 107 acres in crops with a herd of ten cows; his less-successful neighbor, sixty-year-old Lyman Nettleson, who in 1930 after eleven years in the town was tax delinquent on his ten acres valued at $255; Harold Cook, the twenty-nine-year-old son of a successful Danish immigrant farmer who worked 160 acres, 70 in crops, valued at $3,186 in 1930; and Wayne Sommerville, who had only started farming in the town sometime between 1925 and 1930.[37] However, farmers were actually less likely than other cutover residents to be on relief. In light of the damage the Depression did to the image of farming in the cutover (chapter 5), it was ironic that people working in town, in the woods, or in other occupations had a proportionately greater presence on the relief rolls.[38]

Since the need was so widespread among rural people there was no stigma attached to receiving relief. When asked a half-century later to identify the difference between reliefers and others, Larry Garneau, who farmed in the town of Drummond in Bayfield County in the late 1930s, laughed and said, "We never gave it a thought. We knew they were hard up . . . we were too." Even an official of the Rust-Owen Lumber Company admitted that "it is no disgrace to be on relief under the conditions prevailing the past few years."[39]

Like elsewhere in the United States people in the cutover particularly approved of the Civilian Conservation Corps (CCC). One corpsman who worked building a park in northern Wisconsin called it "the Greatest Idea to come out of Franklin D. Roosevelt's New Deal." The CCC operated about seventy-five camps in the cutover with 200 to 250 men each. Most were recruited from outside the region, but local communities supplied older, more skilled workers. For some people in the cutover this sort of assistance was a safety net that got them through the worst of the Depression. Tony Gonia, for instance, used his CCC earnings to save the Taylor County farm on which he still lived in 1983. By one means or another, all four of the farmers just identified from the town of Lenroot still managed to operate farms in the town in 1940.[40]

But even among those who were able to hang on, many farm people in northern Wisconsin continued to depend on government assistance, as indicated by their high relief rates in 1940. Was this because they were lazy and shiftless and selling their votes for handouts, as the Park Falls newspaper claimed earlier in the decade?[41] An investigator in Dunn County, adjacent to the cutover, who addressed the question of why so many people were still on relief in 1936 despite the introduction of federal assistance programs, concluded that reliefers were not shiftless. On average, farmers in the group she surveyed had owned their operation for twenty years and most had tried to develop their farms commercially by heavily mortgaging both their lands and herds. They had borrowed as much as they could from family and friends but suffered from the impact of low commodity prices and drought (which, however, was not so severe farther north in the cutover). Many were old or ill.[42] Indeed, a state-wide survey in the late 1930s, based on a sample including Sawyer and Forest counties from the cutover, reported that the age of most family heads on relief exceeded the rural median, and that half were "unemployable," two-thirds of whom were disabled (and presumably had at least deserved relief in the 1920s). For example George and Augusta Rau had a twenty-two-acre farm in the town of Molitor in Taylor County. After George died in 1935 and Augusta was institutionalized, county officials claimed that "the couple lived in the town of Molitor for years and were always a town burden. Both were mentally deficient and never capable for caring for themselves." The town calculated that between 1902 and 1935 the couple received $2,456.34, mostly in "aid," but occasionally firewood, sowing, and exemption from taxes.[43] This evidence did not support blaming the victims for being reliefers, but did make people think that the physical environment of the cutover, if it did not drive people literally mad, could not provide their sustenance.

Especially to people outside the region, the idea that the Depression was worse in the cutover than in most parts of the United States was furthered by the fiscal problems encountered by towns and counties in northern Wisconsin. Increased expenditures for public assistance occurred simultaneously with a decreased ability to collect revenue. As land values declined, tax delinquency became a serious problem in northern Wisconsin in the 1920s. A widely cited study reported that taxes went unpaid in 1927 on almost one quarter of the land in seventeen northern Wisconsin counties. Even more alarming, private parties purchased the tax certificates on less than one fifth of the delinquent land; the remainder, under Wisconsin law, had to be purchased by the counties (with the revenue going to the town or other taxing unit in which the land was located).[44] Some of these certificates, both publicly and privately held, were eventually redeemed by payment of the delinquent taxes and interest, but the developing pattern was clear: the counties were becoming significant owners of land, from which they would cease to receive any tax income.

The cycle of declining land values, increased tax burden, and rising tax delinquencies intensified in the 1930s, as the situation in Forest County revealed. Between 1927 and 1936, 327,000 acres in this county left the tax rolls (this included not only land taken by the county for tax deed but, increasingly, tax-delinquent land which avoided sale for tax deed by transfer to the federal government as part of reforestation programs that will be discussed in chapter 5). This transfer left only 274,000 taxable acres of rural land in 1936, on a quarter of which the owners had not paid taxes for 1935 or an earlier year. The general decline in land values, furthermore, meant that this land was worth less—in 1936 the per-acre assessed value for agricultural land in Forest County was half what it had been in 1927. County and town governments cut spending by about one third between 1927 and 1936, but the result was still an increasing per-acre tax burden relative to true value—an increase of over 20 percent on all classes of property in the county during the ten-year time span. Overall, in 1929 the ratio of taxes to the value of farm land and buildings was about 10 percent greater in the cutover than statewide in Wisconsin. The growing tax burden, of course, increased the likelihood of further tax delinquency. Of the $207,000 levied for 1936 on rural property in Forest County, only 74 percent had been collected by July 31, 1937.[45]

The pattern in Forest County was general, if less extreme, throughout the cutover. By 1938, 43 percent of the total acreage of the cutover had left the tax base. The total value of real estate in these counties had declined by one third in the previous decade, compared to a one-fifth decline statewide.[46] Identifying a further 1.3 percent decline in 1939, Price County's Committee on Equalization reported to the County Board that "the decline in the value of real estate is due in the main to changes in land use and increase in the exempt land."[47] By law, counties could collect for their own purposes only 1 percent of even the decreased value of what taxable land remained (excluding the cost of debt service). By the late 1930s, therefore, many cutover counties were struggling to remain solvent. Observers questioned whether they had the resources to provide schools, roads, and other services, especially given the widespread need for these services among so many of their residents.

For many settlers in northern Wisconsin, the hard times of the 1930s ended their efforts to farm in the cutover. Norwegian immigrant Hans Skinvik developed a successful farm near Minong in Washburn County while also working as a logger. By 1930, however, he was in his sixties, and all his children had moved away. A son persuaded him to stop farming, move to Milwaukee, and work for five more years in the Boston Store. In 1940 Larry Garneau's father-in-law, a Swedish immigrant who farmed part-time in the town of Drummond in Bayfield County while working in the Rust-Owen lumber mill, simply gave his farm to someone who would assume the mortgage and moved into the village of Drummond. A small overgrown field with the remains of rusting farm equipment was

Figure 4.1. W. A. Rowlands, a critic of unrestricted farming in the cutover, took this photo of an abandoned farm in northern Wisconsin in the 1930s or 1940s. (State Historical Society of Wisconsin, photo WHi (X3) 50585)

all that remained of his farm when visited in the fall of 1988. Abandoned farms began to appear across the cutover (Figure 4.1). The enumerator in the town of Grow in Rusk County was asked in 1930 to explain the drop he reported from 135 to 115 farms in the town. "I know I found empty houses when I was going around last spring," he replied. People told him that "they can't make a living on the land and enough to . . . pay such hight [sic] taxes."[48]

Young people, in particular, left cutover farms. Northern Wisconsin farmers had relatively large families and relatively small farms, so there were limited opportunities for youths to receive all or part of the family farm as a legacy (intergenerational transfer of land will be discussed in chapter 6). Many young people, furthermore, did not want to follow their parents' vocation. In the town of Mason in Bayfield County, according to Knute Anderson, the first generation of settlers "grubbed and they toiled and they slaved and they got 60 acres all cleared . . . [with] an old ramshackle house all falling down. . . . The young ones said there got to be a better way to make a living." Some of these young people moved to cities and villages within northern Wisconsin. When John Kushala, who had been farming in the town of Lake in Price County, died in 1931, eight of his ten children were living in nearby Park Falls. His neighbor Herman Buecher had died a year earlier, and six of his seven children were reported as living "in the immediate vicinity." But many other young people scattered outside the cutover. Sarah Martin, who grew up on a farm near Minong in Washburn County, related that in the 1930s, "my brothers and sisters basically moved South to find jobs and money—they ended up picking cotton." When Mrs. John Bernklau died in 1933 in the Sugarbush district seven miles from Park Falls, one of her four children was still at home, but the others had left Wisconsin. Of the eight children of Sarah Martin who survived childhood, her eldest son Raymond took over the family farm in 1953 and the other seven dispersed. Overall, the extent that young people left northern Wisconsin can be seen in the age distribution of the region's population: in 1930 there were 17,708 rural farm people aged 10–14 in the cutover; in 1940 there were 10,982 such persons aged 20–24. Females left in particular: in 1940 there were better than six men for every four women aged 20–24 on cutover farms. Such a pattern was general in rural America, but not so pronounced in more settled regions. Mostly migrants to the region themselves, the parents of these children understood their reasons for leaving and "accepted it," according to Frank Richardson, pastor of a Chippewa County congregation in the 1920s.[49]

Entire communities ceased to exist. The Croatian settlement of Velebit, about five miles east of Eagle River in Vilas County, into which at least seventeen families moved between about 1915 and 1925, disappeared by the early 1930s. In the 1990s all that remains of Velebit are the ruins of seven farm buildings along mostly unpaved Forest Service roads and trails.[50] The "Severson Community," a pseudonymous settlement apparently in Florence County and closely studied by a social scientist in the late 1930s, had a similar history. Eighteen farmers settled in Severson, all but four between 1913 and 1922, and developed a vibrant community. But hard hit by the Depression, most turned to government assistance programs in the 1930s. Six saw their farms foreclosed between 1926 and 1936. In the summer of 1939, only one farm was still operating. "The meadows, where once the farmers plowed and planted, are covered with scattered stands of young white and Norway pines," the visiting social scientist reported. "The uncultivated cutover has grown up into brush even more impenetrable than before." Similarly, in 1977, seventy-seven-year-old Walter McGee, who came to the town of Springbrook in 1907, recalled, "I'd guess that about 400 acres opened up between here and Gull Lake in those days. Now it's all grown up to jack pine. . . . So many people gave up."[51]

However, unlike some distressed parts of the country, northern Wisconsin did not become depopulated during the 1930s. In fact, the number of residents in the cutover, which had stagnated during the 1920s, grew 7 percent to 339,000, about the national rate of growth. The rural farm population managed to remain unchanged. What happened, in part, was that the collapse of the nation's industrial economy in the early 1930s encouraged a "back-to-the-land movement," especially to places like the cutover where rumor had it that refugees could practice subsistence agriculture. Douglas County offered its own homestead plan, selling county-owned land for $2 an acre. "Are You Afraid of Losing Your Job?" asked a classified *Milwaukee Journal* advertisement for the Ladysmith Land Company; "Buy a Farm and Be Content." Referring to northern Clark County, the land salesman for the John S. Owen Lumber Company continued to insist at the bottom of the Depression that a "settler with small means moving on to land in this section of Wisconsin [had] a better chance of ultimate success" than anywhere else in the country. Consequently, the Park Falls newspaper reported in late 1931 that "practically every shack in the woods is being occupied either by trappers or settlers." Overall, between 1930 and 1935 the number of farms in the cutover increased by 22 percent to 32,716, and there were still 31,530 farms in the region in 1940.[52]

Altogether in the cutover in 1940 there were about 23,600 people— 7 percent of the population—who had arrived since 1935. About half had moved from outside Wisconsin, most from Minnesota, the Chicago area, and the Upper Peninsula of Michigan. The cutover was not the target of large-scale, long-distance relocation, seen most famously at the time by the Okie migration to California.[53] Some two hundred Kentuckians did move to northern Wisconsin during this period, maintaining a connection which had begun when Kentucks settled in Forest and Langlade counties in the 1890s.[54] With its distinctive speech and colorful family feuds, this group was still seen in 1940—negatively—as "a breed apart." Kentucks created the threatening image, disproportionate to their numbers, of Appalachia coming to the cutover.

As was the case with the back-to-the-land movement in other parts of the country, many of these new settlers in northern Wisconsin were not serious farmers. They saw themselves as temporarily eking out a semi-subsistence existence, squatting on or renting cheap land, or perhaps living on part of a relative's farm. For example, an inquiry to the Price County Clerk from a prospective purchaser in Kenosha asking about buying county-owned land emphasized that, with $100 per month in some form of assistance from the federal government, the purchaser "dont half [sic] to make a living off of the land." Furthermore, many of the new migrants who were more serious about agriculture did not have the resources to farm successfully. Price County officials also received an inquiry on behalf of 20 to 40 drought-ravaged South Dakota farmers seeking to relocate together who had no money and wanted that non-existent commodity, "homestead land." Olaf Anderson recalled that in northern Polk County such refugees from the Dakotas took "what was left over," mostly farms that other people had lost. The fifty or so set-tlers attracted by Douglas County's offer of cheap public land clustered around Dairyland, described at the end of the decade by the WPA *Guide* as "a small village of tarpaper shacks in the midst of charred stumps." Overall, of the males who moved to northern Wisconsin in the second half of the 1930s, 20 percent were unemployed in 1940, compared to 12 percent of such migrants in all parts of the state. Straining as they already were to help one another, cutover residents generally did not welcome such newcomers. The Price County authorities, for their part, carefully excluded newly arrived residents from eligibility for general assistance.[55]

These sorts of settlers often did not persist for very long. Olaf Ander-son's neighbor Olaf Severson characterized them as "ne'er-do-wells" who shifted their residence from year to year. A reopened factory in Milwaukee, a CCC job in Wyoming, or an offer to live with an in-law in Des Moines might take these people away from northern Wisconsin. When the enumerator for the town of Grow in Rusk County was asked again in 1933 to explain a reported sharp decline in the number of farms in the town, he explained that there were many "abandoned farms mostly small and new places and several of these were bachelors when they can get anything else to do they don't farm."[56] People liv-ing on such farms cleared little land and produced few products for market. In fact, they had a negative effect on agricultural development in the cutover to the extent that the properties they left behind when they moved on contributed to the image of the region as filled with abandoned farms.

But the back-to-the-land movement also brought permanent settlers and positive accomplishments to northern Wisconsin. Severson admitted that descendants of some 1930s migrants from the Dakotas still lived in the Luck area in the late 1980s. Conrad and Mabel Leafbled impulsively bought a farm outside of Iron River in Bayfield County which was being abandoned in 1938 by a friend. Reality soon set in. "We sat on the steps [with] tears on our cheeks. . . . They left us with one old horse, seven heifers, and no milk cows." But the Leafbleds borrowed another horse and bought a tractor with help from Mabel's brother. Entirely with their own and their son's labor, the Leafbleds electrified the farm, purchased milking equipment, and developed a business delivering dairy products to tourist cabins and hotels and residences in Iron River which supported them for twenty-three years. Born in 1898, Ed Pudas had grown up on a farm in the Finnish community of Oulu in Bayfield County. He left the farm for six years in the 1920s and early 1930s for a variety of jobs, marrying in New York in 1931. Like so many others, he returned home during the depths of the Depression in 1933. Claiming he had gained confidence from his off-farm work experience, he remained to operate the family farm for thirty-four years. In the town of Spirit in Price County, Carl Rhody was in his early twenties and, in his words, did not want "to spend his life taking jobs where he could find them." Adept at what would be termed in the 1990s as "bottom fishing," he acquired two adjacent farms by tax deed sale and distress sale. By selling his car and the hay from his semicleared land while continuing to work in the woods in the winter and borrowing $100 from his father, he was able to own the properties outright in a few years and became a successful farmer.[57]

The experience of the forty-two farm operators in the town of Bayfield in Bayfield County who were enumerated in 1936 but not 1935 clarifies the experience of people who moved back to the land in the Wisconsin cutover. The town reported a net growth of thirty "farms" between 1935 and 1936. Were these "farms" really places where agriculture was practiced? "Just where to draw the line" regarding the definition of what was a farm had "always been a problem," admitted the enumerator. As Table 4.2 shows, most of these new "farmers" only cut hay for others or raised garden crops—especially cabbage—for themselves on "abandoned clearings of homesteaders and those left by camps." "Many of the owners," the enumerator reported, "have work or business in the city" of Bayfield. Several had not actually moved into the town during the preceding year, as at least five had been listed in 1935 but on second thought crossed out by the enumerator. Apparently, by slightly increasing their output in 1936, they crossed the "line" to qualify as farmers, although most were no longer listed as such in 1940. However, of the small group who appear to have been primarily committed to farming (these had 6.4 people on average residing on their farms, compared to 3.1 on the other categories of farms), two thirds persisted until 1940. During this period, they increased their acreage in oats, hay, and corn on average from eight to thirteen.[58] Indeed, not all of the apparent growth in number of farms and population in the cutover should be dismissed as unrelated to serious attempts at farming. Between 1929 and 1939, in northern Wisconsin there was an increase of 16 percent—120,000 acres—in harvested acreage (although the large growth in number of farms meant that the average number of acres harvested per farm declined slightly).[59]

This growth was in part due to the ability of some established cutover farmers to survive and even expand their operations despite the hardships of the 1930s. The despair that induced some farmers to give up, surrender their property, and migrate from the region was not the norm in the cutover. Many instead clung to their farms with remarkable tenacity. "I shurly did not come over here in brush and stumps to clair and put the ground in cultivation and live [leave] it stay for some body eles," wrote one of Ben Faast's settlers at Ojibwa. "I intended to make a Home for my self, in acount of me not working in city."[60]

For one thing, farm operators could take advantage of land vendors' offers to write down debts in order to get nonperforming land contracts and mortgages off their books. By refinancing their loans for less acreage, lower interest rates, or smaller principal, some cutover farmers were able to continue to live on their farms. For example, Vernon Nolan had been farming forty acres near Sheldon purchased from the Northwest-

Table 4.2. Persistence of New Farm Operators, Town of Bayfield, 1936–1940

Type of "farm"	Mean No. of Cows	Mean No. of Acres	STATUS IN 1940	
			Present	Gone
Essentially hayfield	0.1	23	2	6
Essentially garden for home consumption	0.4	24	6	19
Genuine farm	2.2	49	6	3

Source: Annual Enumeration of Agricultural Statistics, Town of Bayfield, Bayfield County, 1935, 1936, 1940, SHSW.

ern Lumber Company in 1919. He struggled throughout the 1920s to meet his payments, frequently becoming delinquent and once having the sheriff sell tax certificates on his land that he had to redeem. In 1934, three years after he should have paid off his contract, Nolan struck a deal with Northwestern Lumber: for $71 in cash the company wrote off most of the principal Nolan still owed, forgave unpaid interest for 1931–1934, and gave Nolan the deed to his farm.[61]

Farm development also often benefitted from Depression conditions: Carl Rhody recalled that land clearing advanced during the 1930s because opportunities for time-consuming off-farm work declined. Herman Schlomann cleared more land on his farm in the town of Grow in Rusk County, built a new house with electricity and indoor plumbing in 1934, and bought a tractor. In 1940 he cropped thirty-six acres, compared to twenty-two in 1930. He had increased his herd from eight cows in 1925 to eleven in 1933 to sixteen in 1938 (his son recalled thirty by 1940). Ole Sommers made similar improvements on the farm in Sioux Creek, Barron County, that he had taken over from his father-in-law in 1923. He built a new barn in 1929 (and enlarged it in 1940), added a silo in 1930, purchased fifty more acres during the 1930s, bought a new mower in the late '30s and a tractor in 1943, added running water to the barn and farmhouse in 1940, and increased his herd from two cows in 1928 to twenty-two by 1944. His son was still operating the farm in 1970.[62]

Determination, resourcefulness, and of course luck explained how these farmers were able to survive and sometimes even expand their operations during the Depression. As much as possible, cutover farm families intensified the practice of "making do," by which yeoman farmers had always kept the full impact of the market at arm's length. Objects would be recycled for different uses, consumption would be adjusted to available resources, neighborhood sharing would increase, and ways would be found to accomplish tasks without spending cash.[63] For example, in the cutover in the 1930s still-abundant hunting and fishing resources increased in importance as nutritional sources. But the largest burden of "making do" fell on women. In the late 1920s and 1930s, Anna Pratt Erickson, who farmed with her husband near Athens in Marathon County, adjacent to the cutover, saved money by disconnecting the farmhouse's phone, making soap, and sewing more of her family's clothing out of flour and sugar sacks. When she purchased a new object it was a pressure cooker, which enabled her to intensify canning, a traditional yeoman farm woman's activity.[64]

Also significant were more direct contributions to farm production by women, as well as by children. On Harvey Dueholm's father's farm in northern Polk County, "hen money" from farm women selling eggs and chickens was vital for survival.[65] Harvey's father was able to enlarge his barn in 1937 and buy eighty adjoining acres in 1938, which became Harvey's home when he married in 1940. William Rohlik struggled economically on his farm in the town of Birchwood in Washburn County, especially after his wife died in 1931. But his daughter Rose contributed her salary as a teacher to the family economy, and the farm remained in the family to pass on to William's eldest son. On the Goldsworthy farm near Three Rivers in Oneida County, the addition of eight tourist cottages to what had been a dairy farm provided essential income, although it "required a lot of work" from all family members, according to then-teenager Walt Goldsworthy.[66]

Just like many individual cutover farmers managed to survive the Depression, not all places in the region met the fate of Velebit and the Severson Community and lost most of their population. In 1940, on the Antigo Flats surrounding the city of Antigo and extending north-westward in Langlade County, and on the West Shawano Upland south of the city extending into Shawano and Marathon counties, settlers practiced viable agriculture in well-settled communities with, in the words at the time of a social-scientist observer, "a degree of prosperity."[67] For example, seven land survey townships in south central Langlade County—about 250 square miles—together had an average rural farm population of about twenty-four people per square mile. This density was similar to that of the well-developed counties of southern and eastern Wisconsin, which had between nineteen and twenty-six rural farm people per square mile.[68] This region supported such a level of population because it was mostly cleared and in farms; by 1933 in the town of Antigo, only about one quarter of the land was forested.[69]

Several factors contributed to the pattern of success in this area. It was adjacent to older, well-established sections of east-central Wisconsin. Soils—such as the Antigo Silt Loam on the Antigo Flats—were very good. Timber harvesters had built a network of roads and railroads through the region. These links, in turn, connected the region with the Chicago market for dairy products. Organized in the 1920s, the Antigo Milk Producers Cooperative enabled farmers to sell cheese and fluid milk in the Chicago market at prices above what they had been receiving. The success of this cooperative encouraged other such enterprises, such as

Figure 4.2. Mr. and Mrs. Fred Goodwill and their children (right) proudly pose in front of their home near Antigo, June 1, 1933. (State Historical Society of Wisconsin, photo WH (W6) 21512)

the cooperative grocery that did $177,000 in business in 1937. Antigo also had a cooperative hatchery, feed warehouse, and maple syrup evaporating plant. Finally, the region's relative success in the 1930s was due to the fact that it had been largely developed before 1920; more-established settlers were better able to weather the downturn of the 1920s and 1930s, and the region had little undeveloped land to attract poor newcomers. Although a few back-to-the-land types found small plots near the city of Antigo in the 1930s, overall in five of the seven well-developed Langlade County townships just mentioned total population peaked in 1910 or 1920.[70] Farms in this region increasingly resembled those in the older portions of the state. In Langlade County as a whole (including less developed districts in the northern part of the county) during the 1930s, herd size increased to 7.8 cows (9 on farms with any dairy cows); in Shawano County it increased to 11.2 (12 on farms with any dairy cows). Shawano exceeded the statewide rate of increase, and its herds were actually larger by 1940, on average, than the 10.8 dairy cows on the typical Wisconsin farm. An average cow in Shawano County in 1940 produced 702 gallons of milk, 7.5 percent greater than the state average, and cows in Langlade County were not far behind by producing on average 629 gallons (up from 502 in 1930).[71]

The experience of ongoing farmers on the Antigo Flats, on the one hand, balanced that of back-to-the-land grubbers in the town of Bayfield, on the other hand, and consequently overall migration patterns in northern Wisconsin during the interwar years resembled those of the United States as a whole. The common—and contradictory—images of the cutover as "abandoned" by ruined farmers and overpopulated by an immobile "stranded" population were both exaggerations.[72] The data in Table 4.3 show that in the first four decades of the twentieth century rates of horizontal mobility by farmers, at least in the communities selected as representative for study, fell within the common range in the United States.[73] Since the towns selected for study in Sawyer County include most of the Wisconsin Colonization Company's territory, it seems that the reports of wholesale abandonment of the land by its settlers were exaggerated or anecdotal. Furthermore, it appears that—like elsewhere in nineteenth- and twentieth-century America—residential stability of farm operators increased as the community matured. Understandably, more established farmers were less likely to relocate. In the case of the cutover, this meant that there was more turnover of farm operators in the prosperous days *before* 1920 than in the distressed period afterwards.

The cutover was also similar to other places in that horizontal mobility decreased during economic downturns. John Styczinski, who started farming in Rusk County in 1908 on land bought from the Faast Land Company, recalled that conditions were "tough" during the Depression, but that he stayed on his farm because there were no better prospects elsewhere. (In the long run, Styczinski was able to prosper, enlarging his herd to forty cows before turning his farm over to his son in 1956.) A rural mail carrier around Ojibwa, in Sawyer County, noted this pattern in 1932 when he reported that "we have had more desertion in the past than there is now."[74] In fact, nationwide the growth in rural population which occurred during the 1930s was more the result of increased retention on farms, especially in less commercially oriented regions such as the cutover, than it was the result of massive numbers of new settlers coming "back-to-the-land."[75]

Table 4.3. Residential Stability, Farm Operators, Selected Cutover Towns, 1900–1940

	n =	Percent Remaining	Percent Remaining as Farmers
Rusk County (towns of Dewey, Grow, Marshall, Big Falls)			
1900–1910	42	29	29
1925–1935	401	51	n.a.
1930–1940	393	61	53
1910–1925	160	21	n.a.
1925–1940	401	42	36
Sawyer County (towns of Ojibwa, Radisson, Lenroot)			
1910–1920	98	33	33
1925–1935	192	41	n.a.
1930–1940	207	51	45
1910–1925	99	21	n.a.
1925–1940	192	35	30

Source: U.S. Manuscript Census, 1900, 1910; Wisconsin Department of Agriculture, Annual Enumeration of Agricultural Statistics, 1925, 1930, 1935, 1940; tax ledgers, Rusk County, 1930, 1940; Sawyer County, 1910, 1920, 1930, 1940, ARC, UWEC.

Overall horizontal mobility rates—not just those of farm operators—also showed that the cutover was not unusual compared with the norm in the United States. In a pattern similar to that of farm operators, overall migration *from* the cutover between 1935 and 1940 was close to the national average of 13 percent, and only half that of devastated regions like the high plains and eastern Oregon and Washington. Furthermore, despite the appearances created by the back-to-the-land movement, migration *into* the cutover actually was at a little lower than the national rate (although close to that of the state and the Midwest as a whole). Consequently, net migration was slightly negative, but at less than half the rate of loss from the central plains or the southeastern coastal plain.[76]

Those families which did leave the cutover in the 1930s did not necessarily abandon the goal of becoming yeoman farmers. In general, most rural farm migration in the north central state in the late 1930s resulted in relocation to another rural farm location.[77] More specifically indicative of the continued commitment to yeoman farming even among struggling cutover farmers was their involvement in the federally sponsored scheme to settle the Matanaska Valley in Alaska. In 1935, 201 families drawn mostly from relief rolls in the Great Lakes cutover, 68 of them from Wisconsin, went by train and boat to an area sixty miles north of Seward, where they drew lots for forty- and eighty-acre homesteads on which they had to build their homes and barns. "This is a godsend," said Earl Barry of Oconto County as he left Wisconsin with his wife and seven children. "Life has been discouraging," said Frank Bailey, another migrant; "maybe I'll have some of the same kind of pioneer spirit as my parents." The success record of these colonists was mixed: twenty-three families of the Wisconsin group remained in 1948, seven in 1985, few as full-time farmers. Put together by bureaucrats and drawn from residents of three states, the Matanaska colonists lacked the social ties, especially of family and ethnicity, which initially sustained most new American farming communities. But the migrants to Alaska showed the remarkable commitment to earning an independent living from the land that characterized settlers of the cutover. "I loved it out there," emphasized Grace Morrison, who left after three years only because of her husband's dissatisfaction. Grace eventually relocated, not insignificantly, back to Washburn County in northern Wisconsin.[78]

This commitment by farmers to living in the cutover and the degree of residential stability it encouraged requires a reexamination of the tax delinquency problem. Actually, while tax shortfalls were real problems for towns and counties in the cutover, the source of the problem was not primarily individual farmers. A 1929 study of Bayfield County, focused on the town of Pilsen, noted this pattern. The report concluded that most of the 156 farms in the town had been tax delinquent at one time or another during the 1920s. But it emphasized that almost all these delinquencies were cleared up before the farm could have been lost for taxes and that only 7 percent were actually encumbered for taxes on January 1, 1929. The major problem area, rather, was undeveloped properties owned by individual speculators and by land companies. Two thirds of the land descriptions in the former category and one third in the latter category were delinquent. The report concluded that "agricultural land as a whole is paying its taxes remarkably well."[79] There was a similar pattern in Rusk County, even when the analysis is limited to developed properties, as Table 4.4 shows. Owners did not pay their 1930 taxes on almost one third of these property descriptions in three sample towns (about 80 percent of which were farms). But a significant percentage of these delinquent taxes were paid before tax deeds were sold on June 9, 1931 (the towns of Marshall and Grow encouraged this by foregoing interest and penalties). Over the next few years, before the transfer of title by tax deed became final, at least 40 percent of the original owners were able to repurchase the tax deed and secure their property. Overall, less than one third of the owners of land who did not pay their 1930 taxes as scheduled eventually lost their property, and only three of these properties—2 percent of the original delinquencies—passed off the tax rolls into the hands of the county. Not much of the shrinking tax base in Rusk County was the result of abandoned farms.[80]

Similarly, a closer look at the records of the Union Mortgage Loan Company, whose 1934 demise appeared to epitomize the failure of cutover farming, suggests that the company's problems were not entirely or even primarily the fault of northern Wisconsin farmers. Most of the company's losses came from operations of dubious legality which were not directly related to financing cutover settlers. One example was the "Lake Property" in Chippewa County, adjacent to the cutover. In 1916 UML loaned George Lake $15,000 on a four-hundred-acre property for

Table 4.4. Disposition of Tax Delinquent Developed Property, Rusk County, 1930 (towns of Grow, Dewey, and Marshall)

	Number Retained by Original Owner	Number Possibly Lost
Developed properties	448*	
Tax delinquent properties	144	
Delinquencies voided	2	0
Redeemed by June 7, 1931		
By owner	63	0
By other	0	4
Subtotal	63	4
Sold for tax deed		
Repurchased by owner	30	0
Repurchased by institution	0	16.5
Repurchased by other individual	0	16.5
Title to private owner	0	7
Title to county	0	3
Disposition unclear	0	2
Subtotal	30	45
Recapitulation	95	49

*1930 U.S. Census of Agriculture reported 369 "farms" in these towns.
Source: Rusk County, Treasurer's Records: Tax Sales Records, 1930, ARC, UWEC.

which he had paid $40,000 a few years previously (hardly the typical cutover farm!). This loan enabled Lake to pay off a $10,000 mortgage due to Northwestern Mutual Life and other smaller obligations. The key figure in the transaction appeared to have been lumber magnate John S. Owen, a former director of UML. Owen had originally sold Lake the property and taken back a second mortgage for $9,000. When a 1922 fire caused $7,400 of damages to the farm, Owen persuaded the president of UML to endorse over the insurance proceeds to satisfy this second mortgage. UML foreclosed on the first mortgage and took possession of the farm in 1927 when Lake and a series of speculators who subsequently bought the property defaulted on their payments. However, due to the fire losses and general decline of property values in the 1920s, the $18,000 owed to UML on the property was "much more than the value of the mortgaged premises" the company now possessed. UML's new president declined counsel's opinion to proceed legally against Owen since he was too powerful and "might endeavor to hurt us if he so inclined." Insider Owen got his money out of the "Lake Property"; the company was stuck paying taxes on a farm it was unable to resell.

Meanwhile UML was making large loans in the Dakotas which violated its own lending guidelines. Two loans to the bankers and real estate developers Hugh and M.C. Egan of Beach, North Dakota, which UML's president later maintained in a personal letter were "fraudulent," were the most spectacular examples of this practice. In 1919 Hugh Egan received a $22,000 loan on 2,240 acres in Wilbaux County, Montana, which he valued at $44,600; M.C. Egan got $36,000 "to pay a part of the purchase price" on 5,570 undeveloped acres he valued at $86,347. These two loans represented almost half the business the company wrote in 1919. This unwarranted risk badly hurt UML; the company became a major Montana landowner when it took possession of these properties by foreclosure in 1922–1923. The mortgages eventually had to be written off as total losses, leaving the company to report a net loss of over $100,000—on $50,000 in revenues—in 1929.[81] It was these activities, of dubious legality and undertaken at least five hundred miles from the Wisconsin cutover, that drove UML into eventual bankruptcy.

The 1920s and 1930s were difficult times for farm people in northern Wisconsin. The fracturing of the growth nexus which had characterized the previous two decades discouraged many settlers and left some economically distressed. But these problems were not new in the history of rural America or confined to the cutover in the 1930s. At previous times and in other places in American history, yeoman farming—relatively small-scale and diversified, based on family labor, linked to but not dominated by the market, economically and socially dependent on other farmers in the community—had survived vicissitudes. The conservative values it was based on often were advantageous in surviving these vicissitudes, since they encouraged yeoman farming communities not to change and thereby expose themselves to potentially serious mistakes. Some of the advantages of this survival mechanism helped the cutover sidestep the worst blows of income losses and property value declines in the 1920s. Cutover farmers intensified the family economy and reliance on supplemental off-farm work which had always characterized them, and looked for new sources of income such as tourism. These practices showed that some cutover farmers had achieved their goal of resembling family farmers in more developed parts of rural America. Their attachment to their communities kept them from abandoning their farms and joining the peripatetic migration which made such an impact on the national consciousness in the 1930s.

But the spirit of yeoman farming was not enough to resist the ravages of the Great Depression. The still-incomplete nature of settlement in northern Wisconsin meant that the region could not rebound from the stress of the early 1930s as ably as could other poor but more mature rural regions, such as Union County in southern Illinois, examined by anthropologist Jane Adams. As Larry Garneau said about his wife's parents, Swedish immigrants who farmed in the town of Drummond in Bayfield County, "They just had a lot of hope and if the Depression had not come they probably would have been ok."[82] State and federal governments had decided by 1920 not to subsidize directly the cost of land purchase and clearing in the cutover, leaving newly arrived settlers, in particular, undercapitalized. The economic downturn exposed the inherent physical limitations of the region, just as melting snow sometimes showed naive settlers the true nature of the land they had bought. A farming venture which was risky but possible at 1914–1919 commodity price levels now became futile. The situation appeared even worse than it actually was because of a crisis in public finance among cutover municipalities. This crisis was a legacy of a local governmental system inherited from the lumber era and sustained by the now exploded expectation that population would grow rapidly enough to fill in an elaborate infrastructure. Farmers were not for the most part responsible for starving their local governments by nonpayment of taxes, but they suffered from the resulting deterioration of services and growing public image that they were living in an impoverished region. Government assistance came from Madison and Washington, but largely in the form of relief programs which were so heavily utilized for such an extensive period that cutover residents apparently would never be able to stand on their own feet. As state, and especially federal governmental policy shifted to restricting the number and output of farms in the 1930s, the agricultural future of the cutover became problematic.

5 | A New View of the Cutover, 1925–1940

I can show you
where Dillinger sweated
at Little Bohemia

Where Mayor Kelly
rubbed his belly
and shot
well bodyguarded rounds of golf
  Robert Peters, "Eagle River, Wisconsin: 1930"[1]

The headline on the front page of the *New York Times* on April 23, 1934, announced, "Dillinger is Surrounded in a Forest in Wisconsin: National Guard Called." For the next week, the focus of the *Times* and other U.S. newspapers was on northern Wisconsin. The most notorious criminal in the country, John Dillinger, had escaped from a shootout with agents of the nation's premier law enforcement agency, the Federal Bureau of Investigation, and vanished into the cutover.

The details of this incident and how it was presented to the American public reveal a great deal about the cutover in the 1930s and its relationship to the rest of the United States. They dramatically illustrated the way in which the region was presented to Americans as backward and dangerous. The investigations of social scientists in the 1920s and 1930s seemed to give substance to these journalistic accounts. Together the picture they presented of the cutover justified—indeed, seemed to necessitate—that outside planners and government officials step in with new public policies and redirect the way in which northern Wisconsin was developing. People living in the region, however, especially farmers still attached to the dream of yeoman agriculture, were not altogether enthusiastic about this chain of events.

Wanted for a series of bank robberies and jail breaks, in mid-April 1934 Dillinger and nine cohorts quietly drove to Little Bohemia, which the

New York Times described as a "backwoods resort" just off United States Highway 51 on Little Star Lake, one mile from Manitowish Waters in Vilas County. Emil Wanatka, a small-time Chicago speakeasy operator who had married a local girl, ran the resort and recognized Dillinger. Disdaining the local authorities, Wanatka impressed an in-law to drive him fifty miles to Rhinelander, where he telephoned to the FBI office in Chicago. Hastily arranged flights swiftly brought planeloads of special agents to Rhinelander, where they commandeered five cars (two of which broke down) for the trip to Little Bohemia on Sunday night, April 22. The agents fanned out on three sides of the lodge, but became cold and confused and aroused a barking dog. The agents shot and killed one innocent local resident and wounded two others when they stepped out of the lodge to go to their cars. An alerted Dillinger and his colleagues leaped from a second floor window onto a snowbank in the rear of the building. Taking advantage of what the *Times* described as a "blizzard" and "impassable woods," they escaped along the unguarded lake side of the lodge. Ignoring reports from local residents that their prey had fled, the agents continued to besiege Little Bohemia for several hours until they finally broke in and discovered only three molls shaking with fear.[2]

Dillinger quickly escaped into Minnesota; his confederate Baby Face Nelson killed a G-man and hid for a few days at the "shack" of Ole Catfish, an Ojibway who lived near the Lac du Flambeau reservation, before making his getaway. They left behind panic in northern Wisconsin. Jack Plano remembered that "I can recall going fishing the day after that shootout with a buddy. Both of us kept wondering if John Dillinger, with a pistol in either hand, would likely jump out of the bushes at any moment and confront us." London newspapers reported that "lumberjacks with pickaxes" and "red Indians" with "bows and arrows" had joined in the chase. Criticism mounted against the FBI both in Washington and in northern Wisconsin. The Lakeland Development Association of Mercer forwarded to the Justice Department a petition charging the agents with negligence and "criminal stupidity" in not seeking local assistance and in allowing the fugitives to escape. The *Times* reported "natives laughing loud, long and bitterly"; the article's author quoted an unnamed source with a hick accent derisively describing the FBI agents as "revenooers." A coroner's jury eventually ruled that the death at Little Bohemia was accidental, but only after assistant FBI director Hugh Clegg and other agents inaccurately left the impression in their testimony that the shooting had occurred during a "crossfire" at the lodge.[3]

Press accounts about Dillinger and his pursuers increased the existing public perception that northern Wisconsin was a region of lawlessness. A 1913 investigation headed by state senator Howard Teasdale had found twenty-one municipally tolerated brothels in a segregated vice district in Superior, the largest such concentration in the state.[4] No place in the United States had a more lurid reputation than Hurley, a mining-based community in Iron County on the Michigan border, which had long boasted of being the "toughest place in the world." Its extensive and wide-open saloons, gambling, and prostitution made it the setting for Edna Ferber's popular novel *Come and Get It*. Prohibition-related problems enhanced Hurley's image. Newspaper readers in Milwaukee in 1920 read about federal and county officials prosecuting one another over responsibility for a death in a raid on a Hurley saloon. In 1938 after the repeal of Prohibition, 80 of the 115 establishments in Hurley's business district were saloons.[5] In Hurley and elsewhere in Wisconsin, gambling was illegal, but in the cutover in was widely tolerated. "Each year at the Lincoln County Fair," recalled Jack Plano, "one of the most popular attractions was the ever present Bingo tent. . . . The police were reluctant to enforce the anti-gambling laws since the majority of the townspeople seemed to accept [reject?] them."[6]

As a result of these sorts of activities, the cutover appeared as Sodom to most Wisconsinites. After a trip through northern Wisconsin in 1926, Albert O. Barton, a prominent Progressive journalist in the state, privately denounced the numerous "moonshine joints often run by high-powered crooks, who boldly defy the law and debauch the neighborhood" and the "large percentage of men and women in the region [who] are making their living making moonshine."[7] Newspaper reports from northern Wisconsin in the Milwaukee newspapers during the interwar years, when not about forest fires, hunting accidents, or bear attacks, usually featured crime. Representative headlines included: "Three Are Shot in Antigo Street"; "Gunman Slain Robbing Cafe"; "Aged Farm Brothers Whip, 'Torture,' Gunmen, Kill One: Fists, Hatchet Conquer Guns and Hot Pokers."[8]

In the popular mind in the 1920s, crime was associated with the enforcement—or nonenforcement—of the Prohibition laws. Wisconsin as a whole was less than enthusiastic about Prohibition, compared to most parts of the United States, but northern Wisconsin in particular appeared to be a "wet" region. Voters in the cutover gave only lukewarm support to enforcing the state's Prohibition law, the Mulberger Act, in a referendum in November 1920 (Table 5.1); the Yes vote in all but one cutover county was below the state average. After Prohibition went into effect, as a sparsely settled region in proximity to Chicago and the Twin Cities, the cutover was an ideal location for the production or transshipment from Canada of beverages outlawed by the Mulberger and Volstad acts. Especially as their economic woes mounted, most cutover residents were not too particular about how they earned income. According to the historian of the town of Three Lakes in Oneida County, residents believed that the "ends justified the means," and that bootlegging was necessary for "survival." Knute Anderson recalled that around Luck, in northern Polk County, "making moon" from potatoes was a "sideline for some people." An anonymous contributor to the history of Forest County described fourteen stills in and around Crandon during "the bootleg alcohol days" which focused on supplying the Twin Cities market. A Crandon pastor reported in 1928 that "the whole County is honey-comb[ed] with Bootleggers, it seems impossible for local authorities to cope with the situation." The Chicago and Northwestern express train which crossed the county was known locally as the "Whiskey Northern." When Prohibition finally ended in Price County, the Park Falls newspaper cynically editorialized that it "will mean little to Park Falls" since the city "has not been dry."[9]

Reports about violence and corruption which resulted from this widespread ignoring of the Prohibition laws helped give northern Wisconsin a negative image. The Milwaukee newspapers prominently featured stories about police raids and other violence at stills and speakeasies in the cutover. These articles displayed such headlines as, "Two Chicago Gangsters Shot in North," an account of a shootout at a Shawano-area roadhouse related to factional fighting within the teamsters union. Stories about the involvement of public officials in these sorts of activities

Table 5.1. Referendum on Prohibition Enforcement, November 2, 1920

	Yes (%)	No (%)	Percent of State Vote
Cutover	63.5	36.5	10.7
Milwaukee	71.7	28.3	20.4
Rest of the state	67.2	32.7	68.9
Wisconsin	67.7	32.3	

Source: Wisconsin Blue Book, 1921 (Madison, 1921), 226–27.

created an aura of corruption about all of northern Wisconsin. Particularly unsavory were the publicly aired charges and counter-charges between competing political factions in Forest County in the 1920s. In 1925 a candidate backed by the Connor Lumber and Land Company ousted County Judge James Walsh, a central figure in the "Crandon Bunch" faction, charging the incumbent with drunkenness, financial ties to moonshiners, and having a sexual relationship with a teenage girl. The following year, a grand jury investigation of corruption led to 170 indictments, mostly for prohibition violations, and 40 convictions. Former county board member Joseph Sherman went to state prison for adultery and cohabitation. Then in 1928, Governor Fred R. Zimmerman removed County Sheriff William Clawson from office for malfeasance amid Connor-instigated charges that Clawson took bribes from bootleggers, tipped-off moonshiners about raids, drank heavily himself, and allowed prisoners to escape from the county jail.[10]

Familiarity with the region from bootlegging activities led organized crime leaders like Dillinger to vacation in northern Wisconsin. Al Capone reportedly spent $250,000 in the 1920s for a four-bedroom fieldstone house with machine-gun portals and an eight-car garage six miles south of Courderay on Cranberry Lake in Sawyer County. His brother Ralph had a lodge near Mercer, a few miles from Dillinger's hideaway at Little Bohemia.[11] The spread of the highway network in northern Wisconsin (chapter two) made the region especially attractive to vacationers like the Capones, who understandably did not want to rely on public transportation. Crime barons also found a generally tolerant, even welcoming public attitude. In 1990, John Blork, who helped build Al Capone's lodge and worked there for nine years, still insisted, "I have never worked for nicer people."[12] Public officials were similarly accommodating. In the fall of 1933, Joseph Wilkie, who had recently moved to the Sugarbush area in Price County, was found dead in the woods. He had been shot in the back of the head with his own gun and found kneeling, an obvious gang execution. A cooperative coroner's jury ruled it an accidental death, caused by Wilkie tripping and his gun discharging when it hit a tree limb![13]

Even ostensible anticrime efforts in the cutover left observers wondering whether northern Wisconsinites knew the difference between civilization and savagery. For example, in 1939 a "posse" of Sawyer County residents spent two weeks tracking down a fugitive escaped felon, Augie Buelow. Buelow killed two volunteer deputies before the posse found and killed him. A newspaper photographer then snapped what was captioned as a "ghastly" photo of eight proud and grinning posse members hunched over Buelow's dead body, their rifles stacked on the corpse, as if at the successful conclusion of a deer hunt. The intensity of the emotional relief from surviving the dangers of the chase could explain the posse's inappropriate pose, but even a local historian conceded that the photo publicly revealed "much that was very ugly" about Sawyer County.[14]

Press coverage of the Dillinger episode in 1934 further reinforced in the public mind the idea that the cutover was isolated, exotic, lawless, and dangerous. The necessity of airlifting agents to Rhinelander and then having them struggle over bad roads in rickety cars to the scene of Dillinger's hideout pointed out the cutover's distance from "civilization." Indeed, the *Milwaukee Journal* characterized Vilas County as "ideal for a game of hide and seek between outlaws and officers."[15] The snow conditions—in late April!—that reportedly assisted Dillinger's escape gave the impression that northern Wisconsin was in the Arctic. The involvement of Native Americans in the story further suggested wild, "uncivilized" conditions. The *Milwaukee Journal* played to the stereotypes of its readers by printing a photograph of Ole Catfish's "shack" and its litter-strewn yard.[16] Readers who followed press reports of the incident could not have missed the point that both Emil Wanatka and the FBI avoided involving local law-enforcement officials. Reports over the previous decade of the cutover's lawlessness made outsiders or newcomers reluctant to trust anyone in northern Wisconsin.

When not seen as dangerous, the cutover increasingly appeared exotic to outsiders. This view developed before 1920 (chapter 3), and subsequently received encouragement from the growing emphasis on promoting tourism in the region. Early in the century, Chicago newspapers told about a "hodag," a mythical 185-pound seven-foot-long lizardlike beast, in captivity at Ballard Lake resort near Rhinelander.[17] During the interwar years, purple-prose journalism, encouraged by local boosters looking for tourists, spread the image of the cutover as a place of exotic practices. For example, in 1930 the *Chicago Tribune* described the area around Lac du Flambeau in Vilas County as "the nation's last frontier." It reported that "the far north of Wisconsin has changed little since . . . voyageurs travelled its streams."[18] During the same year the *Milwaukee Journal*'s Sunday magazine serialized the novel *Flambeau*, a "fascinating northwood's romance." Its protagonist had "deep-dyed hatreds and consuming passions that seethed in his blood [and] made a veritable beast out of him."[19]

Some of the exotic aspects of the cutover placed the region in an outwardly benign light, but with invidious undertones. For example, President Calvin Coolidge spent ten weeks during the summer of 1928 at Cedar Lake Lodge, thirty miles south of Superior on the Brule River in Douglas County. Coolidge fully enjoyed his holiday, and the subsequent national publicity pleased local boosters, especially those interested in developing tourism as an alternative or supplement to farming in the region's economy.[20] But newspaper reporters assigned to Coolidge made the cutover seem attractive because of its wild and isolated quality. They described laborious twice-a-week journeys of almost an hour by the President in order to transact public business and meet with officials who had made the long journey from Washington to Superior. Local "color" stories featured Ojibway Indian lore. Reporters were amazed that night temperatures in late August fell close to freezing; the *New York Times* characterized the day before Coolidge left the Brule in early September as a "bleak, cold day."[21]

Press coverage of both Coolidge and Dillinger's experience in northern Wisconsin emphasized the presence of Native Americans in the region. Like the Coolidge visit, the continued existence of Indians had an ambiguous effect on the image of white settlers in the cutover. The exotic crafts and rituals of native peoples attracted tourists to northern Wisconsin, helping the economy of the white settlers.[22] But their presence suggested that these settlers were still living on the margins of civilization. The Milwaukee newspapers treated Indians as curiosities, giving them only trivial coverage. "Indian Mother Saves Bleeding Child With Buckskin Tourniquet," was the headline of one of the few items about Native Americans.[23]

From the perspective of native people themselves, the decades of white influx were clearly sad times. Indian communities lost integrity as whites bought large portions of reservations that had been alloted to individual Indians as a consequence of the General Allotment Act of 1887. By 1940 barely one third of the land at Lac du Flambeau was indisputably owned by Indians. Indian-owned tracts, furthermore, were noncontiguous and, as a result of inheritance practices, often in shared ownership among many of the allottees' descendants. On their reservations, therefore, Native Americans lived checkerboard-fashion among the recreational homes of whites, unable to use their land effectively for timber-cutting or other purposes. At Lac Courte Oreilles, furthermore, many families had lost their ancestral homes and had to relocate in the

1920s when construction of a hydroelectric dam flooded almost one tenth of the reservation. The 1919 flu epidemic also struck them particularly hard—over 10 percent of the reservation's population died. There was little understanding in the white community about these developments.[24] But in spite of these problems, Native Americans survived in northern Wisconsin. The census of 1940 reported 5,234 Indians living in the cutover, up about 4 percent from 1930 and about 10 to 15 percent from 1905 (chapter 1).[25]

As they had done since the time of initial contact, Indians selectively adapted traits and practices from white Americans in order to survive and maintain some cultural integrity. However, few Native Americans were interested in farming, despite the efforts of agricultural extension agents. At Lac du Flambeau, about one third of allottees chose to take their eighty-acre plots in more than one segment, reflecting subsistence customs and hindering the practice of settled agriculture. Furthermore, the strongly held white belief in Indian inferiority undercut white efforts to make Indians farmers like themselves—deep-down, whites felt Native Americans could not succeed at farming.[26] Some Native Americans did earn a tiny income working for white farmers during the late summer potato and cranberry harvests. Others earned cash or store credit by producing traditional crafts or food products. Violet Neu Olkowski, whose father operated a grocery store in Three Rivers in Oneida County from 1892 to 1937, recalled "a flourishing business with the Indians which was strictly barter with no cash exchanged. The Indians got their staples in return for birch bark canoes, baskets, beaded moccasins, wild rice, greens and ginseng roots."[27] Some American Indians also worked as hunting and fishing guides for the tourists on whom the economy of northern Wisconsin increasingly depended. Others exhibited traditional songs and dances at specially arranged powwows for tourists.

The experience in the 1930s of the father of Peter Turner, a Forest County Potawatomi, illustrated what Native Americans in northern Wisconsin had to do to earn a living. The elder Turner worked as an itinerant agricultural laborer, raised beans on contract from a cannery, cut wood in the winter, worked on WPA projects, and spent several weeks every summer dancing for tourists at Wisconsin Dells. After acquiring a car about 1940, Peter's father "started working more places, farther away." During World War II he would work in the government ammunition plant at Baraboo. In effect, Peter's father was following the twentieth-century equivalent of the traditional seasonally-shifting pattern of American Indian subsistence. But, as Peter acknowledged, "that was a tough way to live." Like most Native Americans in northern Wisconsin, the Turners remained in poverty. Then "we came home late one Saturday afternoon from town shopping, all of us, and there was the house burned down. . . . Maybe the whites set it on fire to get rid of us."[28]

The authors of the WPA Guide for Wisconsin summed up the plight of these Native Americans at the end of the 1930s. "Deprived of even the discarded submarginal land originally given them, many Indians are living almost at starvation level. Their only income is derived from selling trinkets, berries, or wild rice, or acting as guides or servants to occasional tourists."[29] Would this also become the ultimate fate of the white settlers who had taken their lands?

Indian-white relations, consequently, were problematic. Many white settlers had only contempt for Native Americans. They saw them as dirty, lazy, thieving, and alcoholic, and blamed them for the forest fires burning across the cutover. "Whites found these reds useful," admitted Nell Peters, who grew up near the Lac du Flambeau Reservation during the 1930s, "for it says you aren't lost if there's somebody worse off than you."[30] A few whites did report positive relations with American Indians. In Burnett County in the late nineteenth century, the members of the Oscar family "were friendly with the Indians who walked past their log cabin, and were always ready to lend a hand to the natives. . . . In return, the Indians would bring game or wild rice to the Oscars." The Johnson family "never locked the doors and mother always left a loaf of bread on the table for any Indian that might stop."[31] Such cordiality, however, seldom produced close relationships, even as whites increasingly infiltrated reservations in the twentieth century and lived in closer proximity to Native Americans. Intermarriage was taboo. Ralph Carpersen recalled a woman who married a Red Cliff Ojibway, a chief and a Christian: "My folks had known the chief's wife when she was a girl, but when she appeared in church, she was ignored. She had crossed the color line and was banished from our lily-white society."[32] White understanding of Native Americans fell victim to this cultural gap in northern Wisconsin as it did throughout rural America. White settlers interpreted Indian shyness as stupidity; they saw Indian expectations of sharing material goods when needed as thievery.[33] Even whites who tried to understand Native Americans came across as patronizing. The WPA Guide, for example, in describing a CCC camp at Lac du Flambeau, concluded that, if "put to work at enterprises they understand, Indians have demonstrated remarkable ability to accomplish cooperative undertakings."[34] In the first half of the twentieth century, northern Wisconsin Indians had little choice but to accept this treatment quietly and exhibit themselves in ways that tourists and other whites expected. They understood what was happening to them, however, and did not like it. Peter Turner's father "had to keep borrowing things from them, like their horses and plows and a sled," but "he really hated them whites around there."[35]

That the cutover was Calvin Coolidge's vacationland and the home of several thousand Native Americans brought out its wilderness qualities and suggested its unsuitability for agricultural settlement. Its isolation and bracing weather, however, made it seem a perfect place for a tuberculosis sanatorium. Lake Tomahawk State Camp opened in Oneida County in 1915, and was described by its first superintendent as a "camp in the wilderness."[36] The best-known tuberculosis sanatorium in the United States was at Saranac Lake in the Adirondacks in New York, a state-designated wilderness area. Uses of the cutover like Lake Tomahawk suggested that northern Wisconsin should develop in the direction of the Adirondacks rather than that of Dane or Trempealeau counties in Wisconsin.

Other qualities which the cutover seemed to have in abundance even more clearly contributed to a negative picture of the region. From Hurley's brothels an image of illicit sexuality spread to all the region's residents, encouraged by the stories of local officials going to jail for sex offenses. Observers openly hinted at widespread incest. "As a result of generations of eugenic carelessness, they lack the fiber to do anything for themselves," reported one field worker. "The way they live is bound to breed degenerates."[37] In the same spirit, the *New York Times* reported "moral squalor" across the region.[38] The cutover's poverty also was vividly impressed in the minds of Americans living outside the region. A New Deal planning agency made selective use of impressionistic evidence to report that most homes in the cutover were very poor, many were tarpaper shacks, and the residents lacked community feeling because many were immigrants separated by barriers of language and distance from one another. The *WPA Guide* described settlers "still living in crude log cabins and tarpaper shacks, . . . piecing out an existence in the backwoods. . . . Often in winter they become snowbound and must be rescued by dog teams."[39] As Americans in the 1930s became concerned about endemic poverty among tenant farmers in the rural South and Okie families abandoning Dust Bowl farms, they projected alleged characteristics of these regions' residents—lazy, stupid, oversexed—onto northern Wisconsin settlers.[40] The conclusion was that farmers in the cutover were part of a "socially undesirable settlement" which created an "unstable culture" that, if not limited, would "create in Wisconsin a class of crackers."[41] A headline in the *New York Times* summed up the grim picture that was emerging: "Wilderness Slums Worry Wisconsin."[42]

Commentators increasingly blamed cutover residents themselves for the conditions in which they lived, an attitude which appeared in the early 1920s (chapter 3) and expanded as economic conditions deteriorated in northern Wisconsin. Social science reports in the 1930s often emphasized anecdotes about settlers who refused to work and demanded government services, even public assistance, as an entitlement. Bushrod W. Allin described such a settler in the town of Wilson in Lincoln County: "He didn't farm; and is reported as saying that he hadn't worked a day in his life and didn't intend to." Geographer Harvey A. Uber reported that in the cutover because of their "culture" (i.e., "inherited traits and capabilities"), "many of the farmers are of a type, that even if placed on good land they could not make a success of farming."[43] Based on these descriptions, it seemed as if the cutover was inculcating a "culture of poverty."

The scholar who most actively developed this view of the cutover and its people in the 1930s was George S. Wehrwein, a student of Richard T. Ely and subsequently his colleague at the Institute for Research in Land Economics and Public Utilities. Wehrwein blasted development policies for "letting the settler locate as he pleased." The result of this practice, he argued, was widespread farm abandonment; consequently scattered, isolated settlers remained on the land. Wehrwein gathered data on three thousand such "isolated" families, and found them often earning little from farming and unable, because of health, age, or gender, to do off-farm work. These settlers contributed little to municipal and school budgets, which in turn were strained to provide costly services to the remote locations in which they lived. There was another, even greater concern to Wehrwein, a close friend of the sociologist and eugenicist Edward A. Ross (another Ely student who later taught at the University of Wisconsin). Because "of the lack of contact with others," Wehrwein argued, "incentives to maintain standards of living and conduct are absent" among "isolated" families in the cutover. Wehrwein feared these settlers would damage the lives of others by drifting into dependency like tenant farmers in the South. "The greatest factor in the tenant situation is the human element. The South has . . . the Negro and a special type of white tenants. . . . These people are not illiterate, inert, thriftless, or shiftless because they are tenants, but they remain tenants because they lack those qualities which enable men to succeed." Large relief rolls convinced Wehrwein that too many of this type of person were present in northern Wisconsin.[44]

Sociologists George W. Hill and Ronald A. Smith developed these themes most fully in their 1941 monograph, *Man in the "Cut-Over": A Study of Family Farm Resources in Northern Wisconsin.*[45] Hill and Smith compared the characteristics of two samples of farmers from one unidentified cutover county, one sample consisting of reliefers and the other of non-reliefers. They found no significant difference in the productivity of the land on which these two groups lived. Rather, they emphasized "the farmer himself" as providing the key difference between relief and non-relief status. Hill and Smith rejected ethnic stereotypes as an explanatory variable, and they allowed that, overall, in the cutover only one fifth of farmers were "agricultural misfits" likely to become dependent on relief. But their explanation about why farmers found themselves in the relief class of their research scheme cast all cutover farmers in a negative light in the eyes of less-than-careful readers of their report. Members of the relief class had values and attitudes which prevented them from becoming economically self-reliant. Half "never had any serious inclination to farm" and were "emotionally biased against farming." They did not belong to community organizations and socialized chiefly among themselves. Their wives scored low on an index evaluating "neatness and general cleanliness of the home," "interest in balanced meals," and similar items. Most alarming to Hill and Smith, "chronic" reliefers in particular had high fertility, confirming "the popular public stereotype." And while they did not explicitly mention incest, Hill and Smith pointed out that the numerous offspring of these chronic reliefers practiced "endogamy." In one community chosen for close analysis, they found "three-fourths of the 40 relief families can be traced to four stem families!" Fifteen of sixteen families in one stem received relief. The authors' message was clear: "replacement is coming, therefore, from the most seriously disadvantaged social class in our population." Given a few years, "agricultural misfits" would dominate the cutover.[46]

This fear was part of a larger concern of policymakers in the first several decades of the twentieth century. Drawing on the work of eugenicists (chapter 3), they believed that the United States was threatened by a syndrome evident in a subculture of women which involved high fertility, low intelligence, and crime. Benign restrictions like institutionalization of women with low IQs could fight the syndrome, but certainly policymakers did not want to allow extensive geographical areas like the cutover to provide the isolation in which it could flourish.[47]

Having concluded that some settlers in the cutover were misfits, it was an easy step for social scientists to begin treating residents of northern Wisconsin more as objects than as people. By the early 1920s, onetime Christian Socialist Richard T. Ely believed that, "like other business men, farmers who have accepted the risk of operating the submarginal land must take their losses."[48] Based on this line of reasoning, social scientists constructed models to determine whether specific settlers would ever pay enough in taxes to balance their costs in road and school operations.[49] For example, one researcher highlighted a situation in which twenty families each paid $10 in taxes and received $185 in services.[50] The fiscal problems of cutover counties were mostly the result of nonpayment of taxes by land companies and individual speculators (chapter 4). However, commentators and officials did not emphasize the pecuniary shortfalls of these institutions, and the timber companies which preceded them, because they demanded little in services from the public treasury. People, on the other hand, needed roads, schools, and even emergency deliveries of firewood. Criticism, therefore, was directed at them. The equations of social scientists also challenged the value of cutover farmers who managed to grow crops for the market: "These submarginal farms add their quota to the general supply, reducing thereby the profits of the farmer on good land as well as on their own."[51]

These attitudes of social scientists were part of a general critique of rural America in the first third of the twentieth century, but were sharper in their criticism of the cutover than of other places. County agents, professors, journalists, and governmental experts wanted to shape rural America into a more "modern," urban mode.[52] Frightened by the frustration expressed by rural people through the Populist movement in the 1890s, these urbanized reformers emphasized the need throughout rural America for better roads, more access to education, improved farming practices, and higher moral standards. They hoped that these policies would at least manintain the level of population in rural America. But by the 1920s many of these reformers became increasingly hostile to the very idea of settlement in northern Wisconsin. Ely's colleague Benjamin Hibbard calculated that even at the relatively rapid pace of development achieved between 1910 and 1920, it would take four hundred years to bring all of the cutover under cultivation.[53] The underlying premise in the approach of these social scientists was the belief that the value of cutover land was set by the market, not its social utility to a farm family. This vision stood in contrast to that of settlers who still desired to become yeoman farmers.[54] Social scientists began to conclude that new public policies were needed for northern Wisconsin, in line with Ely's dictum that "if the use of the land in certain ways leads to undesirable social consequences, it is an undesirable use and should be changed."[55]

Changing conceptions of northern Wisconsin's physical environment encouraged the growth of the belief that the region needed new developmental policies. Both directly and indirectly, Aldo Leopold—whose life and ideas have inspired much of the late-twentieth-century environmental movement—contributed to this rethinking. As a professor of wildlife management in the state university's Department of Agricultural Economics, Leopold expounded the concept of a "land ethic," by which he meant the appreciation of the aesthetic quality of the environment as a system, including both animals and vegetation. James J. Blaisdell had advocated forest preservation in Wisconsin as necessary for people's spiritual well-being (chapter 1); Leopold added an emphasis on preserving nature's beauty. Leopold worked to develop this aesthetic consciousness through his teaching and writing, but also in practice on an abandoned farm he bought in Sauk County, northwest of Madison. This was not literally in the cutover, but Leopold's accomplishments in changing land use in a poor location from agriculture to providing a habitat for wildlife and a source of pleasure for humans provided an example of what could be done as well in the "problem areas" of northern Wisconsin.[56]

Leopold's ideas about land use were influenced by his colleague and close personal friend, George S. Wehrwein.[57] Leopold outlined these ideas in an article in the *Journal of Land and Public Utility Economics*, the organ of Ely and Wehrwein's research institute. Leopold argued that most remaining wilderness areas in the United States, like those in the "poor areas" of the Great Lakes states, were "entirely devoid of either existing or potential agriculture." He questioned the economic and ecological benefits of extending roads into these areas to attract more tourists. Rather, what was necessary, he felt, was careful planning to reverse the ordinary economic process within wilderness areas. "The retention of certain wild areas," he concluded, "will introduce a healthy variety into the wilderness idea itself," preserving as the primary characteristic of wilderness areas the provision of "living in the open" for humans. Leopold positively contrasted this possibility to the "atmosphere of a pioneer" created by attempts at human settlement in the wildnerness.[58]

While Leopold was encouraging people to think differently about wilderness areas, natural events had a similar effect. Drought conditions were not as severe in the cutover in the 1930s as in some other parts of the United States, but they still had a negative impact on agriculture. Beginning in 1929, rainfall was below normal in northern zone of Wisconsin for seven of the next nine years, and temperatures were above average in eight of these years. Correspondingly, potato yields were below normal in every year, corn yields in seven years, and oat yields in eight years.[59] The promises of bountiful harvests presented by early-twentieth-century promotional literature and the first blossoming of grasses and berries in the wake of timber cutting (chapter 1, especially Figure 1.6) now seemed to be cruel hoaxes.

Advocates of reforestation asserted themselves. Forester P. S. Lovejoy ridiculed efforts at sheep ranching in the cutover (chapter 2): "preposterous beyond all words . . . a dominant illusion, developed and protected and defended with fanatic, though genuine, enthusiasm." With insensitivity and hyperbole, he claimed that cutover land "boomers have, no doubt, ruined more families than did the Germans in Belgium [during World War I]." To Lovejoy, the need for the Lake States to import lumber at rising costs pointed to the necessity of reforestation in the cutover.[60]

Scientists also reevaluated the quality of the land in northern Wisconsin. Beginning in 1927, the state Department of Agriculture sponsored a new series of land inventories for Wisconsin counties. The conclusions of these reports were less positive for northern Wisconsin than those contained in the early-twentieth-century reports of the Wisconsin Geological and Natural History Survey (chapter 1). While by no means completely dismissive of agriculture in the cutover, evaluations made in the interwar years strongly tended to emphasize that only limited portions of northern Wisconsin contained land suitable for farming. For example, A. R. Whitson's 1914 soil survey of Bayfield County had emphasized the soils which could produce "magnificent" crops, and concluded that less than 4 percent of the county should be reforested; in 1916 Whitson estimated that 60–70 percent of Bayfield County would eventually be improved for agriculture. By 1929 a land inventory of the same county concluded that only 40 percent of the soils were "good," 23 percent "fair," and 25 percent "poor." A decade later, the State Planning Board identified only about 10 percent of the county's land as "definitely suited for continued crop use," another 15 percent as suitable for crops under special conditions but most of which should be "retired," and almost 75 percent as "submarginal." The later reports began to encourage alternative land uses: the 1929 report stressed that about one fifth of the county then without forest cover could be profitably planted with pine seedlings. These evaluations made their way into more-widely disseminated reports. A 1930s investigation of "rural problem areas," for example, stated flatly that in the Great Lakes cutover, "recourse to agricultural pursuits is unprofitable because of climate and soil conditions."[61]

It seemed as if the more Wisconsinites and other Americans looked at the cutover, the more they did not like what they saw. In 1896 Frederick Jackson Turner had concluded that since no more land was open for settlement the American frontier was closed. With no frontier, Turner predicted, the future was going to be difficult. The patterns of individualism, commitment to democracy, and opportunity for achievement, which owed their existence to the frontier and had shaped the character of Americans and the history of the United States until the 1890s, could no longer be influential. By contrast, promoters of settlement in the cutover emphasized that the region still provided the opportunities which Turner's broad-brush treatment had identified as disappearing (although they pointed out that settlement in any twentieth-century frontier needed more public and private direction than had been necessary in the nineteenth century). By the 1930s, however, Americans had lost confidence that the cutover could provide the opportunities of earlier frontiers. Indeed, observers now felt that the demise of the frontier was not to be feared; rather, its continued existence was a danger. As the events of the 1920s and 1930s seemed to show, the cutover did not provide economic opportunity or encourage democracy. Instead, it impoverished its settlers and provided a seedbed for political radicalism. It promoted an antisocial individualism, characterized by laziness, immorality, toleration of crime, and welfare dependency. It allowed the continued existence of Native Americans, whose successful elimination—to Turner—was one of the great accomplishments of frontier settlers. Its different ethnic groups did not blend together, as they had done on Turner's frontier, but because of low population density were able to maintain their un-American ways. Most seriously, the antisocial qualities of life in the cutover threatened not only the region's residents, but all Americans.

In the middle third of the twentieth century it seemed easy to see why northern Wisconsin did not resemble a nineteenth-century Turnerian frontier. By then foreign immigration had essentially ended. "Free" land from the federal government was no longer available. The climate of the cutover was harsher and its land poorer in quality than that of the prairies which settlers had opened for farming in the nineteenth century. It now seemed time for an entirely new approach to developing and managing what if anything remained of the frontier in the United States.

Public and private planners were confident that their technocratic vision could engineer the cutover in a new and better direction. Agencies such as the state Department of Immigration had played a role from the beginning in directing settlement in the cutover. With the impetus of New Era thinking in the 1920s, planning became more formalized and systematized. Now government programs encouraged and coordinated private business activities rather than challenging or at least regulating them as they sometimes had in the Progressive Era. Part of this new coordination effort involved using the expertise of social scientists to help individual private business managers make better decisions.

Richard T. Ely adapted his thinking to that of the New Era. His Institute on Research in Land Economics encouraged closer ties between businessmen and social scientists and generated private financing for economic research. The institute worked with a trade group, the National Association of Real Estate Boards, to improve the education of real estate salesmen and qualify them for professional autonomy sanctioned by state licensing. This shift in his thinking reflected Ely's longstanding pragmatic, institutional, and evolutionary ideas about economics. But it encouraged the adoption of new public policies for northern Wisconsin in the 1920s. In the context of changing ideas about cutover settlers, scholars such as Ely now encouraged programs unsympathetic to dirt farmers. In reporting on the National Agricultural Conference he attended in 1922, Ely proudly identified the triumph of "sound thinking" reflected in the meeting's endorsement of President Warren G. Harding's proposals for "diversification," "efficiency," and opposition to inflation. By contrast, Ely denounced "vociferous political advocates of farm relief" who used "demagoguery" and the "rhetoric of oppression." Instead of relief for individuals, Ely recommended impersonal public policies which would alleviate the income shortfalls of cutover farms and the fiscal problems of their municipalities. These policies involved limiting further settlement in northern Wisconsin rather than helping settlers who were already there. "Scrap the poorer land," Ely argued, "and confine production to the better land."[62]

To achieve this goal, Ely and other planners strongly advocated the implementation of rural land classification schemes. Ely believed this should be done by a state commission, which would establish the best economic use of rural land.[63] The basis for its decisions would be data from the increasingly numerous reports about Wisconsin's ecological and economic conditions, reports which were also increasingly critical of conditions in the cutover. Therefore, while by no means completely excluding agriculture, by the late 1920s planners emphasized that most of northern Wisconsin was best suited for reforestation or recreational uses. "Lake States Need Forests," the *Milwaukee Journal* agreed editorially, a position which the *New York Times* also endorsed.[64]

A series of measures translated the planners' recommendations into official public policy. After a 1926 report failed to find greater success by settlers sponsored by projects like Ben Faast's compared to other settlers, Dean Harry Russell and the College of Agriculture finally reversed course and began to discourage farm settlement in the north. The Department of Immigration also stopped its recruiting activities. State government and the organized business interests to which it was responsive instead began to promote tourism and reforestation for northern Wisconsin.[65]

If people should not come to northern Wisconsin to farm, promoters at least wanted them to vacation there. The Milwaukee Association of Commerce pledged $10,000 to "aid the movement to advertise the state . . . as a playground second to none in the country." On the county level, for example, Forest County boosters issued a pamphlet, *The Lodge of Nature's Temple,* an allegory about a weary city businessman who is led by Brother Crandon to the temple of the Goddess of Nature, who mends his spirit by sending him out to be refreshed by the woods and waters of Forest County. By the end of the 1920s, about two hundred summer residents had built homes in Forest County, and lakefront lots cost several hundred dollars per acre.[66]

Public policies encouraged reforestation in northern Wisconsin during the 1920s. A series of state parks developed in the cutover, which met with the enthusiastic approval of boosters like the Park Falls newspaper. To make reforestation economically viable, the state Forest Crop Law of 1927 exempted land designated for reforestation from most taxation, channeled a small annual payment from the state to towns in lieu of this tax revenue, and eventually recovered it through a severance tax when second-growth timber was finally harvested. As Wehrwein emphasized in an article written for popular consumption, the goal of these programs was to make "fullest utilization" of land so as to reduce the tax drain from southern to northern Wisconsin.[67]

To assure that large areas would be available for recreation and re-forestation, planners applied to the cutover an urban innovation of the 1920s—zoning. In 1929 the state legislature authorized counties, with the concurrence of affected towns, to adopt rural zoning ordinances. They could now zone land for exclusive forest, recreational, or agricultural use. Governor Walter J. Kohler praised this development as "a deterrent against ill-advised location of farms." The implementation of zoning meant that there could be no further agricultural settlement in forest or recreational zones, although existing "non-conforming" users were allowed to remain.[68]

In 1933 Oneida County was first in the state to implement rural zoning. By 1940, twenty-nine other counties, including all those in the cutover, had followed suit. The process used in Price County was typical. First, the county agent and Main Street businessmen aroused public opinion to support zoning. The *Park Falls Herald* editorialized, "Enough Farms Now," and welcomed guest editorials by George Wehrwein, "More Vacation Land," and "Why We Need to Zone Land."[69] In the late winter of 1934 the county agent chaired a series of ten informational meetings on zoning in different towns around the county, attended by about 470 citizens. Some in attendance expressed doubts. As might be expected, there were concerns that zoning might somehow restrict hunting and fishing. John Cummings of the town of Emory reflected the independent streak in cutover settlers when he warned that "this zoning is the first step toward federal control of everything." But the official minutes reported that the "sentiment" at each meeting was favorable to zoning. Late in April a county-wide meeting about zoning was held at the county normal school building in Phillips. D. van Ostrand, a land dealer, did object to zoning, pointing to an anticipated inrush of homeseekers and the suitability for farming of much of the land tentatively identified for the forest or recreation zones. However another land man, Hugo

Kandutsch (a long-time agent of the Union Mortgage Loan Company), wanted *more* land zoned in these categories, since there was "no chance of farmers ever living there." Hostile feelings toward settlers came into the open. The chair of the county board's agriculture committee argued from the perspective of seeing cutover farmers as objects in a profit-loss calculation. Replying to van Ostrand, he emphasized, "If you can get $4.00 [a forty] from the State [through the Forest Crop Law] you are a whole lot better off than if you would sell a forty to someone and get $5.00 [in taxes] and pay them $60 from the Relief." A Phillips lawyer enthusiastically supported zoning, darkly suggesting that if someone "makes trouble in the community" they should be removed from the "back 40s." In addition to this input received at the public hearing, the county board received written comments. The Soo Line Railroad claimed that over a third of its land in Price County which had been zoned for forestry was inaccurately classified. The railroad reiterated its intention and desire to add to the fifteen hundred farmers it had already settled in Price County. Despite—or perhaps because of—this continued interest in settling farmers, the county board adopted a rural zoning ordinance for Price County.[70]

In 1927 the state legislature authorized the establishment of county forests as one method of reforesting land zoned for forestry.[71] Counties owned extensive tracts of land which had been taken for nonpayment of taxes (chapter 4). In 1929 the legislature allowed this land to be put into county forests and entered under the Forest Crop Law. With land acquired by purchase, tax deed, and trade, Marinette County, for example, entered over fourteen thousand acres in 1930. By 1940 the county forest had grown to over two hundred thousand acres, almost one-quarter of the county's land area. Replanting began with 250,000 seedlings in 1935. Recreational use of the forest was encouraged by establishing several parks and a youth center. State and federal programs in the 1930s put unemployed men to work in the Marinette County Forest in fire protection, camp-building, and trail-clearing activities. By 1940 there was timber to be cut for sale and over $100,000 came to the county from the state under the Forest Crop Law.[72] In Marinette County and elsewhere in the cutover, some people saw much better ways to use the land than farming.

Efforts at encouraging conservation and recreation, especially by tourists, came together in the development of county parks in northern Wisconsin. For example, in Marathon County, bordering the cutover, the Park Commission in the 1930s announced its "desire . . . to have a big comprehensive park system completely covering the county . . . so developed that a big recreation program will be carried on throughout the year."[73] Less ambitious plans in most cutover counties for lakefront swimming beaches, fishing sites, and hiking trails in the woods expanded the nonagricultural uses of northern Wisconsin land.

The federal government also expanded its land holdings in the cutover in the 1930s. Under authorization of the Weeks Law of 1911, in his final hours in office President Herbert Hoover established the Nicolet National Forest in Vilas, Florence, Forest, and Oconto counties. Subsequently, the New Deal emphasized the role national forests could play throughout the country in unemployment relief and environmental protection. By 1940, as a consequence, the Nicolet Forest had grown to 554,247 acres. Late in 1933 President Franklin D. Roosevelt also initiated the Chequemagon National Forest in Taylor, Price, Ashland, Bayfield, and Sawyer counties. Seeing it as an "asset" that would take over "poor lands not fit for agricultural purposes," Price County sold to the national forest county-owned land and served as a nonprofit conduit for additional land it continued to take title to by tax deed or swapping with owners. Other private interests dealt directly with the federal government and were able to make a small profit on their sale. Through these means individuals such as Irene Otto and institutions such as the W.C. Foster Company, both of Chicago, were able to unload large Price County tracts onto the federal government for prices between $1.25 and $1.60 an acre. Price County looked forward to its entitlement to 25 percent of receipts from forestry sales from that part of the national forest within its jurisdiction. Foresters, for their part, believed that the "rehabilitation" of the purchased units would "contribute to the solution of a regional dilemma." Eventually, workers at twenty Civilian Conservation Corps camps in the Nicolet Forest performed conservation and recreation-development tasks. Additionally, from 1934 to 1937 the Forest Service provided work projects at Camp Imogene for 250 "transients" recruited from around Wisconsin, who raised all their own vegetables and some of their livestock. Having been revitalized, the Chequamegon National Forest would become, in the words of the *New York Times*, a "poor man's playground . . . deep in the heart of the Wisconsin cut-over wilds," bringing tourists to the region.[74]

With the development of state programs like rural zoning and state and county parks, in addition to federal programs in the 1930s to combat the Depression (chapter 4), planners had increasingly potent tools to design the future of the cutover. They intensified their work, creating government programs that more directly affected individuals. In the late 1920s and early 1930s the Agricultural Extension Service published a series of special circulars, "Making the Most of ———— County's Land." The headings in the Washburn County circular indicated the direction that its authors wanted the county to move. "Land, the Basis of County Finance" outlined the dismal fiscal condition of Washburn County, like that of most cutover counties, and pointedly highlighted a subsection entitled "State Aid Greatly Exceeds Taxes Paid to State." Agriculture was not ignored; the planners clearly saw a continued farming presence in the area. One section of the circular emphasized how dairy production could be increased by growing more alfalfa. But central to the circular was the section entitled "Forestry, the Major Use for the Bulk of Washburn County Land." This section recommended that county officials create a county forest and utilize the Forest Crop Law. The title of another section in the circular stressed, "Recreation Industry Capable of Further Development." Its conclusions recommended public action to "enhance" the recreation industry, zone rural land, create a county forest, and consolidate rural schools to save money.[75]

Additional reports for other counties elaborated aspects of the overall plan. The "Recreational Plan for Vilas County" concluded that "recreation is Vilas County's biggest business," and that county-owned lands should generate more income from their fishing, hunting, and scenic beauty characteristics. These reports took on an increasingly technocratic tone, with analysis driven by fiscal concerns. A federal government report on land use in Forest County devoted almost 60 percent of its pages to topics related to county finances, zoning, and settler relocation. When it turned to agriculture, it was not positive. In "problem" areas, it concluded that "many of the families have become so accustomed to the subsistence type of farming, that they are not likely to be satisfied or successful on commercial farms." In order to capture the fiscal savings they envisioned, the reports increasingly emphasized school, town, and even county consolidation. These measures were said to be "inevitable," once counties adopted zoning and other land use measures which made many local governmental units "obsolete."[76]

Several comprehensive state and federal reports, and their shorter and popularized versions, promoted rural planning. In 1929 the state legislature created the nation's first office of regional planning and two years later elevated it into the Wisconsin Regional Planning Committee. In 1934 this agency surveyed the state's physical and economic resources and concluded that the northern and central portions of the state were "largely unsuited for agriculture." A section of the report prepared by George Wehrwein identified the cutover as a problem region because of its "isolated" settlers requiring costly governmental services. Another section on land use, therefore, concluded that "there was and is no prospect" to develop "communities" in northern Wisconsin no matter how hard settlers worked. It recommended using zoning and other governmental programs to vacate settlers from poor lands and scattered locations and restrict agricultural expansion to already established communities.[77] In 1939 the tristate Northern Lakes States Regional Committee—which included the ubiquitous Wehrwein—issued a major report, *The Cutover Region of Wisconsin*. The report's survey of local governmental finances, per-capita income statistics, welfare expenditures, and related data painted a bleak picture of the region. This condition was blamed on the "extensive depletion" of forests in northern Wisconsin and "the too great prevalence of an ill-advised agriculture." The report suggested an integrated solution to the problem. It recognized that there were some "splendid farms" in the cutover and that the region's farms as a whole had per-acre outputs close to the state norm. Farm income was low, however, because there were fewer acres per farm in crops than in the rest of the state. Therefore, the report recommended improved "agricultural planning"—extension work, better credit opportunities, more cooperatives—to make more farms viable. This necessitated zoning and relocation so that efforts would not be wasted on agriculturally hopeless places. At the same time, the report argued that "the economy of the region is such that a large proportion of the farmers will find it profitable to combine agriculture with forest work and in part-time employment in recreation." It encouraged, therefore, the continued formation in northern Wisconsin of county, state, and national forests.[78]

National planners were even less nuanced in their evaluations and recommendations for the cutover. Inspired in part by Wisconsin planners' accomplishments, as part of the New Deal the federal government created a National Resources Board. In 1935 this agency presented a striking picture of desolation in the Great Lakes cutover based on worst-case examples ("in one township . . .") and impressionistic evidence (there were "many" tarpaper shacks; "most" homes were "very poor";

there was no community life because settlers were "too weary"). The report's authors concluded that four million acres in the Great Lakes cutover should be turned from farms to forest (a much larger land area than was being farmed in 1935 in the Wisconsin part of the cutover).[79] Similarly, a WPA-sponsored survey of rural "problem areas" drew on stereotypes about northern Wisconsin and had a bleak conclusion about the Great Lakes cutover: "If some of the energy and money spent in extolling the dubious virtues of 'Cloverland' to uninformed buyers had been turned to developing what is now admitted to be the 'Land of Hiawatha,' some of the present troubles of this area could have been avoided. Only through a system of land zoning, such as that used in Wisconsin, can a repetition of wildly speculative land selling schemes be avoided."[80]

The federal Department of Agriculture's widely circulated yearbooks propagated similar views, which reflected ideas about national land use planning developed in the department's Bureau of Agricultural Economics by former cutover researcher Lewis Gray (chapter 4).[81] In the 1938 edition, which featured essays on "soils and men," Wehrwein coauthored a piece which described the cutover in familiar terms: "The soils are generally poor. The isolation of the families and the poverty of the soil reproduce familiar conditions—low family income and correspondingly low standards of living, and inadequate public facilities and services combined with high costs of the services provided." The remedy was publicly owned forests, with farms excluded by zoning and relocation. The 1940 yearbook, *Farmers in a Changing World*, a landmark accomplishment of social science written for a nonscholarly audience, included Gray's essay "Our Major Land Use Problems and Suggested Lines of Action." He reported cutover farmers were not producing for the market, and therefore characterized them as a "redundant" population, part of a "socially undesirable settlement" that created "unnecessary public expenditures for roads, schools," and other services.[82]

As was the case with newspaper and other popular accounts, the wider the audience for social science reports on the cutover, the cruder the picture they gave of its settlers, and the less allowance they made for the viability of any agriculture in the region.[83] From these reports, readers gained the impression that all rural people in the cutover were lazy, ignorant, immoral, and incompetent, with no interest or ability to stand on their own feet as farmers. This conflation of the characteristics of cutover farmers was exaggerated, since profitable agriculture still existed and was even continuing to expand in the cutover at the end of the 1930s.

But the broad-brush picture of cutover farming also contained a kernel of truth: rural people in northern Wisconsin, whatever their degree of success with commercial agriculture, overwhelmingly shared an attachment to yeoman farming and the way of life they hoped it would provide their families. They were open to many of the new practices and technologies that agricultural experts wanted to see expand in rural America, but not entirely for the same reasons as the experts. Cutover settlers did not want change to lead to farm consolidation, rural depopulation, an orientation toward modern consumer goods as ends in themselves rather than means to support family farming, and an increasing inability of rural people to manage their own affairs. They were proud of their community institutions, which the experts tended to overlook in their quest to find a rural world with men taking guidance from county agents at Farm Bureau meetings while their wives attended Homemaker Clubs to learn how to make their farmhouses more citified. Increasingly fearful of the social consequences of their inability to nurture this sort of rural world, social scientists in the 1930s embraced a different vision for the cutover, and therefore encouraged alternative public policies which would eventually undermine yeoman farming in the cutover.

How did people in northern Wisconsin react to the way in which they were portrayed to outsiders and to the governmental policies which were designed to redeem their region? A few voices stood up for the region. An angry letter to the editor of the *Milwaukee Journal* responding to a short story based in Oconto County which the paper was serializing wanted "to know if the person who wrote the story has been in Oconto since 1650." Fear of alienating a source of income inhibited cutover residents from publicly blaming tourists for unattractive aspects of their region, but sometimes they privately expressed such thoughts. Nell Peters, who grew up on a struggling farm in Vilas County in the 1930s, admitted that "after the repeal of prohibition [local] joints [offered] free opening and closing times, and unrestricted gambling and prostitution." But this was to meet an outside demand: "The more freedom, the more money tourists coughed up."[84]

Rural people in the cutover were also cautious about criticizing the new public policies which affected them in the 1920s and 1930s. The *Neillsville Press* in Clark County did denigrate rural zoning as the product of "men seeking to create jobs for themselves" by eliminating "the poor man's haven." But such comments were rare in print. Newspaper opinion generally accepted, even welcomed, the new evaluation of northern Wisconsin. In Price County, for example, Main Street eventually lessened the support it showed in the 1920s for agricultural development, and the *Park Falls Herald* endorsed the creation of state and federal forests in the county and the adoption of the Forest Crop Law. The paper even argued that "the idea is good" to consolidate Price with four other counties.[85]

The general support of cutover editors by 1930 for reforestation stood in dramatic contrast to their position in 1915 at the time of the controversial *Owen v. Donald* decision (chapter 1).[86] Intervening events and the interpretation given to them by social scientists undoubtedly influenced the editors to reevaluate their earlier support for farming over forestry. But it is always dangerous to measure public opinion in the past by reading editorial pages.[87] In this instance, there is more systematic evidence which suggests that support for reforestation was much stronger on Main Street and outside the cutover than on dirt farms in northern Wisconsin.

Wisconsin voters had to approve reforestation. Adoption of the Forest Crop Law first required an amendment to modify the "uniformity" clause of the state constitution of 1848 (article VIII, section I), which the state courts had interpreted as requiring uniform real property tax rates within a taxing jurisdiction.[88] A constitutional amendment, allowing tax "classifications as to forests . . . as the legislature shall prescribe," twice passed the legislature, as required, and went to the state's voters for approval in April 1927. It won the support of 55.6 percent of the electorate.[89]

Voting patterns on the constitutional amendment suggest that cutover voters, especially in rural communities, were not particularly enthusiastic about its adoption (Table 5.2). Eleven of the twenty-three counties in Wisconsin in which voters rejected the amendment were in or adjacent to the cutover. Overall, voters in the cutover and adjacent counties approved the amendment by the slimmest of margins. In the rural towns of the cutover only 47 percent voted Yes, and only 41 percent of voters in rural parts of adjacent counties favored the amendment. The pattern was for the strongest support for the amendment to come from villages and, especially, cities. This was true throughout the state (with the major exception of Milwaukee, where only a lukewarm 57 percent

Table 5.2. Vote on Amendment to Wisconsin Constitution, April 27, 1927

	Yes (%)	No (%)	Total Vote
Cutover	52.3	47.7	42,926
Cities	57.4	42.6	
Villages	60.0	40.0	
Towns	46.5	53.5	
Eight counties adjacent to cutover	49.2	50.8	27,715
Cities	64.3	35.7	
Villages	62.8	37.2	
Towns	41.4	58.6	
Milwaukee County	57.0	43.0	66,841
Rest of the state	57.3	42.7	188,996
Wisconsin	55.6	44.4	326,478

Source: Statements of Board of County Canvassers, in Secretary of State, Election Return Statements, 1926–1927 (series 211, boxes 102–3), SHSW.

of voters cast Yes ballots). Support for the amendment was over 70 percent in Janesville, Kenosha, La Crosse, Oshkosh, Eau Claire, Manitowoc, Stevens Point, and Wausau. In the largest city in the cutover, Superior, 60 percent of the electorate voted Yes, less than in most other major cities in the state but greater than in most rural parts of the cutover.

Economic self-interest explains some of this voting pattern. Residents of relatively urban parts of counties (villages and cities) had the most to lose from land becoming tax delinquent under the pre-1927 system. Taxpayers throughout a county had to makeup the shortfall in a town's budget caused by unpaid taxes. Under the system approved in 1927, potentially delinquent land would now earn a small tax revenue for towns (half paid by taxpayers statewide) and would not become a burden on village and city taxpayers. (Milwaukee was exceptional because by 1927 there was very little rural land remaining in the county that could become a burden on the city's taxpayers, and urban taxpayers would have to pay their share of the state's small annual per-acre payment to towns for land entered under the Forest Crop Law.) Voters in the rural towns, on the other hand, would have their taxes increase to make up for a declining local tax base as land was entered under the Forest Crop Law— the $.20 per acre the town would receive under the new law from landowners and the state would be less than what would be received from landowners (or the county, if they became delinquent) under the pre-1927 tax system. To the degree voters based their decision on this factor, they had internalized the fiscal cost-benefit reasoning about cutover farming that social scientists and planners had emphasized in the 1920s. But, more significantly, rural people in northern Wisconsin were also reluctant to support a measure encouraging reforestation because many remained committed to seeing their neighborhoods develop into farming communities. They knew that forests might provide part-time by-employment for struggling farmers, but their existence would hinder the development of a rural population dense enough to support the cooperative farming practices and interpersonal social bonding on which yeoman farming communities depended. Where this dream still seemed possible, opposition was greatest to the 1927 constitutional amendment. Hence the particularly negative reaction to the amendment in the counties just outside the cutover, especially Clark, Marathon, and Shawano, where 61 percent of the voters turned down the amendment. This area by the late-1920s had largely made the successful transformation to an economy based on dairy farming (chapter 2). In the cutover itself, rural voters in more developed areas, especially in Lincoln, Langlade, Octonto, and Burnett counties, opposed the amendment. In the seven towns on the Antigo Flats in Langlade County, 73 percent of the voters rejected the amendment. If dodging tax burdens had been their primary concern, voters in these towns should have been most enthusiastic *in favor* of the amendment. Correspondingly, the strongest support for the amendment came from voters in the three adjacent northernmost counties of the cutover, Forest, Iron, and Vilas (where 65 percent of the rural electorate voted Yes). The rural parts of these counties had relatively few farms—Forest and Vilas counties had the smallest percentage of their rural population living on farms in 1930 of all cutover counties. Furthermore, in these counties many people who were designated as "farmers" were not committed to agriculture as a vocation. Even the real farmers in these northernmost counties had good reasons by 1927 to conclude that agriculture was not the most promising future for their neighborhoods.

In sum, Wisconsinites responded to proposed reforestation on the basis of a combination of their self-interest and the degree to which they remained committed to preserving yeoman farming. Abstract ideas about good planning or efficient government were less significant. Throughout the state, support for reforestation was strongest in more urbanized areas, where emotional attachments to yeoman farming were weakest and the danger of shifting tax burdens was greatest. But in addition, in rural parts of the cutover and adjacent counties, especially where possibilities for viable agriculture remained, support for reforestation was particularly weak. Most cutover farmers and their families who had cleared land, built up herds, and constructed farm buildings remained committed to allowing farming to expand in northern Wisconsin. They clung to this commitment despite the economic setbacks they had encountered with the agricultural depression of the 1920s and despite the opportunity the Forest Crop Law offered to protect them from having to shoulder some of the tax responsibilities of less-successful farmers in as-of-yet less-developed parts of their region.

6 | The Cutover in the Late 1930s: Last Efforts at Yeoman Farming

The cutover was a different place in 1940 than it had been at the beginning of the twentieth century. As a result of almost a half-century of intensive efforts at agricultural settlement, the region's physical environment had changed, hundreds of thousands of expectant settlers had moved to the region, its social characteristics no longer resembled those of frontier areas, and the public perception in the nation had changed regarding its capabilities. It was now obvious that the cutover was never going to become the bountiful place that early-twentieth-century promoters had envisioned. But tens of thousands of farm families lived in the region. While their labor had not turned the cutover into a region identical to older agricultural parts of Wisconsin, it had made parts of the region into places that a yeoman farmer would recognize. Other families, furthermore, still wanted to try yeoman farming in northern Wisconsin. The still-incompletely developed quality of the cutover provided opportunities within the region for out-of-the-mainstream people, including small groups of single women and African-Americans. A strand of New Deal planning also found in the cutover a place to implement schemes for rural communities. Yeoman farming was not dead in northern Wisconsin.

But the interest of settlers and the programs of some planners were not enough to make northern Wisconsin a land of family farms. In fact, another strand of of New Deal thinking, favorable to limiting agricultural production in order to assist commercial farmers, proved to be the greatest legacy of the federal government's agricultural policy in the 1930s. These developments at the national level fed into the skepticism in Wisconsin toward agriculture in the cutover which was discussed in the previous chapter.

President Franklin D. Roosevelt had broad but ill-defined sympathies towards rural America. His New Deal agricultural programs therefore contained varied and contradictory thrusts. One part of the New Deal's agricultural policy sought to improve the position of commercial farmers. The Agricultural Adjustment Act of 1933 tried to raise prices farmers received by limiting their output through production and marketing agreements. The Soil Conservation and Domestic Allotment Act of 1936 sought the same ends by encouraging the removal of land from cultivation for conservation purposes. In the closing years of the 1930s, the federal government tried to raise prices by buying farm commodities such as wheat for storage in Agricultural Secretary Henry A. Wallace's "ever normal granery." At the same time, the Bureau of Agricultural Economics in the Department of Agriculture oversaw the drafting of comprehensive land use policies for all of rural America. These plans were designed to reduce farm acreage on which operators were unable or unwilling to produce fully for the market, which would therefore raise the prices of the commodities produced on the acreage that remained.[1] Even the cutover farms which were most commercially oriented were not developed enough to benefit fully from the price-boosting programs of the New Deal, and many cutover farms belonged to the type that planners and officials wanted to consolidate and reduce in acreage. The advocates of this aspect of New Deal agricultural policy understood that their programs would reduce the number of Americans on farms, particularly in areas like northern Wisconsin, but felt that this was in the best interests of the people who would be forced out of farming as well as all Americans, rural and urban.

Writing in the late 1930s, Department of Agriculture officials concentrated in the Bureau of Agricultural Research and university land economists estimated that there was a "redundant" population of between five hundred thousand and one million people on "submarginal land" in the United States. According to experts like Lewis Gray and George Wehrwein, this "socially undesirable settlement" did not produce significant crops for market and did not have an acceptable standard of living.[2] These planners felt that this population should relocate, preferably to urban areas, but at least to farms which could earn them higher incomes. In a mid-1930s study of population migration, Bushrod Allin and Carter Goodrich concluded, "The net movement of man-power must be from farm to nonfarm employment if the nation is to progress in an economic sense." Goodrich was firm in believing that there was "no room in commercial farming for a net increase in population."[3] Public policy concern was now the reverse of what it had been in the first decades of the twentieth century: for the advocates of the Country Life movement, the progress of the entire country had depended on maintaining, even increasing, the population level of rural America (chapter 3); for these New Deal planners it depended on *reducing* it. Rural people in the cutover figured prominently as candidates for relocation. The federal government estimated in 1935 that the Great Lakes cutover contained 3,500,000 acres in farms which should be returned to forests and whose "stranded" population should be relocated elsewhere.[4] This relocation was not an end in itself, Allin and Goodrich emphasized, but the means to the end of taking land out of cultivation. In an essay focused specifically on the Great Lakes cutover, Allin allowed that "less emigration is needed in this region than in the Southern Appalachians and the Old Cotton Belt . . . or in the Great Plains" and that the emphasis therefore should be on discouraging further immigration. But he still identified fifteen thousand families in need of relocation to correct past "mistakes."[5] The federal government would assist this movement by buying out these "mistakes," by subsidizing the costs of moving away from them, and by locating and perhaps paying for part of the cost of new homes in more desirable locations.

Federal, state, and county governments in Wisconsin in the 1930s implemented relocation programs. Between 1934 and 1943 the Northern Wisconsin Settler Relocation Project spent $500,000 in federal money to purchase between four hundred and five hundred farms in seven cutover counties.[6] On their own, county governments relocated about two hundred more farmers, often by trading county-owned land for an existing farm. Officials claimed that 98 percent of these people moved voluntarily. Nell Peters recalled moving a short distance in 1935 to another farm in Vilas County, which her father "bought on the installment plan from President Roosevelt's Home Owners Loan Corporation Program" for $350, while he worked for the Works Progress Administration for $70 a month.[7] An estimated 30 to 40 percent of relocated families remained in agriculture as Sam Peters did. About twenty-five were "infiltrated" by federal government programs into established farming communities. Others were subsidized in other ways, and some were left on their own to find new farms. The director of the Settler Relocation Project claimed that "with the supervision given in their farming operations, most of these people succeeded on their new farms." The remainder of the relocated population found nonfarm work in the cutover or factory work in cities, or retired. The Wisconsin Rural Rehabilitation Corporation built "retirement homes" near Crandon and Antigo, in

Langlade County, for relocated farmers who were disabled or retired. In summarizing the results of the program, its director emphasized that "it is estimated that at least one-half of those originally on relief became self-supporting."

New Deal agricultural policy also contained another thrust, one that was more friendly to maintaining small-scale family farmers and assisting tenants and sharecroppers.[8] As part of this aspect of the New Deal, some officials in Washington tried to create planned rural communities in which farming would play a major role. But again, as with most aspects of the New Deal, this idea contained conflicting strands. These conflicts made the success of planned communities—including the one that was built in the cutover—difficult to achieve.

Planned rural communities had a long history in the United States, although few were ever successful. In the late-nineteenth and early-twentieth centuries, the Salvation Army, the Catholic Rural Life movement, the Southern Agrarian intellectuals, and others encouraged the creation of small-scale, cooperative rural colonies. These proposals tended to project a romantic, antiurban attitude. In the first quarter of the twentieth century, visionaries developed more hard-nosed schemes compatible with an urbanizing America. The work of Ebenezer Howard and the Regional Planning Association became well known. Elwood Mead managed two planned communities in California, Durham and Delphi, in the years around World War I, based on his experience with land reclamation projects in Australia. Influenced by Richard T. Ely, Wisconsin officials rejected Mead's model in planning for resettlement of returning World War I veterans (chapter 3). Planners influenced by Ely emphasized careful social science research, a regional rather than community focus, less rather than more land in farms, and only indirect government involvement. Milbourn L. Wilson, a student of Ely's, directed a widely reported project at Fairway Farms in Montana during the 1920s. Rural planning, therefore, came from several not-altogether-compatible directions.[9]

The essays in a 1939 volume, *Agriculture in Modern Life*, reflected the range of thinking about agricultural problems in the 1930s, which in turn influenced the decade's self-consciously created rural communities. Ralph Borsodi expressed the romantic, antiurban strain when he argued that the basic problem facing farmers was not the economy but the quality of life on their farms. "We need a new program," he urged, "which places the current interests of human beings ahead of the development of the perfect future industrialized state, and which does not assume that the expansion of industry should have priority over the happiness of the people who have to live today." Agricultural economist and geographer Oliver E. Baker, a staff member of the Bureau of Agricultural Economics, had a different tone and perspective. His heavily statistical section emphasized rural "debt, depletion of resources, and a trend toward depopulation." The application of "science" was the remedy for these problems. Milbourn Wilson adopted a middle ground which was somewhat hazy in its specifics: "The task of today is one of combining some dependent specialization with some individual responsibility, in joining some group and cooperative activity with some personal self-sufficiency."[10]

With encouragement coming from mixed directions, planners in the early 1930s tried to design new rural communities which would respond to the economic distress evident in rural America. In Wisconsin, there was interest in formalizing what many cutover farmers had been doing for decades: building rural communities which combined farming and forestry. For instance, P. G. Beck and M. C. Forster surveyed conditions in "the Lake States Cut-Over Area" and did not recommend relocation for all "stranded" farm families. Instead, they believed that some families should be "provided with part-time work in a reforestation program which in the end will establish a stable forestry and woodworking industry." Beck and Forster believed that almost half of the farm families receiving relief in the cutover "were considered capable of rehabilitation on the land if given supplementary employment."[11] Such proposals for "forest-farm" communities presented the economic potential of the rejuvenated forests of northern Wisconsin to the public in a benign light. They implied that forest-farm communities would exploit forests not by the rapacious methods of the nineteenth-century lumber barons but by the carefully regulated actions of part-time farmers.

A thoughtful advocate of forest-farm communities in Wisconsin was R. B. Goodman, a lumberman and member of the State Conservation Commission in the 1930s. Goodman envisioned "forest towns," which would replace both ghostlike "sawmill towns" and the "wilderness slums" of scattered stump farmers. These towns would be more compact than existing farm settlements but less compact than sawmill towns. Their residents would be permanent settlers, not transitory as in sawmill towns. They would work in conservation and harvesting of timber while being "part-time subsistence farmers."[12] Goodman put his ideas to work on his timberlands in northeastern Wisconsin. By 1944 he reported that three thousand people formed a "working circle" within a ten-mile radius of the village of Goodman in northwestern Marinette County. "Employment in the Goodman working circle," he explained, "is almost equally divided between farming and the forest industries," which were based on sustained-yield forestry. "More acreage is put into crops each year," he emphasized. This was possible because "mill employment provides for extended leaves of absence for farm planting and the harvesting of crops. In the woods, peak employment is during the winter months."[13]

The strongest impetus for establishing planned communities during the 1930s came from the national level. Eventually over ten thousand settlers inhabited about one hundred New Deal community projects of various types. Some were rural farming communities, although not on reclaimed land as Elwood Mead advocated. Many of these were initiated in the early years of the New Deal by the Federal Emergency Relief Administration (FERA). These projects were often collectivist, encouraged by Resettlement Administration (RA) Administrator Rexford G. Tugwell, who took over responsibility for FERA programs in 1935.[14] Other projects were suburban greenbelt towns, such as Greendale near Milwaukee, which were initiated in the mid-1930s by the RA and reflected the tradition of the Regional Planning Association as well as Tugwell's commitment to an urban rather than rural future for the United States.[15] The romantic strain in planned communities was found in still other proposals for "subsistence homesteads." In these projects, residents combined part-time subsistence farming with work in local industries. As Borsodi explained: "Farming by its intrinsic nature is a part-time occupation; and I don't believe that the grave agricultural problem with which we are confronted today will ever be solved until we begin to apply technological discoveries of modern times to part-time and subsistence farming instead of concentrating them on commercial farming."[16]

The Subsistence Homesteads project had its first home in the Interior Department under the direction of Milbourn Wilson, beginning in August 1932. Wilson, as we have seen, had a vision for rural America somewhere between that of the romantic agrarians and that of industrial-model modernizers. He directed several programs with somewhat different thrusts during his tenure in Washington between 1930 and 1953— for instance, he came to Subsistence Homesteads from directing the wheat section in the Agricultural Adjustment Administration, where he worked on crop reduction as part of the first thrust of New Deal agricultural programs discussed above.[17] As a result of his education under Ely and his experience in Montana, he was also deeply interested in land policy, and worked closely with the social scientists who were encouraging emigration from poor regions like the cutover.[18] Reflecting this perspective, he had no sympathy with Mead's schemes to build rural communities on land that would be added to the agricultural base by reclamation. At Subsistence Homesteads, in contrast to Tugwell, Wilson stressed increasing farm ownership rather than encouraging communal projects.[19] His programs met with the endorsement of Ely as well as conservative intellectuals among the Southern Agrarians and the Catholic Rural Life movement who were skeptical of industrialization and favored a more decentralized America.[20] Wilson had some success initially—Borsodi himself proposed a project near Dayton, Ohio.[21] After Wilson left Subsistence Homesteads in 1934 and the program became part of the RA in 1935, RA Administrator Tugwell, who was skeptical about the chances for success of rural planned communities, moved the program toward more centralized direction. At the same time, Assistant Administrator Lewis Gray stressed the necessity of *removing* poor farmers from their land rather than encouraging new communities.[22] For his part, Tugwell pushed for the homesteads to build producer cooperatives to furnish their residents with nonfarm employment as part of his national economic plan of decentralizing industry in the United States. A few of these projects, like Granger Homesteads in Iowa, were successful, but most, like the well-publicized fiasco at Arthurdale in West Virginia, were economic failures.[23] Tugwell became unpopular with some hard-nosed social scientists, conservative intellectuals, and romantic agrarians who disliked paternalistic control by the government over homesteads and resettled farmers, and—most significantly—with conservative politicians. In 1937 he was ousted and the RA reorganized into the Farm Security Administration (FSA) and brought into the Department of Agriculture. Community settlement projects moved to the back burner in the FSA, where the emphasis now was on rural land retirement, rehabilitation of existing commercially viable farms, and assisting tenants to become farm owners. These programs were coordinated by careful planning in the Bureau of Agricultural Economics supervised by Wilson, now Under Secretary of Agriculture.[24] As the New Deal lost political momentum after the 1938 mid-term elections, Congress voted first to prohibit new planned community projects and then to terminate the program.[25] In sum, New Deal programs for building new rural communities had conflicting inputs and changing directions of implementation.

Early in the New Deal years, advocates enthusiastically planned for subsistence homesteads in northern Wisconsin. A Wisconsin-based non-profit corporation, working in conjunction with the State Conservation Commission and Department of Agriculture, put together the Wisconsin Forest-Farm Homestead Plan. This scheme aimed to relocate "isolated" cutover settlers to better locations in the cutover where they could combine subsistence farming with 100 to 150 days per year of work in the expanding network of county, state, and federal forests.[26] The United States Regional Forester in Milwaukee asserted that "the national forests of this region alone could provide work for possibly forty such communities, or about 32,000 people" for twenty years.[27] However, in March 1934 the comptroller general in Washington ruled that such projects were illegal when run by local organizations. Incubating projects were either centralized, with resulting loss of local support, as in the case of Borsodi's community near Dayton, or abandoned, as in the case of the Wisconsin Forest-Farm Homesteads.

In his critique of the Wisconsin program, George Wehrwein showed that social scientists who were involved with it had less romantic expectations for it than did Borsodi. Wehrwein saw the project as helpful primarily in its relocation of "isolated" settlers and consequent reduction in school and other public expenses. Like the advocates of rural out-migration discussed above, he wanted a reduction in the number of small farmers more than the creation of reinvigorated yeoman farming communities. "When it comes to resettling an entire community," Wehrwein argued, "it will be found that there is not only submarginal land but there are also submarginal people."[28] In sum, the first involvement by Wisconsin with subsistence homesteads highlighted the different strains of thinking which lay uncomfortably behind the program. Its planning also provided the basis for the only subsistence homestead project that was actually built in Wisconsin, the Drummond Forest Project.[29]

The town of Drummond in Bayfield County was the site of large-scale lumbering operations in the late-nineteenth and early-twentieth centuries by the Rust-Owen Lumber Company (chapter 1).[30] Having exhausted the surrounding forests, the company closed its sawmill in the unincorporated village of Drummond in 1930 and a smaller planing mill in 1933. Much of the heavily transient work force of the mills migrated to nearby cities such as Ashland or to remaining lumbering areas on the upper peninsula of Michigan. The population of the town of Drummond declined from 1,054 in 1930 to 776 in 1940.

But Drummond also included a group of about fifty families who, beginning around 1915, had developed small farms on cutover land purchased from Rust-Owen. The chief wage earner in most of them continued to work in the sawmill or the woods and, in the words of a long-time resident who grew up in Drummond during the 1920s, would "maybe ship a little bit of cream" and maintain a garden, chickens, "a beef or two," and a dairy cow for their own consumption. I "can't tell you anybody," he recalled, "who made a living . . . on a farm that didn't have . . . some other income."[31] In the early 1930s the farms in the town of Drummond in the aggregate had about five hundred acres in crops and about 125 cows.[32] This group of residents was attached to Drummond: the rural farm population of the town declined only from 334 to 302 during the 1930s. They all gathered during the 1930s at the annual Farmers' Picnic[33] (Figure 6.1). A Drummond resident in the late 1930s described the "fine spirit of friendliness" in the community. She emphasized her neighbors' "cheerful adjustment to circumstances." "Those who found returns too slow have left for

Figure 6.1. Drummond Farmers Club Picnic, 1917. (Drummond Historical Society)

other work," she asserted. "The sturdier ones, who love this country, remain and form an interesting community."[34] In sum, as a classic "stranded" community, Drummond presented an ideal opportunity for New Deal community planners.

In 1935 the RA initiated the Drummond Forest Community. The project was one of two nationwide which subsequently were administered by the United States Forest Service. The community resembled Camp Imogene in the Nicolet National Forest (chapter 5), but was more organized and designed for permanent residence by families. It consisted of thirty-two homes on twenty-acre lots, largely built with WPA funds. Five acres were initially cleared on each lot, from which planners expected the residents to produce most of their food requirements and perhaps have a little extra to sell to summer tourists. An informal arrangement with the Forest Service promised approximately half-time employment for householders in the community. "I had a lot of garden stuff," recalled one resident, "and I trapped, and I had 13 days [a month] with the Forest Service" as well as work in a souvenir shop.[35] The program was popular; "it sounded great," recalled one resident of Drummond. Getting a place in the community enabled Larry Garneau to get married; "we stalled our marriage because we didn't have a place to live."[36] Mrs. Alfred Fruechtl, who had lived in Drummond since 1922, believed that the "lucky ones" were getting farms in the community. When interviewed in 1988, Harry Sanders—who was still living on his original homestead— fondly recalled the community meetings and socials at the schoolhouse. The community was almost fully occupied throughout the late 1930s.[37]

But the Drummond Forest Community was not a long-term success. Only a half-dozen residents remained in 1944, and the government decided to terminate the project and sell the homesteads to their residents. The results from the farming component of the homestead plan, in particular, were disappointing. In 1938 the annual agricultural enumeration reported seventy-one farms in the town of Drummond, twenty-six of them twenty-acre lots. Of these twenty-six, none had more than an acre in potatoes, none had field crops, and only six had cows. Forest community farms at best averaged $100 per year in sales, where $300 had been projected. By 1940, the enumeration found only thirty-eight active farms in the town, suggesting that lots in the Forest Community were no longer considered "farms." Queried about this drop, the enumerator cryptically reported that "they have been sold to the Government."[38] It was difficult to farm successfully. Harry Sanders found that the soil was stony and that there was no market for dairy products. "It froze off in July," Larry Garneau explained about his 1940 crops. "By golly they came back, and they froze off again in August," he laughed.[39]

Settlers emphasized that the Drummond Forest Community was not an economic success because they did not earn enough from their work for the Forest Service. The Forest Service did not "fulfill their promise on the time" that would be available for residents to work, according to Hans Pederson. "If the Forest Service had turned on a lot of work," Larry Garneau believed, the settlers "would have been happy, whittled out a little farming and gardening, cut wood."[40] The formal evaluation of the Drummond Forest Community, however, found that families averaged over $550 a year from work in the national forest, substantially more than had been anticipated. In fact, despite the shortfall in farm sales, total income for the community residents averaged a little higher than the projected $969 per year.[41] The problem was that the Chequamegon Forest did not yet offer possibilities for commercial logging. The only available work was in forest service rehabilitation projects.[42] The Forest Service therefore was unable to increase hours or wages in the early 1940s, when World War II–stimulated industries began to offer better opportunities to Drummond settlers. The settlers perceived the Forest Service as cheap and preferred to move to jobs, for instance, in shipyards at Superior about fifty miles away.

The Drummond Forest Community had solid accomplishments. The Chequamegon Forest Ranger, in the words of the project's evaluator, believed that "virtually every family was better off after its stay in the community." It was the "best housing they ever had in their lives," Hans Pederson pointed out (Figure 6.2). Living conditions were much better than in company housing in the village, where, in the words of Harry Sanders, people were slaves to Rust-Owen. Indeed, most of the homes were still occupied a half-century later (at over $7,000 per tract they were expensive for the government to build, although not as costly as the average subsistence homestead). Settlers in the community generally earned the income that officials had projected for them at the outset of the project. Furthermore, the community was popular with its residents. Its design was consistent with the work experience of many of its residents, like Harry Sanders, who were used to combining agriculture, work in the forest, and other by-employment. It did not have manufacturing or other communal economic features that burdened other Tugwell-inspired subsistence homesteads. Unlike some other projects, it buildings were well adapted

Figure 6.2. Family moving into their home in Drummond Forest Project, May 1937. (Drummond Historical Society)

to the environment in which they were constructed. "Many families indicated that they disliked leaving the community," the evaluation reported, and they "asked about the possibility of returning after the war."[43]

But the Drummond Forest Community project was not able to revitalize yeoman farming in the cutover. Just as Ben Faast's plans for agricultural communities (chapter 3) had been rooted in the agricultural prosperity of the World War I years, the plans for Drummond were based on the bleak conditions of the Depression years in the cutover (chapter 4). In both instances, economic conditions unexpectedly changed and the plans were undermined. In the case of Drummond, as the project's evaluator pointed out, "Fairly good depression incomes were received. But depression incomes are not enough."[44]

New Deal programs were significant in northern Wisconsin. Thousands of cutover settlers avoided material deprivation because of them. The CCC helped to transform the landscape of the region. The Drummond Forest project was an imaginative and relatively well-managed effort to create a new community for some of its residents. But the most significant New Deal agricultural programs, which were aimed at well-established, demonstrably commercial farms, did not help the cutover. Those New Deal programs which were focused more on smaller and poorer farmers were disorganized and underfunded. An important component of them, furthermore, worked against further agricultural development in the cutover by encouraging migration out of farming and out of the region. All of the New Deal programs had the effect of bringing the outside world and its more strictly commercial economy into the cutover—federal relief checks for the poor, crop allotment benefits for the better-off, planners to design new communities, bureaucrats to manage new agencies, federal ownership of large sections of land in new national forests, and so forth. These developments would make it difficult to sustain, much less expand, yeoman farming in the cutover after 1940.[45]

A small number of African-Americans showed interest in settling in northern Wisconsin during the 1930s.[46] Their involvement with the region was not as part of any subsistence homestead project, for New Deal planned communities were strictly segregated. It was a spillover, rather, from rural to urban, South to North migration which characterized the experience of African-Americans beginning in the years around World War I. This interest by blacks in the cutover says something about their goals and capabilities, reflects on race relations in the cutover, and shows that promoters were still trying to encourage yeoman farming. However, just as with the residents of the Drummond Forest Community, the number of these settlers was small and their efforts to earn a living in the cutover met with difficulties. Indeed, if they had been more numerous and successful, African-Americans would probably have strengthened the negative image of the cutover which became part of the American imagination in the interwar years.

The great migration of blacks away from the rural South increased the African-American population of Wisconsin. As was the case everywhere, most of these migrants came to cities; most blacks in Wisconsin lived in Milwaukee, where they were tightly compressed into a decaying neighborhood immediately north of the central business district.[47] The Depression struck particularly hard at this community. In 1940, 29 percent of black males in Milwaukee aged fourteen and over were unemployed, compared to 13 percent of whites. Of those who did have jobs, 56 percent worked as unskilled and domestic workers, compared to 20 percent of whites.[48]

Given their rural backgrounds in the South and the poverty in which they lived in Milwaukee, it is not surprising that some African-Americans joined in the "back-to-the-land" movement of the 1930s, which particularly affected the cutover. Between 1930 and 1935 there was a 50 percent increase in the number of Wisconsin blacks operating farms. Two thirds of this increase came in the cutover, where the number of African-American farmers more than doubled, to 178. Most of these new farmers migrated from the Milwaukee ghetto. They had the resources, however, to operate only the poorest type of farm: between 1930 and 1935 the average value of black-operated farms in Wisconsin declined from 40 percent of the value of white-operated farms to only 25 percent.[49]

There was a place for African-Americans in the cutover because their numbers were not large enough to seem threatening to whites. Small communities of rural blacks had been accepted since the antebellum period.[50] Hard-pressed land vendors and local governments, furthermore, could not afford to be choosy to whom they sold land. One such vendor was the John S. Owen Company and its affiliate, the John S. Owen Lumber Company. Working through their Milwaukee representative, real estate agent William Kimpel, the Owen companies sold farms to African-Americans in the town of Hoard, in northern Clark County.[51] We can sense the gleam in the eyes of Owen's director of land sales when he learned "of the negro with a thousand dollars" and confessed to Kimpel that "I hope we can get hold of the thousand dollars or a large part of it." It was also his judgment that whites in the town of Hoard accepted black newcomers. He reported that a group of prospective black settlers "visited with a neighbor up there who treated them well."[52]

As was often the pattern among cutover settlers (chapter 2), many of these African-Americans had known one another previously and wanted to settle in close proximity. One of the first of the group to buy was B. J. Holliday, characterized by Owen's land salesman as "a preacher in Milwaukee" who "conducts a large church down there." Several of Holliday's relatives and parishioners expressed interest in land nearby. In 1934 his son-in-law tried to buy a tract, but could not complete the down payment. By the end of 1935, however, another black, William Landrum, had purchased 80 acres to the south of Holliday, and to the east George Shelton, one of his vestrymen, was renting twenty acres with an option to buy. In 1936 Kimpel reported "three negro prospects," perhaps including the two blacks, Oliver Moore and Webster Johnson, who shortly thereafter purchased land in the section diagonally to the northwest of Holliday's. In 1940 Holliday bought forty more acres diagonally northeast of his original purchase, which on the east adjoined the land of Forest Mynor, who had purchased it from the John S. Owen Company in 1932.[53]

The experience of these African-Americans who purchased cutover land differed in some respects from that of other cutover settlers. The Owen interests treated them as special, regularly identifying them as "negroes" or "colored men" in correspondence and even in their land sales ledger, where no one else was identified by race or ethnicity.[54] The settlers themselves also chose to behave distinctively. Most of them remained in Milwaukee rather than moving immediately to their land in Clark County. They also paid for their land differently. In the 1930s the Owen companies generally sold land on seven-year contracts, usually with at least a partial balloon payment rather than by regular amortization. Most purchasers paid a lump-sum down payment of $50 to $100, but African-Americans generally made their down payments in small monthly installments of $5 to $10, or rented with their payments to be credited to the down payment. Once they had completed the down payment, in practice, or often by the terms of their contracts, they paid principal and interest monthly. Since the black settlers were usually still living in Milwaukee, Kimpel generally collected these small monthly payments, somewhat in the manner of an insurance debit. These practices were certainly patronizing on the part of the Owen companies, but they also show that the companies could be flexible and fit their terms of sale to meet the needs of African-American settlers. For their part, the black purchasers apparently believed that their chances for success in the cutover would be greater if they had paid all or much of their purchase price before beginning farming. They understood, more so than many cutover settlers, that they would need cash to get by for several years before their farms could support them.

Prior to 1940, apparently only Mynor actually settled in Clark County.[55] His struggles exemplified the experience of blacks who purchased land in the town of Hoard. In 1935, after farming for two years, he had only two acres in corn and one in hay and owned just one cow, compared to an average herd in the town of eleven head. By 1944 he had four acres in corn, ten in oats, and eight in hay, as well as a potato patch. But perhaps because by 1944 the farm had to support twelve people, Mynor never made a payment on his land contract and finally lost his farm by foreclosure in March 1945. Holliday, Shelton, and Landrum were also frequently delinquent in their payments, but managed to pay enough so that the John S. Owen Company issued Holliday his deed in 1940 and Shelton in 1942.

After World War II all three actually lived in Clark County on farms with newly built barns. In 1948 Holliday had a herd of twelve cows and Shelton had a herd of seven. Landrum, however, who still owed money to Owen on his purchase price, was recorded as having "no crops" and lived with seven others on one of the few farms in the town without electricity.[56] In the 1950s Landrum was receiving public assistance. Webster Johnson and Oliver Moore were never able to complete their purchases, but the Owen companies subsequently transferred their properties to other African-Americans. One of these men, John L. Pitts, despite the interruption of a term in the state prison, was living on his land by 1950 and still making payments on his land contract in the late 1950s, when the record of his account ceases.[57] In 1950, the bloc of farms operated by Holliday, Pitts, Shelton, and Landrum adjoined the farms of Paul Lampkins, who had purchased Mynor's place in 1945, and James Goodman, who did not buy from the Owen interests but whose surname suggests he was an African-American. These apparently were the six black farmers in Clark County enumerated on the 1950 United States Census.

What was the significance of this attempt at African-American settlement in the cutover? The struggles of the handful of blacks who did farm in Clark County highlights their determination and tenacity, as well as the wisdom of their decision not to move to their farms during the burst of the back-to-the land movement of the early 1930s, but wait until the relatively good years of World War II. Their record compares favorably to that of all settlers in those years—only eleven of fifty-one land purchasers from the John S. Owen Lumber Company in 1931–1932 eventually received deeds to their land. That these African-Americans chose to settle in the cutover shows that the still-partially developed quality of northern Wisconsin allowed space for marginal social and economic groups like blacks, and that developers and local officials and residents were reasonably tolerant. But the redemption of the cutover as a region of yeoman farmers was not going to come from large numbers of African-American settlers. Like most back-to-the-land migrants in the 1930s, blacks generally had too few economic resources to succeed. Statewide in Wisconsin between 1935 and 1940, the number of black farmers declined 34 percent, almost five times the overall rate in the state. It was by their own choice that more African-American migrants from the rural South did not settle on farms in the North, even in places like the Wisconsin cutover where inexpensive land was still available. It is true that many foreign immigrants found the lifestyle offered by the cutover to be attractive, but most African-Americans were not about to underconsume for ten years, as many immigrants were willing to do, in order to own forty acres of stumps.[58] It was not that blacks in the United States were not eager to farm; freedmen had clearly expressed their desire, even expectation, to own small yeoman farms. But these farms would have been in a place African-Americans were familiar with and in which they thought they had a stake. The real opportunity for African-Americans to become yeoman farmers was lost fifty years before a handful of descendants of freedmen tried to farm in the Wisconsin cutover.

Northern Wisconsin in 1940 was no longer a frontier. In many respects it had come to resemble the older rural areas of southern Wisconsin, although its movement in this direction had been retarded by the depressed economic conditions of the interwar years and had become obscured to outsiders. The cutover, however, had not become a fully settled region of yeoman farmers. Its social and economic characteristics still differed from those of the rest of Wisconsin, and in some respects the divergence was growing. It was ironic, furthermore, that some of the characteristics it did increasingly share with other parts of rural America had the effect of gradually weakening the yeoman farming lifestyle.

By 1940 the cutover did not show most of the demographic characteristics of a frontier which had been evident in the region in 1920 (chapter 2). The sex ratio, at 114 in the cutover compared to 104 throughout Wisconsin, was more evenly balanced (Table 2.1).[59] The age structure was no longer as disproportionately youthful (Table 6.1). Where less than 20 percent of the cutover's population had been forty-five or older in 1920, 28 percent was by 1940, essentially similar to the statewide aver-

Table 6.1. Age Structure of Wisconsin's Population, 1940 (percentages)

Age	Wisconsin	Northern Wisconsin
Under 21	35.7	39.4
22–44	35.7	32.7
45 and over	28.6	27.9

Source: U.S. Bureau of the Census, *Sixteenth Census of the United States (1940): Population,* vol. 2: *Characteristics of the Population,* pt. 7 (Washington, D.C., 1943), 553, 578–92.

age. The declining influx of young families into the cutover and the increasing out-migration by young adults accounts for this pattern. Most significantly, fertility had decreased in the cutover (Table 6.2) For the rural farm population, already by 1930 it was lower than the comparable statewide rate. This trend would continue when the baby boom began in the 1940s, which disproportionately increased births in urban and suburban Wisconsin.[60]

However, many social practices traditionally found in rural America—not just on the frontier—were still clearly evident in northern Wisconsin on the eve of World War II. Demographically this was seen in the pattern of seasonality of births (Figure 6.3). The rhythms of work associated with the seasonality of nature affected the rate of sexual activity among cutover couples, and consequently conceptions and births, as it had among rural people for thousands of years.[61] The seasonality of births in the cutover exaggerates the statewide pattern and parallels that throughout rural Wisconsin. In the late 1930s, cutover couples were most active sexually in August, at the height of northern Wisconsin's brief summer. Then the duties of the harvest, the growing shortness of the days, the increasing confinement to often crowded farmhouses, and the nutritional shortfalls brought on by lack of fresh food in winter led to a

Table 6.2. Indices of Fertility in the Cutover, 1920–1950

	1920	1930	1940	1950
Total population	131	119	123	109
Basis for calculation	6 AND UNDER	4 AND UNDER	4 AND UNDER	UNDER 1 YEAR
	females 18–44	females 15–44	females 18–44	unmarried females, 14 and older
Rural farm population	n.a.	99	100	101
Basis for calculation	n.a.	UNDER 1 YEAR	4 AND UNDER	4 AND UNDER
		married females 15 and older	females 15–44	females 15–44

Note: Total population of Wisconsin = 100.
Sources: Fourteenth Census of the United States, 1920, vol. 3: *Population* (Washington, 1922), 1124–30; *Fifteenth Census of the United States, 1930: Population,* vol. 3, pt. 2 (Washington, 1932), 1320–32; *Sixteenth Census of the United States, 1940: Population,* vol. 2, pt. 7 (Washington, 1943), 574–92, 612–16; *Census of Population, 1950,* vol. 2, pt. 49 (Washington, 1952), 121–25, 131.

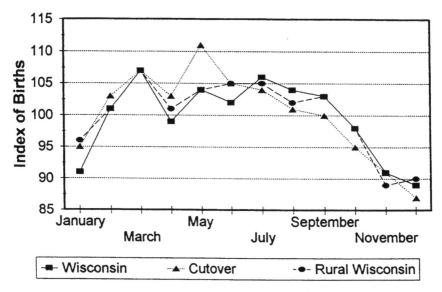

Figure 6.3. Index of seasonality of births, 1938–1939 (100 = monthly expectation). (*38th Report of the State Board of Health of Wisconsin*. [Madison, 1941],
128–29, 134–39. Rural Wisconsin calculations for forty-eight counties for 1939
only)

steady decline through March in the rate of conceptions. With the
belated arrival in April of spring in the cutover, warmer temperatures,
the increasing use of automobiles as road conditions improved, and the
feasibility of outdoor rendezvous made sexual encounters more frequent, and consequently the rate of conception finally rose.

In their labor patterns, as in their demographic patterns, rural residents of northern Wisconsin on the eve of World War II maintained
many familiar practices. For instance, family members provided most
of the labor force on cutover farms, as they had in 1920. In the last week
of March 1940, hired help was present on only 7.4 percent of farms in
the cutover, compared to 21.2 percent of farms statewide.[62] A farmer
who had retired in 1920 would also have been comfortable with what
was grown on cutover farms just before World War II. While at the urg-
ing of agricultural extension agents and other specialists alfalfa was becoming more common, most cutover farmers still depended on clover
and timothy to feed their dairy cows. They grew oats for their horses,
which still supplied most of the power on cutover farms. Short-season

hybrid varieties of corn were still new and had not yet made an impact. Consequently, restrained by the length of the growing season, cutover farmers grew relatively less corn than farmers statewide in Wisconsin. The use of commercial fertilizers and herbicides was also still uncommon in northern Wisconsin.[63] In 1939 only about 9 percent of cutover farmers used commercial fertilizer, compared to almost 20 percent of all Wisconsin farmers.[64]

To be sure, farming in the cutover on the eve of World War II had changed since 1920. Like their counterparts throughout North America but at a slower pace, northern Wisconsin farmers gradually relied more on machinery. The content of probate inventories of farmers who died in Taylor County in 1936–1937, compared to those of farmers who died twenty years previously, shows this pattern (Table 6.3). Items such as mowers and plows, which most farmers owned in 1915–1916, were now essentially universal. Items such as binders and cultivators, which only a minority possessed in 1915–1916, were common by 1936–1937. Even items such as hay loaders and manure spreaders (important because of the lack of commercial fertilizer), which only a few farmers owned in 1915–1916, were found on about half of the farms of Taylor County decedents by 1936–1937. This greater availability of machinery helped

Table 6.3. Percentages of Farmers with Selected Items of Farm Equipment, Taylor County, 1915–1916 and 1936–1937

	1915–1916	1936–1937
Horse	72.7	84.0
Mower	68.2	96.0
Plow	63.6	88.0
Rake	54.5	64.0
Harrow	36.4	56.0
Cultivator	36.4	68.0
Binder	27.3	64.0
Hay loader	8.0	48.0
Manure spreader	4.5	48.0
Truck	4.5	4.0
Tractor	0	24.0
Mean Herd Size	7.14	9.64
n =	22	25

Source: Taylor County Court Case Files, 1878–1946 (boxes 10–12, 30–32), ARC, UWEC.

this group of Taylor County farmers to increase their herd sizes about 35 percent between 1915–1916 and 1936–1937. Tractors, however, were still uncommon (although not absent, as they had been in 1915–1916). The census of 1940 reported tractors on less than one fourth of all Taylor County farms, which was about the average for the cutover. Throughout Wisconsin, by contrast, about 45 percent of farms were worked with tractors.[65] The relative lack of expensive equipment such as tractors kept the total value of machinery on northern Wisconsin farms well below the state average: in 1945 cutover farms had machinery worth only 56 percent of machinery on the average Wisconsin farm, and had slipped from 62 percent in 1910. In sum, the increase in mechanization on farms in the cutover in the interwar years was largely consistent with, and encouraged, the expansion of yeoman farming, with its limited capitalization and heavy reliance on family labor.

The paucity of tractors on cutover farms highlighted another significant point: the cutover in 1940 was still a poor region. The value of the average cutover farm's land and buildings was about $3,000, just 47 percent of the value of the average Wisconsin farm.[66] Furthermore, while cutover farms had increased in value faster than the statewide rate between 1900 and 1920 (chapter 2), their value relative to the average farm in the state was unchanged between 1920 and 1940 (Figure 6.4). A factor in this slow pace of development was the tendency for cutover farmers to spend more of their time in off-farm work than other farmers in Wisconsin, either out of preference for mining or woods work or out of necessity because of Depression conditions. In 1935, when less than one third of all Wisconsin farmers reported off-farm work, most farmers did this type of work in fifteen of the eighteen cutover counties, and reported significantly more days than other farmers working off their farms. Part-time off-farm work was usually common in newly settled farm regions in the United States, but its continuing significance in the cutover highlighted the incomplete development of the region after fifty years of effort.[67]

As the cutover moved away from resembling a frontier but remained poor and incompletely developed as a region of yeoman farming, there were opportunities for single women to operate farms.[68] To be sure, some apparent farm ownership by women was a smokescreen to hide male control. Maud Ferguson Pratt, while teaching in Bayfield County in the 1890s, fronted for a lumber company by filing a homestead claim on which she was paid "half its value" when it was proven up. "A lot of

Figure 6.4. Andres farm near Conrath, Dec. 11, 1948. Rocks removed from fields have been gathered along fence lines, and second-growth forest is visible in the background. (State Historical Society of Wisconsin, photo WHi (X3) 50581)

schoolteachers took advantage of this law," she admitted, "and filed both for timber and homestead" claims.[69] On the Great Plains, women often used this opportunity to increase the amount of their family's land or acquire some land for themselves to bring to their marriage. But in contrast to the situation on the plains, in the cutover little land was taken by homesteading by anybody, and the significance of women homesteaders was limited. But probably more so than on the plains, some single women actually operated farms in northern Wisconsin.[70] The *Milwaukee Journal* endorsed this practice in 1904, arguing that farming would not "unsex" women, who had the brains to hire men for back-breaking work.[71] In these early years of the century, Ed L. Peet, for many years an indefatigable promoter of Burnett County land, reported that twenty single women from Minnesota, mostly former schoolteachers (and who were "not afraid of light soil"), had settled in the town of Lincoln. This group stood out on the 1910 U.S. Census. Ten women who were divorced, widowed, or had absent husbands were farmers in the town of Lincoln (four other women without husbands, but with other occupations, were heads of households). In keeping with the background of cutover settlers, eight of these women were immigrants and the other two were second-generation Americans. As the *Journal* indicated, male labor was usually necessary for these farms to succeed: seven of these women farmers had sons or sons-in-law aged 14 or older living with them (two of the other three lived with another adult woman).[72]

Two decades later single women still had a presence in the rural cutover. The back-to-the-land movement brought some unmarried women to rural northern Wisconsin. Theresa Langford and her three children in 1935 moved to the Three Rivers area in Oneida County, near where her mother lived and her brother farmed. Theresa lived for a while in an old schoolhouse, working as a farmer's housekeeper, harvesting beans and potatoes, and collecting relief. In 1939 she married Robert Cullum.[73] Like Theresa, many of these single women lived on their own only for a brief time. For instance, in the town of Lenroot in Sawyer County, Theresa Sterling had lived on her father's farm since he had moved to the town sometime between 1900 and 1910. Then in 1935, at age fifty-eight, she was identified as living there alone, with twenty-three acres in crops and two cows. Five years later, the farm's operator was Theresa Decker, and now there were two people living there. Theresa, apparently, had found a spouse.[74] Other women, however, lived on their own for extended periods of time. Theresa's neighbor in the town of Lenroot, Ola Frets, operated a seventy-nine-acre farm throughout the interwar years, generally with about twenty acres in crops. In Marathon County, bordering the cutover, Anna Pratt Erickson operated a farm sporadically for about twenty-five years, in periods after the death of her first husband and her divorce from her second. She relied on the labor of her children, work exchange with neighbors, and hired men until her son Morris took over the farm in the early 1940s.[75]

Widowhood was the most common reason for women to become farm operators, and this circumstance became more frequent as the cutover's population aged. Many widows quickly left their farms. For example, when Robert Wood died in Taylor County in 1917, he left his wife and nine children on a ten-acre farm. The widow found herself with "no means to pay taxes" for "this year or last year," and while the estate was still in probate she successfully petitioned the county court to be allowed to sell it, distribute the net proceeds in accordance with the intestate laws, and move to Sioux City, Iowa.[76] But other widows remained on their land for long periods of time, especially if they had male children to help them. Emma Ingebretson Larson was in her early thirties with six young children when her husband died in the early 1910s. She stayed on her farm in the town of Crystal in Washburn County, planted a "big garden" especially with potatoes, maintained a herd of about ten cows, and made butter and sold it. "You might say I raised the kids myself," she reported proudly.[77]

Statistics gathered from several towns in Bayfield County suggest the extent of farming by single women in the cutover on the eve of World War II. Women operated only two of the forty-three farms in the town of Drummond. But female farmers were more common in the more developed towns of Washburn (on 10 out of 115 farms) and Oulu (on 15 out of 205 farms). In Oulu the average-sized herd on a woman's farm was a respectable 5.4 cows, and in Cable the largest herd in the town—twenty cows—belonged to a woman.[78] In northern Wisconsin there was a niche within yeoman farming for independent women. But female-operated farms were the antithesis of what agricultural experts and planners wanted to see: farms large enough and productive enough for men to "support" their wives without the input of much productive female labor, as was the ideal in urban, industrial America. The presence of this deviant type of farming deepened suspicions about northern Wisconsin already aroused by the region's endemic poverty.

What sort of a standard of living did these cutover farms actually provide for the families who lived on them? As with machinery, cutover farms almost always had the basic items for family living. In 1940 privies or flush toilets were as common on a cutover farm as anywhere in Wisconsin; only 3 percent of cutover families had to use the bushes. Almost all the memoirs of settlers agree with Florence Dale Burmeister, who came with her parents to Washburn County in 1899, that "we always had plenty to eat." The ability of cutover farms in the late 1930s to provide about 60 percent of their residents' food needs helped keep diets sufficient. Furthermore, automobiles were almost as common on cutover farms as throughout rural Wisconsin. But there is also no question that many modern conveniences were often absent from northern Wisconsin farms. Women, in particular, felt these shortcomings, as limited financial resources often went to the barn before they went to the farmhouse. For instance, only 11 percent of cutover farmhouses had running water in 1940, compared to 19 percent of all Wisconsin farms. The U.S. Census that year categorized 47 percent of cutover farmhouses as in need of major repairs, compared to 31 percent of farmhouses throughout the state and only 16 percent of all Wisconsin homes. Social scientists used these data to create indexes which showed the primitiveness of life in the cutover.[79]

One aspect of the standard of living in which northern Wisconsin lagged was electrification. The relatively dispersed population of the region made the initial capital costs of electrification exorbitantly high. The new farmhouse in 1923 on the Anderson farm in northern Polk County had been wired for electricity, but the supply never came. In 1928, in the seven cutover counties served by the Lake Superior District Power Company, only forty farms were electrified. Most cutover farmers relied on kerosene lanterns for light ("like holding a candle," recalled Olaf Anderson) and gasoline engines (which were a struggle to start on cold winter mornings) for water-pumping and other power needs. A few farms, such as Roy Meier's in Price County, had small electric generators of their own (about 880 cutover farms were so equipped in 1940).[80] When the New Deal decided to encourage rural electrification through the programs of the Rural Electrification Administration (REA), farmers in the cutover and neighboring counties were quick to take advantage of the opportunity.[81] Disdaining officials' doubts about the abilities of rural people to manage power plants and high-voltage lines, northern Wisconsin farmers drew on their experience in cooperatives to create organizations which would control the generation and transmission as well as the distribution of electric power. In Clark County, for instance, at the instigation of county agricultural agent Wallace Landry, farmers organized one of the largest electric cooperatives in Wisconsin, which was probably the first such cooperative to build a generating plant.[82] In sum, the experience of rural people in the cutover in obtaining electricity for their farms supports historian Mary Neth's argument that the successful introduction in the Midwest of the new technology of rural electrification depended upon the existing strength of socially conservative yeoman farming.[83]

Electrification programs began to make a difference on cutover farms. Although only 28 percent of northern Wisconsin farms had electricity in 1940, compared with 49 percent of all Wisconsin farms, electricity was rapidly becoming a common feature. For instance, in Rusk, Taylor, and Price counties, most farms were electrified in 1944, where only between 9 and 15 percent had been in 1938.[84] On the Anderson farm in Luck, the kids thought electricity was "just wonderful" and went around turning on all the lights just to see how they worked; when the REA's "high line" came through southern Price County in 1941, Roy Meier traded his electric plant for a tractor.[85]

The electricity grid which slowly developed across northern Wisconsin was one way in which the cutover was linked, quite literally, with the outside world. Of course, it was harder for a cutover farmer to be well informed about events outside the region than a farmer in a more densely settled, prosperous part of Wisconsin. Sarah Martin, who grew up on a farm near Minong in Washburn County, admitted that "it was hard to hear about the [World] War, especially living out in the sticks; it was very hard to get newspapers and radios that far out." Face-to-face encounters were the important sources of information in traditional rural communities like the cutover. Sarah Martin explained that in her community, "We found out most of our information at church or at the Bear's Cabin—a store."[86] But more formal modern sources of communication and information were not absent from the cutover and gradually gained influence. By the early 1930s, cutover farms were almost as likely to take a weekly newspaper as were farms throughout Wisconsin.[87] To be sure, the national and especially the international news content of these papers was not large, but most carefully involved their rural readers in the regional community by regularly running columns reporting events in rural neighborhoods.[88] Cutover radio listeners had few local stations to tune in to, and therefore, as Roy Meier recalled, wound up listening to Chicago or Milwaukee stations, which provided them with a more cosmopolitan perspective. The railroad network which crisscrossed northern Wisconsin (Figure 1.5) also kept the region in touch with the rest of the country. As early as 1904, the *Phillips Times* in Price County regularly ran advertisements for special excursion packages for visitors to the St. Louis World's Fair. Articles in the paper reported on events at the fair and on people from Price County who visited it.[89] Closer to home, during the 1920s the Soo Line railroad ran weekend excursions from northern Wisconsin to the Twin Cities. The railroad also brought the larger world to the cutover: for example, following the end of the regular season in 1924, the St. Louis Browns baseball team barnstormed across northern Wisconsin.[90] Interregional connections continued during the Depression, reflected by the Park Falls newspaper's coverage of the Century of Progress World's Fair in Chicago.[91] Transportation was also adequate enough for rural people to interact among themselves within northern Wisconsin. As a resident of the town of Piehl in eastern Oneida County emphasized about the years between 1910 and 1930, "The people of Piehl were not isolated, though they only had corduroy roads. . . . Travel was not a problem," he explained, "since there was daily two-way train service to Rhinelander," sixteen miles away.[92] The Park Falls newspaper illustrated this practice when it reported that during one week in January 1929 eight women from the town of Fifield visited Park Falls on one day, and nine women on another.[93]

In sum, balance is needed for a fair evaluation of the standard of living on cutover farms on the eve of World War II. The basis for comparison needs to be kept in mind. Standard of living indexes ranked the cutover lower than southern Wisconsin, the core of a relatively prosperous farming state. But the indexes put cutover farms ahead of those in all of the southeastern United States; most of Texas, Oklahoma, and the Southwest; and the western Great Plains. In general, they rated northern Wisconsin farms as comparable to those in southern Illinois and Indiana. In Union County in southern Illinois, for instance, a region of poor fruit and vegetable farms but vibrant community life, only 4 percent of farms had running water in the farmhouse, 15 percent electricity, and 19 percent tractors in 1940.[94] Cutover farms met the basic needs of their residents. As Ed Pudas explained, the Depression years "were always not so rosy perhaps" on the family farm in Washburn County, "but I can't say we ever went hungry."[95] Furthermore, we must keep in mind that the expectations of cutover settlers were limited; their definition of success was not based on material accumulation. "We didn't have a lot of money," Margaret Pike admitted, "but we had all these good things," such as popcorn, fudge, a pipe organ in the house, and visits to the circus.[96] When Carl Stassel was interviewed in 1959, he had seventy-four years of perspective to evaluate the meaning of change for the quality of life in the area around Sheldon, in Rusk County. His conclusion was that when he and his neighbors had struggled to survive by combining farming and work in lumber camps, people "lived better than many folk do today."[97]

For many rural people in the cutover this quality of life was enhanced by involvement in community activities. Churches were often "the center of life" in a community, as a pastor recalled about rural Chippewa County in the 1920s.[98] There were 840 congregations in the cutover in 1940.[99] The thinness of the population in many parts of northern Wisconsin and the continued attachment of many settlers, particularly immigrants, to the particular denomination in which they had been raised meant that many of these congregations were relatively small. The average cutover congregation had about 165 members in the late 1930s.[100]

This situation led to cries from within and outside northern Wisconsin that the cutover was "overchurched."[101] For instance, in the late 1930s near Luck in northern Polk County, theological and liturgical divisions between "happy Danes" and "holy Danes," combined with the widespread desire to have a church within walking distance, meant that the community had two congregations affiliated with the Danish Evangelical Lutheran Church in America and two other congregations affiliated with the United Danish Evangelical Lutheran Church in America.[102] The large number of congregations and the limited financial resources of cutover residents produced a shortage of clergy in northern Wisconsin. In Price County in the early 1920s, for instance, only five of the thirty Protestant churches had full-time pastors, and five pulpits were vacant. Throughout northern Wisconsin in 1940, there were only about half as many clergy as there were congregations.[103]

Church people in the cutover adapted to this situation by "yoking" congregations and sharing pastors. At Luck, for instance, the four Lutheran congregations were served by two ministers, Pastor J. M. Firtz and Pastor Jens F. Andraesen. The experience in the 1920s of an Episcopal priest, Father Samuel Evans, is illustrative of this pattern. Evans was based in Medford, Taylor County, where he was vicar of St. Mary's, and also served Episcopal congregations to the north at Westboro, Prentice, Park Falls, and Mellen, in Price and Ashland counties. Between Labor Day and Memorial Day during 1923–1924, Evans led Sunday services about twenty-one times at Medford, usually for about forty congregants. He was at Park Falls on seventeen Sundays, at Mellen on twelve, and at Westboro on two. He also held services at his churches fourteen times on weekdays and holy days. On many Sundays he had to rush to be in different churches at different times—on three occasions he preached at Medford in the morning and sixty miles away at Mellen in the evening. These congregations were still yoked in a similar pattern in 1940.[104]

One consequence of having clergy divide their time among several congregations was that laypeople in the cutover had to take responsibility for church affairs. More so than in more settled rural areas, laypeople in northern Wisconsin shaped their own religious lives.[105] For instance, on every Sunday but two when Father Evans was absent from Medford, parishioners held Sunday school, with about half as many in attendance as when their pastor was present. Even the strictest of clergymen had to bend to some of the wishes of their parishioners. There was a small but revealing incident at Zion Evangelical Lutheran Church in Winter, Sawyer County, in the 1930s. Dagmar Noel and another fourteen-year-old girl "were caught wearing our new lipstick to church." They were chastised and consequently quit as Sunday school teachers, "but soon came back because there were so few teachers. We still wore our lipstick—but real lightly."[106]

Lay people's organizations played important roles in cutover churches. At West Denmark Lutheran Church in Luck in 1914 the Young People's Society subscribed $1,500 and free labor for the construction of a *Gymnastik Sal* (gymnasium). Furthering the holistic spirit of the Danish Folk School tradition, this building served as a social center, lecture hall, theater, and gymnasium. Christ Birkholm taught Danish gymnastics and folk dancing there until the late 1930s.[107]

Women's groups were the most significant lay organization in most cutover churches. In his annual report in 1925 the pastor at Zion acknowledged that "the Ladies Aids have been our most active organizations. Truly it might be said of them that they are the backbone of the church, at least in a financial way." When twenty-six families founded Sheldon Church of Christ in 1922, the Ladies Aid raised the money to buy an old bank building in town for use as a meeting place. In 1932 it sold the bank building and loaned $400 to the congregation towards building a new church. At St. Francis of Assisi Roman Catholic Church in Flambeau, the oldest church in Rusk County, the Catholic Altar Society kept alive the congregation of about fifty families, raising money through dinners, raffles, bingo, and donations, and paying for hymnals, fuel oil, insurance, cemetery cleaning, building repairs ($27.20 in 1938 to redecorate the sacristy)—whatever needed to be done. At Zion, the pastor pointed out in his 1933 annual report that despite the ravages of the Depression, "the Ladies Aide still found it possible to pay for paint and labor for decorating our place of worship, and remunerate Bible School Teacher for board and services."[108]

Churches in the cutover gained strength as time passed. The percentage of the population affiliated with a congregation gradually increased, and individual congregations emerged from the Depression stronger than before. Sheldon Church of Christ, which was used to having a minister visit from Holcombe every other Sunday, was able to hire its first full-time pastor in 1943. In 1936 Zion Lutheran in Winter purchased a parsonage for its pastor. In 1938 the congregation, which had been worshipping for a decade in the basement of its uncompleted church, agreed to take a $1,300 loan from the Mission Board of the Augustana Synod (to be paid off by the Ladies Aid) to finish construction. West Denmark Lutheran Church recovered from a lightning fire which destroyed the church building in September 1937. Within weeks the congregation voted to rebuild and subscribed $2,013 and 194 days of free labor. The rebuilding effort brought together the congregation, which had been divided for over a decade by a controversy within the Danish Evangelical Lutheran Church in America over the qualifications needed for ministerial ordination. Reconstruction was completed in time for a confirmation service on May 29, 1938.[109]

One function of cutover churches was to regulate public and private morality. The Reverend Nels Benson, pastor at Zion during the early 1930s, was typical of cutover clergymen in denouncing "tavern fellowship, dancing, card playing and other questionable phases of our local community life." Although Benson did not explicitly mention illicit sexuality among his roster of sins, he perhaps alluded to it by explaining how the other problems "pluck away the good seed" from the church.[110] The message of Pastor Benson and his brethren in the pulpit had some effect. Despite the popular view from outside the cutover that the region was a land of licentiousness, lust was not unchecked in northern Wisconsin. On the eve of World War II, illegitimacy rates were close to the statewide average, and divorce rates were actually lower than in Wisconsin as a whole.[111] Some local residents put the blame for the image and some of the reality of illicit sexuality in the cutover on outsiders—sweaty-palmed tourists who had read the coy allusions to loose sex in descriptions of northern Wisconsin and came north on their vacations anticipating a good time. Robert Peters, who was an adolescent growing up near Eagle River in Vilas County in the late 1930s, recalled the local disdain for vacationers who took up casually with local girls, sometimes impregnating them. "The glamorous allure of city life," he lamented, "destroyed many of these girls." His sister Nell explained that "by seducing one of these rich guys, they thought they'd marry and spin off to Chicago or Milwaukee to a life of wealth and pampering." Among themselves, young people in the cutover had their own standards. Referring to the consorts of tourists, Robert Peters explained that "no hard-working local male would marry such used goods."[112] Some sexual encounters, of course, took place among young people in northern Wisconsin. But when pregnancy resulted, local standards dictated that a shotgun wedding follow. When Edith Martin, who grew up on a farm near Minong, found herself pregnant at sixteen in 1942, "mom and dad didn't say too much." But after "talking to Pastor Olson about the situation" they went ahead and arranged a wedding.[113] In general, immigrants to the rural Midwest in the late nineteenth century followed stricter standards of premarital sexuality than they had done in Europe, a pattern reinforced by their gradual absorption of Victorian moral standards in America.[114] A few decades later, settlers in the cutover, by their restricted but not prudish sexual behavior, followed the pattern of their predecessors in rural America.

One of the major goals of yeoman farmers from the time of the first British settlement in North America had been to provide their male progeny with the land necessary to set up their own farms in their parents' community.[115] In the nineteenth century native-born Americans began to put more emphasis on providing their sons with financial resources, with often only one son inheriting land and the others outmigrating. Immigrants, however, clung to the yeoman pattern of trying to establish all their heirs as farmers, which often involved fragmenting their estates.[116] Hence immigrants generally had lower migration rates out of their communities of birth than did native-born Americans, a pattern which was evident in the cutover in the migration pattern of the residents of seven towns in Rusk and Sawyer counties previously analyzed (Table 4.3).

Cutover settlers brought yeoman values about inheritance to the cutover. For instance, Joe Zelinka, of the town of Riverview in Oconto County, required in his 1931 will that his male heirs live together on the family farm in separate houses with one barn. They would "farm together each as member of family," he prescribed, "with no selling right of any land." If any tried to sell or divide the property, he would be "put out." Over time, some cutover settlers were able to implement the traditional yeoman pattern of land transfer, albeit without the draconian restrictions of Zelinka. When he was interviewed in 1969, seventy-six-year-old Guy Campbell lived on 640 acres in the town of Trego in Washburn County, most of which had been farmed by his father, who had moved there from South Dakota in 1902. Guy's son lived on an adjacent eighty-acre farm which he had inherited from his grandfather. Guy proudly reported that "these are both now large and well cultivated farms, having been hewed out of the wilderness by the Campbells since my father purchased them in 1901."[117] But most cutover farmers were not able to replicate this aspect of yeoman farming. Their farms were too small to begin with to subdivide among heirs, and their financial resources were too limited for them to purchase additional land for their sons (Guy Campbell's father had been unusual in making a large initial purchase, 320 acres, at a low price, $2.50 an acre).

Patterns in farmers' estates probated in Taylor County illuminate this situation and show the strategies cutover farmers chose to deal with its limitations. In sharp contrast to the pattern at that time in more agriculturally developed parts of Iowa, only a decreasing minority of farmers bothered to write wills. In 1915, 68 percent of the thirty-four deceased farmers allowed their estates to be distributed in accordance with the intestate laws, and 73 percent of fifty-nine farmers did so in 1935.[118] Intestate descent encouraged fragmentation of property: Wisconsin laws in the 1930s essentially assigned one third of real and personal property to the widow in such instances, and divided the rest of the estate equally among the children, subject to the widow's life use of that part of the real property designated as "homestead." Among the sixteen cases in Taylor County in which there was a will and the deceased was survived by both a wife and children, in four instances the deceased essentially divided his property among his children, and in only one of the instances was able to give at least forty acres to more than one son. Property was concentrated for at least eventual descent to a favored son in six instances, usually subject to provision for the widow. In six instances the deceased essentially left all his property to his wife, and if the four women's wills in the samples were an accurate indication, this property eventually was usually evenly divided among the children ("share and share alike," as more than one testator wrote) upon her death. In sum, more than one son seldom inherited enough land from his father to farm in the cutover. However, faced with this inability to follow the ideals of yeoman agriculture, only a minority of cutover farmers chose to concentrate their limited legacy into a viable farm for a favored son, often preferring to ensure that their widow was sufficiently provided for. The result was generally fragmentation of small estates.

This fragmentation necessitated intrafamily cooperation among the heirs. "Usually one or two of the children buy out the interests of the other," explained the Taylor County Judge. These arrangements were "most always made outside of any court proceedings."[119] Joe Zelinka understood the necessity for this cooperation when he insisted in his will that "members of family will fight brush, stumps, and stones that keep them busy so they will not fight among themselves." Sometimes the support of the entire community was necessary to ensure a harmonious and effective transfer of property, especially if a poor widow had to be taken care of.[120] For instance, C. O. Gray died intestate in the town of Jump River, Taylor County, in 1935, leaving forty acres appraised at

$1,500. The farm's handful of livestock and equipment were auctioned for $315 and an automobile worth $250 remained. The estate paid out $365 in debts and expenses, leaving exactly the $200 legally due to Mrs. Gray before the rest of the personal property (in this instance, nothing) would be divided among her and her children. This balance existed because the local funeral director and lawyer only charged the estate nominal fees (and the appraisers conveniently decided the automobile was worth $250). Mrs. Gray was left with the automobile, $53.62 in cash as an administratrix's fee, and the life use of the farm, which would not have to be sold to settle the estate (although, of course, she lacked the equipment to farm it).[121]

Of course, the transfer of property from one generation to the next was not always harmonious. The experience of the children of widower Joseph Lang, who died intestate in the town of Little Black, Taylor County, in 1936, was revealing. Joseph left a prosperous, unmortgaged eighty-acre farm and a herd of sixteen cows. His heirs were one son and five daughters, to one of whom he had given *inter vivos* a $2,900 mortgage loan, the kind of assistance which often caused problems among heirs. In this instance, the attorney for the estate's executor concluded, "It is quite evident that the heirs are discordant and have other purposes and motives than to co-operate in closing this estate." Joseph's son Frank had been living on the farm with his father and apparently wished to continue operating it. In order to reduce the value of the estate and therefore make it easier for him to purchase his siblings' shares, Frank claimed $3,500 for wages and expenses while he had worked the farm during the illness that preceded his father's death, including mileage for transporting his father to the hospital! He eventually settled for $1,428 (from the sale of the estate's personal property), $300 in cash from his sisters, and some other assets of the estate. Meanwhile, with the support of most of his sisters, Frank offered to buy the intact farm. He was blocked by his sister who was indebted to the estate (who apparently preferred to see it liquidated and apply her share to reduce her debt) and the executor, who thought that Frank's neighbors had deliberately helped him by underappraising the farm (he noted a cow appraised at $35, which he felt was worth $60, and which indeed was eventually auctioned for $53). Eventually the residual assets of Joseph Lang's estate— the farm itself and his daughter's note—were divided among the six children. Frank Lang presumably bought out his sisters (it was he who had purchased much of the farm's equipment at auction). Frank had cash from the $1.00-per-day wages he earned from the estate for working the farm and from his settlement with the estate for expenses; he could also raise money by mortgaging his share of the farm.[122] In this case, with only one son, the Lang farm remained within the family. But the transfer came at the expense of family harmony and, perhaps most ominously, by Frank's commercialization of the family economy when he collected money for taking his father to the hospital to die.

What happened to the children of cutover settlers who found no place for themselves, or wanted no place for themselves, on the family farm or nearby land? Men tended to look for nonagricultural jobs in the region. After five years of marriage in 1930, Wade Crane found himself in Barron County with "nothing but two more children." "Dad couldn't pay me" to work on his farm, so Wade labored as a hired man. "About November, they say we can't afford to pay you much," he recalled, "how about you work for your board and room for the winter?" Frustrated, Crane took the postal exam, which led to a thirty-year career with the Post Office.[123] Young women tended to look for employment farther away. Nell Peters, for instance, enlisted in the army immediately following graduation from Eagle River High School.[124] As time passed, more and more young people of both sexes of cutover settlers went farther afield. For example, individuals from the cohort of school graduates in Ladysmith, Sawyer County, in the 1930s were more likely to eventually live outside Wisconsin than their counterparts from the 1920s (Table 6.4). In all, by the 1930s in the cutover perhaps only about one child in four remained as an adult near where he or she had grown up.[125]

A similar migration pattern emerges from the church records of Oulu Evangelical Lutheran Church, in Bayfield County. The Finns who moved

Table 6.4. 1962 Whereabouts of Graduates of Our Lady of Sorrows School, Ladysmith, Wisconsin (percentages)

| | DATE OF GRADUATION | |
	1920–1925	1935–1939
Ladysmith and vicinity	22	24
Elsewhere in Wisconsin	24	12
Outside Wisconsin	27	47
Deceased or location unknown	27	18
n =	37	68

Source: Compiled from data in *Golden Jubilee Commemorative, Our Lady of Sorrows Church and School, Ladysmith, Wisconsin, 1912–1962* (Ladysmith, 1962).

to Oulu and joined the church showed remarkable stability: of the twelve original families of 1903, and of the thirty-nine families which subsequently joined, almost all before 1920, eighteen were still present in 1940, and four others were represented by adult children. Overall, however, few of the children of these Finns followed their parents into the church. The original members had 79 children and the subsequent members had 126 children (reflecting, incidently, the cutover's declining fertility). Almost all these children were born before 1920. Correspondingly, 206 young people were confirmed at Oulu between 1921 and 1939. But only thirteen children of members had joined the church by 1940. Some of the nonmembers, of course, were still too young; others attended services without undertaking membership; and others preferred the fellowship of the hard-drinking, secular Finns who comprised a large segment of the town's population. But many had moved from Oulu, as the church records sometimes indicated. For example, of the twenty-three children baptized in 1938 and 1939, only seven had been born in Oulu; the others came from as far away as Chicago, apparently brought back for baptism by their parents who had moved away.[126]

These migrants should not be thought of as failures. Olaf Severson pointed to numerous success stories among the "large, capable families" raised on farms near Luck before World War II. Eight children grew up on the forty-acre Clausen farm, for example, one of whom became a propane gas millionaire. Despite the farming failure of their father, the eventual occupations of the children raised on the Ravenholt farm included, among others, physician, journalist, and U.S. Senate staff member.[127] Robert Peters went on from Vilas County to a distinguished career as a poet and professor of literature. But as the aging generation which had initially settled the cutover looked around in 1940, its members had to be disappointed in the limited extent to which their children had been able to follow them on the land.

What did people who grew up in northern Wisconsin in the interwar years think about their experience? Few who felt deprived and frustrated and moved as far from the cutover as they could as soon as they were able have left personal accounts; the cutover was part of their life they wanted to forget. Robert Peters is something of an exception. His memories of Vilas County in the 1930s are not bitter, but intensely honest and certainly unromantic. "That we might starve was a common fear," he admits. He has no fond memories of one-room schoolhouses: "The stench of soiled wool, stale long johns, and unwashed bodies permeated" them. At the annual Christmas pageant Robert's speech is boring and gets short applause. "Visits from local families were rare," he remembers, and anyway the neighbors were narrow-minded, anti- Semitic, and petty thieves. Community gatherings ended in drunken fights, not warm family fellowship. As a young adolescent struggling with homoerotic feelings, Robert was introduced to sex. Like life in the cutover in general, he characterizes his early sexual experiences—not without fondness or respect—as harsh and unromantic. Sections of his narrative describing the birth of animals, insemination, and castration parallel accounts of Robert's learning to "talk dirty," observing semipublic sexual intercourse in a tavern, and experiencing his first ejaculation. The bewildering advice he receives from his father is to "fuck" the neighbor's daughter as soon as he can.[128] Robert Peters expressed his simultaneous fascination and repulsion with this aspect of life in the cutover in his later poem, "That Family," about neighbors who "never wiped their asses clean—there was no paper," and whose mother wore only a single, dirty dress. "That family took me fishing, taught me sex in the barn, and invited / me swimming. We showed our asses to the girls and called them / 'moons.' I loved that family."[129]

But when placed in its context, Peters's experience was atypical. Even by the standards of a poor town in a poor county, the Peters family was poor. There were nine acres in crops and one cow on their farm in 1937, the year Robert focuses on in his narrative. Across the town of Lincoln that year, the average farm had about eighteen acres in crops and five cows.[130] The Peters' isolation certainly had something to do with the unusual fact that they lived adjacent to the family of Robert's uncle but did not get along with their kin (in the early 1940s Robert's aunt would accuse his sister Nell of trying to murder her). By his own admission, Robert was "different," "sensitive," and "pathetically shy."

Even discounting their tendency to romanticize the "good old days," most first-hand voices present a more positive description of the cutover. Olaf Severson "always went barefoot" around his farm in Luck during the summer, but does not associate this with poverty. He remembers learning to walk with the grain of newly cut oats so as not to hurt his feet and, when on the way to school on fall mornings, jumping from warm spot to warm spot where cows had slept in the "night pasture." Harvey Dueholm admits he grew up on a "very poor" farm in Polk County, but remembers how much his father "loved the land." In his words, Harvey "held to me all these years" the memory of taking lunch to his father working in the fields, and seeing him always sit and run his hands through the soil before he would eat and stress that he wanted to be buried there. On his death bed, his father recalled to Harvey how he had gone to bed hungry in Denmark and swore that would never happen to his family in the United States.[131] Fiction written by people who grew up in the cutover also shows this attitude. Most of it does not have the literary sophistication of Robert Peters's poems or memoirs. But incidents this writing focuses on—rebuilding barns after fires, celebrating when men returned from absentee work, neighbors coming to help with dramatic childbirths, everyone enjoying the natural beauty of the landscape—clearly project a much more positive feeling for northern Wisconsin than Peters communicates.[132]

Epilogue

The farms are ploughed under, bulldozed, erased.
The trees are gone. The creeks diverted. Grass
    where the slops were thrown is still fire-green.
My parents are dead.

  Robert Peters, "Now"[1]

Farming in the United States changed dramatically in the half-century after World War II. Farms became larger and machinery more common and more expensive. Consequently the capital needed to farm expanded greatly. Chemical fertilizers and herbicides became more potent and widely used, while genetically engineered seeds increased agricultural productivity. Farms specialized more in one commodity; few grew any of the food consumed on the farm. Overseas markets expanded in importance. Government assistance—and, correspondingly, regulation—increased in significance. Social changes paralleled these economic and technological developments. The number of farmers dramatically declined; population density became too thin to maintain rural communities; shopping, schooling, and socializing shifted to ever-more-easily-accessible urban locations. With the costs of machinery and land so enormous, it became difficult for even the children of successful farmers to take over family farms. The family economy system and the networks of community labor-sharing which had undergirded yeoman farming disappeared.[2]

Farming in northern Wisconsin after 1945 reflected all these changes. Indeed, many of the changes were more pronounced in the cutover than elsewhere in rural America, since it was less strongly developed in 1940 and many planners and officials thought it particularly needed change. However, the changes did not have the results anticipated by planners in 1940. Furthermore, the very enormity of the transformations in the cutover created more space there than in other regions for the continuation of practices not in alignment with the thrust of post–World War II American agriculture. Some small-scale farming survived in the region, and some of the special qualities of northern Wisconsin remained, attracting a variety of people to the region for many of the same reasons which inspired settlers to take up cutover farms almost a century before.

In 1940 the U.S. House of Representatives empaneled a select committee to study interstate migration by "destitute" and "indigent" Americans. The committee heard testimony about the cutover at hearings in Chicago in the late summer. Witnesses from several different perspectives outlined to the committee the existing conditions and future possibilities for northern Wisconsin.[3]

The committee was concerned about the cutover as both a source and a target of undesirable migration. It heard testimony from the secretary of the Wisconsin State Planning Board that seventy-eight thousand people migrated out of the cutover between 1910 and 1930, and received a written statement from the director of the Lake States Forest Experiment Station describing the cutover as a "breeding place of migrants." The director reported an additional "5,000 miners that would like to go somewhere" but had no opportunities or resources to move. At the same time, in a somewhat paradoxical pattern, the committee also learned that in the 1930s people "began to flock back to the land" in the cutover—"Kentuckians are coming into Forest County. Polish people are coming into Armstrong Creek." Witnesses characterized this development as undesirable. "These people are chiefly squatters," claimed the Forest Experiment Station director. "They do not have any money. They become a burden on the county." The committee heard directly from one such migrant, Andrew Batjes. A forty-one-year-old unskilled and unemployed Chicagoan with a wife and four children, Batjes moved to Wisconsin and worked as a casual farm laborer from June to November 1939. He intended to stay permanently "to better myself," but when he found it was a "lean season" he went on relief for a month and collected $36 before returning to Chicago.[4]

In their testimony, witnesses outlined for the committee different scenarios for the future of the cutover. D. B. Osborne, who operated a 670-acre farm thirteen miles from Superior, presented a bright picture for farming possibilities in Douglas County, where the county owned "at least 100,000 acres of just as good land as there ever was on earth." Osborne claimed that at least a dozen farmers from his home state of Nebraska, "whipped" by agricultural conditions there, had already successfully relocated to his neighborhood. His recommendation was "that the Government go in and take over every bit of that good land from

the county, cut it up into about 80 acre tracts, clear about 20 acres of it
. . . [and] sell it to a good farmer at about $3,000 or $3,500 an 80 . . . on
an amortized-payment plan."

The Forest Experiment Station Director, Raphael Zion, proposed a
program similar to that at Drummond (chapter 6). "I do not see why the
Government could not let people settle on that agricultural land" in the
national forests which was suitable for farming. "Of course, they might
not make an economic existence from agriculture," he allowed, "but by
working in addition on roads, at fire protection, reforestation, cutting,
and so forth, they could make a fairly good living." But the message from
Wisconsin planners was negative. M. W. Torkelson, secretary of the State
Planning Board, stated flatly in respect to the cutover that "we do not
believe any large amount of migration into there is desirable." He and
University of Wisconsin land economics professor Walter A. Rowlands
explained the public programs Wisconsin had developed for dealing with
the cutover: relocation of "isolated" settlers, reforestation, and increasing the acreage in crops on those farms still considered viable (Figure
4.1)[5] The testimony of the witnesses at these hearings clearly outlined
alternative ways northern Wisconsin could develop over the next several
decades. Public policies for the cutover would follow most closely the
recommendations of Torkelson and Rowlands, but the vision of these
experts for the region would be achieved only incompletely.

There continued to be agriculture in the cutover after 1940. Some farms
expanded and prospered. Certainly in contrast to the preceding two
decades, the early 1940s were good times; high wartime commodity
prices finally raised the incomes of many cutover farmers. We "farmed
every piece we could get ahold of," recalled Roy Meier about farmers in
his community in southern Price County. Between 1940 and 1947 factory cheese production in the cutover increased by 37 percent, compared
to 31 percent growth statewide. The earnings from this increased output brought a modest prosperity to many cutover communities. Describing the Chetek area in Barron County, adjacent to the cutover, in 1949,
B. M. Apker proudly pointed out that "we now have a thriving little city
surrounded by one of the best farming countries in the state of Wisconsin." These were conditions advantageous for yeoman farming, which
continued for several decades in parts of the cutover. Writing in 1969
about the farming community of Kief in Rusk County, which had been
settled by Polish immigrants about 1900, a local historian emphasized

the community's prosperity and continuity, rooted in its inhabitants' "capacity for drudgery" and lack of ambition. These farmers showed adaptability: their crop mix changed as the use of short-season hybrid varieties of corn brought the midwestern corn belt into the western part of the cutover, and the replacement of horses with tractors sharply reduced the acreage in oats. The continuing viability of farming in northern Wisconsin, based on the spirit of yeoman farming combined with adaptation to changing technology, was recognized in 1987 when the annual Wisconsin Farm Progress Days attracted forty thousand visitors to adjacent family farms near Cumberland in Barron County, the northernmost site for the exhibition in its thirty-four-year history.[6]

But the overall picture of agriculture in the cutover after 1940 was not that of the triumph of yeoman farming. In the half-century after 1940 the number of farms and acreage in farms retreated much faster in northern Wisconsin than in the state as a whole. Where there had been 31,530 farms in the cutover in 1940, there were only 7,830 in 1991 (the statewide decrease was from 187,000 to 79,000). By 1991 the cutover had only 46 percent of the acreage in farms that it had in 1940, compared to 76 percent in all of Wisconsin. Of the fourteen counties in Wisconsin with the fewest acres in farms in 1991, eleven were found in the cutover (the other three were in the Milwaukee metropolitan area); with the exception of Taylor County, the cutover counties clustered near the bottom of Wisconsin's counties when ranked on most agricultural indexes, just as they had in 1900.[7] The planners and state officials who in their testimony at the 1940 hearings wanted agriculture curtailed in the cutover had their wishes fulfilled.

Furthermore, what farming continued in the cutover increasingly was not of the yeoman type. Some cutover residents continued to live on farms, but gave less and less effort to farming. The history of the Gustafson farm in the town of True in Rusk County reveals this pattern. Beginning in 1905, Charles Gustafson, a son of Swedish immigrants, built up a modest but successful farm. He cleared and stumped his land, built a barn and numerous other out-buildings, electrified the farm in 1939, and managed a herd of a dozen cows. At 68, Charles sold the farm in 1944 to his son-in-law, who lived on the place but concentrated on his water-system contracting business rather than agriculture. The products of the farm went mostly for family consumption; in 1966 the herd was sold and the barn torn down. There was a similar pattern on the Frank Loomis farm in the town of Cassian in Oneida County. The county took title on tax deed to the farm's 120 acres and moved Loomis and his house to the plot in 1939, in exchange for his existing farm elsewhere, in order to reduce public expenses by getting the Loomis family closer to a school. Loomis raised strawberries, maintained a few cows, chickens, and horses, and grew the crops needed to feed his animals. He spent most of his time, however, working at carpentry and masonry jobs. The next owner of the farm, Jim Busche, bought a tractor but generally operated the farm in a similar manner while working full-time at the St. Regis Paper mill in Rhinelander. In a variation of this pattern, Frank Johns worked in lumber mills all his life, then inherited his father's farm near Phillips in Price County, retired in 1958 and, in his words, "just farmed."[8] For an increasing number of part-time farmers across the cutover, farming became a hobby rather than an essential complement to seasonal off-farm work as had been envisioned at the 1940 hearings by advocates of subsistence homesteads.

Those cutover farmers who did work their farms full-time also increasingly did not resemble the model of yeoman farmers. Realizing that income per cleared acre was almost the same in the cutover as in southern Wisconsin, experts in the 1930s who wanted to expand agriculture in northern Wisconsin encouraged larger-scale farming where they felt that a farmer was capable and located on good land.[9] The result after World War II was an explosion in the size of cutover farms. Commenting in 1976 on her community in Florence County of two hundred mostly retired people, the daughter of an 1880s Swedish settler pointed out that "those who do farm do it on a much larger scale." Indeed, whereas cutover farms had been smaller than the statewide norm in 1940, a half-century later, in fourteen of the eighteen cutover counties, farms were *larger* than the statewide average. These larger farms required more machinery. Irv Holman, a visitor to the 1987 Farm Progress Days in Barron County, explained that "I was born on a farm over 60 years ago, but this is a fantastic change. . . . The selection and brands of machinery is something, but the size is amazing." The consequences can be seen in 1995 on the Maly farm on the Antigo Flats in Langlade County (chapter 4): a computer-directed milking parlor for five hundred cows, a curtain-free stall barn and a pit for 2.7 million gallons of manure and other wastes, 480 acres in corn and 500 acres in hay. The three Maly brothers operate the farm with only two full-time and two part-time hired hands.[10] The era of family labor and neighborhood exchange has ended.

The alternative for farmers without the capital or desire to operate dairy farms on the scale of the Maly brothers was to turn their land over to grazing horses ridden for recreation, raising Christmas trees, growing orchards, or raising specialized vegetables such as ginseng or pumpkins. Most of these farmers depend primarily on off-farm income, often a job held by their wife. Such part-time farming is not a new practice in the cutover (chapter 2). But what made the cutover somewhat distinctive from most other parts of rural America in 1940 became common among the remaining family farmers in all of the United States in the 1990s. Ironically, part-time farming, which experts had seen as backward and wanted eliminated from northern Wisconsin in 1940, has become the only way for many American farmers to remain on their land.

As farming changed, the population of the cutover did not grow. Fewer that 350,000 people lived in northern Wisconsin in 1990, essentially the same number as in 1940, and the region's share of the state's population had fallen from 10.8 percent to 7.1 percent. There were significant social changes related to these demographic changes. As fertility declined and pressure mounted to save money by reducing the number of units of government, schools began consolidating before World War II. In his 1939 annual report, the Price County Superintendent of Schools reported the closing of two rural schools, reducing to sixty-eight the number of such schools in his county, and said that he would encourage further consolidations. This trend accelerated in the early 1940s: Rusk County had eighty-nine rural schools in 1932 and only fifty-seven in 1944, while county-wide enrollment fell from 3,198 in 1932 to 2,145 in 1944. After World War II the number of school districts plunged across the cutover. By the 1964–1965 school year, there were only six one-room rural schools left in the region. The number of school districts in the region decreased from 1,041 in 1937 to 78 in 1967.[11]

No longer could the bonds of rural neighborhoods be fostered by school pageants and district business meetings in one-room schoolhouses. The neighborhood "wasn't the same. It made a difference," lamented Lars Kailberg, who experienced school consolidation in Barron County in the 1940s and 1950s. "I felt so bad," admitted a long-time school board member in Rice Lake. "They've lost something that was dear to them; it was their community center." With school consolidation, the daily rhythm of life now centered more on urban places with schools, like Rice Lake, encouraging the expansion of urban and commercial attitudes into the countryside once dominated by the values of yeoman farming.[12]

For the people in the cutover committed to yeoman farming these were sad developments. Roy Meier pointed out in 1979 that "we work independently of each other much more than we did." When interviewed in 1978, Harvey Dueholm, who had taken over operation of his family's farm in northern Polk County in the 1930s, lamented that "the day of the poor farmer is past." He felt that farm life had become "cold"; one of the worst things for Harvey was the "loss of the neighborhood." Sharing work, socializing with neighbors, and sending kids together to rural schools had ended. It was an "entirely different feeling now." Harvey's four sons lived near him, some on the land his father had started clearing in 1906, but none farmed full-time. "The family farm is in trouble," Harvey concluded.[13]

The advocates of reforestation in 1940 would have been more pleased than yeoman farmers like Harvey Dueholm with the direction of change in the cutover. By the 1990s, forests grew on about ten million acres in northern Wisconsin, five times the area occupied by farms. About a quarter of this total was private land entered under forest crop–type laws initially enacted in the late 1920s. Burned-over stumpland now existed only in the memories of long-time residents. But forests also reclaimed farm land. In the town of Argonne in Forest County, for example, where 40 to 50 potato farms had flourished around 1920, already by the 1950s few farms remained. Referring to the "sand barrens" of Washburn County, in 1996 a Wisconsin Department of Natural Resources forester observed, "Now you drive through, and you wouldn't know they used to be farms."[14]

Reforestation encouraged recreational uses of land in northern Wisconsin, another goal for many planners of the region in the 1930s. In the early twentieth century wealthy vacationers came by train to elegant resort hotels and picturesque private "lodges." During the interwar years, the increase in automobile travel brought middle-class tourists from Chicago and Milwaukee to "light housekeeping" cabins. Post–World War II affluence greatly increased the number of these vacationers—by the 1990s almost 60 percent of residences in Vilas County, for instance, were primarily recreational homes and 80 percent of new construction in Sawyer County was lakefront cabins. Vera Kringe, who farmed for forty-five years with her husband, Lloyd, in the town of Cedar Lake in the northeast corner of Barron County, explained this pattern. "When I first came up to this area" about 1940, she pointed out, "I looked around and said this won't be farming area very long because the rich will come up here and see what they have up here and they'll want it. That's exactly what happened."[15]

These economic and social changes helped to eliminate the conditions in the cutover that pre–World War II commentators feared would produce antisocial behavior. Sociological researchers in Price County in the 1950s reported fewer but larger farms, decreased "physical isolation," and less "clustering of nationality groups." Reflecting the dominant sociological perspective of that era, they favorably concluded that the decline in farm population was a "population adjustment" that was a part of a "basic adjustment to the problem situation."[16] Within this framework, the demise of yeoman farming was a depersonalized "adjustment" to abstract forces.

Before World War II, especially when writing for general audiences, prognosticators painted a rosy future for the cutover—provided that their policies were implemented. Already in 1939, Samuel Lubell and Walter Everitt reported that as a result of rural zoning in the cutover "counties are financially sound, relief rolls have been slashed, tax delinquency has been reduced to a minor irritant." In the 1950s, after summarizing the public programs that had reshaped northern Wisconsin and boasting of the region's natural resources, Walter Rowlands (who had testified at the 1940 Congressional hearings) predicted that "someday, someone will bestow on this giant 'Empire of the North' a new name—a name much more keeping with the contributions it has already made and will continue to make to the future welfare of all the people in America."[17]

The reality of conditions in northern Wisconsin in the decades after World War II differed from these predictions. In 1937 the State Planning Board projected a gain of nineteen thousand people in the cutover between 1930 and 1960; in actuality, population *declined* by twelve thousand in those decades. Since they drastically underestimated the postwar growth of the Milwaukee suburbs and the areas in and around Madison and Green Bay, the 1937 planners thought the cutover would have 9.5 percent of the state's population in 1960; actually, it had only 7.7 percent.[18] The people who did live in the cutover, furthermore, did not achieve the prosperity Rowlands and others predicted. In 1990 residents of the eighteen cutover counties on average had between 49 and 80 percent of the gross income of the average Wisconsinite; residents of only two counties averaged more than 75 percent of the state's average. The five counties in Wisconsin with the lowest per-capita income—Forest, Burnett, Iron, Rusk, and Sawyer—were all in the cutover.[19] In sum, the new economic plan for the cutover which deemphasized farming and stressed reforestation and tourism did not attract new residents to northern Wisconsin or enrich the ones who already lived there.

Ironically, the development of a stronger, more diversified economy in the post–World War II cutover, in particular one that included manufacturing, might have been assisted by the continuation of yeoman farming. Economic historian Paul Salstrom has recently argued that the loss of small-scale farming, which had been supplying most of the needs of the region's work force, hurt Appalachia's economy after 1945 by increasing labor costs in the manufacturing sector.[20] He offers post–World War II Japan as an alternative model, where rapid expansion in manufacturing coexisted with the continuation of a large government-subsidized small-scale agricultural sector. Closer to home, anthropologist Jane Adams has reported that in Union County, Illinois, in a poor farming region in the southern part of the state, agriculture and industry grew together during a brief period in the 1940s and 1950s, with small farmers receiving essential supplemental income from manufacturing jobs.[21] However, throughout the poorer parts of rural America, as in the cutover, the effect of New Deal agricultural programs was to spread the cash economy and undermine semisubsistence farming. In Appalachia, according to Salstrom, this development combined with environmental limits and shortages of capital to destroy the viability of the small-scale agriculture which could have boosted the growth of manufacturing. When interviewed in the town of Spirit in Price County in the 1970s, Roy Meier still believed that small-scale farming was viable, not just as a hobby or sideline but as an integral supplement to forest or lumber mill work, as Raphael Zion had advocated at the 1940 Congressional hearings. Meier understood that such a pattern would keep his neighborhood more populated and discourage the proliferation of vacant farmhouses, which he sadly pointed out as he gave his interviewer a tour of the neighborhood.[22] The adoption of an economic pattern such as that advocated by Salstrom and Meier, however, depended upon the policies of corporations and governments beyond the influence of cutover residents and largely unsympathetic to them as a result of the view of the cutover predominant in the popular mind by 1940. For whatever reason, little manufacturing developed in northern Wisconsin after World War II. Furthermore, Superior, the largest city in the cutover, was tied with Duluth to the fortunes of Great Lakes shipping, which did not get the boost expected in the 1950s from the creation of the St. Lawrence Seaway. As Superior's population declined to twenty-seven thousand in

1990, only 77 percent of what it had been in 1980 and 68 percent of what it had been in 1910, the rural cutover could not benefit indirectly from urban growth.

The emphasis, rather, would be on promoting forestry and recreation, which would exacerbate some problems in northern Wisconsin and create others. The forest that regrew in northern Wisconsin consisted largely of such species as jack pine, birch, and aspen (Figure 1.4). Its appearance was certainly better than that presented by charred stumpland in the 1920s, but popular opinion began to see these forests as monotonous and lacking desirable "big trees." Critics claimed that the limited variety of species was deliberately designed to benefit timber companies, which critics also targeted for clear-cutting state and county forests and unfairly exploiting tax breaks initiated by the forest crop laws of the 1920s. The types of forest which regrew in northern Wisconsin, furthermore, encouraged an explosion in the deer population; these deer, in turn, increasingly damaged the crops on the farms that remained in the cutover, and discouraged the introduction of other large mammals, such as moose.[23] In addition, an economic focus on natural resource extraction, encouraged by the rejuvenated timber industry, led to other problems in northern Wisconsin. In the 1980s and 1990s mining interests pushed state and county governments for permission to dig for zinc beneath the surface of the cutover. These proposals raised concerns about environmental damage, particularly to the interests of Native Americans and hunters and fishermen. Critics feared that mining threatened to return the cutover to the economic boom-or-bust days of the timber era of the late nineteenth century. In general, to many cutover residents renewed interest in natural resource extraction seemed to be another example of outsiders—multinational companies like Exxon—trying to shape their lives.[24]

Its growing economic reliance on tourism was similarly problematic for northern Wisconsin. Tourists and vacationers from suburban Chicago and Milwaukee reshaped the cutover into alignment with their vision of what it should be like. Like Native Americans in the interwar years, by the end of the century all residents of northern Wisconsin had to present themselves in ways that tourists expected. As Bob Korth, a University of Wisconsin Extension agent working with lake associations, pointed out in the mid-1990s, visitors "have a certain mental image of what the north is all about."[25] Meanwhile, jet-skis and fishing boats with beer kegs for ballast filled northern Wisconsin lakes, while Indian gaming casinos offered a tamer version of the illegal and exotic which pre–World War II visitors expected to find in the cutover. Seasonal homes surrounded once-pristine lakeshores, creating clutter and damaging the habitat for the very fish the tourists want to catch.

Residents of northern Wisconsin have also increasingly found themselves unable to afford to live in their own communities—the value of lakefront property in Forest County quadrupled between 1985 and 1995, and the rise in home prices in Forest and four adjacent counties between 1990 and 1994 was 20 percent greater than it was statewide.[26] All in all, cutover residents increasingly resembled the economically dependent and culturally subservient population of tourist destinations like the West Indies. Reduced to seasonal labor at low wages, many residents of the cutover scrambled to survive by "working the system"—pilfering from employees, submitting false insurance claims, relying on public assistance. "You make your own scam," explained Nell Peters of Eagle River, in Vilas County. "It's called *tret,* what the butchers trim from steaks. It's an important part of surviving in the Northwoods."[27]

Anger was one response to this dependent situation. Historian Paul Glad, in the recent comprehensive history of Wisconsin, identified the "suppressed resentment" of cutover residents toward "messy" tourists, who seemed to chain them to businesses—motels, fishing boats, roadside attractions—with high rates of failure.[28] We saw Robert Peters acknowledge that he had such feelings about vacationers in Vilas County in the late 1930s (chapter 6). A "safe" target for this anger appeared in the 1980s when federal court decisions acknowledged the right of the Chippewa people to fish outside of state restrictions on lakes within the territory they had ceded to the United States. Rock-throwing and name-calling by whites toward Native Americans marred the spring spearfishing seasons for several years in the late 1980s.[29] In sum, the elimination of yeoman farming from the cutover did not eliminate the social and economic problems that had seemed to bedevil the region in the interwar years.

The termination of yeoman farming did not completely eliminate from northern Wisconsin the spirit of its early-twentieth-century settlers or their attachment to its land. The still-undeveloped quality of the region in the 1980s and 1990s provided space for people who wanted to live in the country and have a lifestyle somewhat different than what was prescribed by the agribusiness world.

This pattern can be seen in the experience of some women in the cutover in the decades after World War II. Carrying on the tradition of the community of single women farmers in early-twentieth-century Washburn County, Karen Kringe took over her family's dairy farm near Rice Lake in Barron County. While most farm women, in the cutover and across the United States, were marginalized in the productive side of farming by changes in agriculture which eliminated small-scale female endeavors such as poultry raising, Kringe demonstrated another effect of that agricultural change—the increase of mechanization made it physically possible for some women to increase field work. In any event, Kringe not only ignored the people "irritated by a woman trying to farm" but lived openly with her lesbian lover. "We are pretty well established here now," Kringe believed by 1993, and provided a model for other farmers. "We have a neighbor down the road, really he and his wife are partners. Twenty years ago, she would have still been looked on as more property."[30] On this neighbor's farm, at least, the mutuality of work roles characteristic of yeoman farming in the cutover before 1940 increased in the post–World War II years, in spite of the efforts of agricultural experts to encourage separation of gender roles and the effects of economic change in eliminating women's traditional productive roles.

After World War II the movement of African-Americans from the rural South to urban locations became a torrent, but for those blacks who wanted to farm, the cutover was the kind of place to try. Echoing the efforts of the black community in the town of Hoard in Clark County in the 1930s and 1940s, in the 1990s African-American Dan Blakey farmed near Gromton in Clark County. Blakey, who grew up on a farm in Minnesota, struggled to hold onto several central Wisconsin farms before a white widow, Ruth Searls, offered to make him a partner and let him take over her farm. From his share of the farm's income, in two years Blakey bought the farm's herd and machinery, and when interviewed in 1991 hoped to buy Searls's land and buildings.

Groups outside the mainstream of post–World War II American society also found space in the cutover, showing that the fears of some critics of cutover settlement were justified. Near Luck in northern Polk County, site of strong Danish farming communities in the interwar years, the Anathoth Catholic Worker Community moved onto fifty-seven acres in the 1990s and focused on protesting a navy nuclear submarine communications station in the Chequamegon National Forest near Clam Lake in Ashland County. Seeking cheap farm land, adherents of religious sects which follow nonmechanized agricultural practices have also moved to Northern Wisconsin, such as 140 Mennonite families who settled in northern Clark County, adjacent to the cutover.

At least one unit of government tried to encourage the continuation of this kind of family farming in the cutover. In the late 1980s Burnett County's Project Farmland tried to take people from places like Illinois or Indiana who wanted to begin or continue farming and match them with farms for sale in or near Burnett County. Its appeal was to older farmers alienated from the post–World War II changes in American agriculture and younger farmers frustrated by the high initial capital costs now necessary to enter farming. In a manner more restrained yet still reminiscent of the hyperbolic publicity given the cutover at the beginning of the twentieth century (chapter 1), the project's national advertising campaign emphasized Burnett County's inexpensive land, peaceful environment, and slow pace of life.[31] Sustaining some agriculture in their region remained important to the residents of Northern Wisconsin.

The cutover also attracted settlers who desired a rural lifestyle but did not particularly want to farm. Some people sought privacy and independence in the northwoods, in the manner that so alarmed moral and fiscal standard-setters in the interwar years. In the town of Wilkinson in Rusk County, Peggy and Dan Thearlin chose to live with their children in a small secluded house. They worked thirteen miles away in Rice Lake but preferred to live in Wilkinson because, in Peggy's words, "you can really relax because you're removed from the hectic lifestyle. . . . We have nature all around us, and we have each other. That's living for us." The Thearlin's "neighbors" included Bill Reed and his girlfriend, who lived on an unpaved road in a trailer without running water or a toilet. "I can make it here," Reed explained, raising chickens, growing vegetables, and scouring farm fields for leftovers. He also labored as a farm hand and in the woods for cash—his yearly income in the early 1990s was about $2,000—or items like cheese or gas in trade. "I know how to live in this kind of environment," he insisted to an interviewer. Another "neighbor" was Bill Duesselman, a disabled veteran with emotional scars from his service in Vietnam. "I can't deal with the public," he admitted. "The people up here, they understand and accept me." He did logging work but stressed, "I'm fortunate in that I have benefits coming in. It's hard to make it up here otherwise."[32]

Other cutover settlers in recent decades desiring peace and quiet were men and women who grew up on cutover farms, migrated elsewhere as young adults to find jobs, and then retired to northern Wisconsin. Margaret Kehoe Clemons, for instance, who was born on a farm in the town of Bass Lake in Washburn County in 1907, returned there in 1962 after living her adult years in Milwaukee. She enjoyed the "company of our relatives and of old friends." Walt Goldsworthy, after working for thirty-two years at International Harvester in Chicago, retired in 1978 and built a small house "on the old farm" near Three Rivers in Oneida County. Larry Garneau, who lived on one of the subsistence homesteads in the Drummond Forest Project in the 1930s, retired back to Drummond in the 1980s, where he became president of the local historical society.[33]

These return migrants to northern Wisconsin showed their identification with the cutover as a special place. Farming in the cutover in the early twentieth century helped to shape this identity. Indeed, one of the fears of cutover critics in the interwar years had been that the settlers identified too much with the region and resisted relocation. In the 1980s this identification came across in the frequency of the use of "northwoods" and similar terms to define the region. At least 2 percent of commercial telephone listings in all cutover counties except Burnett (and over 5 percent in Vilas County) used the term, which seldom appeared south of the counties adjacent to the cutover.[34]

The "making do" spirit of yeoman farming continued to be found in the cutover at the end of the twentieth century. For instance, small rural church congregations continued to maintain separate existences, sharing pastors. In the late 1980s one clergyman served the Presbyterian churches in Winter, Couderay, and Radisson, in Sawyer County. Every Sunday morning a Wesleyan pastor preached at Stone Lake and at Edgewater, farther west in Sawyer County. This practice was also growing in the Catholic church, as the number of priests declined in the dioceses of Superior and Green Bay. In Sawyer County, for example, Father Hugh Briody said four masses each weekend at churches in Winter, Radisson, and Couderay. In sum, because of their experience of struggling and never becoming part of a fully developed farming region, rural people in northern Wisconsin may have found themselves in a more secure position in the 1990s than their counterparts on the Great Plains, for example, where declining population density has threatened to end a way of life that has existed for a century.

What conclusions should we draw from the story of the efforts of thousands of farm families to settle in the Wisconsin cutover? It is too simplistic merely to invoke a mismatch of people and natural resources leading to universal failure.[35] Northern Wisconsin is not "naturally" destined for a particular human use. In the first half of the twentieth century, some farmers successfully used cutover land to gain the resources needed to support their families and participate in community, regional, and even national life. In doing so they did not ignore the environment, nor did they seek to overwhelm it with the most advanced capitalist techniques, as "suitcase farmers" did on the Great Plains in the 1920s. Rather, they chose to live in northern Wisconsin because of the region's natural beauty, and saw themselves restoring the natural balance in the wake of capitalist exploitation by lumber companies.

Faced with the fact that there was some successful farming in the cutover, we could blame individuals for the undeniable failures which also occurred. The logic is that since some farmers were able to make it, all could have—it was "the man on the land, not the land" that counted. In this explanation, the settlers themselves were responsible for failure because of their stupidity—choosing poor land for their farms—or developers were irresponsible for selling such land to settlers.[36] These explanations come close to blaming the victim.

In sum, to explain why farming in the cutover did not develop to the extent that boosters predicted it would in 1900, too much emphasis should not be placed on the shortcomings of the natural resources of the region for agriculture, real as they were in many respects. The focus should not even be on how people misunderstood those natural resources, although that was undoubtedly a problem. The emphasis should be on the limited social, economic, and political resources available to the settlers as a group. These resources were not strong enough for the settlers to build yeoman farming communities in the face of economic and technological changes and the attitudes and public programs that encouraged these changes, which began to transform all of American agriculture before World War II and which increased their impact in the second half of the twentieth century.

The success of the cutover as a farming region depended on the success of many farmers. Achieving the goal of yeoman farming required that neighborhoods, sections, and counties eventually be thoroughly settled. This density was necessary to maintain the practices—work sharing, marketing cooperatives, rural schools—that made yeoman farmers into a community. It was also necessary to increase the value of existing yeoman farms so their operators had the financial resources to participate in community activities. That most parts of the cutover did not become completely settled, therefore, is more than an indicator of a problem; it was a *cause* of the failure of yeoman farming to succeed. Indeed, the success of individual farmers, especially after 1940, increasingly came as a result of not following the model of yeoman farming, which further undermined its viability for others.

There were several reasons why yeoman farming did not develop in the cutover on the scale it needed to succeed. In general, Euro-American settlement in northern Wisconsin was belated: in the decades of the late nineteenth century when farming successfully spread across the prairies, the focus on lumbering discouraged family farms from northern Wisconsin. When yeoman farming finally began to appear in the cutover in the 1890s, the timing was bad: in the subsequent twenty years relatively high commodity prices were falsely alluring, and then twenty years of depressed conditions were problematic for farmers everywhere in the United States. The interest of planners and government officials was double edged: their sympathy for yeoman farming was accompanied by, and by the time of influx by settlers into the cutover was overwhelmed by, an emphasis on transforming all of rural America along more "modern," efficient lines. The mood of the country soured toward the type of people living in the cutover: immigration was severely restricted in the 1920s and images of Okies and Kentucks aroused fears in the 1930s. All of these factors were nationwide in their effect on rural America but had their greatest impact on the cutover in particular. Northern Wisconsin was vulnerable because it was recently settled, poor, and still underpopulated. Consequently, public policies which discouraged agriculture and encouraged other land uses affected northern Wisconsin sooner than other places. These programs relieved the distress of many families but also pointed the way toward a movement away from family farming further encouraged by the economic and technological developments following World War II.

The effort to make northern Wisconsin into a land of yeoman farmers was a small, sad part of the history of farming in the United States in the twentieth century. It was poignant for the thousands of families who struggled with stumps and increasingly hostile evaluations of what they were trying to do. It was pregnant with meaning for the future direction of American agriculture.

Notes

Abbreviations

ARC   Area Research Center
SHSW   State Historical Society of Wisconsin
UML Papers   Union Mortgage Loan Company Papers, Area Research
             Center, University of Wisconsin–Eau Claire
UWEC   University of Wisconsin–Eau Claire
UWGB   University of Wisconsin–Green Bay
UWM   University of Wisconsin–Madison
UWRF   University of Wisconsin–River Falls
UWSP   University of Wisconsin–Stevens Point
WMH   *Wisconsin Magazine of History*

Introduction

1. Chuck Duprow, "In the Sticks: Pair Enjoy Challenge of Running Lone Farm in Town of Wilkinson," *Eau Claire Leader Telegram,* 21 Feb. 1993, F1ff.

2. Idem, "Town in Decline, But Living On," ibid., C1ff. Town level farm statistics are calculated from Wisconsin Crop Reporting Service, Annual Enumeration of Agricultural Statistics, 1923–, SHSW.

3. B. M. Apker, "Reminiscences," typescript, ARC, UWEC.

4. See the suggestive ideas of Yi-fu Tuan, *Space and Place: The Perspective of Experience* (Minneapolis, 1977). For an example of the use of the concept of place by a political scientist in developing social science theory, see John A. Agnew, *Place and Politics: The Geographical Mediation of State and Society* (Boston, 1987), 25–61. The concept is used by an elected official to advocate a new style of public life in the 1990s based on "cooperation" that comes from "the project of inhabiting a place" (Daniel Kemmis, *Community and the Politics of Place* [Norman, Ok., 1990], 80).

5. *History Collections of Washburn County,* 2 vols. (Shell Lake, Wis., 1980), 2: 511–12.

6. Eldon Marple, *The Visitor Who Came to Stay* (Hayward, Wis., 1971), 69. Even as it was being settled, the cutover was ignored in theoretical analysis of American agricultural settlement. Isaiah Bowman (*The Pioneer Fringe* [New York, 1931]) discussed "modern pioneering" on the high plains, in Oregon, and elsewhere, but omits discussion of the cutover. Subsequently, the cutover has been ignored and misunderstood by scholars. Even as perceptive a historian as Samuel P. Hays has dismissed the "fragile community life" of the Great Lakes woodlands before 1940 ("Human Choice in the Great Lakes Wildlands," in Susan L. Flader, ed., *The Great*

Lakes Forest: An Environmental and Social History [Minneapolis, 1983], 310–11). Hays is correct, however, that "the history of the Great Lakes wildlands is hampered by the lack of historical inquiry."

7. For a recent sophisticated overview of the changes from subsistence to "yeoman" to "capitalistic" farming in U.S. history, see Allan Kulikoff, *The Agrarian Origins of American Capitalism* (Charlottesville, 1992), esp. 1–59.

8. Thomas A. Lyson and William W. Falk, eds., *Forgotten Places: Uneven Development in Rural America* (Lawrence, 1993).

9. Ed Pudas, "Autobiography" (c. 1976), typescript ARC, UWRF.

10. Knute Anderson, interview, Luck, Wis., June 1989 (notes in possession of the author; Anderson is a pseudonym); Wendell Berry, *The Unsettling of America: Culture and Agriculture* (San Francisco, 1977).

1. The Cutover in 1900

1. Cited in Robert Gard and Mary Gard, *My Land, My Home, My Wisconsin* (Milwaukee, 1978), 72.

2. *Milwaukee Journal,* 12 March 1900; quotations from pp. 1, 17, 4.

3. "High Praise for Northern Wisconsin," *Phillips Times,* 27 Dec. 1902 (reprint from *Milwaukee Sentinel*); Ernest Luther to K. L. Hatch, 2 June 1912, Ernest Luther Papers, SHSW; A. R. Whitson et al., *Reconnaissance Soil Survey of North Part of North Central Wisconsin,* Wisconsin Geological and Natural History Survey Bulletin no. 50 (Madison, 1916), 78; James O'Neil, "The Future of Northern Wisconsin," *Proceedings of the 46th Annual Meeting, 1898,* SHSW (Madison, 1899); Richard Runke to George Lehnert, 28 Feb. 1906, 30 March 1906, Richard Runke Papers, ARC, UWSP; John G. Owen to I. E. Sassman, 8 Jan. 1909, John S. Owen Papers (box 174), ARC, UWEC.

4. On the physical geography of Wisconsin see Lawrence Martin, *Physical Geography of Wisconsin,* 3d ed. (Madison, 1965). A good brief introduction is Ingolf Vogeler, with others, *Wisconsin, A Geography* (Boulder, 1986), 24–50. Useful specialized works include Francis D. Hole, *Soils of Wisconsin* (Madison, 1976) and John T. Curtis, *Vegetation of Wisconsin* (Madison, 1971).

5. Ernest Luther to K. L. Hatch, 30 April 1912, Luther Papers; Fred Etcheson, typescript of interview, 30 July 1970, ARC, UWEC.

6. Hole, *Soils of Wisconsin,* 24.

7. In addition to the sources previously cited on the physical geography of Wisconsin, see esp. Eric A. Bourdo, Jr., "The Forest the Settlers Saw," in Susan L. Flader, ed., *The Great Lakes Forest: An Environmental and Social History* (Minneapolis, 1983), 3–16.

8. For different characterizations of the cutover climate, compare Board of Immigration, Vilas County, *Vilas County Handbook for the Homeseeker* (n.p., c. 1897), 7; and Robert J. Schlomann, *The Thread of Love* (Oshkosh, Wis., 1986), 27.

9. Useful introductions to Wisconsin Indians can be found in Robert E. Bieder, *Native American Communities in Wisconsin, 1600–1960* (Madison, 1995); Nancy Oestreich Lurie, *Wisconsin Indians* (Madison, 1980); and William H. Hodge, "The

Indians of Wisconsin," in the *Wisconsin Blue Book 1975* (Madison, 1975), 95–192. On the relationship between Native American society and the physical environment of northern Wisconsin see Charles E. Cleland, "Indians in a Changing Environment," in Flader, ed., *The Great Lakes Forest*, 83–95; and Harold Hickerson, *The Chippewa and Their Neighbors: A Study in Ethnohistory* (New York, 1970). The social, economic, and nutritional importance of wild rice is discussed in Thomas Vennum, Jr., *Wild Rice and the Ojibway People* (St. Paul, 1988); and James W. Oberly, "Land, Population, Prices and the Regulation of Natural Resources: The Lake Superior Ojibwas, 1790–1920," paper presented at the Columbia University Seminar on Economic History, New York, May 1994, pp. 9–13, esp. table 3. See also Robert Gough, "Gathering Wild Rice: Indian Culture and Wisconsin Agriculture," in Tom McKay and Deborah E. Kmetz, eds., *Agricultural Diversity in Wisconsin* (Madison, 1987), 16–23 (the author of the last cited piece is a different individual than the author of the present study.)

10. Cited in Vennum, *Wild Rice*, 260.

11. Cited in ibid., 290.

12. *History Collections of Washburn County*, 2 vols. (Shell Lake, Wis., 1980), 2:333.

13. Calculated from *Tabular Statement of the Census Enumeration . . . of the State of Wisconsin . . . 1905* (Madison, 1906), 2–62; Indian Census Rolls, 1880–1940, National Archives, Washington, D.C., microcopy 595, roll 238: LaPointe; roll 173: Menominee, Oneida, and Stockbridge-Munsee.

14. *History of Northern Wisconsin*, 2 vols. (Chicago, 1881), 1:170.

15. Robert Dessureau, *History of Langlade County* (Antigo, Wis., 1922), 9.

16. Vennum, *Wild Rice*, 204, 239–45.

17. For a sequence different than that in the cutover, in which a largely self-sufficient, poverty-free, homogeneous, and isolated community of farm owners underwent "devastating" rural industrialization and conversion to commercial agriculture beginning in the mid-1870s, see Ann Potts Malone, "Piney Woods Farmers of South Georgia, 1850–1910: Jeffersonian Yeomen in an Age of Expanding Commercialism," *Agricultural History* 60 (1986): 51–84.

18. Mrs. Edward Porter, *The March of Civilization: A Story of the Development of the Cornell Country* (Cornell, Wis., 1916), n.p.

19. The standard history is Robert F. Fries, *Empire in Pine: The Story of Lumbering in Wisconsin, 1830–1900* (Madison, 1951). Succinct and more recent treatments are Robert L. Nesbit, *The History of Wisconsin*, vol. 3: *Urbanization and Industrialization, 1873–1893* (Madison, 1985), 46–88; and Michael Williams, *Americans and Their Forests: A Historical Geography* (Cambridge, Eng., 1989), 193–237. The era of extracting natural resources from northern Wisconsin also included a mining frontier in Ashland and Iron counties, an extension of the much greater mining activity in Michigan on the Gogebic Range (Vogeler, *Wisconsin: A Geography*, 99–103).

20. William Cronon, *Nature's Metropolis: Chicago and the Great West* (New York, 1991), 200–203.

21. Michael J. Goc, *Where the Waters Flow* (Friendship, Wis., 1991), 58–59; Ralph W. Hidy et al., *Timber and Men: The Weyerhaeuser Story* (New York, 1963), 93.

22. Nesbit, *Urbanization and Industrialization*, 47–48; J. M. Dodd, "Ashland Then and Now," *WMH* 20 (1944–45): 193.

23. Ellis B. Usher, "Marvelous Progress Made in Northern Wisconsin, " *Milwaukee Journal*, 10 July 1904, p. 2.

24. David M. Gates et al., "Wildlife in a Changing Environment," in Flader, ed., *Great Lakes Forest*, esp. 62–72.

25. Paul Fussel, *The Great War and Modern Memory* (New York, 1975), 256–69.

26. C. Luther Fry, *The Old and New Immigrant on the Land* (New York, 1922), 39; Hans Pederson interview, Drummond, Wis., 24 October 1988 (tape on deposit), ARC, UWEC (Pederson is a pseudonym); W. H. Baler, quoted in George Gilkey, "History of Merrill," 436–37, in Gilkey Papers, ARC, UWSP.

27. Clifford E. Ahlgren and Isabel F. Ahlgren, "The Human Impact of Northern Forest Ecosystems," in Flader, ed., *Great Lakes Forest*, 33–51; Frank Krueger, "Reminiscences" (1951), in Krueger Papers, ARC, UWGB.

28. Stephen J. Pyne, *Fire in America: A Cultural History of Wildland and Rural Fire* (Princeton, N.J., 1982), 199–218.

29. "Memoirs of Albert L. Stouffer" (1958), in *History Collections of Washburn County*, 1: 153, 157; Robert Peters, *Crunching Gravel* (San Francisco, 1988), [iv]; Vilas County Board of Immigration, *Vilas County Hand Book for the Homeseeker* (n.p., n.d. [c. 1897]), 24; [Walt Goldsworthy, ed], *The Pine, the Plow, and the Pioneer* [Three Rivers, Wis. 1984], 43. See also Schlomann, *Thread of Love*, 38–41; and more generally, Walter H. Ebling et al., *A Century of Wisconsin Agriculture, 1848–1948*, Crop Reporting Service Bulletin no. 290 (Madison, 1948), 11–12.

30. Bieder, *Native American Communities in Wisconsin*, 157–64, 203–5.

31. Jack P. Greene has emphasized this theme in his work in early American history. See, e.g., "Independence, Improvement, and Authority," in his *Imperatives, Behaviors, and Identities: Essays in Early American Cultural History* (Charlottesville, Va., 1992), 181–207.

32. Yi-fu Tuan, *Passing Strange and Wonderful: Aesthetics, Nature, and Culture* (Washington, D.C., 1993), 144–49.

33. Randall Rohe, "Lumber Towns in Wisconsin," *Old Northwest* (Winter 1984–85): 419–37; Arlan Helgeson, *Farms in the Cutover: Agricultural Settlement in Northern Wisconsin* (Madison, 1962), 12–17; James B. Smith, "The Movements for Diversified Industry in Eau Claire, Wisconsin, 1879–1907: Boosterism and Urban Development Strategy in a Declining Lumber Town" (M.A. thesis, UWM, 1967); Kurt Daniel Kortenhof, *Long Live the Hodag! the Life and Legacy of Eugene Simeon Shepard: 1854–1923* (Rhinelander, Wis., 1996), 49–62 (on Rhinelander).

34. Nesbit, *Urbanization and Industrialization*, 71, 80, 82–83, 110–13; Robert C. Ostergren, "Geographic Perspectives on the History of Settlement in the Upper Middle West," *Upper Midwest History* 1 (1975): 27–39, esp. 36–37; Joyce I. Bart, "Culture and Continuity at Knox Mills, Wisconsin (1864–1931)," typescript (1985), SHSW, pp. 14–15.

35. Bart, "Culture and Continuity," 11; James R. Donoghue, "The Local Government System of Wisconsin," *Wisconsin Blue Book 1968* (Madison, 1968), esp. 90–96; James Willard Hurst, *Law and Economic Growth: The Legal History of the Lumber Industry in Wisconsin, 1836–1915* (Cambridge, Mass., 1964), 524–26.

36. Fries, *Empire in Pine*, 123; Ebling et al., *Century of Wisconsin Agriculture*, 11–12; A. R. Reynolds, *The Daniel Shaw Lumber Company* (New York, 1957), 47–48, 141–

42; Duane D. Fischer, "The John S. Owen Enterprises" (Ph.D. diss., UWM, 1964), 86; Price County Agricultural and Dairy Statistics, 1880–1906, manuscript, ARC, UWEC.

37. Carol Lofgren, *Historical Album: Stone Lake, Wisconsin: Recollections of People and Places and Times Gone By* (Stone Lake, 1977); "The Skinvik Family," student paper no. 203, Edward Blackorby Collection, ARC, UWEC; Wilfred L. LeBeau, "A German Farmer Pioneer in Northern Wisconsin," *WMH* 38 (1954): 239–44; "Pioneer Citizen Dies," *Phillips Times*, 29 Jan. 1921, p. 1; Price County Agricultural and Dairy Statistics, 1880–1901, ARC, UWEC; Gilkey, "History of Merrill." See also Howard R. Klueter and James J. Lorence, *Woodlot and Ballot Box: Marathon County in the Twentieth Century* (Wausau, Wis., 1979), 170.

38. Hurst, *Law and Economic Growth*, 480–481. An excellent modern study of pre-1900 settlement in the cutover is S. J. Linton, "The Swedish Element in Wisconsin: The Trade Lake Settlement," *Swedish Pioneer Historical Collections* 30 (1979): 254–61.

39. Goc, *Where the Waters Flow*, 59–60.

40. See David B. Danbom, *Born in the Country: A History of Rural America* (Baltimore, 1995), 114.

41. John W. Bennett and Seena B. Kohl, *Settling the Canadian-American West, 1890–1915: Pioneer Adaptation and Community Building* (Lincoln, Nebr., 1995), esp. 16–20. See also Barbara Allen, *Homesteading the High Desert* (Salt Lake City, 1987), esp. 33–35, a study of Lake County, Oregon, in the early twentieth century.

42. Calculated from the *Annual Reports of the Commissioner of the General Land Office*, 1867–1900. I am indebted to James Oberly for supplying me with these data.

43. Hurst, *Law and Economic Growth*, 13–142; Paul Wallace Gates, *The Wisconsin Lands of Cornell University* (Ithaca, N.Y., 1943). For the Canadian experience see R. J. Burgar, "Forest Land-Use Evolution in Ontario's Upper Great Lakes Basin," in Flader, ed., *Great Lakes Forest*, 177–93. Specific evidence to the infrequency of settlers gaining title by government entry can be found in Price County, List of State Lands, 1879–1948, folders no. 3 and 4, ARC, UWEC. Between April 1, 1925 and Nov. 8, 1926, for example, one description was obtained from the federal government by final homestead, two by timber-stone entry, and one by commuted homestead. Forty-four properties had been patented from the state government between May 1, 1911 and April 30, 1912, but this number fell to twenty-two by 1919–1920, to only one by 1927–1928, and to none by 1940–1941.

On the lack of free government land for farmers after 1890, see Benjamin Horace Hibbard, *A History of the Public Lands Policies* (New York, 1927), 542–43, 565–66. Counties in Wisconsin would eventually become significant landowners as a result of taking title for tax delinquency, and subsequently became retailers of land, but such sales were infrequent at the beginning of the twentieth century.

44. *Report of the Forestry Commission of the State of Wisconsin* (Madison, 1898), 18. See Williams, *Americans and Their Forests*, 372; Nelson Van Valen, "James J. Blaisdel, Wisconsin's Eclectic Environmentalist, " *WMH* 74 (1991): 297–311; Peter A. Fritzell, "Changing Conceptions of the Great Lakes Forest," in Flader, ed., *Great Lakes Forest*, 274–94; Vernon Carstensen, *Farms or Forests: Evolution of a State Land Policy for Northern Wisconsin, 1850–1932* (Madison, 1958), 5–45; F. G. Wilson, "Zoning for Forestry and Recreation," *WMH* 41 (1957–58): 102–6.

45. State *ex re.* Owen v. Donald, 160 Wis. 21. See Carstensen, *Farms or Forests,* 53–89; and, esp. Hurst, *Law and Economic Growth,* 579–85.

46. Carstensen, *Farms or Forests,* 47–53.

47. A. R. Whitson et al., *Soil Survey of the Bayfield Area,* Wisconsin Geological and Natural History Survey Bulletin no. 31 (Madison, 1914).

48. Whitson, *Reconnaissance Soil Survey.*

49. A. R. Whitson et al., *Soil Survey of Northern Wisconsin,* Wisconsin Geological and Natural History Survey Bulletin no. 55 (Madison, 1921).

50. For an insightful discussion of a specific example of how natural scientists can change the classification of phenomena where "the data had not changed, so the reversal of opinion can only record a revised presupposition about the most likely status," see Stephen Jay Gould, *Wonderful Life: The Burgess Shale and the Nature of History* (New York, 1989), 168–72.

51. W. A. Henry, *Northern Wisconsin: A Hand-Book for the Homeseeker* (Madison, 1896). See John W. Jenkins, *A Centennial History: A History of the College of Agricultural and Life Sciences at the University of Wisconsin–Madison* ([Madison], 1991), 35–36.

52. E. J. Delwiche to E. L. Luther, 25 Nov 1935, Luther Papers (box 2), SHSW; "Wisconsin Farmers' Institutes for 1911–1912," Wisconsin Farmers Institutes Bulletin no. 25 (Madison, 1911), 14–15, "Wisconsin Farmers' Institutes for 1912–1913," Bulletin no. 26 (Madison, 1912), 14–15, "Wisconsin Farmers' Institutes for 1910–1911," Bulletin no. 24 (Madison, 1910), 14. See Wilbur H. Glover, *Farm and College: The College of Agriculture of the University of Wisconsin: A History* (Madison, 1952), 149–59.

53. *Thirtieth Annual Report of the Agricultural Experimental Station of the University of Wisconsin* (Madison, 1913), 92. See Glover, *Farm and College,* 211.

54. *Twenty-ninth Annual Report of the Agricultural Experimental Station of the University of Wisconsin* (Madison, 1912), 64–66. See Jenkins, *A Centennial History,* 69–70.

55. E. L. Luther to K. L. Hatch, 24 Dec 1912, Luther Papers (box 1). Capitalization in original.

56. Edward H. Beardsley, *Harry L. Russell and Agricultural Science in Wisconsin* (Madison, 1969), 121–36.

57. E. J. Delwiche, "The Growing of Wheat in Northern Wisconsin," Wisconsin Agricultural Experiment Association, *11th Annual Report* (Madison, 1913), 32–37.

58. Helgeson, *Farms in the Cutover,* 32–34; Kortenhof, *Long Live the Hodag!,* 65–67.

59. *Vilas County Handbook for the Homeseeker,* 3, 39; Ed L. Peet, comp., *Burnett County, Wisconsin* (Grantsburg, Wis., 1902), 6; Report of the Committee on Advertising, 1920, in Price County Board of Supervisors Papers (box 6), ARC, UWEC.

60. Helgeson, *Farms in the Cutover,* 20–21; *Wisconsin Blue Book 1927* (Madison, 1927), 304–305; Mark Davis, "Northern Choices: Rural Forest Country in the 1920s, Part I," *WMH* 79 (1995–96): 3–31, esp. 26. For a memoir which highlights the social significance of county fairs in the cutover see Nell Peters with Robert Peters, *Nell's Story: A Woman from Eagle River* (Madison, 1995), 86–88.

61. Ebling et al., *Century of Wisconsin Agriculture,* 11–12; Robert Nesbit, *Wisconsin: A History,* 2d ed. (Madison, 1989), 471.

62. Fischer, "John S. Owen Enterprises," 402–405, 544–50; Reynolds, *Daniel Shaw Lumber Company*, 34–37; Gates, *Wisconsin Pine Lands of Cornell University*, 239–42; Helgeson, *Farms in the Cutover*, 44–48.

63. Agreement, Wisconsin Central Railroad Memo of 1912, Small Collection, no. 38, ARC, UWEC.

64. Lucile Kane, "Selling Cut-Over Lands in Wisconsin," *Business History Review* 28 (1954): 236–47; Helgeson, *Farms in the Cutover*, 48–52. See also Kane, "Selling the Wisconsin Cutover," *WMH* 40 (1956–57): 91–98.

65. Helgeson, *Farms in the Cutover*, 7–8, 42–43; Klueter and Lorence, *Woodlot and Ballot Box*, 171–74; D. O. Thompson and W. H. Glover, "A Pioneer Adventure in Agricultural Extension: A Contribution from the Wisconsin Cutover," *Agricultural History* 22 (1948): 124–28; Jerry Novak, comp., *History of the Moquah Area* (Ashland, 1966), 8–9.

66. Harold Martin Troper, *Only Farmers Need Apply: Official Canadian Government Encouragement of Immigration from the United States, 1896–1911* (Toronto, 1972), 107–11. See also Bennett and Kohl, *Settling the Canadian-American West, 1890–1915: Pioneer Adaptations and Community Building* (Lincoln, Nebr., 1995).

67. M. F. Beaudoin, interview, 29 Nov. 1950, transcript, SHSW.

68. W. A. Henry, "Agricultural Possibilities of Central and Northern Wisconsin," Wisconsin Farmers Institute Bulletin no. 17 (Madison, 1903), 141–51.

69. *Burnett County, Wisconsin: A Souvenir* (Minneapolis, [1915]), 3–4; *The Story of the Per Ola Settlements in Forest County Wisconsin* (n.p. [Crandon], n.d. [1917]), 7; Peet, *Burnett County, Wisconsin*, 11; "The Round Lake Country," *Upper Wisconsin* 1 (no. 3, c. 1917): 7; *Vilas County Handbook*, 21; Helgeson, *Farms in the Cutover*, 67–81. Since the time they initiated settlement in North America, Euro-Americans had myopically believed that their own actions could mitigate harsh climates (Karen O. Kupperman, "The Puzzle of the American Climate in the Early Colonial Period," *American Historical Review* 87 [1982]: 1262–89).

70. *Vilas County Handbook*, 3; *Northern Wisconsin*, 3; *Burnett County, Wisconsin: A Souvenir*, 144; *Per Ola Settlements*, 3. On the bleak social conditions at this time in the industrial sector that encouraged immigrant factory workers to think about relocating to northern Wisconsin, see S. J. Kleinberg, *The Shadow of the Mills: Working Class Families in Pittsburgh, 1870–1907* (Pittsburgh, 1989), esp. 12–40. Emphasizing that material abundance could enable potential settlers to live the independent lives they desired was a tactic of promoters from the outset of European colonization of North America. See Jack P. Greene, "Early South Carolina and the Psychology of British Colonization," in *Imperatives, Behavior, and Identities*, 87–112.

71. Jane Marie Pederson, *Between Memory and Reality* (Madison, 1992), has recently described such a rural lifestyle in two communities in Trempealeau County in west central Wisconsin.

72. Schlomann, *Thread of Love*, 17; [Goldsworthy], *Pine, Plow. and Pioneer*, 73–74; Crosby quoted in D. W. Sawtelle, "Tour Through Northern Wisconsin" (1918), in Richard T. Ely Papers (microfilm reel 184), SHSW. For an almost identical sales experience with Crosby see Gilkey, "History of Merrill," 506.

73. Beaudoin interview, transcript, pp. 5, 2.

74. Julius Rosholt to Directors of Union Mortgage Loan Company, 1 July 1913, UML Papers, Administrative Subject File: Annual Reports, ARC, UWEC. See Robert J. Gough, "Mortgage Banking in the Wisconsin Cutover Region: Union Mortgage Loan Company, 1905–1935," *Essays in Economic and Business History* 5 (1987): 46–57.

75. Herman F. Schlegelmilch to L. A. Pecore, 18 Nov. 1910, Union Mortgage Loan Papers, General Correspondence; Schlegelmilch to Evald Hammar, 11 June 1913, ibid., Loan Series, no. 380. See also Schlegelmilch to F. O. Burger, 4 Dec. 1912, ibid., General Correspondence.

76. U.S. Bureau of the Census, *Fifteenth Census of the United States (1930): Agriculture*, vol. 2, pt. 1 (Washington, 1932), 736–47, 790–93.

77. Herman F. Schlegelmilch to John Miller, 9 Nov. 1918, Union Mortgage Loan Papers, Loan Series, no. 771.

78. U.S. Bureau of the Census, *Thirteenth Census of the United States (1910)*, vol. 7: *Agriculture* (Washington, 1913), 914–33.

79. Kim Rosholt Papers, ARC, UWEC; Land and Timber Holdings, vol. 233, Land Sales (box 3, folder 5), Holt Lumber Company Papers, ARC, UWGB; Kane, "Selling Cut-Over Lands," 238, 244–45 n. 32; Land Sales Records, Northwestern Lumber Company, ARC, UWEC (based on first sixty sales in 1914 and all fifty-two sales in 1918); questionnaires in Richard T. Ely Papers (microfilm reel 185), SHSW; Sherwood William Sheer, "A Survey of Settlers Progress in Upper Wisconsin" (Ph.D. diss., UWM, 1924), 5.

80. John S. Owen Lumber Company Land Contract Sales Book, Owen Papers; A. R. Owen to J. R. McQuillan, 29 Aug. 1919, ibid., vol. 175; Fischer, "John S. Owen Enterprises," 544–50.

81. John G. Owen to J. E. Wade, 8 Mar. 1909, Owen Papers (box 174).

82. William J. Starr, Record of Mortgages Held, 1904–1925, ARC, UWEC.

83. *Iron River, Wisconsin, 1892–1992* (n.p., [1992]), 7–8.

84. C. S. Bostwick to J. T. Homer, 15 Mar. 1933, Owen Papers (box 225).

85. D. W. Cartwright to Union Mortgage Loan, 20 Oct. 1925, Loan Series no. 2443, Union Mortgage Loan Papers (original emphasis); Stefonik cited in Kurt Kortenhof, *Sugar Camp, 1891–1941: The Origins and Early History of a Northern Wisconsin Community* (Eau Claire, [1994]), 31.

86. Donald Holt to Robert J. Gough, 26 July 1990, in possession of the author.

87. Kane, "Selling Cut-Over Lands," 236, 247. Consistent with his overall view of the cutover, Helgeson (*Farms in the Cutover*, 49–52) clearly implies that AIC was not successful, without attempting precise calculations.

88. Holt Lumber Company Papers (box 3, folders 4 and 5). Holt's policy was to adjust the book value of its lands, diminishing them for cash received on land contracts and increasing them for the amount of taxes the company had to pay on them and also, apparently, for changes in market value; its Wisconsin lands, consequently, almost doubled in book value between Jan. 6, 1917 and Dec. 31, 1920; ibid., vol. 215. These records are separate from those the company maintained based on initial cost of the land.

89. Without presenting details, the study of the John S. Owen Company's land sales operations has concluded that they "made money" through 1920 and then "lost money every year" (Fischer, "John S. Owen Enterprises," 549).

90. C. D. Moon to Northwestern Lumber Company Stockholders, 1 June 1932, Northwestern Lumber Company Papers, ARC, UWEC.

2. Building a New Life in the Cutover, 1900–1920

1. C. E. ("The Land Man") Tobey to the Editor, *Phillips Times*, Feb. 24, 1900, p. 4.

2. U.S. Bureau of the Census, *Thirteenth Census of the United States (1910)*, vol. 3: *Population* (Washington, D.C., 1913), 1082–95, vol. 7: *Agriculture* (Washington, D.C., 1913), 1914–20.
The "cutover" has been delineated by many different boundaries. The present definition, which follows closely the limits of the northern highlands physiographic division, is based on an area whose residents went through a common historical experience. These eighteen counties were the least developed in Wisconsin in 1900 by several measures, grew the fastest between 1900 and 1940, and—with one exception—lost farmland between 1940 and 1990 at a rate above the statewide average. The seven counties bordering the cutover were significantly more developed in 1900 and, although they grew rapidly between 1900 and 1940, lost farms at a rate lower than the statewide average between 1940 and 1990.

3. David B. Danbom, *Born in the Country: A History of Rural America* (Baltimore, 1995), 161–67; U.S. Bureau of the Census, *Historical Statistics of the United States, 1607–1976* (Washington, D.C., 1976), 457.

4. U.S. Bureau of the Census, *Fourteenth Census of the United States (1920)*, vol 1: *Population* (Washington, D.C., 1921), 666–77; ibid., vol. 6, pt. 1: *Agriculture* (Washington, D.C., 1921), 460–66; idem., *Thirteenth Census (1910)*, vol. 7: *Agriculture* (Washington, D.C., 1913), 914–20 (calculations for 1900 use the towns in Chippewa County which were set off as Gates [Rusk] County in 1901); *WMH* 6 (1922–23): 104–6.

5. *Iron River, Wisconsin, 1892–1992* (n.p., [1992]), 35–36. The Elred Klaussen Papers, SHSW, contain the correspondence of the Eldred Company's frustrated farm manager.

6. *Fourteenth Census (1920)*, vol. 3: *Population* (Washington, 1921), 1124–30.

7. Report of the First Wisconsin Land Mortgage Association (1915), in the Richard T. Ely Papers (microfilm reel 185), SHSW; B. M. Apker, "Reminiscences," (typescript, 1949), ARC, UWEC.

8. For a close examination of clustered settlement by Swedes in Isanti County, Minnesota, just two counties to the west of the cutover, see Robert C. Ostergren, *A Community Transplanted: The Trans-Atlantic Experience of a Swedish Immigrant Settlement in the Upper Middle West, 1835–1915* (Madison, 1988), 15–19, 155–189. For the Midwest in general, see Mary Neth, *Preserving the Family Farm: Women, Community, and the Foundations of Agribusiness in the Midwest, 1900–1940* (Baltimore, 1995), 82–85.

9. Lars Kailberg, interview, Rice Lake, Wis., 22 July 1988, ARC, UWEC (Kailberg is a pseudonym); *Tabular Statement of the Census Enumeration and the Agricultural, Dairying and Manufacturing Interests of the State of Wisconsin* (Madison, 1906) [*1905 State Census*], pt. 1, p. 81; *Fourteenth Census (1920)*, vol. 3: *Population*, 1135; Eunice Kanne, comp., *Pieces of the Past: Pioneer Life in Burnett County* (Friendship, Wis., 1988); S. J. Linton, "The Swedish Element in Wisconsin: The Trade Lake Settle-

ment," *Swedish Pioneer Historical Quarterly* 30 (1979): 254–76; Joe Mills, *The Lithuanians in Oneida County, Wisconsin* (Chicago, 1992), 1.

10. Hans Pederson, interview, Drummond, Wis., 24 Oct. 1988 (tape on deposit), ARC, UWEC (Pederson is a pseudonym); [Walt Goldsworthy, ed.], *The Pine, Plow, and Pioneer* [Three Lakes, Wis., 1984], 63; Carl H. Rhody, *The Saga of Spirit Valley: The Story of My Father* (Ogema, Wis., 1980), 41; Jack C. Plano, *Fishhooks, Apples, and Outhouse: Memories of the 1920s, 1930s, and 1940s* (Kalamazoo, Mich., 1991), 12; *1905 State Census; Fourteenth Census (1920)*, vol 3: *Population*, 1136. Both state and federal censuses identify as such Poles, Bohemians, and other nationalities born within the German, Austrian, and Russian empires.

On the importance of intra-group cooperation and work sharing among immigrants in the rural Midwest in the early decades of the twentieth century, see Mary Neth, *Preserving the Family Farm: Women, Community, and the Foundations of Agribusiness in the Midwest, 1900–1940* (Baltimore, 1995), 82–84, 88, 93–94.

11. Richard Runke to W. H. Driessen, 8 June 1911, Richard Runke Papers, ARC, UWSP; Robert J. Schlomann, *The Thread of Love* (Oshkosh, Wis., 1986), 34; Peter A. Speek, *A Stake in the Land* (New York, 1921), 173–74; Roy R. Meier, interview, Spirit, Wis., 21–23 March 1979 (tape on deposit), Wisconsin Agriculturalists Oral History Project, SHSW. For a similar pattern among Norwegian-Americans, see Jane Marie Pederson, *Between Memory and Reality: Family and Community in Rural Wisconsin, 1870–1970* (Madison, 1992), 35–39; and Jon Gjerde, *From Peasants to Farmers: The Migration From Balestrand, Norway, to the Upper Middle West* (Cambridge, 1985). By contrast, John W. Bennett and Seena B. Kohl (*Settling the Canadian-American West, 1890–1915: Pioneer Adaptations and Community Building* [Lincoln, Nebr., 1995], 33–39) explicitly follow Frederick Jackson Turner on the homogenizing effect of the frontier, and argue that ethnic differences among settlers on the northern Great Plains became muted relatively quickly and remained evident chiefly in benign expressions of "heritage."

12. Meier interview; *1905 State Census*, pt. 1, 198; C. Luther Fry, *The Old and New Immigrant on the Land* (New York, 1922), 42. On political radicalism among Finns, see John I. Kolehmainen and George W. Hill, *Haven in the Woods: The Story of the Finns in Wisconsin* (Madison, 1951), 118–35; and Lowell K. Dyson, *Red Harvest: The Communist Party and the American Farmer* (Lincoln, Nebr., 1982), 26.

13. Kolehmainen and Hill, *Haven in the Woods*, 84.

14. Ed Pudas, "Autobiography" (c. 1977), ARC, UWRF, 7; *1905 State Census*, pt. 1, 72, 108; *Montreal River Miner*, reprinted in Works Progress Administration, comp., *Historical Survey of the City of Hurley and Iron County* (n.p., 1937), 44.

15. *Fourteenth Census of the United States (1920)*, vol. 3: *Population*, 1136. See Robert Peters, *Crunching Gravel: Growing Up in the 1930s* (San Francisco, 1988), 91–93.

16. *1905 State Census*, pt. 1, 209; *Radisson Courier*, 24 June 1919; Wisconsin Crop Reporting Service, Annual Enumeration of Agricultural Statistics, 1930, SHSW (ARC, UWEC). See also "The History of Kief: A Polish Settlement in Rusk County, Wisconsin," student paper no. 95, Edward Blackorby Collection, ARC, UWEC (author's names have been removed from papers in this collection to protect privacy).

17. D. W. Sawtelle, "A Trip Through Northern Wisconsin to Investigate Credit Needs of the Settlers," typescript, July 1918, in Ely Papers (reel 184); Jean Sanford

Replinger, ed., *History of the Rural Schools of Rusk County* (Ladysmith, Wis., 1985), 116; Peters, *Crunching Gravel*, 91.

18. Pederson, *Between Memory and Reality*, 108–14; "Development of Agriculture," *Wisconsin Blue Book, 1927* (Madison, 1927), 56–57.

19. Quoted in "The History of a Northern Wisconsin Farm," student paper no. 1956, Blackorby Collection, p. 16; Sawtelle, "Notes on Settlers: 2d Trip to Northern Wisconsin," typescript, June 1918, Ely Papers (reel 184); Fry, *Old and New Immigrant*, 45.

20. Julie Paylin, *Cutover Country: Julie's Story* (Ames, 1976). Although written in the style of a novel, *Cutover Country* appears to be nonfiction according to its library cataloging classification.

21. On the demographic fluctuations in communities on the northern Great Plains settled contemporaneously with the cutover, see Bennett and Kohl, *Settling the Canadian-American West, 1890–1915*, 108–16.

22. Robert E. Bieder, *Native American Communities in Wisconsin, 1600–1960* (Madison, 1995), 172–75; Robert E. Ritzenthaler, *The Potawatomi Indians of Wisconsin*, 2d ed. (Milwaukee, 1962; reprint from the Bulletin of the Milwaukee Public Museum 19 [1953]: 99–184), 106–8, 137, 159–63; James A. Clifton, *The Prairie People: Continuity and Change in Potawatomi Indian Culture, 1665–1965* (Lawrence, Kans., 1977), 309–11; Alexander Morstad, *The Reverend Erik Olsen Morstad: His Missionary Work Among the Wisconsin Pottawatomie Indians* (Clearwater, Fla., [1971], 13–55.

23. For a good recent study, especially relevant because it covers Clark County, adjacent to the cutover, see Jan Coombs, "Frontier Patterns of Marriage, Family, and Ethnicity: Central Wisconsin in the 1880s," *Journal of Family History* 18 (1993): 265–83.

24. *Fourteenth Census of the United States (1920)*, vol 3: *Population*, 1124–30; Juris Veidemanis, "A Twentieth Century Pioneer Settlement: Latvians in Lincoln County, Wisconsin," *Midcontinent American Studies Review* 4 (1963): 15. Veidemansis's calculations are based on church records.

25. A. Bobjeg, "Danes in Polk County, Wisconsin" (1907), trans. Olaf Severson, typescript courtesy of Olaf Severson, Luck, Wis. (Severson is a pseudonym).

26. Calculated from data in State of Wisconsin, *Report of the Bureau of Vital Statistics, 1905–1906* (Madison, 1906), 25–26. In general, see Richard M. Bernard, *The Melting Pot and the Altar: Marital Assimilation in Early Twentieth-Century Wisconsin* (Minneapolis, 1980); and Pederson, *Between Memory and Reality*, 42–46.

27. Kailberg interview; marital status of farmers calculated from the manuscript "United States Census, 1900 and 1910" (National Archives, Washington, D.C.) for the towns of Dewey, Ojibwa, and Radisson; Joe Volkac to First Wisconsin Land Mortgage Association, 10 Aug. 1925, Eau Claire County Circuit Court, First Wisconsin Land Mortgage Association, Liquidation Proceedings, 1913–1929 (box 7, folder 5), ARC, UWEC.

28. State of Wisconsin, *Report of the Bureau of Vital Statistics, 1912–1913* (Madison, 1913), 19, 38–41; "Eidsvold Once Bustled With Timber-Cutting Activity," *Eau Claire Leader-Telegram*, 31 Oct. 1987, p. 7A; *Fourteenth Census (1920)*, vol 3: *Population*, 1124–30; *Thirteenth Census (1910)*, vol. 3: *Population*, 1052–95; Thomas Pomietlo,

"Survival: The Immigration Experience of Anna Bednaczyk and Amelia Bednaczyk Pomietlo, 1912–1932" (student paper, UWEC, 1994), 28–29.

Gerard Bouchard ("Family Reproduction in New Rural Areas: Outline of a North American Model," *Canadian Historical Review* 75 [1994]: 475–510) has identified large fertility growth as a key component in the "open system" he finds characteristic of frontier areas. Other characteristics of his model which were present in the cutover were owner-operated family farms and nuclear families. Less evident (chapter 6) was his characteristic of land transmission, through varied means, on an egalitarian basis to all sons.

Eric Plotzer has reported that nationwide in 1930 a key variable in a regression equation explaining most fertility variation among rural families was capital input into agricultural production, which was low in the cutover ("Fertility and Agricultural Structure in 1930," *Rural Sociology* 51 [1986]: 156–68).

29. "The Skinvik Family," paper no. 203, Blackorby Collection.

30. Daniel Scott Smith," Life Course, Norms, and the Family System of Older Americans in 1900," *Journal of Family History* 4 (1979): 285–98; Steven Ruggles, "The Transformation of American Family Structure," *American Historical Review* 99 (1994): 103–28.

31. Deborah Fink and Alicia Cariquiry, "Having Babies or Not: Household Composition and Fertility in Rural Iowa and Nebraska, 1900–1910," *Great Plains Quarterly* 12 (1992): 157–68.

32. Nell Peters with Robert Peters, *Nell's Story: A Woman from Eagle River* (Madison, 1995), 14–16.

33. Pederson interview; Richard T. Ely, "Private Colonization of the Land," *American Economic Review* 8 (1918): 533; Sherwood William Shear, "A Survey of Land Settlers' Progress in Upper Wisconsin" (Ph.D. diss., UWM, 1924), 5; *Wisconsin Blue Book, 1901* (Madison, 1901), 242–47.

34. *Fourteenth Census (1920),* vol. 6, pt. 1: *Agriculture* (Washington, 1922), 460–66.

35. Ibid., 460–80.

36. UML Papers, Loan Series no. 1329; Report of the First Wisconsin Land Mortgage Association, 1915, typescript, Ely Papers (reel 185).

37. For a very bleak scholarly assessment of the cutover in 1920, see John R. Borchert, *America's Northern Heartland: An Economic and Historical Geography of the Upper Midwest* (Minneapolis, 1987), 61.

38. *History Collections of Washburn County,* 2 vols. (Shell Lake, Wis., 1980), 1:153, 167; classified advertisement for Wisconsin Land and Realty Exchange, *Milwaukee Journal,* 23 Sept. 1920; "The History of a Northern Wisconsin Farm," paper no. 1956, Blackorby Collection; Edward H. Beardsley, *Harry L. Russell and Agricultural Science in Wisconsin* (Madison, 1969), 121–36; Annual Report of the Price County Agricultural Agent, 1920, County Board Papers (box 6), ARC, UWEC; "Price County Gets TNT," *Phillips Times,* 18 Oct. 1919; "Lots of Noise in Price County," ibid., 1 April 1922, p. 1; Ed Pudas, "Autobiography," 16.

39. Ralph Owen Memoirs, typescript, ARC, UWEC; Kailberg interview; *Swedish-American Post,* 4 Oct. 1898, translation courtesy of Lars Kailberg; *History Collections of Washburn County,* 1:158; Mrs. Frank van Slate to George Gilkey, 6 June 1959, George Gilkey Papers, ARC, UWSP. Of the 238 fires officially reported in Price

County in 1926, "railroads" and "clearing" were identified as the two most common causes ("Summary of Forest and Marsh Fires for the Year 1926," Price County Small Series no. 13 (folder 10), ARC, UWEC). In general, see Stephen J. Pyne, *Fire in America: A Cultural History of Wildland and Rural Fire* (Princeton, N.J., 1982), 199–218. Pyne is most disparaging of cutover farmers, who are described as comprising "a lethal parody of settlement."

40. On the family as a labor system in the rural Midwest before World War II, see Neth, *Preserving the Family Farm*, 17–39, and Jane Adams, *The Transformation of Rural Life: Southern Illinois, 1890–1990* (Chapel Hill, N.C., 1994), 96–107. Nancy Grey Osterud, in "'She Helped Me Hay It as Good as a Man': Relations among Men and Women in an Agricultural Community," in Carol Groneman and Mary Beth Norton, eds., *'To Toil the Livelong Day': American Women At Work, 1780–1980* (Ithaca, N.Y., 1987), 87–98, stresses the "economic mutuality" between rural men and women in the late nineteenth century.

41. Phillips Centennial Committee, *Phillips, Wisconsin . . . 1876–1976* (Phillips, 1976), 35; *Radisson Courier*, 24 Jan. 1919 (supplement); Larry Garneau, interview, Drummond, Wis., Oct. 1988 ARC, UWEC (Garneau is a pseudonym); Edna Hatlestad Hong, "A Nostalgia Almanac," *Wisconsin Trails* (Spring 1978): 24–26. In a pattern which seems similar to what prevailed in the cutover, Gjerde (*From Peasants to Farmers*) argues that among rural Norwegian-Americans the labor of children became more important than it had been in Norway, due to the lesser availability of hired help in the United States, which in turn kept Norwegian-American children at home longer and contributed to the predominance of nuclear families among rural households. Deborah Fink (*Agrarian Women: Wives and Mothers in Rural Nebraska, 1880–1940* [Chapel Hill, N.C., 1992], 150–51) emphasizes physical coercion by fathers to exploit labor from their children. I found no evidence in the cutover of the whippings by fathers, and children's resistance by running away that Fink reports for rural Nebraska. For the Canadian-American "heartland" in Montana, Alberta, and Saskatchewan, which was settled approximately contemporaneously with the cutover, anthropologists Bennett and Kohl present a more balanced conclusion: "[t]he matrix of family relationships in the context of labor and cash needs was a flexible and adaptive one" between the needs of parents and the desires of children (*Settling the Canadian-American West*, 97–99).

42. Garneau interview; Nellie E. Batt, "Early History of Minong," in *History Collections of Washburn County*, 2:572; Eldon Marple, *The Hayward Lakes Region* (Hayward, 1979), 27; potato statistics calculated from Annual Enumeration of Agricultural Statistics, 1925 (tabulations by Mark Rose); *Fourteenth Census (1920)*, vol. 6, pt. 1: *Agriculture*, 474–80; Rhody, *Spirit of Saga Valley: The Story of My Father*, 56.

43. Marple, *Hayward Lakes Region*, 25–26; Replinger, ed., *History of the Rural Schools of Rusk County*, 155–56; Pudas, "Autobiography," 73; U.S. Bureau of the Census, *Fifteenth Census of the United States (1930): Agriculture*, vol. 3, pt. 1 (Washington, 1932), 553–57. For a similar subsistence pattern in Polk County in the 1920s, see Harvey Dueholm, interview, Madison, November–December 1978, Wisconsin Agriculturalists Oral History Project, SHSW.

44. Arnold R. Alanen and William H. Tishler, "Farming the Lake Superior Shore: Agriculture and Horticulture on the Apostle Islands, 1840–1940," *WMH* 79

(1996): 162–203; Mark E. Bruby et al., *Heritage Resources Management, 1989,* United States Forest Service, Nicolet National Forest, *Cultural Research Survey Report* no. 7 (Rhinelander, 1990), 362; *Superior Tyovaen Osustaiminalehti,* 22 June 1933, cited in Kolehaimen and Hill, *Haven in the Woods,* 62 (for how Finns out-migrated from the Keweehaw Peninsula in upper Michigan after an unsuccessful 1912–1913 strike, see Larry Lankton, *Cradle to Grave: Life, Work and Death at the Lake Superior Copper Mines* [New York, 1991]); Peters, *Crunching Gravel,* [v]; *History Collections of Washburn County,* 2:498; Mary Roach, quoted in "History of the Town of Atlanta" (1960), student paper no. 1857, Blackorby Collection; Fred Etcherson, interview near Hayward, Wis., 30 July 1970, ARC, UWEC; *Radisson Courier,* 24 Jan. 1919 (supplement).

45. Cf. Mary Beth Pudup, "The Limits of Subsistence: Agriculture and Industry in Central Appalachia," *Agricultural History* 64 (1990): 61–89.

46. Pederson, *Between Memory and Reality,* passim; *Phillips Times,* 28 March 1902.

47. "Memoirs of W. J. Davies," *History Collections of Washburn County,* 1:171.

48. "Urges More Crop Acres Be Added," *Park Falls Herald,* 30 March 1936; *Memories of Forest County* (n.p., 1980), 183–84; [Goldsworthy], *Pine, Plow, and Pioneer,* 53.

Luderus was the regular first baseman for the Philadelphia Phillies from 1911 through 1919. Overall in thirteen big league seasons he batted .277, hitting .315 on the pennant-winning Phillies team of 1915 and batting .435 in the World Series that fall (*The Baseball Encyclopedia,* 10th ed. [New York, 1996], 1286–87).

49. Walter Ebling, "The Development of Agriculture in Wisconsin," *Wisconsin Bluebook, 1929* (Madison, 1929), 50–74, esp. 71; Ebling et al., *A Century of Wisconsin Agriculture, 1848–1948,* Wisconsin Crop Reporting Service Bulletin no. 290 (Madison, 1948), 40–41; Robert M. Dessureau, *History of Langlade County* (Antigo, 1922), 307.

50. "Stanley—Vegetables," in Tom McKay and Deborah Kmetz, eds., *Agricultural Diversity in Wisconsin: A Catalog to Accompany the Cooperative Exhibit Culture and Agriculture* (Madison, 1987), 44–46; [Mrs. Spencer Thompson], *Sheldon, Wi., 1909–1959* [Sheldon], 1959).

51. Batt, "Early History of Minong," 572; *Fourteenth Census (1920),* vol. 6, pt. 1: *Agriculture,* 474–86. See the expansive description of the activities of the Cranberry Lake Development Company, six miles southeast of Phillips in Price County, in "Harvesting Cranberries," *Phillips Times,* 24 Sept. 1921, p. 1.

52. Leighton D. Morris, comp., "White Pines and White Tails: A Social Study of Sawyer County," (1957), pp. 80–82, ARC, UWEC; Peters, *Nell's Story,* 139–40.

53. Dessureau, *History of Langlade County,* 88–91.

54. Howard R. Klueter and James J. Lorence, *Woodlot and Ballot Box: Marathon County in the Twentieth Century* (Wausau, 1977), 146–48; Rhody, *Spirit of Saga Valley,* 73–74; *Fourteenth Census (1920),* vol. 6, pt. 1: *Agriculture,* 474–80; Michael J. Anuta, *East Prussians From Russia* (Menominee, Mich., 1979), 115–19; *Phillips Times,* 24 May and 27 Sept. 1902, 24 Jan., 31 Jan., 7 Feb., 14 Feb., 23 May, 30 May, and 26 Dec. 1903, 9 April and 17 Dec. 1904; Ebling et al., *Century of Wisconsin Agriculture,* 50.

55. Elva Lessard, *Fifield, 1876–1976* (Fifield, 1976), 46; "A History of Fifield," paper no. 1092, Blackorby Collection. For an attempt to boost sheep ranching, see *Phillips Times,* 6 Jan., 24 March, 21 April, and 15 Sept. 1900, 27 April 1901.

56. Ebling et al., *Century of Wisconsin Agriculture,* 61–64.

57. Jerry Novak, ed., *History of the Moquah Area* (Ashland, Wis., 1966), 15; Kolehaimen and Hill, *Haven in the Woods,* 54; C. A. Paul to Union Mortgage Loan Company, 15 Nov. 1915, Loan Series no. 1284, UML Papers; Mills, *Lithuanians in Oneida County.*

58. For prices see Table G in Eric E. Lampard, *The Rise of the Dairy Industry in Wisconsin* (Madison, 1963), 455.

59. Robjerg, "Danes in Polk County," 22; Pudas, "Autobiography," 11; *Fourteenth Census (1920),* vol 6, pt. 1: *Agriculture,* 467–77.

60. Klueter and Lorence, *Woodlot and Ballot Box,* esp. 151–55; Lampard, *Rise of the Dairy Industry,* 284–85.

61. *History Collections of Washburn County,* 2:510; Pudas, "Autobiography," 131; Pederson, *Between Memory and Reality,* 82.

62. *History Collections of Washburn County,* 2:510. For a visual indication of the spread of creameries compare the maps in *Fourteenth Annual Report of the Agricultural Experimental Station of the University of Wisconsin* (Madison, 1897), facing p. 148; and *Report of the Wisconsin Dairy and Food Commission, 1924* (Madison, 1924). In general, see Ebling et al., *Century of Wisconsin Agriculture,* 67–74.

63. Meier interview; Ebling, "Development of Agriculture in Wisconsin," 73.

64. Neth, *Preserving the Family Farm,* associates commercialized farming with increased patriarchy, beginning in the first decades of the twentieth century and triumphing after World War II. But Fink, *Agrarian Women,* sees oppressive patriarchy as a constant on nineteenth- and twentieth-century farms. Katherine Jellison (*Entitled to Power: Farm Women and Technology, 1913–1963* [Chapel Hill, N.C., 1993]) describes a similarly constant patriarchy, but grants women greater success at resisting it (in part by the adaptations of technology). Glenda Riley (*The Female Frontier: A Comparative View of Women on the Prairie and the Plains* [Lawrence, Kans., 1988]) identifies a less oppressive "domestic focus" as defining rural women's work regardless of place or type of farming, in contrast to men, but stops her analysis in 1915. Adams (*Transformation of Rural Life*), like Neth emphasizes changes in the gendered nature of work on American farms after World War II, but does not see them as completely disadvantageous for women because, by asserting themselves, women were able to maintain important roles.

65. Sally McMurry, *Transforming Rural Life: Dairying Families and Agricultural Change, 1820–1885* (Baltimore, 1995), 194–224.

66. *Peitojakoti,* Dec. 1920, cited in Kolehmainen and Hill, *Haven in the Woods,* 59.

67. In general, on the important economic contributions made by farm wives to their families see Joann Vanek, "Work, Leisure, and Family Roles: Farm Households in the United States, 1920–1950," *Journal of Family History* 5 (1980): 422–31.

68. Neth, *Preserving the Family Farm,* 60–62.

69. Robjerb, "Danes in Polk County," 21; Kailberg interview; *Peltojakoti,* Dec. 1920, cited in Kolehmainen and Hill, *Haven in the Woods,* 59.

70. Elise Kramolis Lajcak, "Moquah—As I Remember It," in Novak, ed., *History of the Moquah Area,* 37–38; Mary Bedore, "Farm Life in 1900," (typescript), Marie Procheska Family Papers, ARC, UWGB.

71. Charlotte G. Borst, "Wisconsin Midwives as Working Women: Immigrant Midwives and the Limits of a Traditional Occupation, 1870–1920," *Journal of American Ethnic History* 8 (1979): 24–59; Paul Nagel, *I Remember, I Remember: History and Lore of Jump River, Wisconsin* (n.p., 1986), 78. See the "Price County Midwives' and Physicians' Reports," 1888–1903, ARC, UWEC. In 1940, almost half the births in Wisconsin attended by a midwife took place in the cutover (*Thirty-Ninth Report of the State Board of Health of Wisconsin* [Madison, 1942]).

72. Pomietlo, "Survival," 16–17; *History Collections of Washburn County*, 1:141–42; Carol Lofgren, *Historical Album: Stone Lake Wisconsin* (Stone Lake, 1977), 30; Anderson interview; Meier interview; G. E. Anderson to E. C. Hart, 20 April 1909, vol. 174, Owen Papers; Margaret Pike, "Remembrances of a Life," (typescript, 1992), p. 1, ARC, UWEC; Alvina Schmidt, interview, Bloomer, Wis., March 1989, Memories About the 1920s Project (tape on deposit), Chippewa Valley Museum, Eau Claire, Wis.; Carl Rhody, *Saga of Spirit Valley*, pt. 2: *Hard Times, Good Times* (Ogema, Wis., 1982), 43.

73. Cf. Adams, *Transformation of Rural Life*, to Fink, *Agrarian Women*, esp. 115–28. An intermediate position, emphasizing "ambivalence" in the attitudes of farm women in frontier situations, is Bennett and Seena, *Settling the Canadian-American West*, 50–54. Underlying Fink's analysis is a belief in the static influence, beginning at least in the early nineteenth century, of the "agrarian myth," which emphasized the importance of the labor of individual farm families and made women and children susceptible to male exploitation. By contrast, Adams, Neth, Pederson, and other recent scholars emphasize the importance of the labor exchange system among farm families.

74. Charles Patterson, interview, Rice Lake, Wis., July 1989 (tape in possession of the author; Patterson is a pseudonym); *Iron River, Wisconsin*, 18; Adams, *Transformation of Rural Life*, 70–71.

75. Allan Kulikoff, "The Transition to Capitalism in Rural America," *William and Mary Quarterly*, 3d ser., 46 (1989): 120–44.

76. Schlomann, *Thread of Love*, 51; *1905 State Census*, pt. 1, pp. 593–602.

77. Dennis Nodin Valdes, "Betabelleros: The Formation of an Agricultural Proletariat in the Midwest, 1897–1930," *Labor History* 30 (1989): 536–62; Adams, *Transformation of Rural Life*, 117–19, 130.

78. Rhody, *Spirit of Saga Valley: Hard Times, Good Times*, 85.

79. Bedore, "Farm Life in the 1890s"; Ron Duff Martin, "History of Sarah Elizabeth Neal Martin" (student paper, UWEC, 1990), 5; Peters, *Nell's Story*, 57–58.

80. *Rusk County Schools*, 155–56; "Memoirs of Eve Stuart," *History Collections of Washburn County*, 2:377; Rhody, *Saga of Spirit Valley: The Story of My Father*, 55–58; Peters, *Crunching Gravel*, 107; Kailberg interview.

81. In fifteen of the twenty-two inventories of farmers's property taken for probate purposes in Taylor County in 1915–1916, a mower was mentioned, and twelve times a rake was mentioned (one farm had two rakes) (calculated from Taylor County Probate Files, ARC, UWEC).

82. Nagel, *I Remember, I Remember*, 212–13.

83. Stouffer, "This I Remember," *History Collections of Washburn County*, 1:158. Six of the twenty-two Taylor County inventories of 1915–1916 contained a binder, one of them a half-share.

84. See Mary Neth, "Gender and the Family Labor System: Defining Work in the Rural Midwest," *Journal of Social History* 27 (1994): 563–77; Neth, *Preserving the Family Farm,* 23–24; Adams, *Transformation of Rural Life,* 84–89; Bennett and Seena, *Settling the Canadian-American West,* 89–93.

85. *History Collections of Washburn County,* 2:338–44; Garneau interview. Not all absent spouses were faithful in remitting or returning to their farms with their off-farm earnings, which further increased the pressure on their wives to be providers. Nellie Bednaczyk recalled that in the early 1920s on their farm near Lublin in Taylor County, "I took over the man's job for Father went back to the mines again . . . he didn't send a penny for us; but we managed very nicely" (Pomietlo, "Survival," 19).

86. On the family economy, see Steven Mintz and Susan Kellogg, *Domestic Revolutions: A Social History of American Family Life* (New York, 1988), 87–91. On the significance of "working out" in a newly developing agricultural region see, e.g., Bennett and Seena, *Settling the Canadian-American West,* 99–101.

87. Neth, *Preserving the Family Farm,* 32; Pomietlo, "Survival," 24–25. For a discussion of how "social networks" directed young farm women to urban work see Alan A. Brookes and Catharine A. Wilson, "'Working Away' from the Farm: The Young Women of North Huron, 1910–30," *Ontario History* 77 (1985): 281–300.

88. Manuscript U.S. Census, 1910; Annual Enumeration of Agricultural Statistics, 1940, town of Grow (such situations account for many of the relatively few nonnuclear households in the early years of settlement in the cutover; for instance, in 1910 on the farm of widow Louise Olsen, in the town of Dewey, the oldest son was only twelve, but Louise's brother Louis Shawson lived with the family).

89. Rhody, *Saga of Spirit Valley: Hard Times, Good Times,* 105; *Rusk County Schools,* 90; *History Collections of Washburn County,* 1:161–63; Schlomann, *Thread of Love,* passim.

90. *The Impact of Her Spirit: An Oral History by the Wisconsin Extension Homemakers Council* (River Falls, Wis., 1991), 22.

91. Meier interview; Roy R. Meier, "History of the Herd of Spring Brook Farm" (typescript, 1977), Meier Papers.

92. *Iron River, Wisconsin,* 18; Schlomann, *Thread of Love,* 28; *History Collections of Washburn County,* 544–45; Kailberg interview; Nagel, *I Remember, I Remember,* 168–69. For a good discussion of the centrality of neighborhood work exchange integrated with community social interactions in a fruit and vegetable–growing area of the Midwest before World War II, see Adams, *Transformation of Rural Life,* 49–70; for a similar pattern in a frontier region settled contemporaneously with the cutover, see Bennett and Kohl, *Settling the Canadian-American West, 1890–1915,* 121–22.

93. *Impact of Her Spirit,* 75; *History of Moquah,* 35–36. Nancy Grey Osterud ("Gender and the Transition to Capitalism in Rural America," *Agricultural History* 67 [1993]: 14–27) argues convincingly that women's work was critical to maintaining yeoman-type farming against the inroads of the "capitalist market."

94. Erven J. Lane, "The Sorenson Community: A Glimpse of Northern Wisconsin in Process," *Land Economics* 25 (1949): 193–209; Kailberg interview.

95. Pederson, *Between Memory and Reality,* 150–51; J. Sanford Rikoon, *Threshing in the Midwest, 1820–1940: A Study of Traditional Culture and Technological Change* (Bloomington, Ind., 1988), 83–134; Neth, *Preserving the Family Farm,* 148–67.

96. Pudas, "Autobiography," 133; "Memoir of Herman Swan," *History Collections of Washburn County*, 1:167; Severson interview; Meier interview.

97. Mark Davis, "Northern Choices: Rural Forest County in the 1920s, Part I," *WMH* 79 (1995–96): 3–31, esp. 27; Kolehmainen and Hill, *Haven in the Woods*, 53–55, 91–96, 135–50; Dyson, *Red Harvest*, ch. 3; Pederson, *Between Memory and Reality*, 54, 78, 86–88; Samuel Mermin, "Consumer Cooperatives in Northern Wisconsin," *Monthly Labor Review* 45 (1937): 1327–44; Dale E. Treleven, "Agricultural Cooperatives in Wisconsin," in Kmetz and McKay, eds., *Agricultural Diversity in Wisconsin*, 78; Paul W. Glad, *A History of Wisconsin*, vol. 5: *War, a New Era, and Depression* (Madison, 1990), 152, 175, 177–78, 409; Speek, *Stake in the Land*, 138–41.

98. Pudas, "Autobiography," 107–12; Medford Co-operative Creamery Company Records, 1915–1965, ARC, UWEC; Flambeau Valley Farms Cooperative Records, 1925–1980, ARC, UWEC.

99. Mermin, "Consumer Cooperatives in Northern Wisconsin," 1327–44.

100. Report of the Commissioner of Insurance, in *Wisconsin Public Documents, 1913–14*, vol. 7 (Madison, 1916); Trade Lake Mutual Fire Insurance Company Papers, ARC, UWRF.

101. Eldon Marple, *The Visitor Who Came to Stay* (Hayward, Wis., 1971); Kailberg interview.

102. Erich Lenz, interview, Merrill, Wis., 1970 (tape on deposit, SHSW).

103. Dueholm interview. On rural neighborhoods, see Neth, *Preserving the Family Farm*, 53–62.

104. See McMurry, *Transforming Rural Life*, 224–231.

105. *Fifteenth Census (1930): Agriculture*, vol. 2, pt. 1 (Washington, D.C., 1932), 794–99; *Phillips Times*, 24 Nov. 1923; Mary Neth, "Leisure and Generational Change: Farm Youths in the Midwest, 1910–1940," *Agricultural History* 67 (1993): 163–83 (for a visual presentation of the expansion of the paved road network in northern Wisconsin between 1924 and 1940 see Glad, *War, a New Era, and Depression*, 212–13); Elizabeth A. Perkins, "The Consumer Frontier: Household Consumption in Early Kentucky," *Journal of American History* 78 (1991): 486–510. For a somewhat different interpretation, see Michael Berger, *The Devil Wagon in God's Country: The Automobile and Social Change in Rural America, 1893–1929* (Hamden, Conn., 1979), which sees the introduction of the car as intensifying social interaction, but in doing so overcoming an alleged pre-existing "isolation" in the country and encouraging "individualism" among rural people.

106. F. C. Johnson, "Experiences of a Pioneer Physician in Northern Wisconsin," *Wisconsin Medical Journal* 38 (1939): 584; Nagel, *I Remember, I Remember*, 197–205. See also Neth, *Preserving the Family Farm*, 66.

On the significance of women's roles in farm communities at this time in general, see Mary Neth, "Building the Base: Farm Women, the Rural Community, and Farm Organizations in the Midwest, 1900–1940," in Wava G. Haney and Jane B. Knowles, eds., *Women and Farming: Changing Roles, Changing Structures* (Boulder, Colo., 1988), 339–55.

107. Mary Roach quoted in student paper no. 1859, Blackorby Collection; *Rusk County Schools*, 109, 137; Neth, *Preserving the Family Farm*, 69. See Records of Rusk County Joint School District no. 3, Cloverleaf School, 1916–1958, ARC, UWEC. For

example, twenty-one citizens attended the 1932 annual meeting, which after debate rejected a proposal to electrify the school. In general, see Wayne E. Fuller, *The Old Country School: The Story of Rural Education in the Middle West* (Chicago, 1982).

108. Report of the Price Country Superintendent of Schools for 1920, Price Country Board Papers; *Fourteenth Census (1920)*, vol. 8: *Population* (Washington, 1922), 1124–30.

109. Frank Richardson, interview, Waverly, Ohio, August 1987 (tape on deposit), ARC, UWEC (Richardson is a pseudonym); Dueholm interview; [Goldsworthy, ed.], *Pine, Plow, and Pioneer*, 15; U.S. Bureau of the Census, *Religious Bodies: 1936*, vol 1: *Summary and Special Tables* (Washington, D.C., 1941), 846–49; idem., *Religious Bodies: 1916*, pt. 1: *Summary and General Tables* (Washington, D.C., 1919), 327–28.

110. LaVerne H. Marquart, *Wisconsin's Agricultural Heritage: The Grange, 1871–1971* (n.p., 1972), esp. 34–35; Records of the Homestead Grange, no. 684, 1914–1918, SHSW; Meier interview. See also Dessureau, *History of Langlade Country*, 88–91.

Donald B. Marti, *Women of the Grange: Mutuality and Sisterhood in Rural America, 1866–1920* (New York, 1991), shows how the Grange throughout the United States provided farm women with opportunities both to promote separate women's activities and to interact with men in advocating interests mutually shared as rural residents. Neth (*Preserving the Family Farm*, 129) describes Midwest Grange chapters as "community based."

111. *History Collections of Washburn County*, 1:178; *Phillips Times*, 27 Oct. 1900, 9 July 1904; Price Country Budget for 1929, Papers of the Board of Supervisors (box 10), ARC, UWEC; Rhody, *Saga of Spirit River: Hard Times, Good Times*, 36–37.

112. Kanne, *Pieces of the Past*, 79–80; Carolyn Crotteau, *Historical Album: Cameron Centennial, 1879–1979* (n.p., 1978), 177; Bruby, *Heritage Resources Management*, 364–65; *Phillips Times*, 13 June 1925, p. 1; *Rusk County Schools*, 105; Neth, *Preserving the Family Farm*, 68. On the social significance of charivaris, see esp. Pederson, *From Memory to Reality*, 206–17.

113. Dueholm interview.

114. *History Collections of Washburn County*, 1:161.

3. The Shaping of the Cutover by Agricultural Experts, 1895–1925

1. For an overview of the Country Life movement see David B. Danbom, *Born in the Country: A History of Rural America* (Baltimore, 1995), 167–75. A fuller treatment of the reformers' motives is found in idem., *The Resisted Revolution: Urban America and the Industrialization of the Countryside* (Ames, Iowa, 1979). See also William L. Bowers, *The Country Life Movement in America, 1900–1920* (Port Washington, N.Y., 1974), which portrays the reformers as less committed to modernizing rural America than as to resisting the inevitable forces of "industrialization."

Recent studies of failed agricultural settlement in the twentieth century include Paula M. Nelson, *After the West Was Won: Homesteaders and Town Builders in Western South Dakota, 1900–1917* (Iowa City, 1986); Barbara Allen, *Homesteading the High Desert* (Salt Lake City, 1987); Michael L. Olsen, "The Failure of An Agricultural Community: Johnson Mesa, New Mexico," *New Mexico Historical Review* 58 (1983):

113–32; Frank Norris, "On Beyond Reason: Homesteading in the California Desert, 1885–1940," *Southern California Quarterly* 64 (1987): 297–312; and Marshall Bower, "Turnover of Pioneers and Property in a Marginal Nevada Farming Community," *Yearbook of the Association of Pacific Coast Geographers* 42 (1980): 45–57.

2. On the activities of the reorganized Board of Immigration, see Arlan Helgeson, *Farms in the Cutover: Agricultural Settlement of Northern Wisconsin* (Madison, 1962), 85–89.

3. B. G. Packer, "An Empire in Waiting" (typescript), Department of Agriculture, Administration, Immigration Division Records, 1920–1930 (folder 1), SHSW; B. G. Packer and E. J. Delwiche, *Farm Making in Upper Wisconsin: Hints for the Settler,* Agricultural Experimental Station Bulletin no. 290 (Madison, 1918). Packer frankly discouraged settlement in the central sands region of Wisconsin, such as in Jackson County, but continued to insist until the mid-1920s that there was plenty of good land farther north.

4. *Fourth Biennial Report of the State Board of Immigration* (Madison, 1915), 13.

5. Ibid., 3.

6. Immigration Division Records, 1920–1930 (folder 1). Packer's agency became a division of the Department of Agriculture in 1915.

7. *Wisconsin Blue Book, 1923* (Madison, 1923), 255; Byron Selves to R. G. Johnstad, 26 Jan. 1928, Division of Immigration to Johnstad, 10 Feb. 1928, Immigration Division Records (folder 1). Prompted by the Division of Immigration, the Wisconsin Real Estate Brokers Board formally warned the Burnett County Abstract Company about this solicitation.

8. *Fourth Biennial Report,* 22; *Farm Making in Upper Wisconsin,* 71; *Wisconsin Blue Book, 1925* (Madison, 1925), 319; *Blue Book, 1923,* 256; Householder to Rudolph Carlson, 16 Mar. 1928, Division of Immigration Records, 1920–1930 (folder 1).

9. Marion Clinch Calkins, "Protecting Immigrant Settlers," *Survey* 45 (Nov. 20, 1920): 277. See also Peter A. Speek, *A Stake in the Land* (New York, 1921), 97–101.

10. Wilber H. Glover, *Farm and College: The College of Agriculture of the University of Wisconsin: A History* (Madison, 1952), 218–25; Edward H. Beardsley, *Harry L. Russell and Agricultural Science in Wisconsin* (Madison, 1969), 97–101.

11. The annual reports of the county agent during the 1920s and early 1930s are in the Price County Board Papers, ARC, UWEC.

12. In general see Charles E. Rosenberg, *No Other Gods: On Science and American Social Thought* (Baltimore, 1976), 153–95.

13. Glover, *Farm and College,* 276–78.

14. Ernest Luther, "Draft Biography of Dean Russell" (typescript), Ernest Luther Papers, SHSW. See Beardsley, *Harry L. Russell,* 142–44.

15. Lars Kailberg interview, Rice Lake, Wis., 22 July 1988 (tape on deposit), ARC, UWEC (Kailberg is a pseudonym).

16. See the petition of the Price County Taxpayers Association, 2 May 1921, Price County Board Papers, box 6.

17. Luther to H. L. Russell, Dec. 1915 (draft); Luther to K. C. Hatch, 2 June 1912, Luther Papers (box 1). Russell told Luther not to enter future competitions.

18. "New Agricultural Journal for Upper Wisconsin Issues 1st Number," *Phillips Times,* 17 Oct. 1925, p. 1.

19. This and the following paragraphs are based on Robert J. Gough, "Richard T. Ely and the Development of the Wisconsin Cutover," *WMH* 75 (1991): 2–38. See also Dorothy Ross, *The Origins of American Social Science* (Cambridge, Eng., 1991), 98–118.

20. Richard T. Ely, "Private Colonization of the Land," *American Economic Review* 8 (1918): 522–48.

21. Ronald Sandfort, "The Entrepreneurial Activities of Ben Faast: A Visionary Banker, Colonizer, and Community Developer of Northern Wisconsin" (MST thesis, UWEC, 1974), 10–39.

22. See, e.g., B. F. Faast, "Practical Policies of Land Colonization," *Journal of Land and Public Utility Economics* 1 (1925): 300–307.

23. Faast, "Financing the Undeveloped Timber Sections of the Middle West," typescript enclosure to Richard T. Ely, 16 June 1917 (microfilm reel 56), Richard T. Ely Papers, SHSW; Householder, "Wisconsin Land Mortgage Associations as a Means of Financing Newly Arrived Settlers" (typescript, 1923), Immigration Division Records, 1920–1930 (folder 7); "Report of Results for Year 1920," and "Bonds Sold in Each Year" (typescripts), Eau Claire County Circuit Court, First Wisconsin Land Mortgage Association, Liquidation Proceedings, 1913–1929 (box 13, folder 5), ARC, UWEC.

24. On New Era programs in rural America, see David E. Hamilton, "From New Era to New Deal: American Farm Policy Between the Wars," in Lawrence E. Gelfand and Robert J. Neymeyer, eds., *Agricultural Distress in the Midwest: Past and Present* (Iowa City, 1986), 19–54, esp. 24–33; and idem., "Building the Associative State: The Department of Agriculture and American State-Building," *Agricultural History* 64 (1990): 207–18.

25. Sandfort, "Entrepreneurial Activities of Ben Faast," 39–47; Susan O. Haswell and Arnold R. Alanen, "Colonizing the Cutover: Wisconsin's Progressive-Era Experiments in Rural Planning," *Landscape Journal* 14 (1995): 171–87, esp. 177–81. See the promotional materials, internal reports, circular letters, and other materials in the Wisconsin Colonization Company Papers, ARC, UWEC.

26. See, e.g., *Radisson Courier*, supplement for 24 Jan. 1919: "Farm Development and Land Clearing."

27. Ibid; Wisconsin Crop Reporting Service, Annual Enumeration of Farm Statistics, 1923–, SHSW; Wisconsin Department of Agriculture, Land Appraisers' Reports, 1920–1925, SHSW; Town of Radisson, Tax Assessment Ledgers, 1920, 1930, ARC, UWEC.

28. B. M. Apker, "Reminiscences" (typescript), ARC, UWEC.

29. Land Appraisers' Reports, 1920–1925.

30. Marion Clinch Calkins, "Colonization Projects in Wisconsin," *Survey* 45 (1921): 480–85; Speek, *Stake in the Land,* esp. 52–65. While touring northern Wisconsin with Speek, Ely's assistant was told by a Faast employee that churches were discouraged because they "take from the settler money which he seriously needs for the development of his farm" (David W. Sawtelle, "Tour of Northern Wisconsin in the Investigation of Land Settlement" [typescript, July 1918] [reel 184], Ely Papers).

31. Michael F. Beaudoin, interview, Park Falls, Wis., 29 Nov. 1950 (transcript), p. 9, SHSW.

32. A. B. Cox, "A Trip Through Northern Wisconsin to Investigate Credit Needs of Settlers" (typescript, July 1918); D. W. Sawtelle, "A Tour Through Northern Wisconsin in the Interest of Land Settlement" (typescript, Aug. 1918), both in Ely Papers (reel 184).

33. Ibid.; Calkins, "Colonization Projects."

34. Faast to Farmers on Wisconsin Colonization Company Land, 1 June 1921; Wisconsin Colonization Company, "Your Record of Progress" (1924), Wisconsin Colonization Company Papers.

35. Sawtelle, "A Tour Through Northern Wisconsin."

36. Ibid.

37. Cox, "Trip Through Northern Wisconsin," 11–12.

38. Ely, "Thoughts About Immigration," *The Congregationalist* 79 (1894): 13–14. On Ely and immigration restriction, see Lee Benson, "Historical Background of Turner's Frontier Essay," *Agricultural History* 25 (1951): 50–82, reprinted in Lee Benson, *Turner and Beard: American Historical Writing Reconsidered* (New York, 1960), 41–91, esp. 74–75, 85–86.

39. Petition to President Wilson, Nov. 1914 (copy) (reel 49), Ely Papers.

40. Nine eugenic studies are reprinted, with a thoughtful introduction, in Nicole Hahn Rafter, ed., *White Trash: The Eugenic Family Studies* (Boston, 1988). See Mark H. Haller, *Eugenics: Hereditarian Attitudes in American Thought* (New Brunswick, N.J., 1963).

41. R. T. Ely, B. H. Hibbard, and A. B. Cox, *Credit Needs of Settlers in Upper Wisconsin,* Wisconsin Agricultural Experiment Station Bulletin no. 318 (Madison, 1920).

42. Ely to Fabian Franklin, 9 June 1920 (reel 71), Ely Papers.

43. Faast to Harry L. Russell, 10 Mar. 1919, Wisconsin Colonization Company Papers, addendum. See Beardsley, *Harry L. Russell,* 131–32; Sandfort, "Entrepreneurial Activities of Ben Faast," 69–70. Faast had a history of interfering with university publications regarding northern Wisconsin. In 1915, for example, he had effected modifications in a bulletin prepared by Delwiche, getting an emphasis added that, among other points, new settlers should not immediately try to remove stumps but should plant clover between them (Faast to Russell, 26 May 1915, Wisconsin Colonization Company Papers, addendum).

44. Faast to Prof. W. A. Scott, 18 Dec. 1921, ibid.; Ely, "Public and Private Colonization," *National Real Estate Journal* 25 (Mar. 12, 1923), 42. See Benjamin G. Rader, *The Academic Mind and Reform: The Influence of Richard T. Ely in American Life* (Lexington, Ky., 1966), 207–8.

45. Ely to Faast, 22 Nov. 1919, 11 Dec. 1919 (reel 69), Ely Papers.

46. Ely to Faast, 20 Jan. 1920, Wisconsin Colonization Company Papers, addendum. See Sandfort, "Entrepreneurial Activities of Ben Faast," 77–79.

47. Paul W. Glad, *History of Wisconsin,* vol. 5: *War, a New Era, and Depression, 1914–1940* (Madison, 1990), 203.

48. Bill G. Reid, "Franklin K. Lane's Idea for Veteran's Colonization," *Pacific Historical Review* 33 (1964): 447–61; "Proposals for Soldiers Settlement during World War I," *Midamerica* 46 (1964): 172–86; "Agrarian Opposition to Franklin K. Lane's Proposal for Soldiers Settlement, 1918–1920," *Agricultural History* 41 (1967): 167–79.

49. Sandfort, "Entrepreneurial Activities of Ben Faast," 61–62. Mead endorsed Faast's approach to land colonization, but emphasized that he could not do it "as a private enterprise" and was entitled to "public aid" (Mead to Faast, 12 Apr. 1923, Wisconsin Colonization Company Papers, addendum).

50. Ely to U.S. Representative A. P. Nelson, 10 July 1919 (reel 69), Ely Papers; B. L., "Wisconsin Plans for Land Settlement," *Outlook* 42 (1919): 432. See Rader, *Academic Mind and Reform*, 203–4; Helgeson, *Farms in the Cutover*, 91–92.

51. *Wisconsin State Journal* (Madison), 27 May 1920.

52. Richard T. Ely, "An American Land Policy," in Elisha M. Friedman, ed., *America and the New Era: A Symposium on Social Reconstruction* (New York, 1920), 127–49.

53. Sandfort, "Entrepreneurial Activities of Ben Faast," 62–63.

54. Ibid., 64–67.

55. Ely to Paul Popenoe, 15 May 1917 (reel 56), Ely Papers; Ely, "What is Bolshevism?" *Review of Reviews* 62 (1920): 497–501; Merle Curti and Vernon Carstensen, *The University of Wisconsin: A History*, 2 vols. (Madison, 1949), 2:201; Herbert B. Margulies, *The Decline of the Progressive Movement in Wisconsin, 1890–1920* (Madison, 1969), 203–4, 213–14; Rader, *Academic Mind and Reform*, 97–98, 185–86, 190; Glad, *War, a New Era, and Depression*, 40–44, 54.

56. Roy R. Meier, interview, Spirit, Wis., 21–23 March 1979 (tape on deposit), Wisconsin Agriculturalists Oral History Project, SHSW; Ely to Mark Cresap, 30 July 1920 (reel 71), Ely Papers. Voting results are calculated from *Wisconsin Blue Book, 1909* (Madison, 1909), 558; *Wisconsin Blue Book, 1913* (Madison, 1913), 270–71; *Wisconsin Blue Book, 1917* (Madison, 1917), 141–301; and *Wisconsin Blue Book, 1921* (Madison, 1921), 120–64.

57. Ely to Mrs. T. S. McMahon, 16 June 1920 (reel 71), Ely Papers.

58. *Milwaukee Journal*, 6 Aug. 1925. See Curti and Carstensen, *University of Wisconsin*, 2:223–29, 341–42; and Rader, *Academic Mind and Reform*, 210–12.

59. C. Luther Fry, *The New and Old Immigrant on the Land: A Study of Americanization and the Rural Church* (New York, 1922), 60, 63, 78–80. If this work is indicative, the ecumenism of rural church reformers in the 1920s, which called on denominations to stop competing for members in the country, did not extend to the Catholic church. For background, see Brian W. Beltman, "Rural Church Reform in Wisconsin During the Progressive Era," *WMH* 60 (1976): 3–20, and James H. Madison, "Reformers and the Rural Church," *Journal of American History* 73 (1986): 645–68, esp. 660 on the role of Fry. On the Institute for Social and Religious Research, see ibid., 668–72; and Lowry Nelson, *Rural Sociology: Its Origin and Growth in the United States* (Minneapolis, 1969), 47–51.

60. Madison, "Reformers and the Rural Church," 665–68.

61. P. S. Lovejoy to Richard T. Ely, 4 Sept. 1921 (reel 72), Ely Papers.

62. I am indebted to Susan Hasweld for this quotation, which can be found in the Henry C. Taylor Papers (box 38), SHSW.

63. Grover, *Farm and College*, 328.

64. Sandfort, "Entrepreneurial Activities of Ben Faast," 70–73. The report is an attachment with Birge to Board of Regents of the University of Wisconsin, 15 July 1919 (copy) (reel 68), Ely Papers.

65. Taylor to Ely, 5 Mar. 1920 (reel 70), Ely Papers.
66. Grover, *Farm and College*, 329; Nelson, *Rural Sociology*, 34–41.
67. Charles Josiah Galpin, *Rural Social Problems* (New York, 1924), 251–84.

4. Struggles with Adversity, 1920–1940

1. Archibald MacLeish, *Land of the Free* (New York, 1938), 25.
2. Carl Rhody, *The Spirit of Saga Valley*, vol. 2: *Hard Times—Good Times* (Ogema, Wis., 1982), 63; H. F. Schlegelmilch to Charles Shaver, 10 Dec. 1918, Loan Series no. 1800, UML Papers, ARC, UWEC; Richard Runde to Robert Peacock, 21 Jan. 1920, Richard Runde Papers (box 1), ARC, UWSP; loan totals calculated from documents in UML Papers. In general, see Paul W. Glad, *The History of Wisconsin*, vol. 5: *War, a New Era, and Depression, 1914–1940* (Madison, 1991), 129–30.
3. U.S. Bureau of the Census, *Historical Statistics of the United States*, 2 vols. (Washington, D.C., 1976), K504, p. 1:511, K265, p. 1:483, K353, p. 1:489, K17, K36, p. 1:463. On the impact of the agricultural depression in the early 1920s see David B. Danbom, *Born in the Country: A History of Rural America* (Baltimore, 1995), 186–89, and, in an older but more detailed treatment, James H. Shideler, *Farm Crisis, 1919–1923* (Berkeley, Calif., 1957), esp. 46–75.
4. "The Kroll Family: German Wisconsin Settlers" (1972), student paper no. 950, Edward Blackorby Collection, ARC, UWEC; B. P. Apker, "Reminiscences" (typescript, 1949), ARC, UWEC. On population decline in rural America in the 1920s see Danbom, *Born in the Country*, 196–97.
5. Herman F. Schlegelmilch to A. E. Leonard, 7 Feb. 1924, Loan Series no. 2220, UML Papers; *Fifteenth Census of the United States (1930): Population*, vol. 3, pt. 2 (Washington, D.C., 1932), 1328–32; *Fifteenth Census of the United States (1930): Agriculture*, vol. 2, pt. 1 (Washington, D.C., 1932), 736–41, 748–51.
6. Ibid., vol. 2, pt. 1, pp. 10, 736, 748–51; *Historical Statistics*, K596, p. 1:522.
7. *Phillips Times*, 4 Feb. 1922, p. 1, 7 Jan. 1922, p. 1, 4 Oct. 1924, p. 1.
8. Ibid., 20 Feb. 1920, p.1, 22 June 1922, p.1, 27 Oct. 1923, p.1, 22 Nov. 1924, p.1, 18 Aug. 1923, p.1.
9. Ibid., 4 Feb. 1922, p.1, 11 March 1922, p.1, 1 Aug. 1925, p.1.
10. C. E. Arnold to Thomas G. Barland, 25 Apr. 1921, 2 Nov. 1921, Loan Series no. 2072, UML Papers; calculations from the John S. Owen Lumber Co. Land Contract Sales Book, John S. Owen Papers, ARC, UWEC.
11. F. G. Johnson, "Experiences of a Pioneer Physician in Northern Wisconsin," *Wisconsin Medical Journal* 38 (1939): 582; Loan Series no. 1527, Northwestern Lumber Company Records, ARC, UWEC. See Mrs. Archie Mallo to Northwestern Lumber Co., 15 May 1938, and George Hipple to Mrs. Archie Mallo, May 17, 1938, ibid.
12. Robert J. Gough, "Mortgage Banking in the Wisconsin Cutover Region: Union Mortgage Loan, 1905–1935," *Essays in Economic and Business History*, 5 (1987), 50–51.
13. Ronald Sandfort, "The Entrepreneurial Activities of Ben Faast: A Visionary Banker, Colonizer, and Community Developer of Northern Wisconsin" (MST thesis, UWEC, 1974), 90–114; Arlan Helgelson, *Farms in the Cutover: Agricultural Settle-*

ment in Northern Wisconsin (Madison, 1962), 62–64; Edwin M. Tainter to First Wisconsin Land Mortgage Association, 12 Jan. 1928, Eau Claire County Circuit Court, First Wisconsin Land Mortgage Association, Liquidation Proceedings, 1913–1929 (box 7, folder 4), ARC, UWEC; "Farmer of Ojibwa" to First Wisconsin Land Mortgage Association, 27 Mar. 1928 (box 9, folder 1), ibid.; Analysis of collateral with the state treasure [*sic*], (manuscript), [c. Mar., 1928] (box 13, folder 5), ibid.; Edward H. Beardsley, *Harry L. Russell and Agricultural Science in Wisconsin* (Madison, 1969), 135–36.

14. For an overview of the Great Depression in rural America, see Danbom, *Born in the Country,* 197–202.

15. Robert J. Schlomann, *The Thread of Love* (Oshkosh, Wis., 1986), 67; Frank Richardson, interview, Waverly, Ohio, Aug. 1987 (tape on deposit), ARC, UWEC (Richardson is a pseudonym); Roy S. Meier, interview, Spirit, Wis., 21–23 Mar. 1970 (tape on deposit), Wisconsin Agriculturalists Oral History Project, SHSW; *Park Falls Herald,* 22 Aug. 1930, p. 1, 7 Nov. 1930, p. 1.

16. U.S. Bureau of the Census, *Sixteenth Census of the United States (1940): Agriculture,* vol.1, pt. 1 (Washington, D.C., 1942), 894–900, vol. 2, pt. 1 (Washington, 1942), 446–53; M. E. Anderson to Ralph Owen, 8 Apr. 1933, Owen Papers; Holt Lumber Company Papers, Land Sales (Wisconsin) (box 3, folder 5); Inventory of Lands, 31 Dec. 1922 (box 3, folder 4), ARC, UWGB.

17. Martin quoted in Ron Duff Martin, "History of Sarah Elizabeth Neal Martin" (student paper, UWEC, 1990), 10; Olive Blaylock to Union Mortgage Loan Company, 6 Feb. 1930, Loan Series no. 2308 UML Papers; Melvin Teel to First Wisconsin Land Mortgage Association, 23 Dec. 1927, (box 7, folder 4), First Wisconsin Land Mortgage Association, Liquidation Proceedings; J. J. Roseman to First Wisconsin Land Mortgage Association, 23 Mar. 1928, (box 9, folder 1), ibid.

For good recent detailed descriptions of the impact of the Depression on other rural regions, see Jane Adams, *The Transformation of Rural Social Life: Southern Illinois, 1890–1990* (Chapel Hill, N.C., 1994); and Pamela Riney-Kehrberg, *Rooted in Dust: Surviving Drought and Depression in Southwestern Kansas* (Lawrence, Kans., 1993), 89–100.

18. [Price County] Summary of Forest and Marsh Fires for the Year 1926 (typescript), Price County Small Series 13 (folder 10), ARC, UWEC; Jack C. Plano, *Fishhooks, Apples and Outhouses: Memories of the 1920s, 1930s, and 1940s* (Kalamazoo, Mich., 1991), 122–23.

19. I. A. Leech to First Wisconsin Land Mortgage Association, 12 April 1928, First Wisconsin Land Mortgage Association Liquidation Proceedings (box 9, folder 2); L. Stankowski to First Wisconsin Land Mortgage Association, 3 Mar. 1928; Martin Pydo to First Wisconsin Land Mortgage Association, 15 Mar. 1928 (box 9, folder 1), ibid.; A. L. Stapleton to M. J. Leinenkugel, 5 Dec. 1927 (box 7, folder 3), ibid.

20. *Park Falls Herald,* 3 July, 30 Oct., 6 Nov., 13 Nov., 4 Dec., 25 Dec. 1931, 15 Jan., 5 Feb. 1932; Audie Christianson to Ladysmith Creamery, 2 June 1934, Flambeau Valley Farms Cooperative, Records, 1925–1980 (box 1, folder 2), ARC, UWEC; E. Pfeifer to Peterson Cash Store, 24 Dec. 1940 (box 1, folder 3), ibid.; Paul Nagel, *I Remember, I Remember: History and Lore of Jump River, Wisconsin* (n.p., 1986), 69;

George W. Hill and Ronald A. Smith, *Man in the 'Cut-Over': A Study of Family Farm Resources in Northern Wisconsin,* University of Wisconsin Agricultural Experiment Station Research Bulletin no. 139 (Madison, 1941), 51–52. For similar patterns in southwestern Kansas see Riney-Kehrberg, *Rooted in Dust,* 59–66, 112–17; for Union County, Illinois, see Adams, *Transformation of Rural Social Life,* 143.

21. Petition from the town of Harmon, Nov. 1931, in Papers of the Board of Supervisors, Price County (box 11), ARC, UWEC; *Park Falls Herald,* 19 June 1931, p. 1, 11 Aug. 1933, p. 1, 17 Nov. 1933, p. 1.

22. *Park Falls Herald,* 3 Feb 1933, p. 1.

23. E.g., ibid., 21 March, 4 Apr. 1930.

24. Ibid., 25 Dec. 1931, 26 May 1932.

25. Ibid., 19 Aug. 1932, p. 1; Reno to Emma Swenson, 23 Aug. 1932, Olin Swenson Papers, 1932–1933, ARC, UWEC.

26. In general, see John L. Shover, *Cornbelt Rebellion: The Farmers' Holiday Association* (Urbana, Ill., 1965), 90–92, 129–30, 156.

27. *Park Falls Herald,* 24 Feb. 1933, p. 1.

28. Ibid., 19 May 1933, p. 1, 3 Nov. 1933, p. 1. See Glad, *War, a New Era, and Depression,* 409–19, and A. William Hogland, "Wisconsin Dairy Farmers on Strike," *Agricultural History* 35 (1961): 24–34.

29. Olaf Severson interview, Luck, Wis., June 1989 (notes in possession of the author; Severson is a pseudonym); *WPA Guide,* 437; *Park Falls Herald,* 6 Oct. 1933, p. 1; Petitions to Price County Board, Aug. 1932, Apr. 1934, Jan. 1935, Papers of the Price County Board of Supervisors.

30. Papers of the Price County Board of Supervisors, passim. See Susan Schlaefer, "Price County Outdoor Relief, 1926–1932" (student paper, UWEC, 1986). For the limited role of public assistance in Forest County during the 1920s, see Mark Davis, "Northern Choices: Rural Forest County in the 1920s, Part I," *WHM* (1996): 3–31, esp. 30.

31. For the impact of federal assistance programs, see James T. Patterson, *The New Deal and the States: Federalism in Transition* (Princeton, N.J., 1969), 31–33, 50–51, 74–75, 85–87; for their implementation in Wisconsin see Glad, *War, a New Era, and Depression,* 394–96, 462–72. Price County details are found in the Board of Supervisors Papers, boxes 12, 13, and 14. Relief policies were explained in front page articles in the *Park Falls Herald,* 21 Oct. 1932, 10 Nov., 17 Nov., 24 Nov. 1933, 1 Mar., 22 Nov. 1935. A model study of how these programs worked in an upper Midwest county is found in D. Jerome Tweton, *The New Deal at the Grass Roots: Programs for the People in Otter Tail County, Minnesota* (St. Paul, 1988), 37–133. For other regions of the country see Riney-Kehrberg, *Rooted in Dust,* 67–88, 100–111; and Adams, *Transformation of Rural Social Life,* 144–56.

32. Glad, *War, a New Era, and Depression,* 371.

33. See the map in J. H. Kolb and Edmund deBrummer, *A Study of Rural Society, Its Organization and Changes* (Boston, 1935), 371.

34. Calculated from data in table 28 in Wisconsin State Planning Board, *Cutover Region of Wisconsin* ([Madison], 1939), 116.

35. For a different experience in Otter Tail County, see Tweton, *New Deal at the Grass Roots,* 164.

36. Price County Board of Supervisors Papers; J. Webster Johnson and others, *Land Program for Forest County, Wisconsin,* United States, Department of Agriculture, Technical Bulletin no. 687 (Washington, D.C., 1938), 49.

37. Tax Assessment Ledger, Lenroot, Sawyer County, 1930, ARC, UWEC; Wisconsin Crop Reporting Service, Annual Enumeration of Agricultural Statistics, Lenroot, Sawyer County, 1925, 1930, SHSW; U.S. Manuscript Census, Lenroot, Sawyer County, 1910, 1920; Sawyer County Welfare Office, Relief Roll, 1932–1934, ARC, UWEC.

38. Carle C. Zimmerman and Nathan L. Wheeten, *Rural Families on Relief,* Works Progress Administration, Division of Social Research, Research Monograph no. 17 (Washington, D.C., 1938), 16–20.

39. Larry Garneau, interview, Drummond, Wis., Oct. 1988 (tape on deposit), ARC, UWEC (Garneau is a pseudonym); Oliver Olson to C. T. Yarnall, 16 Nov. 1940, Owen Papers, vol. 224, ARC, UWEC.

40. David Rowe, "Pages from My Past," *WMH* 71 (1986): 216; Carol Ahlgren, "The Civilian Conservation Corps and Wisconsin State Park Development," ibid., 187–204; Sara Saetre, "The Happy Days of the CCC," *Wisconsin Trails* (July/Aug. 1983): 19–23. For attitudes toward the CCC see also the positive article in the *Park Falls Herald,* 4 June 1935 (reprint from the *Antigo Herald*).

41. *Park Falls Herald,* 3 Nov. 1931, 3 June 1932, 3 Feb., 9 June 1933.

42. Carol L. Shafer, "These Country People on Relief," *Survey Graphic* 25 (1936): 512–15, 538–39.

43. George W. Hill and Ronald A. Smith, *Rural Relief Trends in Wisconsin From 1934 to 1937* (Madison, 1939); Taylor County Probate Court, case file no. 3285, ARC, UWEC.

44. B. H. Hibbard and others, *Tax Delinquency in Northern Wisconsin,* Wisconsin Agricultural Experiment Station Bulletin no. 399 (Madison, 1928), 11.

45. Johnson et al., *Land Program for Forest County,* 24–29, 36–37; *Fifteenth Census (1930), Agriculture,* vol. 2, pt. 1, pp. 790–93.

46. Calculated from data in *Cutover Region of Wisconsin,* 30–32.

47. Report of the Committee of Equalization, 19 Aug. 1937, Price County Board of Supervisors Papers (box 14).

48. "The Skinvik Family," student paper no. 203, Blackorby Collection, ARC, UWEC; Garneau interview; W. P. Hanson to Walter Ebling, [Oct. 30, 1930], in Annual Enumeration of Agricultural Statistics, 1930, Grow, Rusk County.

49. Knute Anderson, interview; Drummond, Wis., Oct. 1988 (tape on deposit), ARC, UWEC (Anderson is a pseudonym); *Park Falls Herald,* 12 Feb. 1931, 17 Jan. 1930, 20 Jan. 1933; Martin, "History of Sarah Elizabeth Martin," 10; *Fifteenth Census (1930): Population,* vol. 3, pt. 2, pp. 1328, 1332; U.S. Bureau of the Census, *Sixteenth Census of the United States (1940): Population,* vol. 2, pt. 7 (Washington, D.C., 1943), 612–16; Jane Marie Pederson, *Between Memory and Reality* (Madison, 1992), 93–95; Richardson interview.

50. Mark E. Bruhy et al., *Heritage Resources Management, 1990,* U.S. Department of Agriculture, Forest Service, Nicolet National Forest, Cultural Resources Survey, Report no. 7 (Rhinelander, Wis., 1990).

51. Erven J. Long, "The Severson Community: A Glimpse of Northern Wisconsin in Process," *Land Economics* 25 (1949): 193–207; *History Collections of Washburn County,* 2 vols. (Shell Lake, Wis., 1980), 2:462.

52. *Sixteenth Census (1940): Population,* vol. 2, pt. 7, pp. 574–78, 612–16; *Milwaukee Journal,* 12 Jan. 1930, p. V4; Federal Writers Project, *Wisconsin: A Guide to the Badger State (WPA Guide)* (New York, 1941), 432; G. E. Anderson to Axel Lonquist, 16 Nov. 1933, Owen Papers, vol. 133; "Land Clearing Operations Are Heavy: Indicate 'Back to the Land' Movement," *Park Falls Herald,* 18 Dec. 1931, p. 1; *Sixteenth Census (1940): Agriculture,* vol. 1, pt. 1, pp. 894–900. A detailed account of this phenomenon in another state is Pamela Webb, "By the Sweat of the Brow: The Back-to-the-Land Movement in Depression Arkansas," *Arkansas Historical Quarterly* 42 (1983): 332–45. It is placed into national context in Lorraine Garkovich, *Population and Community in Rural America* (New York, 1989), 91–92.

53. Donald J. Bogue et al., *Subregional Migration in the United States, 1935–1940,* vol. 1: *Streams of Migration Between Subregions* [Oxford, Ohio, 1953], 99.

54. Joanne S. Stuttgen, "Kentucky Folksongs in Northern Wisconsin" (M.A. thesis, UWEC, 1986), 20–30; Asher E. Treat, "Kentucky Folksongs in Northern Wisconsin," *Journal of American Folklore* 52 (1939): 1–50; Jason Barnet, "Kentucky Migrants to Northern Wisconsin" (student paper, UWEC, 1993).

55. John S. Border to A. M. Jacobson, 24 Feb. 1932,; Tom Davis to Joshua Jones, 18 May 1933, Price County General Correspondence, 1928–1937 (box 2), ARC, UWEC; Olaf Anderson, interview, Luck, Wis., June 1989 (notes in possession of the author; Anderson is a pseudonym); *WPA Guide,* 432; Bogue, *Subregional Migration,* cliii.

56. Severson interview; Martin Webb to Walter Ebling, 11 Oct. 1933, Annual Enumeration of Agricultural Statistics, Grow, Rusk County, 1933.

57. *Iron River, Wisconsin* (n.p. [1992]), 168; Ed Pudas, "Autobiography" (typescript, 1977), ARC, UWRF; Rhody, *Saga of Spirit Valley,* 2:150–225.

58. O. G. Mills to Walter Ebling, 3 Nov. 1936, Annual Enumeration of Agricultural Statistics, Bayfield, Bayfield County, 1936.

59. *Sixteenth Census (1940): Agriculture,* vol. 1, pt. 1, pp. 894–900.

60. Elie Buggie to First Wisconsin Land Mortgage Association, 13 Mar. 1928, First Wisconsin Land Mortgage Association Liquidation Proceedings (box 9, folders 1 and 2).

61. Land sale no. 1660, Northwestern Lumber Company Papers, ARC, UWEC. See also, e.g., V. Podisiadly to First Wisconsin Land Mortgage Association [Mar. 1928]; First Wisconsin Land Mortgage Association Liquidation Proceedings, 13 Mar., 30 Mar. 1928, (box 9, folders 1 and 2).

62. Rhody, *Spirit of Saga Valley,* 2: 157–59; Schlomann, *The Thread of Love;* Annual Enumeration of Agricultural Statistics, Grow, Rusk County, 1925–1938; "Progress of a Marginal Farm in Barron County," student paper no. 156, Blackorby Collection, ARC, UWEC.

63. On the importance of "making do" in rural America, especially by women, during the Depression, see Adams, *Transformation of Rural Social Life,* 137–41; Deborah Fink, *Agrarian Women: Wives and Mothers in Rural Nebraska, 1880–1940* (Chapel Hill, N.C., 1992), 106–10; Mary Neth, *Preserving the Family Farm: Women,*

Community, and the Foundations of Agribusiness in the Midwest, 1900–1940 (Baltimore, 1995), 30, 270.

64. Ibid., 203–4.

65. Harvey Dueholm, interview, Madison, Wis., Nov.–Dec. 1978 (tape on deposit), SHSW.

On the enhanced importance of income produced by farm women during the 1930s, see Mary Neth, "Gender and the Family Labor System: Defining Work in the Rural Midwest," *Journal of Social History* 27 (1994): 568; Deborah Fink and Dorothy Schwieder, "Iowa Farm Women in the 1930s: A Reassessment," *Annals of Iowa* 49 (1989): 570–90, esp. 572–79; and Fink, *Agrarian Women*, 106–10.

66. "They Were Strong and Good: A Short History of the John Riohlk Farm" [c. 1977], student paper no. 1516, Blackorby Collection; [Walt Goldsworthy, ed.], *The Pine, the Plow, and the Pioneer: A History of Three Lakes and Clearwater Lakes, Wisconsin, 1881–1984* [Three Lakes, 1984], 72–73.

67. Loyal Durand, Jr., "The West Shawano Upland of Wisconsin: A Study of Regional Development Basic to the Problem of Part of the Great Lakes Cutover," *Annals of the American Association of Geographers* 34 (1948): 135–63.

68. *Sixteenth Census (1940): Population*, vol. 2, pt. 7, pp. 612–16. The townships were T.30 N., R.11 E., and 12E.; T.31 N., R.10 E., 11 E., and 12 E.; and T.32 N., R.10 E., and 11 E.

69. Wisconsin Department of Agriculture and Markets, *Land Economic Inventory— Langlade County, Wisconsin: Forest and General Cover Map—T.31 N. R.11 E.* ([Madison], 1933).

70. Durand, "West Shawano Upland"; Rudolph K. Froker, "Antigo Milk Products Cooperative" (typescript [1944]), in Ernest Luther Papers (box 1), SHSW; *WPA Guide*, 355.

71. *Sixteenth Census (1940): Agriculture*, vol. 1, pt. 1, pp. 915, 918, 921.

72. On "stranded" farmers in the Wisconsin cutover see, e.g., Farm Security Administration, *The Resettlement Administration* (Washington, D.C., 1935), 17–18; on farms "abandoned" in the cutover see, e.g., G. S. Wehrwein and J. A. Baker, "The Cost of Isolated Settlement in Northern Wisconsin," *Rural Sociology* 2 (1937): 253–65.

73. Ten-year persistence rates for farmers in twenty-five communities reported in secondary sources, unadjusted for deaths, range from 22 percent (Sugar Creek, Illinois in the 1850s) to 83 percent (Dedham, Massachusetts, in the 1690s), with rates of 40–50 percent most common in the nineteenth century. One study with twentieth-century coverage (Richard Bremer, "Patterns of Social Mobility: A Case Study of Nebraska Farmers," *Agricultural History* 49 [1974]: 529–43) reported rates of 34 percent, 35 percent, 46 percent, and 43 percent, respectively, for the first four decades of the twentieth century. Riney-Kehrberg (*Rooted in Dust*, 193), reported 52 percent persistence in five towns in southwestern Kansas during the 1930s. On the high plains in the Dakotas, Montana, Saskatchewan, and Alberta, settled contemporaneously with the Wisconsin cutover, John W. Bennett and Seena B. Kohl (*Settling the Canadian-American West, 1890–1915: Pioneer Adaptation and Community Building* [Lincoln, Nebr., 1995], 16–17, 75–76, 246), believed that at best 25 percent of settlers established "long-lasting agricultural enterprises."

74. "Family History of John Styczinski," (1971), student paper no. 656, Blackorby Collection; Crane, testimony to the Public Service Commission of Wisconsin, case 2-R-63 (closing the Omaha train station at Ojibwa), 5 Feb. 1932 (transcript), Wisconsin Colonization Company Papers, ARC, UWEC. See also Riney-Kehrberg, *Rooted in Dust,* 140.

75. Garkovich, *Population and Community,* 92.

76. Donald J. Bogue, *The Population of the United States* (Glencoe, Ill., 1959), 376, 391–96. Bogue defines migration as moving to another county, whereas in the previous paragraph of the text I define migration as moving to another municipality, so the resulting migration rates are not directly comparable.

77. Edmund deS. Brummer, "Internal Migration in the United States, 1935–40," *Rural Sociology* 13 (1948): 9–22.

78. Rudolph A. Christiansen and Sydney D. Staniforth, *The Wisconsin Resettlement Program of the 1930s: Relocation to the Matanaska Valley in Alaska,* University of Wisconsin, Department of Agricultural Economics Bulletin no. 50 (Madison, 1967); Tom Lawin, "State Farmers Met the Challenges of Alaska," *Eau Claire Leader-Telegram,* 8 June 1985, pp. 1E, 8–9E; Orlando W. Miller, *The Frontier in Alaska and the Matanaska Community* (New Haven, Conn., 1975), esp. 65–84.

79. *Land Economic Inventory of Northern Wisconsin: Bayfield County,* Wisconsin Department of Agriculture and Markets Bulletin no. 100 (Madison, 1929), 77.

80. Rusk County, Treasurer's Records: Tax Sales Records, 1930, ARC, UWEC.

81. Gough, "Mortgage Banking in the Wisconsin Cutover Region," 54–55. Although there is no evidence, arson must be suspected in the fire at the Lake Property.

82. Garneau interview; Adams, *Transformation of Rural Social Life.*

5. A New View of the Cutover, 1925–1940

1. Robert Peters, "Eagle River, Wisconsin: 1930," in *What Dillinger Meant to Me* (New York, 1983), 1.

2. *New York Times,* 23 Apr. 1934, p. 1; 24 Apr. 1934, p. 1. These articles are major sources for John Toland, *The Dillinger Days* (New York, 1963), 261–84. See also *Milwaukee Journal,* 23 Sept. 1934, p. 1, an accurate and straightforward account. An important recent book, G. Russell Girandin with William J. Helmer, *Dillinger: The Untold Story* (Bloomington, Ind., 1994), 145–51, has no new revelations on this incident.

3. *New York Times,* 25 Apr. 1934, pp. 1, 3; 26 Apr. 1934, pp. 1, 3; *Milwaukee Journal,* 28 Apr. 1934, p. 1; Jack C. Plano, *Fishhooks, Apples, Outhouses: Memories of the 1920s, 1930s, and 1940s* (Kalamazoo, Mich., 1991), 110. See also "North in Uproar as Dillinger Dodges Nest," *Park Falls Herald,* 27 Apr. 1934, p. 1. Robert Peters was a ten-year-old farm boy in Vilas County in 1934. His reaction to Dillinger, as conveyed in his later poems, was different than Plano's (for Peters, see chapter 6). Peters compares Dillinger to Robin Hood ("What Dillinger Meant to Me"), treats him not with fear but with fascination and respect, and finds him physically attractive ("Night Visitor" and "Snow Image"). For Peters, the cutover is poor and hard and crude ("Gangsters / came to Eagle River / but not one singer / writer or painter"—"Eagle River, Wisconsin: 1930"). Dillinger therefore fits in well, and as a

socially deviant figure is someone with whom Peters, as a teenager struggling with homoerotic feelings, can identify. Peters' poems on this theme have been collected in *What Dillinger Meant to Me*.

4. Paul Hultass, "Sin in Wisconsin: The Teasdale Vice Committee of 1913," *WMH* 49 (1965): 139–51, esp. 144.

5. William F. Thompson, *The History of Wisconsin*, vol. 6: *Continuity and Change, 1940–1965* (Madison, 1988), 14; *Milwaukee Journal*, 28 Oct. 1920, p. 1; 3 Nov. 1920, p. 10.

6. Plano, *Fishhooks, Apples, Outhouses*, 91, 94.

7. Cited in Paul Glad, *History of Wisconsin*, vol. 5: *War, a New Era, and Depression* (Madison, 1990), 218.

8. *Milwaukee Journal*, 1 Sept. 1934, p. 1; 18 Nov. 1935, p. 5; 2 Dec. 1935, p. 1. In general, at this time the *Journal's* "journalism" was on a par with that of the *National Enquirer* in the 1990s. See, e.g., "New Edison Device to Talk with Dead," 1 Oct. 1920, p. 29, and "Trysts Forbidden, Girls Go on Orgy of Mass Hysteria," 23 Aug. 1934, p. 1. For a contemporary impression from the cutover of the poor quality of the Milwaukee newspapers at this time, see Robert Peters, *Crunching Gravel: Growing Up in the 1930s* (San Francisco, 1983), 78.

9. *Oneida County: Centennial History Edition, 1887–1987* (n.p., n.d), 153; Knute Anderson, interview, Luck, Wis., July 1989 (notes in possession of the author; Anderson is a pseudonym); *Memories of Forest County* [n.p., 1980], 32–35; Mark Davis, "Northern Choices: Rural Forest County in the 1920s, Part II," *WMH* 79 (1996): 109–38, esp. 109–14; *Park Falls Herald*, 1 Nov. 1933.

10. *Milwaukee Journal*, 21 July 1932, p. 1; 22 July 1932, p. 2; Davis, "Northern Choices, Part II," 122–34.

11. Bill Bottoms, "Good Manners Required Here," *West Wisconsin Magazine* (Aug./Sept. 1990): 14–15, 37; Kathleen S. Abrams, "Al Capone's Hideout," *Wisconsin Trails* (Spring 1980): 6–7.

12. Cited in Bottoms, "Good Manners," 37.

13. "Mystery Surrounds Sugarbush Shooting," *Park Falls Herald*, 20 Oct. 1933, p. 1; "Accidental Death Verdict Returned," ibid., 27 Oct. 1933, p. 1; "Crime Expert Holds Wilkie Was Slain," ibid., 3 Nov. 1933, p. 1.

14. *Superior Evening Telegram*, 29 June 1939, p. 1. A full retrospective account of the incident is Rick Olivo, "Panic stalks a city as killer is stalked in the woods," *Sawyer County Record* (Hayward), 1 July 1981. Similarly, Michael Lesy has marshalled photos of late-nineteenth-century Jackson County to stress the pathological in its society, especially its fascination with morbid subjects (*Wisconsin Death Trip* [New York, 1973]). Lesy is seriously myopic (literally), but the point is that if his use of photos could convince people in the 1970s that Jackson County in the 1890s was degenerate, how easy must it have been for similar photos taken in the 1930s, like that of Buelow's body, to convince contemporary Americans that residents of the cutover were sadists?

15. *Milwaukee Journal*, 24 Apr. 1934, p. 1.

16. Ibid., 26 Apr. 1934, p. 14.

17. Kurt Daniel Kortenhoff, *Long Live the Hodag! The Life and Legacy of Eugene Simeon Shepard: 1854–1923* (Rhinelander, Wis., 1996), 111–17.

18. Reprint in *Milwaukee Journal*, 12 Sept. 1934.

19. *Milwaukee Sunday Journal Magazine,* 23 Apr. 1930.

20. See, e.g., "Predict Increase in Tourist Trade," *Park Falls Herald,* 8 June 1928, p. 1.

21. *New York Times,* 1 July–11 Sept. 1934, quotation, 10 Sept. 1934, p. 23. See Walt Harris, *The Chequamegon Country, 1659–1976* (Fayetteville, Ark., 1976), 268–72, for a detailed account of Coolidge's visit. In actuality, the *Milwaukee Journal* reported overnight lows only in the mid-40s at Duluth during the last week of August and first week of September, although temperatures inland at Coolidge's cottage may have been a little lower. The visit also highlighted outsiders' contemptuous views of northern Wisconsinites. Coolidge's Secret Service agents reportedly pulled their guns and required spectators to raise their hands over their heads when the President walked from his car into church, his only public appearances during the summer (*Park Falls Herald,* 13 July 1928, p. 1). After worship, Coolidge met once with members of the Head of the Lakes Ministerial Association. In the words of a pastor who was present, the president "shot from one door to the other like that," shaking the hands of those present before they realized what happened (Frank Richardson, interview, Waverly, Ohio, August 1987 [tape on deposit], ARC, UWEC [Richardson is a pseudonym]).

22. See, e.g., "First Indian Pageant August 1st–13th Now On," *Phillips Times,* 2 Aug. 1924, p. 1.

23. *Milwaukee Journal,* 5 Dec. 1930, p. 1.

24. James W. Oberly, "The Lac Courte Oreilles Chippewa and the Resources of the Chippewa River Valley," in Mark Lindquist and Martin Zanger, eds., *Buried Roots and Indestructible Seeds: The Survival of American Indian Life in Story, History, and Spirit* ([Madison], 1993), 60–72; Tim Pfaff, *Paths of the People: The Ojibway in the Chippewa Valley* (Eau Claire, 1993); Nancy Oestrich Lurie, *Wisconsin's Indians* (Madison, 1987), 25–27, 42, 55–56; Robert E. Bieder, *Native American Communities in Wisconsin, 1600–1960* (Madison, 1995), 195–203; Ronald A. Janke, "Indian Land-Tenure Problems in the United States," in Richard Heer, ed., *Themes in Rural History of the Western World* (Ames, Iowa, 1993), esp. 151–62; Rick Olive, "Spanish Influenza Came to Sawyer County," *Sawyer County Record,* 1 July 1981.

25. U.S. Bureau of the Census, *Sixteenth Census of the United States, 1940: Population,* vol. 2, pt. 7 (Washington, D.C., 1943), 605.

26. J. F. Wojta, "Indian Farm Institutes in Wisconsin," *WMH* 29 (1946): 423–34; Olaf Anderson, interview, Luck, Wis., July 1989 (notes in possession of the author; Anderson is a pseudonym).

27. [Walt Godsworthy, ed.], *Pine, Plow, and Pioneer: A History of Three Lakes and Clearwater Lakes, Wisconsin, 1881–1984* [Three Lakes, Wis., 1984], 5.

28. *Wisconsin Blue Book, 1975* (Madison, 1975), 150–55.

29. Federal Writers Project, *Wisconsin: A Guide to the Badger State* (*WPA Guide*) (New York, 1941), 458. On Indians as tourist "curiosities" in the 1920s, see Michael Dunn III, *Easy Going: Wisconsin's Northwoods—Vilas and Oneida Counties* (Madison, 1978), 22.

30. Nell Peters with Robert Peters, *Nell's Story: A Woman From Eagle River* (Madison, 1995), 53.

31. Eunice Kanne, comp., *Pieces of the Past: Pioneer Life in Burnett County* (Friendship, Wis., 1983), 9.

32. Ralph Carpersen, *A Northern Boyhood* (Niles, Mich., 1993), 128–29. Similarly, Harvey Dueholm recalled that a white man was derisively called "squaw man" if he married an Indian (interview, Madison, Nov.–Dec. 1978; tape on deposit, Wisconsin Agriculturalists Oral History Project, SHSW).

33. In general see Mary Neth, *Preserving the Family Farm: Women, Community, and the Development of Agribusiness in the Midwest, 1900–1940* (Baltimore, 1995), 86–87.

34. *WPA Guide*, 458.

35. *Blue Book, 1975*, 152.

36. Harold Holand, *Rehabilitation at Lake Tomahawk State Camp: A History* (New York, 1945), 9.

37. George Wehrwein and J. A. Baker, "The Cost of Isolated Settlement in Northern Wisconsin," *Rural Sociology* 2 (1937): 258.

38. *New York Times*, 3 June 1934, sec. 4, p. 6.

39. *WPA Guide*, 333, 413; National Resources Board, *Maladjustments in Land Use in the United States*, pt. 6: *Report on Land Planning* (Washington, D.C., 1935), 8–9, 26–28.

40. James N. Gregory, *American Exodus: The Dust Bowl Migration and Okie Culture in California* (New York, 1989), 103–13.

Perhaps not by coincidence, cutover researcher Lewis C. Gray also wrote about this time the classic *History of Agriculture in the Southern United States to 1860* (Washington, D.C., 1933). See Gray and J. D. Black, *Land Settlement and Colonization in the Great Lakes States*, U.S. Department of Agriculture Bulletin no. 1295 (Washington, D.C., 1925). On Gray, a student of Richard T. Ely and Henry C. Taylor, see Richard S. Kirkendall, "L. C. Gray and the Supply of Agricultural Land," *Agricultural History* 37 (1963): 206–14.

41. L. C. Gray, "Our Major Land Use Problems and Suggested Lines of Action," in U.S. Department of Agriculture, *Farmers in a Changing World: The Yearbook of Agriculture, 1940* (Washington, D.C., 1940), 398–415; Robert F. Fries, *Empire in Pine: The Story of Lumbering in Wisconsin, 1830–1900* (Madison, 1951), 178; Carle C. Zimmerman and Nathan L. Whetten, *Rural Families on Relief*, Works Progress Administration, Division of Social Research, Research Monograph no. 17 (Washington, D.C., 1938), xvii.

42. *New York Times*, 3 June 1934, sec. 4, p. 6.

43. Bushrod W. Allin, "The Cutover Region of the Great Lakes States," in Carter Goodrich, ed., *Emigration and Economic Opportunity: The Report of the Study of Population Redistribution* (Philadelphia, 1936), 174–75; Harvey A. Uber, *Environmental Factors in the Development of Wisconsin* (Milwaukee, 1937), 122, 222. Nell Peters explained the perspective of cutover residents. Referring to her parents, who collected money from a variety of public assistance programs including Aid for Families with Dependent Children while raising Nell's two illegitimate children, she wrote that "they believed that since they'd paid taxes for years they deserved money flowing back—the County owed them that" (Peters, *Nell's Story*, 142). In twenty years of farming in Vilas County, Sam Peters probably paid no more than $200 in taxes.

44. George S. Wehrwein, "The Place of Tenancy in a System of Farm Land Tenure," *Journal of Land and Public Utility Economics* 1 (1925): 72–82; idem, "The Economic Status of the Isolated Settler in the Cut-Over Area of Wisconsin," ibid., 15

(1939): 184–94; Wehrwein with J. A. Baker, "The Cost of Isolated Settlement in Northern Wisconsin," *Rural Sociology* 2 (1937): 253–65. See Julius Weinberg, *Edward Alsworth Ross and the Sociology of Progressivism* (Madison, 1972), esp. 149–76.

45. University of Wisconsin Agricultural Experiment Station Research Bulletin no. 139 (Madison, 1941).

46. Ibid., 22, 3, 15–16, 65, 24, 29, 26, 39, 27. Zimmerman and Whetten had previously reported that cutover families on relief were not more likely to contain six or more persons than families in rural American in general (*Rural Families on Relief,* 39, 54, 130).

47. Diana Selig, "Intelligence Testing and Sexual Delinquency, 1908–1918," paper read at the Organization of American Historians annual meeting, Washington, 31 Mar. 1995.

48. Ely, "Worthless Land: What Can We Do for the Men on It," *Country Gentleman* 89 (Oct. 25, 1924): 1–2, 16.

49. E.g., Allin, "Cutover Region," 174–75.

50. Stuart Chase, *Rich Land, Poor Land: A Study of Waste in the Natural Resources of America* (New York, 1936), 127–30.

51. George Wehrwein, "A Land Policy as a Part of an Agricultural Program," *Journal of Farm Economics* 7 (1925): 295.

52. David Danbom, *The Resisted Revolution: Urban America and the Industrialization of the Countryside* (Ames, Iowa, 1979); idem., *Born in the Country: A History of Rural America* (Baltimore, 1995), 168–75, 180–82; Neth, *Preserving the Family Farm,* ch. 4.

53. B. H. Hibbard and others, *Tax Delinquency in Northern Wisconsin,* University of Wisconsin Agricultural Experiment Station Bulletin no. 399 (Madison, 1928), 4–10.

54. For a penetrating theoretical analysis of the simplistic use of the concept of economically "submarginal" land by social scientists in the interwar years, see G. M. Peteson and J. K. Galbraith, "The Concept of Marginal Land," *Journal of Farm Economics* 14 (1932): 295–310. The authors' conclusion pertains directly to the cutover: when a "small farmer" derives "the major share of his income" from off-farm work, his "farm and home, standing as they do somewhat in the nature of a supplementary enterprise . . . permit of production on sub-marginal land in a way that is not probably in any sense uneconomical."

55. Cited in Benjamin Rader, *The Academic Mind and Reform: The Influence of Richard T. Ely in American Life* (Lexington, Ky., 1966), 216.

56. Curt Meine, *Aldo Leopold: His Life and Work* (Madison, 1988); Susan C. Flader, "Aldo Leopold and the Evolution of a Land Ethic," in Thomas Tanner, ed., *Aldo Leopold: The Man and His Legacy* (Ankeny, Iowa, 1987), 3–24.

57. Meine, *Aldo Leopold,* 321–22, 387–88.

58. Aldo Leopold, "Wilderness as a Form of Land Use," *Journal of Land and Public Utility Economics* 1 (1925): 398–407.

59. *Wisconsin Agriculture, Climate, and Land Use,* Wisconsin Department of Agriculture Bulletin no. 238 (Madison, 1943), 27.

60. P. S. Lovejoy, "In the Name of Development," *American Forestry* 29 (1923): 387–93, 447. Lovejoy spread his venom generously: to point out the stupidity of

trying to farm cutover lands in the South, he argued that even "local corn and cotton niggers" preferred migration to the North.

61. A. R. Whitson and others, *Soil Survey of the Bayfield Area,* Wisconsin Geological and Natural History Survey Bulletin no. 31 (Madison, 1914); Whitson and S. Weidman, *Some Facts and Figures about Wisconsin* (1913), cited in Vernon Carstensen, *Farms or Forests: The Evolution of a Land Policy for Northern Wisconsin, 1850–1932* (Madison, 1958), 56; *Land Economic Inventory of Northern Wisconsin: Bayfield County,* Wisconsin Department of Agriculture and Markets Bulletin no. 100 (Madison, 1929), 5; *A Park, Parkway, and Recreation Area Plan,* Wisconsin State Planning Board Bulletin no. 8 (Madison, 1939), pl. xxx; P. G. Beck and M. C. Forster, *Six Rural Problem Areas,* Works Progress Authority, Division of Social Research, Research Monograph no. 1 (Washington, D.C., 1935), 11. See also *Wisconsin Agriculture, Climate, and Land Use,* 26.

62. Robert J. Gough, "Richard T. Ely and the Development of the Wisconsin Cutover," *WMH* 75 (1991), esp. 27–32.

63. Richard T. Ely, "How Do the Economic Limitations of Poorer Agricultural Sections Affect Social Life?" in Dwight Sanderson, ed., *Farm Income and Farm Life: A Symposium on the Relation of the Social and Economic Factors in Rural Progress* (Chicago, 1927), 155–58.

64. *Milwaukee Journal,* 5 Jan. 1930, sec. 1, p. 6; *New York Times,* 5 May 1940, sec. 4, p. 8. See also Neth, *Preserving the Family Farm,* 118–19, 196.

65. Edward H. Beardsley, *Harry L. Russell and Agricultural Science in Wisconsin* (Madison, 1969), 135–36; John W. Jenkins, *A Centennial History: A History of the College of Agriculture and Life Sciences at the University of Wisconsin–Madison* (Madison, 1991), 77–79; Carstensen, *Farms or Forests,* 92–97; Arlan Helgelson, *Farms in the Cutover: Agricultural Settlement in Northern Wisconsin* (Madison, 1962), 111–21.

66. Glad, *War, a New Era, and Depression,* 208–9; Davis, "Northern Choices: Rural Forest County in the 1920s, Part II," 114–22.

67. George Wehrwein, "What Shall We Do With Our Millions of Acres of Tax Delinquent Land?" *Wisconsin Magazine* 9 (Sept./Oct. 1931): 1–2, 13–15. News about state park development ran regularly on the front page of the *Park Falls Herald* in the late 1920s.

68. Glad, *War, a New Era, and Depression,* 209; F. G. Wilson, "Zoning for Forestry and Recreation: Wisconsin's Pioneer Role," *WMH* 41 (1957): 102–6; Carstensen, *Farms or Forests,* 104–13.

69. *Parks Falls Herald,* 22 July, 12 Aug. 1932, 21 Apr., 4 May 1934. As recently as 1929 the *Herald* had editorialized that "there is still plenty of room in northern Wisconsin for the continued development of the dairy industry" (Nov. 15, 1929).

70. See reports in boxes 12 and 13, Price County Board of Supervisors Papers, ARC, UWEC; and *Park Falls Herald,* 16 Mar. 1934, p. 1, 23 Mar. 1934, p. 1. For a similar process in Oneida County, see Carstensen, *Farms and Forests,* 118–22.

71. Carstensen, *Farms and Forests,* 97.

72. Arlan Wooden, "The Marinette County Forest: 1933–1988," *Proceedings of the Fourteenth Annual Meeting of the Forest History Association of Wisconsin, Inc.* (n.p., 1989), 32–36; Carl E. Krog, "The Retreat of Farming and the Return of Forests in Wisconsin's Cutover: Continuity and Change in Marinette County," paper read at

the Northern Great Plains History Conference, St. Paul, 30 Sept. 1994. For a similar development of county forests in neighboring Forest County, see Davis, "Northern Choices: Rural Forest County in the 1920s, Part II," 136–37.

73. I. S. Horgen, "Preserving Natural Landscape in a County Park System," in
Standards of Living: Proceedings of the Thirteenth American Country Life Conference (Chicago, 1931), 111.

74. Kennell M. Elliot, *History of the Nicolet National Forest, 1928–1976* (n.p., 1977),
35–38, 42–48; William E. Shends, "The Lands Nobody Wanted: The Legacy of the
Eastern National Forests," in Harold F. Steen, ed., *Origins of the National Forests*
(Durham, N.C., 1992), 19–44, esp. 29–36; Price County National Forest Formation Records, 1928–1941, ARC, UWEC, esp. Joshua Jones to Fred Herman, 11 July
1931, and Jones to Myron Groesbeck, 26 Feb. 1934; National Forest Reservation
Commission, *Report for the Year Ending June 30, 1930* (Washington, D.C., 1930),
34–35; Samuel Lubell, "In Wisconsin A Forest Playground To Be Created," *New
York Times,* 16 Oct. 1938, sec. 10, p. 2. In general, for developments in forestry policy
in the interwar years see Michael Williams, *Americans and their Forests* (Cambridge,
Eng., 1989), 459–79.

75. *Making the Most of Washburn County Land* (Madison, 1932), 30.

76. *A Recreational Plan for Vilas County,* Wisconsin State Planning Board Bulletin no. 12 (Madison, 1941), 2; J. Webster Johnson and others, *Land Program for
Forest County, Wisconsin,* U.S. Department of Agriculture Technical Bulletin no. 681
(Washington, D.C., 1939), 58; [Samuel Taylor], *Local Government Study in Wisconsin, 1927–1936,* vol. 4: *Summary,* Wisconsin State Planning Board Bulletin no. 13
(Madison, 1943); W. A. Rowlands, "Rural Zoning in Wisconsin," *Wisconsin Blue Book,
1937* (Madison, 1937), 169–83, quote on 183.

77. Wisconsin Regional Planning Committee, *A Study of Wisconsin: Its Resources,
Its Physical, Social and Economic Background* (Madison, 1934), 9, 218–19, 269–74.

78. Wisconsin State Planning Board, *The Cutover Region of Wisconsin: Report of
Conditions and Recommendations for Rehabilitation* ([Madison], 1939), 1, 33–62. In
the mid-1930s the Regional Planning Committee had been reorganized into this
State Planning Board.

79. National Resources Board, *Maladjustments in Land Use in the United States,*
pt. six: *Report on Land Policy* (Washington, D.C., 1935), 8–9, 26–28. For background
on the National Resources Board, see Richard S. Kirkendall, *Social Scientists and
Farm Politics in the Age of Roosevelt* (Columbia, Mo., 1965), 84–85. A sympathetic
summary of these programs is Walter A. Rowlands, "The Great Lakes Region," in
Merrill Jensen, ed., *Regionalism in America* (Madison, 1951), 331–46.

80. Beck and Forster, *Six Rural Problem Areas,* 100.

81. See Kirkendall, *Social Scientists and Farm Politics,* 74–77, 81–83.

82. U.S. Department of Agriculture, *Soils and Men: The Yearbook of Agriculture, 1938*
(Washington, D.C., 1938), 231–56; *Farmers in a Changing World,* 398–415.

83. For a perceptive critique of this social science literature, see Leonard A.
Salter, Jr., *A Critical Review of Research in Land Economics* (Minneapolis, 1948), esp.
78–129, "Land Utilization Research in the Cutovers." Salter identified the use of
unrepresentative samples, the lack of multivariate analysis, confusion of causation
with correlation, tautological and contradictory reasoning, unsupported conclu-

sions, and fuzzy conceptualization (e.g., ignoring the difference between rural-farm and rural non-farm people). More recently, Tony Smith ("Social Scientists Are Not Neutral Onlookers to Agricultural Policy," in Gary Comstock, ed., *Is There A Moral Obligation to Save the Family Farm?* [Ames, Iowa, 1987], 176–86) pointed out biases in social science research caused by biased framing of questions, ideologically driven neglect of relevant dimensions of the problem (e.g., corporate power), and obfuscating retreat to abstract models.

84. *Milwaukee Journal*, 28 Aug. 1928, p. 8; Peters, *Nell's Story*, 153. On the generally negative response in rural America to the Country Life movement, see William L. Bowers, *The Country Life Movement in America, 1900–1920* (Port Washington, N.Y., 1974), 102–24.

85. *Neillsville Press*, cited in Carstensen, *Farms or Forests*, 122–23; *Park Falls Herald*, 17 Feb. 1933.

86. Carstensen, *Farms or Forests*, 97–98, 122.

87. Lee Benson, "An Approach to the Scientific Study of Past Public Opinion," *Public Opinion Quarterly* 31 (1967): 522–67; reprinted in Benson, *Toward the Scientific Study of History* (Philadelphia, 1972), 105–59, esp. 151–57.

88. *Knowlton v. Rock County*, 9 Wis. 410 (1859). A lucid explanation of the constitutional and legal issues involved with the Forest Crop Law, and its long-run significance for tax and fiscal policy in Wisconsin, is Jack Stark, "A History of the Property Tax and Property Tax Relief in Wisconsin," *Wisconsin Blue Book, 1991–1992* (Madison, 1991), 99–165, esp. 125–26.

89. Statements of Boards of County Canvassers, in Secretary of State, Election Return Statements, 1926–1927 (series 211, boxes 102–3), SHSW. Inexplicably, these results were never printed in the *Blue Book*. I am indebted to Cathy Inderberg for locating and transcribing these records. Che Calix assisted in tabulations. I alone am responsible for the analysis. Our tabulations from the manuscript statements differ slightly from results printed in newspapers at the time.

6. The Cutover in the Late 1930s

1. For an overview of this part of New Deal farm policy, see David B. Danbom, *Born in the Country: A History of Rural America* (Baltimore, 1995), 207–17. A more detailed discussion is Theodore Saloutous, *The American Farmer and the New Deal* (Ames, Iowa, 1982), esp. 34–97, 236–53.

2. George Wehrwein et al., "The Remedies: Policies for Private Lands," in U.S. Department of Agriculture, *Soils and Men: The Yearbook of Agriculture for 1938* (Washington, D.C., 1938), 253–56; L. C. Gray, "Our Major Land Use Problems and Suggested Lines of Action," in *Farmers in a Changing World: The Yearbook of Agriculture for 1940* (Washington, D.C., 1940), 398–415. For an overview of resettlement efforts on the national level, see Sidney Baldwin, *Poverty and Politics: The Rise and Decline of the Farm Security Administration* (Chapel Hill, N.C., 1968), 111–14, 214–17.

3. Allin and Goodrich, "A Critique of American Measures," in Goodrich et al., eds., *Migration and Economic Opportunity: The Report of the Study of Population Redistribution* (Philadelphia, 1936), 637; Goodrich, "Toward a Migration Policy," ibid., 667.

4. Farm Security Administration, *The Resettlement Administration* (Washington, D.C., 1935), 7, 18, 25.

5. Allin and Goodrich, "Critique"; Goodrich, "Toward A Migration Policy," 664–65; Bushrod Allin, "Cutover Region," 195–201. For biographical background on Allin, see Richard S. Kirkendall, *Social Scientists and Farm Politics in the Age of Roosevelt* (Columbia, Mo., 1965), 171–73.

6. See L. G. Sorden, "The Northern Wisconsin Settler Relocation Project, 1934–1940," in Ramon R. Hernandez, ed., *Proceedings [of the] Fourth Annual Meeting [of the] Forest History Association of Wisconsin, Inc.* (Wassau, [1979]), 14–17. Less helpful is Rudolph A. Christiansen and Dydney D. Staniforth, *The Wisconsin Resettlement Program of the 1930s: Land Acquisition, Family Relocation, and Rehabilitation*, University of Wisconsin, Department of Agricultural Economics Bulletin no. 52 (Madison, 1968).

7. Nell Peters with Robert Peters, *Nell's Story: A Girl From Eagle River* (Madison, 1995), 12.

8. See Danbom, *Born in the Country*, 216–23; Mary Neth, *Preserving the Family Farm: Women, Community, and the Foundations of Agribusiness in the Midwest, 1900–1940* (Baltimore, 1995), 116–21.

9. In general, see Paul K. Conklin, *Tomorrow A New World: The New Deal Community Program* (Ithaca, N.Y., 1959), 11–89, and, more briefly, Danbom, *Born in the Country*, 162–63, 200–201. On Wilson and Fairway Farms, see Kirkendall, *Social Scientists and Farm Policy*, 12–13.

10. O. E. Baker, Ralph Borsodi, and M. L. Wilson, *Agriculture in Modern Life* (New York, 1939). On Wilson's ideas as moderate between romantic and commercial/industrial models of farming, see Kirkendall, *Social Scientists and Farm Politics*, 23–24. See Wilson's endorsement of the "middle course" between encouraging rural migration to city industries and a back-to-the-land movement to encourage semisubsistence farming in "Planning Agriculture in Relation to Industry," in *National Planning and Rural Life: Proceedings of the Seventeenth American Country Life Conference* (Chicago, 1935), 44.

11. P. G. Beck and M. L. Forster, *Six Rural Problem Areas: Relief—Resources—Rehabiliation*, Works Progress Administration, Division of Social Research, Research Monograph no. 1 (Chicago, 1935), 97–98.

12. R. B. Goodman, "Future Forest Towns in Northern Wisconsin" (April 1934), mimeo in National Forest Formation Records, 1928–1941 (folder 4), Price County Board Papers, ARC, UWEC.

13. Idem, *A Wisconsin Forest-Farm Working Circle* (Goodman, Wis., 1944), 3, 6–8, 20.

14. On the RA under Tugwell, see Kirkendall, *Social Scientists and Agricultural Politics*, 109–17. Recent studies of New Deal planned rural communities include Paul Nieder, "The Osage Farms Project: An Experimental New Deal Community, 1935–1943," *Gateway Heritage* 12 (1991): 50–63; Jeff Hearne, "The Beginning of LaForge: An Experiment in Rural Homesteading," *Missouri Historical Review* 88 (1993): 301–15; Stephen E. Lile, "The Resettlement Farm Project in Kentucky: Preliminary Findings," *Essays in Economic and Business History* 12 (1994): 251–59; J. Rebecca Thompson, "Deshee Farm: A New Deal Experiment With Cooperative Farming," *Indiana Magazine of History* 91 (1995): 380–406; and Brian Q. Cannon,

"Keeping Their Instructions Straight: Implementing the Rural Resettlement Program in the West," *Agricultural History* 70 (1996): 251–67.

15. Conklin, *Tomorrow A New World*, 305–25; Kirkendall, *Social Scientists and Agricultural Politics*, 101.

16. Baker, Borsodi, and Wilson, *Agriculture in Modern Life*, 272.

17. Saloutos, *American Farmer and the New Deal*, 58.

18. Kirkendall, *Social Scientists and Agricultural Politics*, 21.

19. Ibid., 124, 130.

20. Kirkendall, *Social Scientists and Agricultural Politics*, 71; Edward S. Shapiro, "Decentralist Intellectuals and the New Deal," *Journal of American History* 58 (1972): 948.

21. Conklin, *Tomorrow A New World*, 91–130; Saloutos, *American Farmer and the New Deal*, 155–57; Kirkendall, *Social Scientists and Agricultural Politics*, 71–74.

22. Ibid., 72, 112–13.

23. Ibid., 237–55, 294–304.

24. Baldwin, *Poverty and Politics;* Saloutos, *American Farmer and the New Deal*, 164–78.

25. Conklin, *Tomorrow A New World*, 214–33; Baldwin, *Poverty and Politics*, 365–404. George Wehrwein ("An Appraisal of Resettlement," *Journal of Farm Economics* 19 [1937]: 195) favorably quoted descriptions of Tugwell as a "fumbler" who broke promises and operated an agency in administrative "turmoil."

26. Wehrwein, "An Appraisal of Resettlement," esp. 191–92; Christiansen and Staniforth, *Wisconsin Resettlement Program*.

27. "Plan Homesteads for U.S. Forests," *Park Falls Herald*, 19 Jan. 1934, p. 1. See also, "Plan to Move 1,000 Families Out of North Wisconsin Back Woods to Better Farm Lands," *Eau Claire Leader*, 13 Jan. 1934, p. 7.

28. Wehrwein, "An Appraisal of Resettlement," 197.

29. Brief discussions of Drummond can be found in Conklin, *Tomorrow A New World*, 110, Christiansen and Staniforth, *Wisconsin Resettlement Program*, 54–55, and Gordon Sorenson, *Drummond, Centennial, 1882–1982* (Drummond, Wis., 1982), 138–42.

30. Duane D. Fischer, "The John S. Owen Enterprises" (Ph.D. diss., UWM, 1964), ch. 9.

31. Hans Pederson, interview, Drummond, Wis., Oct. 1988 (tape on deposit), ARC, UWEC (Pederson is a pseudonym).

32. Wisconsin Crop Reporting Service, Annual Enumeration of Agricultural Statistics, Drummond, Bayfield County, SHSW.

33. Sorenson, *Drummond Centennial*, 371.

34. Florence S. Little, "My Community As I See It" [c. 1939], typescript in Drummond Community Club Scrapbook, Drummond Public Library and Museum, Drummond, Wis.

35. Larry Garneau, interview, Drummond, Wis., Oct. 1988 (tape on deposit), ARC, UWEC (Garneau is a pseudonym).

36. Garneau and Pederson interviews.

37. Mrs. Alfred Fruechtl, "Personal Observations" [c. 1939], typescript in Drummond Community Club Scrapbook; Harry Sanders, interview, Drummond, Wis., Oct. 1988 (notes in possession of the author; Sanders is a pseudonym).

38. Annual Enumeration of Agricultural Statistics, Drummond, Bayfield County, 1938, 1940; Earl Wisher to Walter Ebling, Oct. 1940 (enclosure), ibid.; Sidney Henderson, "An Experiment in Forest-Farm Resettlement," *Journal of Land and Public Utility Economics* 22 (1946): 15.

39. Sanders and Garneau interviews.

40. Pederson and Garneau interviews.

41. Henderson, "Forest-Farm Resettlement," 15–16.

42. Henry Gilbert White, "Public Forest Homesteads," *Papers of the Michigan Academy of Sciences, Arts, and Letters* 27 (1941): 169–80, esp. 174.

43. Henderson, "Forest-Farm Resettlement," 18; Pederson interview; Sanders interview.

44. Henderson, "Forest-Farm Resettlement," 17.

45. Among scholars, there are conflicting and confusing evaluations of New Deal agricultural planning as it relates to the cutover, especially as it was shaped by the Bureau of Agricultural Economics. I believe that the cutover experience supports Harry C. McDean's conclusion that the BAE "regularly pursued research projects ostensibly scientific, but in fact designed to accomplish preconceived purposes based on unscientific assumptions—even prejudices—about American farm life" ("'Reform' Social Darwinists and Measuring Levels of Living on American Farms, 1920–1926," *Journal of Economic History* 43 [1983]: 79–85, quote on 79). But certainly many scholars are sympathetic to the BAE, especially arguing that it generated the New Deal programs that were at least potentially helpful for small farmers (see, e.g., Gregory M. Hooks, "A New Deal for Farmers and Social Scientists: The Politics of Rural Sociology in the Depression Era," *Rural Sociology* 48 [1983]: 386–402). Part of the problem is that authors focus on different aspects of the BAE's programs at different points in time—McDean is critical of Henry Taylor and Charles Galpin's work in the mid-1920s (chapter 3), while Hooks lauds sociologist Charles Taylor's studies of poor farmers in the late 1930s and early 1940s. But David E. Hamilton sees basic continuities between the BAE's programs in the 1920s and in the 1930s ("From New Era to New Deal: American Farm Policy Between the Wars," in *Agricultural Distress in the Midwest: Past and Present,* ed. Lawrence E. Gelfand and Robert J. Neymeyer [Iowa City, 1986], 17–54, esp. 24–33). Hamilton positively evaluates the technocratic planning which he feels characterized the BAE in both eras, in contrast—for example—to government-mandated New Deal programs associated with the Agricultural Adjustment Adminstration and Tugwell. Kirkendall is also sympathetic to the BAE and sees continuities in it between the Hoover and Roosevelt eras, notably in the role, during both time periods, of Wilson, his hero. However, as a 1960s liberal, Kirkendall praises the BAE in the late 1930s for its typical New Deal spirit of pragmatism and its efforts to bring "science to the service of democracy" (*Social Scientists and Agricultural Politics,* 161–217; see also Jess Gilbert, "Democratic Planning in Agricultural Policy: The Federal-County Land-Use Program, 1938–1942," *Agricultural History* 70 [1996]: 233–50), not for its technocratic aloofness from ill-advised populist and statist programs, as does Hamilton. Expanding her target to the FSA in general, Deborah Fink (*Agrarian Women: Wives and Mothers in Rural Nebraska, 1880–1940* [Chapel Hill, N.C., 1992], 112–13) is critical from a feminist perspective.

46. For a more detailed discussion of the following section, see Robert J. Gough, "Blacks and the Back-to-the-Land Movement in Depression Wisconsin," paper read at the Great Lakes History Conference, Grand Rapids, Mich., April 1989.

47. U.S. Bureau of the Census, *Negroes in the United States, 1920–1932* (Washington, D.C., 1935), 27; idem, *Fifteenth Census of the United States (1930): Population,* vol. 3, pt. 2 (Washington, D.C., 1932), 1305; Joe William Trotter, Jr., *Black Milwaukee: The Making of An Industrial Proletariat, 1915–1945* (Urbana, Ill., 1985), 176–77.

48. Trotter, *Black Milwaukee,* 153, 155.

49. U.S. Bureau of the Census, *Sixteenth Census of the United States (1940): Agriculture,* vol. 1, pt. 1 (Washington, D.C., 1942), 894; [Wisconsin] Governor's Commission on Human Rights, *Negro Families in Rural Wisconsin: A Study of their Community Life* (Madison, 1959), 23–24.

50. Zachary Cooper, *Black Settlers in Rural Wisconsin* (Madison, 1977).

51. Fischer, "John S. Owen Enterprises," 455.

52. Gunder Anderson to W. A. Kimpel, 21 Apr. 1933 (vol. 175), Anderson to Kimpel, 22 Nov. 1932 (vol. 176), John S. Owen Papers, ARC, UWEC. By contrast, another Owen affiliate, the Rust-Owen Lumber Co., did not hide its discrimination against eastern European immigrants, and especially Jews, when selling lakefront property in Drummond.

53. Gunder Anderson to John S. Owen Co., 8 Sept. 1933 (vol. 176), Anderson to Owen Co., 15 May 1934 (vol. 177), Ralph W. Owen to W. A. Kimpel, 30 Nov. 1935 (vol. 118), Owen Papers.

54. Ledger, John S. Owen Lumber Co. Land Contracts. This valuable volume is a recent uncatalogued addition to the Owen Papers.

55. The 1940 U.S. Census reported only three black farmers in Clark County.

56. Annual Enumeration of Agricultural Statistics, Hoard, Clark County, 1935–1948.

57. Ledger, John S. Owen Lumber Company Land Contracts, Owen Papers.

58. Theodore Hershberg and colleagues have shown for cities that comparisons between the success of blacks and immigrants are ahistorical ("A Tale of Three Cities: Blacks, Immigrants, and Opportunity in Philadelphia, 1850–1880, 1930, 1970," in Hershberg, ed., *Philadelphia: Work, Space, Family, and Group Experience in the Nineteenth Century* [New York, 1981], 461–91).

59. *Sixteenth Census (1940): Population,* vol. 2, pt. 7, pp. 574–78.

60. As Table 6.2 identifies, the exact basis for calculating fertility rates changes by decade, but the trend is clear. For the 1940s see Margaret Jarman Hagood and Emmit F. Sharp, *Rural-Urban Migration in Wisconsin, 1940–1950,* University of Wisconsin, Agricultural Experiment Station Bulletin no. 176 (Madison, 1951), table 6. Other poor rural regions in the United States in 1940—the western Great Plains, Appalachia, northern New England, most of Oklahoma—had much higher fertility levels (see *Yearbook of Agriculture, 1940,* 837).

61. For early America, see James A. Henretta and Gregory H. Nobles, *Evolution and Revolution: American Society, 1600–1820* (Lexington, Mass., 1987), 36–37.

62. *Sixteenth Census (1940): Agriculture,* vol. 1, pt. 1, pp. 949–54.

63. See the evocative description of western Wisconsin farming in 1940 by Michael J. Goc, *Where the Rivers Flow* (Friendship, Wis., 1991), 15–20. See also William F. Thompson, "1940," *WMH* 72 (1988): 3–37, esp. 5–12.

64. *Sixteenth Census (1940): Agriculture,* vol 1, pt 1: 949–54.

65. Ibid.; Annual Enumeration of Agricultural Statistics, Drummond, Bayfield County, 1937.

66. *Sixteenth Census (1940): Agriculture,* vol 1, pt 1: 894–900.

67. U.S. Bureau of the Census, *Part-Time Farming in the United States* (Washington, D.C., 1937), 54–55. On the significance of part-time farming in the initial stages of settlement of the northern Great Plains, at the same time as settlement began in the cutover, see John W. Bennett and Seena B. Kohl, *Settling the Canadian-American West, 1890–1915: Pioneer Adaptation and Community Building* (Lincoln, Nebr., 1995), 59–60.

68. For case studies of this phenomenon, see Paula M. Bauman, "Single Women Homesteaders, 1880–1930," *Annals of Wyoming* 58 (1985): 39–53, and H. Elaine Lindgren, *Land in Her Own Name: Women as Homesteaders in North Dakota* (Fargo, N.D., 1991). Sherry L. Smith ("Single Women Homesteaders: The Perplexing Case of Elinore Pruitt Stewart," *Western Historical Quarterly* 22 [1991]: 163–84) has effectively demonstrated the multiple meanings of women as homesteaders, which were also apparent in the cutover, by closely examining the experience of the best-known woman homesteader.

69. *History Collections of Washburn County,* 2 vols. (Shell Lake, Wis., 1980), 2:477–78.

70. On the impossibility of women operating Plains farms, see Fink, *Agrarian Women,* 63–64.

71. *Milwaukee Journal,* 13 Aug. 1904, p. 4.

72. Manuscript, U.S. Census, Burnett County, Wisconsin, 1910.

73. [Walt Goldsworthy, ed.], *The Pine, the Plow, and the Pioneer: A History of Three Lakes and Clearwater Lakes, Wisconsin, 1881–1984* (Three Lakes, Wis., 1984), 51–52.

74. Annual Enumeration of Agricultural Statistics, Lenroot, Sawyer County, 1935, 1940; Manuscript, U.S. Census, Sawyer County, 1910.

75. Tax Assessment Ledgers, Sawyer County, 1920, 1930, 1940, ARC, UWEC; Annual Enumeration of Agricultural Statistics, Lenroot, Sawyer County, 1925, 1935, 1940; Neth, *Preserving the Family Farm,* 34–35, 57, 172–73.

76. Taylor County Court Case Files, 1876–1946 (box 12, case no. 1259), ARC, UWEC.

77. *History Collections of Washburn County,* 2:345–46.

78. Annual Enumeration of Agricultural Statistics, Drummond, Cable, Oulu, and Washburn, Bayfield County, 1937.

79. U.S. Bureau of the Census, *Sixteenth Census of the United States (1940): Housing,* vol. 1, pt. 2 (Washington, D.C., 1943), 739, 767–88; C. P. Loomis, Joseph J. Lister, and Dwight M. Davidson, Jr., *Standards of Living in the Great Lakes Cut-Over Area,* Farm Security Administration and Bureau of Agricultural Economics, Social Research Report no. 13 (Washington, D.C., 1938); *History Collections of Washburn County,* 2:362–63.

80. Olaf Anderson interview, Luck, Wis., June 1989 (notes in possession of the author); Roy S. Meier interview, Spirit, Price County, 21–23 Mar. 1979 (tape on deposit), SHSW; Forrest McDonald, *Let There Be Light: The Electric Utility Industry in Wisconsin, 1881–1955* (Madison, 1957), 292; *Sixteenth Census (1940): Agriculture,* vol. 1, pt. 1: 949–54.

81. For background on rural electrification, see Saloutos, *American Farmer and the New Deal*, 208–11. In a characteristically bizarre argument, McDonald (*Let Their Be Light*, 371–86) argues that the REA *retarded* rural electrification in Wisconsin. But see Lemont Kingsford Richardson, *Wisconsin REA: The Struggle to Extend Electricity to Rural Wisconsin, 1939–1955* (Madison, 1961), esp. 77–80. Even McDonald (*Let Their Be Light*, 382) admits that the REA did help electrify northwestern Wisconsin.

82. Goc, *Where the Rivers Flow*, 108–9.

83. Neth, *Preserving the Family Farm*, 211–12.

84. *Sixteenth Census (1940): Housing*, vol. 1, pt 2: 767–88; Richardson, *Wisconsin REA*, 79.

85. Anderson and Meier interviews.

86. Ron Duff Martin, "History of Sarah Duff Martin" (student paper, UWEC, 1990).

87. Harvey A. Uber, *Environmental Factors in the Development of Wisconsin* (Milwaukee, 1937), 124.

88. On the limited quantity and poor quality of the news read by cutover residents in the interwar years, see Robert Peters, *Crunching Gravel: Growing Up in the 1930s* (San Francisco, 1988), 78.

89. E.g., *Phillips Times*, 2 July, 27 Aug., 3 Sept. 1904.

90. Ibid., 24 Sept. 1921, 11 Oct. 1924.

91. E.g., *Park Falls Herald*, 26 Oct. 1934.

92. *Oneida County: Centennial History Edition, 1887–1987* (n.p., 1987), 128–29.

93. *Park Falls Herald*, 6 Jan. 1928.

94. For the national distribution of indices, see Baker, Borsodi, and Wilson, *Agriculture in Modern Life*, 19; on the material prosperity of Wisconsin in general, see Neth, *Preserving the Family Farm*, 198–200; on Union County, Ill., see Jane Adams, *The Transformation of Rural Life, 1890–1990* (Chapel Hill, N.C., 1994), 208–10.

95. Ed Pudas, "Autobiography" (1977) (typescript), 128, ARC, UWRF.

96. Margaret Pike, "Remembrances of a Life" (1992) (typescript), 304, ARC, UWEC.

97. Quoted in "Golden Jubilee of Sheldon, Wisconsin, 1909–1959" (1959) (typescript), ARC, UWEC.

98. Frank Richardson, interview, Waverly, Ohio, August 1987 (tape on deposit), ARC, UWEC (Richardson is a pseudonym).

99. Calculated from data in Works Progress Administration, Division of Professional and Service Projects, Wisconsin Historical Records Survey Project, *Directory of Churches and Religious Organizations in Wisconsin* (Madison, 1941).

100. Calculated from data in ibid. and in U.S. Bureau of the Census, *Religious Bodies: 1936*, vol. 1: *Summary and Special Tables* (Washington, D.C., 1941), 846–47. Denominations differed in how they defined membership.

101. Charles Patterson, interview, Rice Lake, Wis., June 1988 (tape in possession of the author; Patterson is a pseudonym).

102. Olaf Severson, interview, Luck, Wis., June 1989 (notes in possession of the author; Severson is a pseudonym). Harvey Dueholm categorized the split as between "singing Danes" and "praying Danes" (interview, Madison, Wis., Nov.–Dec., 1978 [tape on deposit], SHSW).

103. C. Luther Fry, *The Old and the New Immigrant on the Land* (New York, 1922), 114; Historical Records Survey, *Directory of Churches*.

104. Compiled from data in Episcopal Diocese of Eau Claire, Scattered Records, ARC, UWEC.

105. One veteran cutover pastor related to me the (apocryphal?) story of a group of parishioners gathered in the church parlor for a post-funeral lunch while the pastor was detained with the deceased's family and unable to give a table grace. Impatient to begin eating, one of the group finally stood up and prayed, "Since no pastor is present, let us give thanks."

106. "Winter, Wisconsin . . . Happy Land," a video history (1995) by Joy Kielcheski, Linda Olson, and Eppy Sundberg (transcript in possession of the author; quote on 12).

107. *History of the West Denmark Lutheran Church, 1873–1973* [Luck, Wis., 1973], 40–41.

108. "The History of the Sheldon Church of Christ," student paper no. 229, Edward Blackorby Collection, ARC, UWEC; Parish Records, St. Francis of Assissi, Flambeau (microfilm), ARC, UWEC; "Winter, Wisconsin" transcript, 9, 11.

109. "History of the Sheldon Church of Christ"; "Winter, Wisconsin" transcript, 12; *History of the West Denmark Lutheran Church*, 43–46. At West Denmark, the altar and other features were the work of noted Danish woodcarver Jes Smidt. Two of Smidt's grandsons who were members of the congregation carved the chancel furniture in the present church after a 1985 fire.

110. "Winter, Wisconsin" transcript, 12.

111. For the years 1938–1942 the illegitimacy rate in the cutover, excluding Indians, was 19.01 per thousand live births to residents and 18.30 for the entire state. For the years 1939–1941 the recorded divorce rate in the cutover was 10.40 per ten thousand residents, and 12.01 for the entire state. Statistics are calculated from the 38th–40th *Annual Reports* of the State Board of Health of Wisconsin (Madison, 1941–1944). Indian illegitimacy rates for 1940–1942 were estimated based on 1938–1939 statistics.

112. Peters, *Crunching Gravel*, 79–80; Peters, *Nell's Story*, 124.

113. Martin, "History of Sarah Duff Martin," 6.

114. Jon Gjerde, *From Peasant to Farmer: The Migration from Balestrand, Norway to the Upper Midwest* (New York, 1985); Jane Marie Pederson, *From Memory to Reality: Family and Community in Rural Wisconsin, 1870–1970* (Madison, 1992).

115. Gerard Bouchard, "Family Reproduction in New Rural Areas: Outline of a North American Model," *Canadian Historical Review* 75 (1994): 475–510. For how this worked in early America, see esp. Christopher M. Jedrey, *The World of John Cleaveland* (New York, 1979).

116. See, e.g., Edward V. Carroll and Sonya Salamon, "Share and Share Alike: Inheritance Patterns in Two Illinois Communities," *Journal of Family History* 13 (1988): 219–32, Mark Friedberger, *Farm Families and Change in Twentieth-Century America* (Lexington, Ky., 1988), 139–40; and Stephen John Gross, "Handing Down the Farm: Values, Strategies, and Outcomes in Inheritance Practices Among Rural German Americans," *Journal of Family History* 21 (1996): 192–217.

117. *History Collections of Washburn County*, 2:451–52.

118. For Iowa, see Friedberger, *Farm Families and Change,* 81. Cutover statistics are based on calculations from Taylor County Court Case Files, 1878–1946 (boxes 10–12, 30–32), ARC, UWEC.

119. M. A. Buckley to F. A. Humble, 14 Mar. 1917, Taylor County Probate Case File no. 1169 (box 12). On the importance of this practice in Iowa, see Friedberger, "Handing Down the Home Place," 518–36.

120. Pederson has described the role of community norms in the land transfer process in Trempealeau County (*From Memory to Reality,* 103).

121. Taylor County Court Case File no. 3365 (box 30).

122. Ibid., no. 3383 (box 31).

123. Wade Crane, interview, Barron, Wis., July 1988 (tape on deposit), ARC, UWEC (Crane is a pseudonym).

124. Peters, *Nell's Story;* see Pederson, *Between Memory and Reality,* 205–24.

125. For a general pattern in the Midwest of increasing distance of migration by children, perhaps developing a few years later than in the cutover, see Mary Neth, *Preserving the Family Farm: Women, Community, and the Foundations of Agribusiness in the Midwest, 1900–1940* (Baltimore, 1995), 264–65.

126. Reconstructed from Records of Oulu Evangelical Lutheran Church, SHSW.

127. Severson interview.

128. Peters, *Chrunching Gravel,* 49, 46, 87–88, 91–93, 79–82. Stylistically, Peters's narrative recalls James Agee and Walker Evans, *Let Us Now Praise Famous Men* (Boston, 1941), which further aligned the cutover in readers' minds with the impoverished South of the 1930s.

129. Robert Peters, "That Family," *What Dillinger Meant to Me* (New York, 1983).

130. Annual Enumeration of Agricultural Statistics, Lincoln, Vilas County, 1937.

131. Dueholm and Severson interviews. For a balanced evaluation of the negative and positive accounts of children who went through the homesteading experience on the northern Great Plains, see Bennett and Kohl, *Settling the Canadian-American West,* 104–7.

132. Paul R. Nagel, *80–Acre Farm: A Saga of Wisconsin* (Eau Claire, 1983); idem, *Farm Growing Up: A Saga of Wisconsin* (Eau Claire, 1993); Roland Coggins, *Dear Tales of Cloverland* (New York, 1968); Jolie Paylin, *Cutover Country: Jolie's Story* (Ames, 1976); idem, *Nels Oskar* (Ames, 1979). Cathy Inderberg assisted me in analyzing some of these works. These novels clearly belong to what Roy W. Meyer has identified as the "God Bless It" tradition of literary descriptions of farm life (*The Middle Western Farm Novel in the Twentieth Century* [Lincoln, Nebr., 1965], esp. 82–87). None show the "anger" or "pain" which Bennett and Kohl (*Settling the Canadian-American West, 1890–1915,* 104) found associated with the autobiographically based fiction of the northern Great Plains.

Epilogue

1. Robert Peters, *What Dillinger Meant to Me* (New York, 1982), 105.

2. For an overview, see David B. Danbom, *Born in the Country: A History of Rural America* (Baltimore, 1995), 233–52. For change in a specific community, see Jane

Adams, *The Transformation of Rural Social Life: Southern Illinois, 1890–1990* (Chapel Hill, N.C., 1994), 185–253. Mark Friedberger, *Farm Families and Change in Twentieth-Century America* (Lexington, Ky., 1988) is relatively optimistic about the survival of family farms, like those he studied in Iowa, because of their ability to adapt, in contrast to the corporate farms in studied in California.

3. U.S. Congress, House, *Hearings Before the Select Committee to Investigate the Interstate Migration of Destitute Citizens,* pt. 3, 76th Cong., 3d sess., 1940.

4. Ibid., 1039, 1042, 1051, 1040, 1056–61.

5. Ibid., 1306, 1305, 1308, 1053, 1038–41. Another suggestion at this time for forest subsistence homesteads is Henry Gilbert White, "Public Forest Homesteads," *Papers of the Michigan Academy of Sciences, Arts, and Letters* 27 (1941): 169–80.

6. Roy R. Meier, interview, Spirit, Wis., 21–23 Mar. 1979 (tape on deposit), Wisconsin Agriculturalists Oral History Project, SHSW; Walter H. Ebling et al., *A Century of Wisconsin Agriculture, 1848–1948,* Wisconsin Crop Reporting Service Bulletin no. 290 (Madison, 1948), 111; B. M. Apker, "Reminiscences" (1949) (typescript), ARC, UWEC; "The History of Kjef: A Polish Settlement in Rusk County, Wisconsin" (c. 1969), student paper no. 95, Blackorby Collection, ARC, UWEC; Gary Johnson, "Farm Exhibition Gets Off to 'Excellent' Start," *Eau Claire Leader-Telegram,* 15 July 1987, p. 1A.

7. *Wisconsin Blue Book, 1993–1994* (Madison, 1993), 616.

8. "The History of a Northern Wisconsin Farm" (1969), student paper no. 1956, Blackorby Collection; "History of a Northern Farm" (1974), student paper no. 233, ibid.; Frank Johns, "Memoir," in Phillips Centennial Committee, *Phillips, Wisconsin* (Park Falls, 1976), 32. For an evocative description of how farming in western Wisconsin changed between 1940 and 1990 see Michael J. Goc, *Where the Rivers Flow* (Friendship, Wis., 1991), esp. 28–30.

9. See, e.g., J. Webster Johnson et al., *Land Program for Forest County, Wisconsin,* United States Department of Agriculture Technical Bulletin no. 687 (Washington, D.C., 1939), 10–14.

10. Grunhild Franzen, "Homestead" (typescript, 1976), p. 6, ARC, UWGB; *Blue Book, 1993–1994,* 616; *Eau Claire Leader-Telegram,* 15 July 1987, p. 1A; "Antigo Dairy Expansion May Be Farm of the Future," ibid., 26 Aug. 1995, pp. 1A-2A. A similar farm in Marathon County, bordering the cutover, was the site of the 1996 Farm Progress Days.

11. Annual Report, 1939, Price County Superintendent of Schools (typescript), Price County Board Papers, ARC, UWEC; Annual Report, 1944, Rusk County Superintendent of Schools, in Jean Sanford Replinger, ed., *History of the Rural Schools of Rusk County* (Ladysmith, Wis., 1985), 203–6; *Forty-second Report of the Superintendent of Public Instruction in the State of Wisconsin* [Madison, 1965], 191; *Wisconsin Blue Book, 1969–1970* (Madison, 1969), 131.

12. Lars Kailberg, interview, Luck Wis., June 1989 (notes in possession of the author; Kailberg is a pseudonym); Charles Patterson, interview, Rice Lake, Wis., July 1988 (tape in possession of the author; Patterson is a pseudonym). For the urbanizing and commercializing effect of school consolidation, see Mary Neth, *Preserving the Family Farm: Women, Community, and the Foundations of Agribusiness in the Midwest, 1900–1940* (Baltimore, 1995), 125–27.

13. Meier interview; Harvey Dueholm, interview, Madison, Nov.–Dec. 1978 (tape on deposit), Wisconsin Agriculturalists Oral History Project, SHSW.

14. *Memories of Forest County* (n.p., 1980), 183–84; Michael Klein, "State Sees Increase in Forests," *Eau Claire Leader-Telegram*, 7 July 1996, pp. 1D-2D.

15. Quoted in Chuck Rupnow, "Life in Angus," *Eau Claire Leader-Telegram*, 26 July 1992, p. 4H.

16. Jon Doerflinger and D. G. Marshall, *The Story of Price County, Wisconsin: Population Research in a Rural Development County*, Agricultural Experiment Station and Agricultural Extension Service Research Bulletin no. 220 (Madison, 1960), 12–13.

17. Samuel Lubell and Walter Everitt, "Wisconsin Revives the Wilderness," *Readers Digest* 35 (Sept. 1939), 59–62; Walter R. Rowlands, "The Great Lakes Cutover Region," in Merrill Jensen, ed., *Regionalism in America* (Madison, 1951), 344–45.

18. *An Analysis of Population Growth in Wisconsin*, Wisconsin State Planning Board Bulletin no. 4 (Madison, 1937), 59.

19. *Wisconsin Blue Book, 1993–1994*, 676. Menominee County, an Indian reservation that was part of Oconto and Shawano counties in 1940, is omitted from this analysis.

20. Paul Salstrom, *Appalachia's Road to Dependency: Rethinking a Region's Economic History, 1730–1940* (Lexington, Ky., 1994).

21. Adams, *Transformation of Rural Social Life*, 244–45.

22. Meier interview.

23. Joe Knight, "Bill Would Turn Back Clock in Forests," *Eau Claire Leader-Telegram*, 3 Jan. 1994, pp. 1B, 3B; Steven Walters, "Private-forest Owners' Tax Breaks May Be Helping Some Corporations," *Milwaukee Sentinel*, 12 Aug. 1993, p. 5A.

24. Keith Schneider, "Concerned About Pollution From Proposed Mine, Indian Tribe Takes on Giant," *New York Times*, 26 Dec. 1994, p. 12A. For how over-reliance on mining in the 1980s in the upper peninsula of Michigan eventually helped to impoverish the region, see Harry K. Schwarzweller and Sue-Wen Lean, "Ontonogon: A Remote Corner of Michigan's Upper Peninsula," in Thomas A. Lyson and William W. Falk, eds. *Forgotten Places: Uneven Development in Rural America* (Lawrence, Kans., 1993), 168–94.

25. Joe Knight, "Buying Surge Damages Ecosystem," *Eau Claire Leader-Telegram*, 9 July 1996, pp. 1A–2A. Suggestive, although focused on an earlier period, is William Cronon, *Nature's Metropolis: Chicago and the Great West* (New York, 1991), esp. 380–83.

26. "Real Estate Booming in Northwoods Region," *Eau Claire Leader-Telegram*, 24 Sept. 1995, p. 10A.

27. Nell Peters with Robert Peters, *Nell's Story: A Girl from Eagle River* (Madison, 1995), 142–43.

28. Paul W. Glad, *History of Wisconsin*, vol. 5: *War, a New Era, and Depression* (Madison, 1990), 219–20.

29. Weston Kosova, "Race Baiting," *New Republic* 202 (June 11, 1990), 16–17; Jim Oberly, "Spearing Fish, Playing 'Chicken,'" *Nation* 245 (June 15, 1989), 844–45; "The Wisconsin Fishing War," *Sports Illustrated* 70 (May 15, 1989), 6.

30. Tim J. Sheehan, "Women in Love," *Eau Claire Leader-Telegram*, 28 Nov. 1992, p. 16E. Adams, *Transformation of Rural Social Life*, emphasizes (in a thrust differ-

ent from that of Neth, *Preserving the Family Farm*) that some women in Union County played an increased though underrecognized role in productive agriculture after World War II. The photograph accompanying the Sheehan article in the *Leader* shows Kringe operating a large piece of machinery.

31. Buz Swerkstrom, "Nuclear Protestors Settle in Rural Luck," *Eau Claire Leader-Telegram*, 15 Aug. 1993, pp. 1H, 4H; Mark Lisheron, "Black Farmer Nets Respect—and Jeers," ibid., 22 June 1991, pp. 1A–2A (reprinted from the *Milwaukee Journal*); Buz Swerkstrom, "Burnett County Hopes to Lure Farmers To Land," ibid., 18 Mar. 1989, p. 8A.

32. Chuck Rupnow, "They Have Come to Love Life of Seclusion," ibid., 21 Feb. 1993, pp. 1A-2A.

33. "Memoir of Margaret Kehoe Clemons" (1964), in *History Collections of Washburn County*, 2 vols. (Shell Lake, Wis., 1980), 2:546–48; [Walt Goldsworthy, ed.], *The Pine, the Plow, and the Pioneer: A History of Three Lakes and Clearwater Lake, Wisconsin, 1884–1984* [Three Rivers, 1983], 72–73; Larry Garneau, interview, Drummond, Wis., Nov. 1988 (tape on deposit), ARC, UWEC (Garneau is a pseudonym). For a similar pattern in Union County, southern Illinois, see Adams, *Transformation of Rural Social Life*, 230–31.

34. Ingolf Vogeler, J. Brady Foust, and Anthony R. de Souza, "The Northwoods Region: A Distinctive Area for Human Settlement," *Wisconsin Dialogue* 3 (1983): 100–115. See Leslie Hewes, *The Suitcase Farming Frontier: A Study in the Historical Geography of the Great Plains* (Lincoln, Nebr., 1973).

35. For a recent argument by a geographer that the cutover "was simply too far north for successful agriculture," see Michael Williams, *Americans and Their Forests: A Historical Geography* (Cambridge, Eng., 1989), 234 (the quotation is from a section entitled "The Assault on the Forests of the Lake States"). The approach of the present study is closer to that of historian James C. Malin, whose work on the settlement of the Great Plains stressed the importance of cultural influences within broad environmental constraints. See esp. "Man, the State of Nature, and Climax: As Illustrated by Some Problems of the North American Grasslands," in *History and Ecology: Studies of the Grasslands* (Lincoln, Nebr., 1984), ed. Robert P. Swierenga, 112–25 (first published in *Scientific American* 74 [1952]).

36. "It was people's ill-founded faith in agriculture and their ill-advised attempt to attract farmers to land better suited to growing trees" that brought "the area's residents to the brink of ruin" (Mark Davis, "Northern Choices: Rural Forest County in the 1920s, Part I," *WMH* [1996]: 5).

Bibliographic Essay

Forty years ago historians first examined the Wisconsin cutover. Vernon R. Carstensen's *Farms or Forests: Evolution of a State Land Policy for Northern Wisconsin, 1850– 1932* (Madison, 1958), and Arlan Helgeson's *Farms in the Cutover: Agricultural Settlement in Northern Wisconsin* (Madison, 1962) surveyed the history of the region from the perspective of state officials and other public policy makers. Taken together, the overall conclusion of these works was that attempts to farm in the cutover were ill-founded and had to be rescued by innovative public programs. This interpretation has subsequently shaped both the popular and scholarly view of the region.

However in the past twenty-five years, consistent with the general change in the direction of writing United States history, historians of rural America have shown more interest in describing and analyzing the lives of ordinary farmers and other settlers. This approach first appeared in the early 1970s in studies of seventeenth- and eighteenth-century America. As an early Americanist, I was impressed by works such as Kenneth A. Lockridge, *A New England Town, the First Hundred Years: Dedham, Massachusetts, 1636–1736* (New York, 1970); Robert A. Gross, *The Minutemen and Their World* (New York, 1976); Christopher M. Jedrey, *The World of John Cleaveland: Family and Community in Eighteenth-Century New England* (New York, 1979); and Darrett B. Rutman and Anita H. Rutman, *A Place in Time: Middlesex County, Virginia, 1650–1750* (New York, 1984). In the 1980s, a "new rural history," which focused on nineteenth-century America, blossomed from studies such as John Mack Faragher, *Sugar Creek: Life on the Illinois Prairie* (New Haven, 1986); Jon Gjerde, *From Peasants to Farmers: The Migration from Balestrand, Norway, to the Upper Middle West* (Cambridge, England, 1985); and Sally McMurry, *Transforming Rural Life: Dairying Families and Agricultural Change, 1820–1895* (Baltimore, 1995). More recently, twentieth-century rural America has been the subject of increasingly sophisticated monographs such as Jane Adams, *The Transformation of Rural Life: Southern Illinois, 1890–1990* (Chapel Hill, 1994) and Mary Neth, *Preserving the Family Farm: Women, Community, and the Foundations of Agribusiness in the Midwest, 1900–1940* (Baltimore, 1995). A model study in this genre is Jane Marie Pederson, *Between Memory and Reality: Family and Community in Rural Wisconsin, 1870–1970* (Madison, 1992), which focuses on two communities in Trempealeau County in west central Wisconsin. Many of the themes from these studies are synthesized in David B. Danbom's sensitive overview, *Born in the Country: A History of Rural America* (Baltimore, 1995).

My effort to reexamine the history of the cutover during the first forty years of the twentieth century from this newer perspective has been assisted by the recent publication of two volumes in *The History of Wisconsin* series: Robert C. Nesbit, *Urbanization and Industrialization, 1873–1893* (Madison, 1985) and Paul W. Glad, *War, a New Era, and Depression, 1919–1940* (Madison, 1990). Howard R. Klueter and James J. Lorence provide insights into the history of the cutover in a scholarly history of an adjacent county in *Woodlot and Ballot Box: Marathon County in the Twenti-eth Century* (Wausau, Wisc., 1977). Perhaps the best scholarship on a community within the cutover is an older article by a geographer, Loyal Durand, Jr., "The West Shawano Upland of Wisconsin: A Study of Regional Development Basic to the Problem of Part of the Great Lakes Cutover," *Annals of the American Association of Geographers* 34 (1948): 135–63. My use of the concept of "yeoman farming" to character-ize the goal of most settlers coming to the cutover is based on ideas in Allan Kulikoff, *The Agrarian Origins of American Capitalism* (Charlottesville, Va., 1992). My approach to the cutover as a "space" for the settlers to shape has been inspired by Yi-fu Tuan, *Space and Place: The Perspective of Experience* (Minneapolis, 1977).

The records of lumber companies and other businesses provide information on how new settlers in northern Wisconsin acquired their farms. In particular, I used the records of the Holt Lumber Company, at the Area Research Center (ARC) at the University of Wisconsin–Green Bay, and the North Western Lumber Com-pany and the John S. Owen Lumber Company, both at the ARC at the University of Wisconsin–Eau Claire (UWEC). A consortium of lumber companies sold their land through the American Immigration Company, which was closely studied dur-ing the 1950s by business historian Lucille Kane. See her "Selling the Wisconsin Cutover," *Wisconsin Magazine of History* 40 (1956–1957): 91–98. An understanding of how these land purchases were financed emerges from the Union Mortgage Loan Company Papers, at the UWEC's ARC, and the records of the First Wisconsin Land Mortgage Association. The State Historical Society of Wisconsin (SHSW) has some of the latter organization's material, but since it was eventually liquidated in bank-ruptcy under state law, many useful records, including correspondence with pur-chasers, wound up at the UWEC's ARC in Eau Claire County Circuit Court records. A well-researched biography of an influential land dealer is Ronald Sandfort, "The Entrepreneurial Activities of Ben Faast: A Visionary Banker, Colonizer, and Com-munity Developer of Northern Wisconsin" (MST research paper, UWEC, 1974).

Once on their land, the experience of settlers can be traced through several series of census materials. The printed and manuscript United States censuses were invaluable for this study. They were supplemented by information in the printed state census, which was taken five years apart from the federal census until 1905. Beginning in the early 1920s, the Wisconsin Department of Agriculture initiated an annual Enumeration of Agricultural Statistics, which contains information of every farm in the state; for the years of my study, these records have been depos-ited at the SHSW. Crop Reporting Service statistician Walter H. Ebling and his colleagues aggregated and analyzed some of these data in *A Century of Wisconsin Agriculture, 1848–1948* (Madison, 1948). Together with much other valuable infor-mation, some of them are also reported annually or biannually in the useful *Wis-consin Blue Book.*

First-hand narratives of life in northern Wisconsin between 1900 and 1940 gave life to the patterns identified from census and other data series. In the church, school, and community histories they have compiled, many local historians included memoirs by early settlers. There is a large collection of such material in the ARC at the UWEC. The richest book-length account of growing up in the pre–World War II cutover is Robert Peters, *Crunching Gravel* (San Francisco, 1988). Also very useful are Robert J. Schlomann, *The Thread of Love* (Oshkosh, Wis., 1986); Jack C. Plano, *Fishhooks, Apples, Outhouses: Memories of the 1920s, 1930s, and 1940s* (Kalamazoo, Mich., 1991); and Carl Rhody, *The Saga of Spirit Valley*, 2 vols. (Ogema, Wis., 1980, 1982). Oral histories were also invaluable. In addition to the interviews I did myself, which will be deposited at the ARC at the UWEC, I found tapes at the SHSW of useful interviews with Roy S. Meier and Harvey Dueholm, among others.

Newspapers provide the historian with useful information about local events and also show how the community wanted to present itself to outsiders. In particular, I used the Park Falls and Phillips newspapers. I focused on Price County newspapers because they can be used in conjunction with an extensive collection of the Price County Board's papers, at the UWEC's ARC, which show how local public officials struggled to promote their region and deal with the impact of economic and environmental reversals.

From the perspective of those who tried to engineer settlement in the cutover rather than live there themselves, the voluminous Richard T. Ely papers at the SHSW, especially for the years 1910–1920, show how the best-known academic economist in the United States viewed the cutover and its settlers. Ely's biography is Benjamin Rader, *The Academic Mind and Reform: The Influence of Richard T. Ely in American Life* (Lexington, Ky., 1966), which can be used in conjunction with Edward H. Beardsley, *Harry L. Russell and Agricultural Science in Wisconsin* (Madison, 1969), and John W. Jenkins, *A Centennial History: A History of the College of Agriculture and Life Sciences at the University of Wisconsin–Madison* (Madison, 1991). Ely, Russell, and others at the University of Wisconsin–Madison encouraged the production in the 1920s and 1930s of a corpus of increasingly negative social science evaluations of the cutover. In some ways the culmination of this work was the well done (and unusually balanced) *Man in the 'Cut-Over': A Study of Family Farm Resources in Northern Wisconsin*, University of Wisconsin Agricultural Experiment Station, Research Bulletin no. 139 (Madison, 1941), by George W. Hill and Ronald A. Smith. A penetrating critique of the deficiencies of much of this social science research can be found in Leonard A. Salter, Jr., *A Critical Review of Research in Land Economics* (Minneapolis, 1948).

For specialized information, I relied on a number of secondary sources, including Robert E. Bieder, *Native American Communities in Wisconsin, 1600–1960: A Study of Tradition and Change* (Madison, 1995); Susan L. Flader, ed., *The Great Lakes Forest: An Environmental and Social History* (Minneapolis, 1983); James Willard Hurst, *Law and Economic Growth: The Legal History of the Lumber Industry in Wisconsin, 1836–1915* (Cambridge, Mass., 1964); Katherine Jellison, *Entitled to Power: Farm Women and Technology, 1913–1963* (Chapel Hill, 1993); Richard S. Kirkendall, *Social Scientists and Farm Politics in the Age of Roosevelt* (Columbia, Mo., 1965); Ingolf Vogeler, with others, *Wisconsin: A Geography* (Boulder, 1986); and Michael Williams, *Americans and Their Forests: A Historical Geography* (Cambridge, England, 1989).

Patterns identified in several recent secondary sources highlight the similarities and differences between the cutover and other rural areas. John W. Bennett and Seena B. Kohl, *Settling the Canadian-American West, 1890–1915: Pioneer Adaptation and Community Building* (Lincoln, Nebr., 1995) examines an area settled contemporaneously with the Wisconsin cutover. Larry D. Lankton, *Cradle to Grave: Life,*

Work and Death at the Lake Superior Copper Mines (New York, 1991) is a study of a region adjacent to the cutover, but with a different economic basis. The settlers on the Plains described by Paula M. Nelson in *After the West Was Won: Homesteaders and Town Builders in Western South Dakota, 1900–1917* (Iowa City, 1986), like their contemporaries in the cutover, had to accept disappointment after initial enthusiasm. As well as having an impact on northern Wisconsin, the Great Depression particularly devastated the farmers discussed in Pamela Riney-Kehrberg, *Rooted in Dust: Surviving Drought and Depression in Southwestern Kansas* (Lawrence, Kans., 1994). See also Richard White, "Poor Men on Poor Lands: The Back-to-the-Land Movement in the Early Twentieth Century," *Pacific Historical Review* 49 (1980): 105–31. Essays examine and compare a number of chronically poor regions, including the Great Lakes cutover, in Thomas A. Lyson and William W. Falk, eds., *Forgotten Places: Uneven Development in Rural America* (Lawrence, Kans., 1993).

Index